CHRISTIAN SOCIALISM

CHRISTIAN SOCIALISM

An Informal History

JOHN C. CORT

ORBIS BOOKS

Maryknoll, New York 10545

The Catholic Foreign Mission Society of America (Maryknoll) recruits and trains people for overseas missionary service. Through Orbis Books Maryknoll aims to foster the international dialogue that is essential to mission. The books published, however, reflect the opinions of their authors and are not meant to represent the official position of the society.

Copyright © 1988 by John C. Cort
Published by Orbis Books, Maryknoll, NY 10545
Manufactured in the United States of America
All rights reserved

Grateful acknowledgement is made for permission to reprint from the following by John Cort:
"Christians and the Class Struggle," from *Commonweal,* July 11, 1984, © Commonweal Foundation.
"A Turning Point in History," from *New Oxford Review,* April 1984, © 1984 by *New Oxford Review* (1069 Kains Ave., Berkeley, CA 94706).
Excerpts from "The Catholic Church and Socialism," appearing in *Dissent,* Spring 1982.
Parts of the text have also appeared in *Religious Socialism.*

Manuscript Editor: Mary Heffron

Library of Congress Cataloging-in-Publication Data

Cort, John C.
  Christian socialism.

  Bibliography: p.
  1. Socialism, Christian.   2. Socialists—Biography.
I. Title.
HX51.C636   1987   335′.7   87-14046
ISBN 0-88344-574-3
ISBN 0-88344-573-5 (pbk.)

To my children
Barbara, Nicholas, Paul, Rebecca, Lydia,
Mary Elizabeth, Alice, David, Susan, and Julia
but most especially to my wife, Helen,
who by working hard and well
made it possible for me to write this book.

Those who neither make after others' goods nor bestow their own are to be admonished to take it well to heart that the earth they come from is common to all and brings forth nurture for all alike. Idly then do men hold themselves innocent when they monopolise for themselves the common gift of God. In not giving what they have received they work their neighbors' death; every day they destroy all the starving poor whose means to relief they store at home. When we furnish the destitute with any necessity we render them what is theirs, not bestow on them what is ours; we pay the debt of justice rather than perform the works of mercy. . . . Of Dives in the Gospel we do not read that he snatched the goods of others but that he used his own unfruitfully; and avenging hell received him at death not because he did anything unlawful but because he gave himself up utterly and inordinately to the enjoyment of what was lawful.

ST. GREGORY THE GREAT

Contents

PART II
THE DEVELOPMENT OF CHRISTIAN SOCIALISM
IN EUROPE AND THE WESTERN HEMISPHERE

Acknowledgments

Other than my wife, Helen, the person to whom I am most indebted is Sister Mary Emil Penet, IHM. As professor of social ethics at Weston School of Theology in Cambridge, Massachusetts, she got me started on this project in 1977. I felt inadequate to the immensity of the job and urged her to collaborate with me. Unfortunately, her teaching load and problems of health made that impossible. The quality of her scholarship and her grasp of property theory are, however, evident in chapter 5. Whatever is valuable in that chapter is mainly due to her and Thomas Aquinas.

Next among my benefactors would be my religious socialist comrade, Gabriel Grasberg, who devoted great quantities of his time and expertise to translations of German works by and about Christian socialists. I am deeply indebted to him, and grateful.

Others who have given me valuable assistance—notably in editing, critique of various parts of the manuscript, or simply in providing useful leads, caveats, or scraps of information—are the following: Orbis publisher Robert Gormley, manuscript editor Mary Heffron, Herbert Kenny, James Luther Adams, Sam Beer, Harvey Cox, Martha Martini, Danièle Hervieu-Léger, Father Frank Murphy, Harry Peer, Ian Rathbone and anonymous members of England's Christian Socialist Movement, officers and members of the International League of Religious Socialists, David Noble, Hans and Klaus Meier, Jacques Chatagner, Robert Vander Gucht, Alfredo Luciani, Tommaso De Francesco, Curt Cadorette, Catherine Costello, Michael Curry, Gary Dorrien, Eve Drogin, John Eagleson, Msgr. George Higgins, Markus Mattmüller, Franz Mueller, Bernard Murchland, Hank Schlau, and Bruce Walker.

Also, Weston School of Theology, which in 1978 named me a Visiting Scholar and has extended my library privileges to the present time, which privileges have been invaluable.

Any factual errors or faulty opinions or conclusions, however, are my responsibility, not theirs.

PART I

THE JUDEO-CHRISTIAN TRADITION

Its Origins, Variations, Challenges, and Implications for Economics and Politics, Including Some Eminent Persons Who Enlarged on the Same

Introduction

For perhaps the first time in American history Christian socialism is front-page news. Curiously, it has become front-page news without ever being mentioned. It appears under the title of "liberation theology" or in a story about some particular liberation theologian who has upset some cardinal in the Vatican or perhaps even the pope. The reporters usually do not mention that the liberation theologian is a Christian socialist, although they will probably mention the word "Marx" or "Marxism" somewhere in the story.

Nevertheless, we are being confronted with some fairly interesting questions, such as, can Christians be socialists? Should they be socialists? If so, what kind of socialist? Marxist, non-Marxist, semi-Marxist? Democratic? And what is meant by "democratic"?

If we are going to address these questions intelligently, and if we are going to write, or read, a whole book about Christian socialism, the first thing we must do is come to some agreement on definitions.

The term "Christian" seems clear enough, despite the wild variety of beliefs that have taken shelter under that word. The root of the word is obvious. Yet some who have called themselves Christian, and who merit mention in any book on the subject, have held views that cannot be reconciled with any traditional view of what Christ taught. Nevertheless, the figure of Christ remains as the focal point.

Neither does this book then require any ticket of admission, doctrine-wise, other than to claim some relation to that figure of Christ. It will, however, try to clarify and distinguish between competing and/or contradictory views of what Jesus Christ really taught. This is no simple exercise, but I will simplify it by accepting fairly literally what the Revised Standard Version of the Bible says he taught, using the New Oxford Annotated Edition, which is perhaps the most acceptable to both Protestant and Catholic scholars.

The word "socialism" is more difficult. Wild variety again confronts us, even among those who take their lead from Karl Marx. At one end of the spectrum are the Leninists, those who tend to favor violent revolution, the dictatorship of the proletariat, and almost total nationalization of property as necessary tools for the construction of a socialist society. These include some Christians, especially in Latin America and other areas of the Third World where democratic reform seems impractical or too difficult.

3

At the other end of the spectrum are Marxists like Michael Harrington or Rosa Luxemburg, who deny that there can be any socialism without democracy, just as they insist that there can be no genuine democracy without socialism. The Democratic Socialists of America have put it as follows:

> As democratic socialists we oppose the claim of Communist countries to be socialist. We are firmly committed to democracy as the only political means to achieve the economic and social power of the people. Thus we oppose bureaucratic and dictatorial state ownership as hostile to socialist emancipation. [*Where We Stand,* merger agreement between the Democratic Socialist Organizing Committee (DSOC) and the New American Movement (NAM), March 20, 1982, at founding convention of Democratic Socialists of America (DSA).]

One definition of socialism is, in fact, the extension of democratic process from the political to the economic sphere of life. Socialism then becomes a *method* based on the assumption that if people are given the opportunity to make economic decisions, they can be trusted to make them, most of the time, so as to provide as much equality, justice, and freedom as are possible in an imperfect world. It follows from this definition that any movement toward the democratization of economic decisions is socialistic, and this would include such phenomena as trade unions and New Deal legislation designed to bring business under some measure of democratic control.

Dictionaries tend to be more restrictive in their definitions. Three typical ones: (1) "a political and economic theory of social organization based on collective or governmental ownership and democratic management of the essential means of production and distribution of goods" (*Webster's Collegiate,* 5th Edition); (2) "a social system in which the producers possess both political power and the means of producing and distributing goods" (*American Heritage*); (3) "a theory or system of social organization that advocates the ownership and control of industry, capital, and land by the community as a whole" (*Random House*).

Emerging from these definitions is the picture of a society in which the means of production and distribution are fairly solidly collectivized under government ownership and control. The dictionaries, however, have not kept up with recent developments. In 1951 the Socialist International, meeting in Frankfurt, drew a more pluralistic picture of socialism. While opting for public ownership where necessary for "controlling basic industries and services," the Frankfurt Declaration insists that "socialist planning does not presuppose public ownership of all the means of production" but welcomes "consumers' or producers' cooperatives" and is compatible with the existence of private ownership in important fields, for instance, in "agriculture, handicraft, retail trade and small and middle-sized industries."

It adds:

Socialist planning does not mean that all economic decisions are placed in the hands of the government or central authorities. Economic power should be decentralized wherever this is compatible with the aims of planning. . . . The workers must be associated democratically with the direction of their industry. [Frankfurt Declaration of Socialist International, in *The New International Review* (Winter 1977), pp. 8–9].

Again the emphasis is on democratic process: "Such planning is incompatible with the concentration of economic power in the hands of the few. It requires effective democratic control of the economy." Note that this statement distinguishes socialism from both capitalist and communist concentrations of economic power.

The first constitution of DSOC, an American affiliate of the Socialist International, included the following: "The realization of humanity's potential requires basic changes, among which are the *social* ownership and *democratic* control of the *decisive* means of production and distribution" (emphasis added). DSA, DSOC's current embodiment, has repeatedly made it clear that it believes that "social ownership" can mean either public or cooperative or worker-owned or worker/community-owned forms of productive and distributive enterprise.

This book will discuss the ideas of Christians who have favored Marxist-Leninist forms of socialism, ideas of those who have interpreted Marx in a more democratic style, and, above all, ideas of those who have come to socialism from non-Marxist traditions rooted directly in Christian and democratic faith.

Christian faith, and especially those elements of it that would encourage a commitment to democratic socialism, is the concern of the first part of this book. This section calls on the Old Testament, the New Testament, the Fathers of the church, Thomas Aquinas, Thomas More, and the more radical figures of the Protestant Reformation.

The second part of the book deals with the development of an explicit Christian socialism in Europe and America in the nineteenth and twentieth centuries, focusing on France, England, German-speaking Europe, and the United States. Latin America and liberation theology are treated only briefly, except for Gutiérrez, because much has already been written about them. Canada deserves a chapter of its own; I have tried to deal with it in chapter 11, "The Convergence of Socialism and Catholicism," drawing on the writings and the thought of Gregory Baum.

In a book of this ambitious, arrogant scope, it is inevitable that much will be missed or neglected. Important books have not been read, but there comes a time when reading becomes the enemy of writing. Important countries and persons have not been mentioned, or have been dismissed too quickly. Whole continents—notably Africa and Asia—whose importance cannot be overestimated, will be almost invisible. Among those omitted or neglected whom I particularly regret, the following stand out:

1. The Jesuit Reductions in Paraguay (1609–1767).

2. African Christian socialists like Julius Nyerere (1922–   ), former president of Tanzania, who in his book *Ujamaa: The Basis of African Socialism* has eloquently expressed a key principle of Christian socialism:

> The foundation, and the objective, of African socialism is the Extended Family. The true African socialist does not look on one class of men as his brethren and another as his natural enemies. He does not form an alliance with the "brethren" for the extermination of the "non-brethren." He rather regards all men as his brethren—as members of his ever extending Family.[1]

I saw one day on the blackboard of an elementary school in the black ghetto of Boston this definition of *Ujamaa,* a Swahili word meaning "Cooperative Economics," which is one of the seven principles of black consciousness: "To build and maintain our own stores, shops and other businesses and to profit together from them." Put that together with Nyerere's Extended Family and you have a pretty good working model.

3. Benigno ("Ninoy") Aquino (1933–83), whose assassination led to the revolution that ended the dictatorship of Ferdinand Marcos. In a 145-page document written in prison to defend himself against the military tribunal that condemned him to death Aquino wrote:

> If I must be labeled I think I will fit the label of a Christian socialist best. My ideology flows with the mainstream of Christian democratic socialism as presently practiced in Austria, West Germany and the Scandinavian countries. . . . It grieves me profoundly to be carelessly branded a Communist by those who never bothered to understand the difference between communism and Christian socialism.[2]

4. Nicholas Berdyaev (1874–1948), an original supporter of the Russian Revolution whose criticisms of Bolshevism led to his exile from the Soviet Union. His books are among the best written on Christian social theory, in his case from a Russian Orthodox viewpoint.

5. Jacques Maritain (1882–1973), the French neo-Thomist who made Catholic social teaching intellectually respectable for a whole generation of Europeans and Americans.

6. George Lansbury (1859–1940), Arthur Henderson (1863–1935), and Sir Stafford Cripps (1889–1952), leaders of the British Labour Party whose strong religious convictions and impressive records, and lives, helped to keep the tradition of Christian socialism alive and well in that party.

I write from a bias that is, theologically, conservative Roman Catholic; politically, democratic with both lower case and capital "d's," and economically, socialist in the sense defined above by the Socialist International, with perhaps a stronger emphasis on worker cooperatives and a weaker one on public ownership. Within these biases I hereby contract to be as fair and objective as possible. This effort will not be a total success. In fact, several readers of the manuscript have already mingled their compliments with charges that my biblical bias is characterized by a sort of naive fundamentalism or is irrelevant to the book's subject, or both.

Faced with such charges I duck behind Bible scholars like Pierre Benoit, director of the *École Biblique* in Jerusalem and author of *Jesus and the Gospel* (New York: Herder & Herder, 1973), and, for a Protestant view, the work of the Anglican theologian Alan Richardson, notably in *The Gospels in the Making: An Introduction to the Recent Criticism of the Synoptic Gospels* (London: 1938) and a shorter, sharper defense of the historical Jesus in Kegley and Bretall's *Reinhold Niebuhr,* from which I quote in Chapter 10.

The conclusion of both Benoit and Richardson, speaking for the more rational defenders of the Gospels as authentic history, is that with all due respect and gratitude for the valid contributions of historical criticism, the claims for that school have gone far beyond reason. Richardson goes so far as to conclude:

> The progress of New Testament research in the 20th century has utterly disposed of the liberal picture of Jesus as in any way historical. The liberal Jesus was a figment of the liberal imagination, the reflection of the liberal critic's own face at the bottom of the well. . . . There is no need to practice deceptions, however pious, in the matter of the miracles of Jesus or in the matter of his Resurrection.[3]

Beyond Benoit and Richardson I rely on an old reporter's ear for the credibility of differing but honest witnesses, some sense of the essential agreements, and a certain gift of faith, which is, after all, not the least useful ingredient.

As for the charge that some concern for the question of Jesus' divinity is irrelevant to the subject of Christian socialism I must politely but vigorously disagree. Whether Jesus was divine or merely human does make a difference. If divine, then we must consider his ideas, and his commandments, very seriously. If merely human, the consideration loses a certain urgency, to put it mildly.

So this is an opinionated history, but all writing of history is by definition opinionated. One dictionary defines it as "a narrative, chronicle or record of events." Which events are included and which excluded depends on the opinion of the historian as to what is important or significant and what is not. This assumes, of course, that under "events" will fall the expression of ideas by various actors in the historical narrative. With this understanding, what follows are the events that, in the opinion of this historian, are most important and/or significant in the history of Christian socialism.

This account will feature a high ratio of direct quotation, which to some may be disturbing and excessive, but I have never trusted even my own competence to render another person's thought with anything like perfect fidelity.

There will be little additional information in the reference notes, mostly just the source of quotations, but one should not neglect them entirely. A few interesting items have been stored there.

CHAPTER 1

The Questions and the Issue

John Ruskin once described Adam Smith, author of *The Wealth of Nations*, as "the half-bred and half-witted Scotchman who taught the deliberate blasphemy: 'Thou shalt hate the Lord, thy God, damn his laws and covet thy neighbor's goods'."[1]

Nothing in *The Wealth of Nations* justifies that description—not literally. Nevertheless, one can understand why Smith infuriated a religious man like Ruskin. Edmund Burke, a distinguished contemporary of Smith, said of this book (whose full title reads *An Inquiry into the Nature and Causes of the Wealth of Nations*), "In its ultimate result, this was probably the most important book that had ever been written."[2] Writing from a very different point in time and political prejudice, the American critic Max Lerner also had a high opinion of its importance: "It has done as much perhaps as any modern book thus far to shape the whole landscape of life as we live it today."[3]

What could justify such tributes? *The Wealth of Nations* contains more than nine hundred pages of intelligent analysis of economic activity in the eighteenth and previous centuries, including subjects as marginal in interest as the average rent of tin mines in Cornwall, the reasons why stockings are cheaply manufactured in Scotland or why codfish are used for money in Newfoundland. In detailed and boring discussion of subjects no longer of interest to most readers it reminds one of Marx's *Capital*. And in impact on the modern world only Marx's *Capital* has had a comparable effect.

Many people assume that Smith was an uncritical spokesperson for business and had little sympathy for workers or common folk. Not so. Speaking of the workers, he wrote, "It is but equity that they who feed, clothe and lodge the whole body of the people should have such a share of the produce of their own labour as to be themselves tolerably well fed, clothed and lodged."[4] His opinion *Smith.* of capitalists was by no means uncritical: "People of the same trade seldom meet together, even for merriment and diversion, but the conversation ends in a conspiracy against the public, or in some contrivance to raise prices."[5]

This apparent lack of bias made Adam Smith the more persuasive when he followed these words with an admonition that gives us a clue as to why Smith so angered John Ruskin:

9

It is impossible indeed to prevent such meetings by any law which could be executed, or would be consistent with liberty and justice. But though the law cannot hinder people of the same trade from sometimes assembling together, it ought to do nothing to facilitate such assemblies, much less to render them necessary. . . . A regulation which enables those of the same trade to tax themselves in order to provide for their poor, their sick, their widows and orphans, by giving them a common interest to manage, renders such assemblies necessary.[6]

Provision for the poor and sick, the widows and orphans, must yield to the necessities of free competition. Thus a traditional Judeo-Christian obligation is cast aside in the hope that employers will be discouraged from meeting together in their own interests.

LAISSEZ-FAIRE THEORY

Smith believed that self-interest, left unchecked by government, except for the most obvious violations of public order, would work out best for everyone in the end. Thomas Carlyle called this "anarchy plus a constable." Consider Smith's own words:

All systems of preference or of restraint, therefore, being taken away, the obvious and simple system of natural liberty establishes itself of its own accord. . . . By directing [his] industry in such a manner as its produce may be of the greatest value, he [the capitalist] intends only his own gain, and he is in this, as in many other cases, *led by an* _invisible hand_ to promote an end which was no part of his intention. . . . By pursuing his own interest he frequently promotes that of the society more effectually than when he really intends to promote it [emphasis added].[7]

And again:

The natural effort of every individual to better his own condition, when suffered to exert itself with freedom and security, is so powerful a principle, that it is alone and without any assistance, not only capable of carrying on the society to wealth and prosperity, but of surmounting a hundred impertinent obstructions with which the folly of human laws too often encumbers its operations.[8]

Mercantilism, the tendency of European governments to impede economic activity with excessive regulation, was in truth a legitimate object of criticism in the eighteenth century. And the pursuit of self-interest does frequently benefit society as a whole. But these truisms did not then and do not now lead to the conclusion that "all systems of preference or restraint" should be stripped away and that the weak should be left only to the beneficent effects of self-interest pursued vigorously by the strong. This, however, was the gospel preached by Adam Smith and believed, ever since, not only by the dominant elements of the Western world but also by much of the dominated. The supply-side economics of President Ronald Reagan, bought by the American voters in the elections of 1980 and 1984, is only one recent example.

The capitalists, of course, were ecstatic. As Harold Laski put it in his *Rise of Liberalism*:

> To have their own longings elevated to the dignity of natural law was to provide them with a driving force that had never before been so powerful. . . . With Adam Smith the practical maxims of business enterprise achieved the status of a theology.[9]

Theology? Surely, some may say, that's going too far, but there is much to be said for the use of the word. Consider the phrase "led by an invisible hand," the phrase that above all others Adam Smith has bequeathed to the study of political economy. What is this "invisible hand"? One flattering critic actually misquoted it as "the divine hand." It seems likely that that is how Smith thought of it, or at least as a natural law of the universe, a force that possessed the awesome power to bring public good out of private greed.

SMITH AND RELIGION

Smith was not, however, a religious man in the usual sense. To Christianity he preferred "that pure and rational religion, free from every mixture of absurdity, imposture or fanaticism such as wise men have in all ages of the world wished to see established."[10] What this "pure and rational religion" is exactly he does not bother to explain beyond, that is, faith in "the invisible hand," and perhaps some vague preference for Greek philosophy that makes one wonder how well he remembered his Plato.

> In the ancient philosophy the perfection of virtue was represented as necessarily productive, to the person who possessed it, of the most perfect happiness in this life. In the modern philosophy it was frequently represented as almost always inconsistent with any happiness in this life; and heaven was to be earned only by penance and mortification, by the austerities and abasement of a monk; not by the liberal, generous and spirited conduct of a man.[11]

By the context it is evident that Smith means Christian philosophy when he speaks of "modern philosophy."

In order to preserve "public tranquillity" the ideal arrangement was to have Christendom split up among "many thousand small sects," since one and even "two or three great sects" could only contribute to "dangerous and troublesome" threats to civil government. It followed that the Middle Ages was a time of the most profound misery for humankind:

> In the state in which things were through the greater part of Europe during the tenth, eleventh, twelfth, and thirteenth centuries, and for some time both before and after that period, the constitution of the church of Rome may be considered as the most formidable combination that ever was formed against the authority and security of civil government, as well as against the liberty, reason, and happiness of mankind.[12]

Although Smith served for ten years as professor of moral philosophy at the University of Glasgow, he seems to have finished his service with a poor opinion of any system of either morals or philosophy, especially if anyone was foolish enough to apply them to economic activity:

> Speculative systems have in all ages of the world been adopted for reasons too frivolous to have determined the judgment of any man of common sense, in a matter of the smallest pecuniary interest.[13]

A very practical man was Adam Smith.

This is but a thumbnail sketch of the mind, and the ideas, that permeate the book that has probably done more than any other "to shape the whole landscape of life as we live it today." But how, one may ask, did it manage to overcome so completely the influence of another book—one that was, and still is, the most popular book in the world? The question assumes a recognition that the Bible and *The Wealth of Nations* are radically at variance, and such a recognition may not be forthcoming at this point. Its demonstration is the subject of the next four chapters. I assume it here in order to clarify and underline the issue with which this book is concerned and the major questions to which Christian socialism addresses itself.

In the eighteenth and nineteenth centuries Christian faith was still relatively strong among the middle classes of the Protestant countries of northern Europe and North America in which the rise of capitalism was most spectacular. Karl Marx had a simple answer as to why capitalism won out over Christianity. He rejected the notion that ideas, religion, or philosophy could determine the modes or relations of production. The reverse was true, he said. This also was a contradiction of the Judeo-Christian faith.

The question remains, how and why did *The Wealth of Nations* defeat the Bible in the battle for the human mind? For an answer we survey the development of economic thought by religious leaders after Aquinas through the eighteenth century.

DEVELOPMENT OF "CHRISTIAN" (?) ECONOMIC THOUGHT

Max Weber (1864–1920), a German economist and sociologist, challenged Marx's notion that modes of production determine the shape of the superstructure of society, namely, its ideas, philosophy, religion, and political institutions. He did this primarily in his book *The Protestant Ethic and the Spirit of Capitalism*. He begins the book by warning us that production for profit is not a useful definition of capitalism because this activity is as old as Adam. This is his definition: "A capitalistic economic action [is] one which rests on the expectation of profit by the utilization of opportunities for exchange" and which involves "the rational capitalistic organization of (formally) free labour."[14] The latter quality is the distinctively modern ingredient.

The *spirit* of capitalism, which in the book becomes an essential part of its definition, Weber defines by quoting at length from the writings of Benjamin Franklin, which contain, he says, "what we are looking for in almost classical purity." The following are highlights:

> Remember that *time* is money . . . *credit* is money . . . money can beget money, and its offspring can beget more, and so on. . . . Remember this saying, *The good paymaster is lord of another man's purse*. . . . The most trifling actions that affect a man's credit are to be regarded. The sound of your hammer at five in the morning, or eight at night, heard by a creditor, makes him easy six months longer" [from *Advice to a Young Tradesman*, 1748; emphasis in original].

> He that idly loses five shillings' worth of time, loses five shillings, and might as prudently throw five shillings into the sea. He that loses five shillings, not only loses that sum, but all the advantage that might be made by turning it in dealing, which by the time that a young man becomes old, will amount to a considerable sum of money [*Necessary Hints to Those That Would be Rich,* 1736].[15]

> I grew convinced that truth, sincerity, and integrity in dealings between man and man were of the utmost importance to the felicity of life. . . . Revelation had indeed no weight with me as such, but I entertained an opinion that, though certain actions might not be bad because they were forbidden by it, or good because it commanded them, yet probably these actions might be forbidden because they were bad for us [*Autobiography*, 1790].[16]

Weber's comment was:

> The peculiarity of this philosophy of avarice appears to be the ideal of the honest man of recognized credit, and above all the idea of a duty of the individual towards the increase of his capital, which is assumed as an end in itself. . . . Honesty is useful, because it assures credit; so are punctuality, industry, frugality, and that is the reason they are virtues.[17]

Some may object, as does Samuel Beer of Harvard, that Weber is unfair to Franklin, that Franklin's aphorisms are no more than a legitimate tribute to thrift and industry. Weber considers this interpretation and rejects it: "It is not mere business astuteness. . . . It is an ethos." I think Weber is more accurate than Beer; the key sentence begins, "Revelation had no weight with me as such," a sentiment that, thus far, was shared by Weber himself. If virtue is virtuous only because it is useful, then for him to whom it is no longer useful it loses all virtue. After all, honesty can sometimes be very costly. It has cost people their heads.

Even more tell-tale of Franklin's "spirit" is the title of his book, *Necessary Hints to Those That Would be Rich*. To be rich is clearly presented as a good in and of itself. On the other hand, one can also identify with Beer's critique of Weber, who no more believes in Christian revelation than Franklin does, but who would have the reader conclude that the desire to be rich is a peculiarly American weakness that has somehow eluded most Europeans. In fairness to Franklin, as Beer has reminded me, I should mention that, whatever his faith or lack thereof, he also gave his readers a humanist version of Judeo-Christian tradition when he wrote:

> All the Property that is necessary to a man, for the Conservation of the Individual and the Propagation of the Species, is his natural right, which none can justly deprive him of; but all Property superfluous to such purposes is the Property of the Publick, who, by their Laws, have created it, and who therefore by other Laws may dispose of it, whenever the Welfare of the Publick shall demand such Disposition. He that does not like civil Society on these Terms, let him retire and live among Savages. He can have no right to the benefit of Society, who will not pay his club [contribution] towards the Support of it.[18]

Weber's point about Franklin's "spirit" as it reflects the spirit of capitalism remains, however, fundamentally correct. All we need do is to contrast his *Necessary Hints to Those That Would be Rich* with the necessary hints that St. Paul wrote to Timothy:

> But if we have food and clothing, with these we shall be content. But those who desire to be rich fall into temptation, into a snare, into many senseless and hurtful desires that plunge men into ruin and destruction. For the love of money is the root of all evils. . . . But as for you, man of God, shun all this" [I Tim. 6:8–11].

Closer in time to Franklin and Adam Smith, Thomas Aquinas was still characterizing this "unlimited lust for gain" as *turpitudo*, moral disgrace and degradation.[19]

The change from Aquinas to Franklin came about slowly, gradually. Martin Luther (1483–1546) was closer to Aquinas in his view of economic activity, but he contributed another idea that ultimately had a profound effect, the idea of "calling." In his *Exegesis of Genesis* he insists that "the milking of cows" is of equal value in the sight of God with the loftiest contemplation of monks in monasteries. He translated verse 20 of the eleventh chapter of the Book of Sirach, using the German word *Beruf*, "calling," for the Hebrew word for "task," a word that had traditionally been translated with some variant of the Latin *opus* or "work."[20]

[margin note: Vocation?]

John Calvin (1509-1564) was like Luther and Aquinas in his insistence that Christianity and the lust for gain were incompatible, but he added some important notions to Luther's idea that commercial enterprise is a calling just as holy as the calling of priests and nuns. He was a more practical man than Luther, trained in the law, and he early recognized what even traditional Catholic theologians were beginning to accept, namely, that the ancient definition and prohibition of usury as *any* interest on loans did not make sense in the sixteenth century, if it had ever made sense. He therefore approved the taking of interest *if* it was reasonable and *if* loans were made without charge to the poor. This removed a great roadblock to commercial activity.

[margin note: his pronouncement?]

Land-holding aristocracy or bourgeoisie—it was clear where Calvin's sympathies lay: "What reason is there why the income from business should not be larger than that from land-owning? Whence do the merchant's profits come, except from his own diligence and industry?"[21]

Calvin's great contribution, however, was the doctrine of predestination. "God not only foresaw," he wrote, "the fall of the first man, . . . but also arranged all by the determination of his own will." Certain men and women he chose as his elect, predestined to salvation from the beginning of time by "his gratuitous mercy, totally irrespective of human merit"; the remainder he consigned to eternal damnation "by a just and irreprehensible, but incomprehensible judgment."[22]

Some of Calvin's more sensitive followers found this doctrine not only incomprehensible but inadmissible. John Milton, for example, protested, "Though I may be sent to Hell for it, such a God will never command my respect."[23] Calvin's commercial converts accepted the teaching with better grace because it soon became evident that the best way to determine who were the elect of God was to see who was blessed by God in this life. The favorite Bible verse was the line from Genesis: "The Lord was with Joseph, and he became a successful man" (Gen. 39:2).

William Tyndale (1492–1536), the Protestant martyr who made one of the first English translations of the Bible, rendered this verse, "And the Lorde was with Joseph, and he was a luckie felowe." The words fall quaintly upon the modern ear, but the phrase is appropriate to Tyndale because he had no sympathy for the notion that later became so popular in Calvinist circles, namely, that one proved one's virtue by holding onto, not by parting with, one's worldly goods. This is what Tyndale wrote in *The Parable of the Wicked Mammon*: "If thy brother or neighbour therefore need, and thou have to help him, and yet showest not mercy but withdrawest thy hands from him, then robbest thou him of his own, and art a thief."[24]

The majority opinion among Protestant Reformers soon turned against this traditional view. Luther denounced begging as a form of blackmail, the Swiss Calvinists declared it illegal, as did Cromwell's Puritan Parliament in 1649, which a few years later legislated punishment for vagrants, whether they were begging or not.

By the seventeenth century English preachers and theologians of the Calvinist persuasion were beginning to anticipate Adam Smith and Ben Franklin. One of the greatest of them, Richard Baxter (1615–1691), wrote a *Christian Directory,* or *Summ of Practical Theologie,* a kind of Puritan answer to the Thomist *Summa.* It includes the following:

> Be wholly taken up in diligent business of your lawful callings, when you are not exercised in the more immediate service of God. . . . To neglect this [bodily employment and mental labor] and say, "I will pray and meditate" is as if your servant should refuse your greatest work, and tye himself to some lesser, easie part. . . . Be every day more careful that you lose none of your time, than you are that you lose none of your gold and silver. . . . If God show you a way in which you may lawfully get more than in another way (without wrong to your soul or any other) if you refuse this and choose the less gainful way, you cross one of the ends of your calling and you refuse to be God's steward and to accept His gifts and use them for Him when He requireth it. You may labor to be rich for God, tho' not for the flesh and sin.[25]

We might interpret this teaching, "All work and no play makes Jack a good Christian—and a rich one."

Richard Steele, a London preacher and contemporary of Baxter, put it with greater pith: "Next to saving his soul [the tradesman's] care and business is to serve God in his calling and to drive it as far as it will go."[26]

Weber concluded, "The Reformation took rational Christian asceticism and its methodical habits out of the monasteries and placed them in the service of active life in the world."[27] Calvinism, he noted, crowned the transfer with a new process of canonization:

> By founding its ethic in the doctrine of predestination, it substituted for the spiritual aristocracy of monks outside of and above the world the spiritual aristocracy of the predestined saints of God within the world.[28]

R. H. Tawney (1880–1962) adds a perceptive observation:

> Calvin did for the bourgoisie of the sixteenth century what Marx did for the proletariat of the nineteenth. . . . The doctrine of predestination satisfied the same hunger for an assurance that the forces of the universe are on the side of the elect as was to be assuaged in a different age by the theory of historical materialism.[29]

John Wesley (1703–1791), founder of the Methodists, did not believe in predestination, but the spirit of Calvinism was so much a part of the intellectual and theological atmosphere of his time that he could not help but reflect it. The following passages, more sharply than any others of the period, reveal the pathos, dilemma, and moral confusion of the age:

> I fear wherever riches have increased, the essence of religion, "the mind that was in Christ," has decreased in the same proportion. Therefore I do not see how it is possible in the nature of things for any revival of true religion to continue long. For religion must necessarily produce both industry and frugality, and these cannot but produce riches. But as riches increase, so will pride, anger and love of the world. . . . For the Methodists in every place grow diligent and frugal. Consequently they increase in goods, and proportionately increase in pride and the desire of the eyes. So, although the form of religion remains, the spirit is swiftly vanishing away.[30]

Wesley was a man with a genuine sense of compassion for the poor. He repeatedly reminded his followers of their obligations to the hungry, the naked, and the homeless. His misreading of the Parable of the Talents, however, as shown in the following passage, demonstrates, first, how far a good man can go off the track because of faulty exegesis and, second, exactly how and why Methodism was confronted with the dilemma that Wesley laments in the previous passage.

> In regards to the use of money, our Lord has given us three rules to guide us. The first of these is, "Gain all you can." Here we may speak like the children of the world. And it is our bounden duty to do this. . . . Having gained all you can, by honest wisdom and unwearied allegiance, the second rule of Christian prudence is, "Save all you can." . . . But let not any man imagine that he has done anything by merely going thus far. . . . Rather, you must add the third rule to the first two. Having first gained all you can, and secondly saved all you can, then you must "give all you can."[31]

A little common sense should have persuaded Wesley that once they have gained all they can and saved all they can, average human beings have lost their appetite for giving all they can. The "desire of the eyes" has long since taken over. And, in fact, how do you arrange to save all you can and give all you can at the same time? Clearly Jesus had something different in mind when he spoke of the duty to increase our talents.

Max Weber was the trailblazer who explored the influence of the Protestant Reformers in the development and triumph of the capitalist spirit. Other scholars reinforced and refined his conclusions, among them Ernst Troeltsch, William Cunningham, and R. H. Tawney. Of these three, Tawney is probably the most interesting. An English economist and devout Anglican, he was admirably situated both geographically and spiritually to evaluate Weber's analysis. His book *Religion and the Rise of Capitalism* is better balanced than Weber's, gives more weight to the economic factor, is more comprehensive and definitely more readable.

Neither Weber nor Tawney tries to absolve Catholics or the Catholic Church from responsibility for the rise of Mammon-worship and the decline of religion. Nevertheless, their conclusion as to the interest of both Protestants and Catholics in economic activity is similar. Weber writes,

> It is a fact that the Protestants, . . . both as ruling classes and as ruled, both as majority and as minority, have shown a special tendency to develop economic rationalism which cannot be observed to the same extent among Catholics either in the one situation or in the other. Thus the principal explanation of this difference must be sought in the permanent intrinsic character of their religious beliefs, and not only in their temporary external historico-political situations.[32]

There is no need to dwell here on the doctrinal differences between Protestantism and Catholicism. We will proceed at once to a review of biblical teaching and the writings of Christian saints and sages who preceded the Reformation. The reader can draw his or her own conclusions. The purpose of this chapter was to raise some basic questions: (1) Is it possible that the theory and practice of capitalism is at odds with the theory and practice of authentic Christian faith? (2) How and why did Adam Smith win the ideological battle so easily? (he wasn't really that brilliant); and (3) Is it possible that democratic socialism, as defined in the Introduction, might be closer to the letter, spirit, and practice of authentic Christian faith than capitalism?

Let us not hide behind rhetorical questions. My answer to questions 1 and 3 is "Yes". To question 2 I would respond, "Smith won the ideological battle because it is the nature of the human animal to seize upon any half-plausible excuse for doing whatever we want to do, and Smith was the first one to come up with a half-plausible excuse."

Smith, however, may have won a battle, but he did not win the war. The war goes on. His contemporary disciples remain locked in confused combat with all sorts of opponents, who demonstrate all sorts of both clear and murky ideas. The issue is to clarify the ideas and define the lines of battle, especially as they can be illuminated and revealed in the light of our Judeo-Christian tradition.

CHAPTER 2

The Old Testament

The fourth chapter of St. Luke's Gospel reports the opening of Jesus' ministry in the synagogue at Nazareth, where he spoke to his fellow Nazarenes:

> And he stood up to read; and there was given to him the book of the prophet Isaiah. He opened the book and found the place where it was written, "The spirit of the Lord is upon me, because he has anointed me to preach good news to the poor. He has sent me to proclaim release to the captives and recovering of sight to the blind, to set at liberty those who are oppressed, to proclaim the acceptable year of the Lord."
> And he closed the book, and gave it back to the attendant, and sat down; and the eyes of all in the synagogue were fixed on him. And he began to say to them, "Today this scripture has been fulfilled in your hearing" [Luke 4:16–21].

This is a significant and dramatic episode. As Jesus started his commentary on Isaiah, Luke reports that "all spoke well of him," but by the time he finished "all in the synagogue were filled with wrath, and they rose up and put him out of the city, and led him to the brow of the hill on which their city was built, that they might throw him down headlong." Christians who preach the social gospel and subsequently find themselves facing a lynch mob can take heart. They stand in the oldest and most respectable of Christian traditions.

POVERTY AND JEWISH TRADITION

The episode is significant because it highlights Jesus' own summary of the meaning of his ministry and sets it solidly on a foundation of Jewish orthodoxy, appealing as he does to the most prestigious of the Hebrew prophets. Jesus quotes from the sixty-first chapter of Isaiah, which was probably not written by the original author (c. 759–694 B.C.) but by a later disciple several hundred years closer to the time of Christ. But Jesus had reason to be confident that he was following the oldest and most respectable of Jewish traditions.

The most venerable Jewish writings showed that concern for the poor was

19

among the essential qualities that God, Yahweh, required of the good and faithful Jew, required of the people of Israel as part of the covenant with that people, the *quid pro quo* for their miraculous deliverance from Egyptian oppression, the necessary return for the gift of the Promised Land and all future favors.

What was meant by the "poor"? Not the lazy poor. "Go to the ant, O sluggard, consider her ways, and be wise" (Prov. 6:6). Not the prodigal poor. "Be not among winebibbers, or among gluttonous eaters of meat; for the drunkard and the glutton will come to poverty, and drowsiness will clothe a man with rags"(Prov. 23:20–21).

One part of Jewish tradition held that poverty was a judgment of God upon the wicked and prosperity a reward for the good.

The righteous has enough to satisfy his appetite, but the belly of the wicked suffers want [Prov. 13:25].

Because the daughters of Zion are haughty and walk with outstretched necks, glancing wantonly with their eyes, mincing along as they go, . . . the Lord will smite with a scab the heads of the daughters of Zion. . . . Instead of perfume there will be rottenness; . . . and instead of a rich robe, a girding of sackcloth [Isa. 3:16–17, 24].

Here we enter the area of ambiguity and the perennial manufacture of excuses and rationalizations as to why one should not be concerned for the poor. Such rationalizations were an affliction of the ancient Jews; they have been a favorite refuge of Christians in all ages. The ancient Jews, however, had the excuse that it was not a strong part of their tradition to believe in life and judgment after death. If God was to reward the good and punish the wicked, he must do so in this life.

The problem, and the ambiguity, are eloquently expressed in the Book of Job. Why do the innocent suffer? "Why do the wicked live, reach old age, and grow mighty in power?" (Job 21:7). The reader, of course, knows that Job's sufferings were simply a test of his faith, the term of a little wager that God made with Satan. In the end Job is rewarded with even greater good fortune than he had known before.

But the dilemma remains and the question remains: Why does the wicked man die "in full prosperity, being wholly at ease and secure, his body full of fat and the marrow of his bones moist"; and why does the poor but good man die "in bitterness of soul, never having tasted of good" (Job 21:23–25)?

The wisdom of the Jews stopped short of resolving the dilemma by righting all wrongs in the afterlife. Their best answer, at least as expressed in Job, was a humble expression of faith in the wisdom and power, justice and mercy of God. Meanwhile, they knew, through their observation of life and experience, that poverty is not always the fruit of sloth, dissipation, pride, and wickedness. It may well be a result of the oppression of the innocent by the wicked, a test of virtue, or a by-product of inexplicable misfortune. The wise would refrain from judgment and treat the poor with compassion, because this was what Yahweh commanded.

Commanded. This statement is the burden of this chapter. Compassion, to the Jews, was not something over and above the commandment. Compassion was commanded by God, required, usually a matter of basic justice. To support this fundamental statement I will quote from fifteen books of the Old Testament ranging over a period of a thousand years.

SCRIPTURAL CITATIONS

First, I quote from three books of the Pentateuch, which Jews call the Torah, the first five books of the Bible, usually credited to Moses, who probably lived in the thirteenth century B.C.

> You shall not wrong a stranger or oppress him, for you were strangers in the land of Egypt. You shall not afflict any widow or orphan. If you do afflict them, and they cry out to me, I [Yahweh] will surely hear their cry; and my wrath will burn, and I will kill you with the sword, and your wives shall become widows and your children fatherless [Exod. 22:21–24].

> You shall not oppress your neighbor. . . . but you shall love your neighbor as yourself: I am the Lord [Lev. 19:13, 18].

> When you reap your harvest in the field, and have forgotten a sheaf in the field, you shall not go back to get it. . . . When you beat your olive trees, you shall not go over the boughs again. . . . When you gather the grapes of your vineyard, you shall not glean it afterward; it shall be for the sojourner, the fatherless and the widow. You shall remember that you were a slave in the land of Egypt; therefore I command you to do this [Deut. 24:19–22].

And again, in a significant linking of God's love and justice, with still another reference to the Egyptian experience:

> He [the Lord your God] executes justice for the fatherless and the widow, and loves the sojourner, giving him food and clothing. Love the sojourner therefore; for you were sojourners in the land of Egypt [Deut. 10:18–19].

One must be careful to note that the commandment does not imply that the poor are always right, as some Marxist writers tend to assume. Moses warns: "You shall not be partial to the poor or defer to the great, but in righteousness shall you judge your neighbor" (Lev. 19:15).

The Psalms were written over a period of perhaps eight hundred years (c. 1300–500 B.C.). Only a few are cited here:

Blessed is he who considers the poor! The Lord delivers him in the day of trouble [Ps. 41(40):1].

Give justice to the weak and the fatherless; maintain the right of the afflicted and the destitute. Rescue the weak and the needy; deliver them from the hand of the wicked [Ps. 82 (81):3,4].

Blessed is the man who fears the Lord, who greatly delights in his commandments! . . . He has distributed freely, he has given to the poor; his righteousness endures forever; his horn is exalted in honor [Ps. 112 (111):1,9].

Happy is he whose help is the God of Jacob, . . . who executes justice for the oppressed; who gives food to the hungry [Ps. 146 (145):5,7].

The Book of Proverbs has sometimes been attributed to Solomon (c. 973–922 B.C.), but it is more likely the work of many authors over many centuries, perhaps as late as the fourth century B.C.

Do not rob [injure] the poor, because he is poor, or crush the afflicted at the gate; for the Lord will plead their cause and despoil of life those who despoil them [Prov. 22:22-23].

In the well-known description of "the good wife" (chapter 31) we find this among her virtues:

She opens her hand to the poor, and reaches out her hands to the needy [Prov. 31:20].

Amos and Hosea (Osee) were prophets who lived during the reign of Jeroboam II (786–746 B.C.). Their denunciations of the wickedness of their time rise to heights of poetic passion. Hosea is especially significant because Jesus, in rebuking the formalism of the Pharisees, twice quotes the words of Hosea (6:6): "I [Yahweh] desire steadfast love [mercy] and not sacrifice" (Mt. 9:13; 12:7). It is evident that Jesus is referring to compassion, love of neighbor. The Hebrew word used by Hosea is *hesed* which the Septuagint scholars translated with the Greek word *eleos*, compassion or mercy. Some confusion has been introduced into this quotation because translators of both the Revised Standard Version and the Confraternity (Catholic) Version have used the correct word, "mercy", when translating Jesus in Matthew but have used the more ambiguous word "love" when translating the original in Hosea 6:6.[1]

This is no semantic quibble. The exponents of individualistic piety are tireless in emphasizing love of God, whereas what Hosea and Jesus are concerned to emphasize is that the love of God requires love of neighbor, and especially love of the poor. With this caveat, here is the citation from Hosea.

What shall I do with you, O Ephraim? What shall I do with you, O Judah? Your love is like a morning cloud, like the dew that goes early away. Therefore I have hewn them by the prophets, I have slain them by the words of my mouth, and my judgment goes forth as the light. For I desire steadfast love and not sacrifice, the knowledge of God, rather than burnt offerings [Hos. 6:4-6].

And Amos:

Thus says the Lord: "For three transgressions of Israel, and for four, I will not revoke the punishment; because they sell the righteous for silver, and the needy for a pair of shoes—they that trample the head of the poor into the dust of the earth, and turn aside the way of the afflicted [Amos 2:6,7].

Amos again, speaking to the rich women of Israel in words that one is not likely to hear in the mouth of a modern preacher:

Hear this word, you cows of Bashan, who are in the mountain of Samaria, who oppress the poor, who crush the needy, who say to their husbands, "Bring, that we may drink!" The Lord God has sworn by his holiness that, behold, the days are coming upon you, when they shall take you away with hooks, even the last of you with fishhooks [Amos 4:1,2].

And finally, by the mouth of Amos, this great exhortation from the Lord:

I hate, I despise your feasts, and I take no delight in your solemn assemblies. Even though you offer me your burnt offerings and cereal offerings, I will not accept them, and the peace offerings of your fatted beasts I will not look upon. Take away from me the noise of your songs; to the melody of your harps I will not listen. But let justice roll down like waters, and righteousness like an ever-flowing stream [Amos 5:21-24].

From what has gone before it is clear that what Amos means by "justice" and "righteousness" is conduct that does not include but scrupulously avoids "oppressing the poor" and "crushing the needy," that includes and scrupulouly pursues "steadfast love" of them.

The great prophet Isaiah (759–694 B.C.), to whom are attributed the first thirty-nine chapters of the Book of Isaiah, strikes a theme similar to that of Amos:

Even though you make many prayers, I will not listen; your hands are full of blood . . . cease to do evil, learn to do good; seek justice, correct oppression; defend the fatherless, plead for the widow [Isa. 1:15–17].

The following curse would seem to be applicable to modern politicians who vote for laws that discriminate against the poor:

Woe to those who decree iniquitous decrees, and the writers who keep writing oppression, to turn aside the needy from justice and to rob the poor of my people of their right, that widows may be their spoil, and that they may make the fatherless their prey [Isa. 10:1,2].

Isaiah's prophetic description of the messianic Christ includes this quality:

He shall not judge by what his eyes see, or decide by what his ears hear; but with righteousness he shall judge the poor, and decide with equity for the meek of the earth [Isa. 11:3,4].

Second Isaiah, also known as Deutero-Isaiah, was written by an unknown poet. Chapters 40 to 55 belong to the end of the Babylonian Exile (722–538 B.C.). Second Isaiah continues the themes stresssed by First Isaiah. One example is particularly touching:

When the poor and needy seek water, and there is none, and their tongue is parched with thirst, I the Lord will answer them, I the God of Israel will not forsake them [Isa. 41:17].

Later disciples finished the book (chapters 56–66) during the fifth century B.C. In a magnificent passage they quote the Lord's response to the complaints of the Jews that their prayers and fasting have not elicited the appropriate response:

Behold, in the day of your fast you seek your own pleasure, and oppress all your workers. . . . Is not this the fast that I choose: to loose the bonds of wickedness, to undo the thongs of the yoke, to let the oppressed go free, and to break every yoke? Is it not to share your bread with the hungry, and bring the homeless poor into your house; when you see the naked, to cover him, and not to hide yourself from your own flesh?

Then shall your light break forth like the dawn, and your healing shall spring up speedily; your righteousness shall go before you, the glory of the Lord shall be your rear guard. Then you shall call, and the Lord will answer; you shall cry, and he will say, Here I am.

If you take away from the midst of you the yoke, the pointing of the finger, and speaking wickedness, if you pour yourself out for the hungry and satisfy the desire of the afflicted, then shall your light rise in the darkness and your gloom be as the noonday. And the Lord will guide you continually, and satisfy your desire with good things, and make your bones strong; and you shall be like a watered garden, like a spring of water, whose waters fail not [Isa. 58:3, 6–11].

I have quoted this long passage for two reasons: first, it is one of the most beautiful and consoling in the entire Bible, especially for believing Jews and Christians who have any concern for social justice, and second, it is perhaps the passage in the Old Testament that most perfectly anticipates the letter and spirit of Jesus' words in Matthew 25, which, as we shall see in the next chapter, provide the surest foundation for Christian socialism.

Two prophets—one from the beginning and one from the end of the sixth century B.C.—are pertinent here. Ezechiel was sent by Nebuchadnezzar in 597 B.C. into exile in Babylon. As a priest, prophet, and exile he fit into the role that many have claimed for him as "the father of Judaism," particularly because of his concern for the Temple and the liturgy. The following passage reveals what the prophet considered most essential in the definition of a good Jew:

> If a man is righteous and does what is lawful and right—if he does not eat upon the mountains or lift up his eyes to the idols of the house of Israel, does not defile his neighbor's wife or approach a woman in her time of impurity, does not oppress any one, but restores to the debtor his pledge, commits no robbery, gives his bread to the hungry and covers the naked with a garment, does not lend at interest or take any increase, withholds his hand from iniquity, executes true justice between man and man, walks in my statutes, and is careful to observe my ordinances—he is righteous, he shall surely live, says the Lord God [Ezech. 18:5-9].

The following quote from Zechariah dates from about 520 B.C.:

> And the word of the Lord came to Zechariah, saying, "Thus says the Lord of hosts, Render true judgments, show kindness and mercy each to his brother, do not oppress the widow, the fatherless, the sojourner, or the poor; and let none of you devise evil against his brother in his heart" [Zech. 7:8-10].

In the Book of Job, Eliphaz the Temanite makes an unjust accusation against Job by way of explaining his great misfortunes. I quote it because, despite its injustice, it demonstrates what a religious Jew of that time (fifth or fourth century B.C.) believed to be serious sin:

> Is not your wickedness great? There is no end to your iniquities. For you have exacted pledges of your brothers for nothing, and stripped the naked of their clothing. You have given no water to the weary to drink, and you have withheld bread from the hungry [Job: 22:5-7].

Jeremiah, one of the greatest of the prophets, became prominent during the reign of Jehoiakim, king of Judah (609-598 B.C.), when he denounced the idolatry of the Jews and predicted the destruction of Jerusalem and the Temple. The Book of Jeremiah was not written by him, but several centuries after he died. The quotation selected is important because it identifies so closely the knowledge of God with fair treatment and justice for the poor:

> Woe to him who builds his house by unrighteousness, and his upper rooms by injustice; who makes his neighbor serve him for nothing, and does not give him his wages; who says, "I will build myself a great house with spacious upper rooms," and cuts out windows for it, paneling it with cedar, and painting it with vermilion. Do you think you are a king because you compete in cedar? Did not your father eat and drink and do justice and righteousness? Then it was well with him. He judged the cause of the poor and needy; then it was well. *Is not this to know me? says the Lord* [Jer. 22:13–16, emphasis added].

By now the point should have been made that the Jews, *throughout their entire history as it is written in the Old Testament*, read the mind and will of God as commanding both justice and compassion for the poor.

We come now to a further development, which is most noticeable in the writings of the minor prophets and in the Book of Tobias, all of which date from the two centuries before Christ. This development is the use of the word *sedakah*, "justice," in speaking of generosity to the poor. However, when the Old Testament was translated into Greek, the word *sedakah* was translated *eleemosyne*, "almsgiving," from which comes the English word "eleemosynary," which Webster defines as "related or devoted to charity or alms."[2] Consequently, early in the history of both the Jewish and Christian religions a shift in emphasis occurred and obligations that were originally given high priority gradually became something extra, something not really required but nice, something that came to be known as "a work of supererogation." Webster's definition (5th ed., 1948) is relevant here: "In the Roman Catholic Church *works of supererogation* are those good deeds believed to have been done by saints, or capable of being done by men, over and above what is needed for their own salvation."

As demonstrated by the following quotations, in which almsgiving is described as *sedakah*, "justice," prophets and scribes of the time immediately preceding Christ, summing up Jewish tradition and its reading of the mind and will of God, gave high priority to consideration for the poor. This consideration was not limited to treating the poor fairly, that is, paying just wages, and so on, but included as an essential ingredient the element of generosity, the sharing of superfluous goods. For an intellectual analysis of how and why this generosity comes under the heading of justice we shall have to wait for the chapters on the Fathers of the Church and Thomas Aquinas. Here we are faced with simpler statements.

The Book of Daniel, written by an anonymous author in the second century B.C., tells of the legendary hero and prophet *Daniel*, an exile at the court of Nebuchadnezzar, king of Babylon (605–562 B.C.). In interpreting a bad dream of the king, Daniel prophesied that Nebuchadnezzar would be "driven from among men and [his] dwelling shall be with the beasts of the field." To ward off this evil judgment Daniel concluded:

> Therefore, O king, let my counsel be acceptable to you; break off your sins by practicing righteousness, and your iniquities by showing mercy to the oppressed, that there may perhaps be a lengthening of your tranquillity [Dan. 4:27].

The Book of Tobit (Tobias), probably written in the second century B.C., is the story of two Jews, father and son, who were captured in Northern Israel and taken to Assyria in the latter part of the eighth century B.C. Tobit thinks he is dying and gives his son Tobias this advice:

> Give alms from your possessions to all who live uprightly, and do not let your eye begrudge the gift when you make it. Do not turn your face away from any poor man, and the face of God will not be turned away from you. If you have many possessions, make your gift from them in proportion; if few, do not be afraid to give according to the little you have. So you will be laying up a good treasure for yourself against the day of necessity. For charity delivers from death and keeps you from entering the darkness; and for all who practice it charity is an excellent offering in the presence of the Most High. . . .
> Do not hold over till the next day the wages of any man who works for you, but pay him at once; and if you serve God you will receive payment. And what you hate do not do to anyone. Give of your bread to the hungry, and of your clothing to the naked. Give all your surplus to charity, and do not let your eye begrudge the gift when you make it [Tob. 4:7-11, 14, 16].

The Confraternity (Catholic) translation of verse 15—"and what you hate do not do to anyone"— is even stronger: "See thou never do to another what thou wouldst hate to have done to thee by another." This verse deserves special mention. It is the reverse, complementary side of the Golden Rule (Luke 6:31 and Matt. 7:12).

Sirach (actually Joshua ben Sirach, which is Hebrew for "Jesus, son of Sirach") wrote the Book of Sirach about 180 B.C. He also makes it clear that almsgiving is merely *sedakah*, "justice."

> Water extinguishes a blazing fire: so almsgiving atones for sin. . . . My son, deprive not the poor of his living, and do not keep needy eyes waiting. Do not grieve the one who is hungry, nor anger a man in want [Sir. 3:29; 4:1,2].

Sirach is most interesting to the student of Adam Smith, however, because of the first two verses of chapter 27:

Many have committed sin for a trifle, and whoever seeks to get rich will avert his eyes. As a stake is driven firmly into a fissure between stones, so sin is wedged in between selling and buying.

One can almost hear Smith muttering, "So what's a little sin compared to the benefits that will be forthcoming from the invisible hand?"

Sirach should also be of interest to the student of Benjamin Franklin:

He who loves gold will not be justified, and he who pursues money will be led astray by it. Many have come to ruin because of gold, and their destruction has met them face to face. It is a stumbling block to those who are devoted to it, and every fool will be taken captive by it [Sir. 31: 5–7].

Conservatives may protest that all these quotations are of no benefit to the socialist argument because they are exhortations or condemnations addressed to individuals; they are not applicable to governments. Secular radicals might well say the same, adding that any remedial action proposed here deals with effects, not causes, with cosmetic, not with structural change.

These protests are weak for several reasons—first of all because governments consist of individuals. In the democracies, individuals elect the individuals who comprise the government. Reinhold Niebuhr has made the point in *Moral Man and Immoral Society* that individuals tend to throw off the constraints of morality when they combine together for collective action, but no respectable theologian would try to justify this or maintain that government executives, legislators, judges, or the voters who elect them are somehow exempt from the moral law. When newly elected politicians place their hand on the Bible and take the oath of office, this action does not somehow free them from the obligation of obedience to what is written in that Bible. Not if the politician is a believing Jew or Christian.

(A note of clarification is in place here: A Christian head of state, or legislator, may believe that personally he or she should turn the other cheek, not resist aggression, as recommended by Jesus in the Sermon on the Mount [Matt. 5:39]. If such persons conclude, however, that they have no right to turn the cheeks of their constituents and support the use of armed forces to resist international aggression, they are not therefore in violation of what might be called the majority opinion of Christian morality. The extreme pacifist view is still a minority opinion, though it daily becomes more popular as the horrors of nuclear warfare become more evident.)

The protests of conservatives and secular radicals are weak for a second reason. The Jews of the Old Testament did not stop short at personal exhortation or condemnation. They took collective action. They enacted and enforced legislation. Their actions were not purely remedial. They dealt with causes. They tried to prevent both poverty and extreme riches from developing. Those who owned productive property were obligated to leave some wheat, some olives, some grapes in the field for "the sojourner, the fatherless and the widow" (Deut. 24:19–22). There was an organized welfare system.

At the end of every three years you shall bring forth all the tithe [tenth] of your produce in the same year, and lay it up within your towns; . . . and the sojourner, the fatherless, and the widow, who are within your towns, shall come and eat and be filled [Deut. 14:28,29].

There was the seventh year, the Sabbath year, when "every creditor shall release what he has lent to his neighbor" (Deut. 15:2), slaves were to be set free (Exod. 21:2–6), and every field, vineyard, and olive orchard shall "rest and lie fallow, that the poor of your people may eat" (Exod. 23:11). There was the Jubilee Year, the fiftieth year, when all fields and houses that had been alienated returned to their original owners (Lev. 25:10ff.). Interest on loans was of course strictly forbidden (Exod. 22:25).[3]

The protests are weak for a third reason. As often as not, the prophets addressed their exhortations and condemnations to the people of Israel as a body or to the kings, the men of power and responsibility, the de facto government. Jeremiah is typical:

And to the house of the king of Judah say, "Hear the word of the Lord, O house of David! Thus says the Lord: 'Execute justice in the morning, and deliver from the hand of the oppressor him who has been robbed, lest my wrath go forth like fire, and burn with none to quench it, because of your evil doings' " [Jer. 21:11, 12].

Hear the word of the Lord, O King of Judah, who sits on the throne of David, you, and your servants, and your people who enter these gates. Thus says the Lord: Do justice and righteousness, and deliver from the hand of the oppressor him who has been robbed. And do no wrong or violence to the alien, the fatherless, and the widow, nor shed innocent blood in this place [Jer. 22:2,3].

Finally, as a summation of the Old Testament view of the right kind of economic life, this lovely, nourishing verse from Ecclesiastes 3:13: "It is God's gift to humankind that every one should eat and drink and take pleasure in all their toil."

When Jesus stood up in the synagogue at Nazareth and quoted Isaiah to justify his mission to the poor, it should be evident from the above citations that Isaiah did not stand alone with him. Jesus was speaking from a great, rich, powerful tradition. He was speaking from the heart of Jewish faith. To that tradition and that faith he added some distinctive accents of his own.

CHAPTER 3

The New Testament

When Mary, pregnant with Jesus, went to visit her cousin Elizabeth, pregnant with John, she said something unusual, something that gives us a foretaste, and perhaps a partial explanation of her son's preoccupation with the poor and the needy. She said,

> My soul magnifies the Lord, . . . He has shown strength with his arm, he has scattered the proud in the imagination of their hearts, he has put down the mighty from their thrones, and exalted those of low degree; he has filled the hungry with good things, and the rich he has sent empty away [Luke 1:46, 51–53].

Some say that Christ had no economic program and no political program. They point to his response to Pilate: "My kingship is not of this world" (John 18:36). They point to the beautiful passage about the lilies of the field: "Do not be anxious about your life, what you shall eat or what you shall drink, nor about your body, what you shall put on. . . . But seek first his kingdom and his righteousness, and all these things shall be yours as well" (Matt. 6:25, 33; cf. Luke 12:22–31).

On a superficial reading it would be hard to find words better calculated to discourage economic planning of any kind, whether capitalist or socialist. But only on a superficial reading. The question is, what does it mean to seek first the kingdom of God and God's righteousness? The answer to that question gives us the key to the economic problem, and to much of the political problem as well.

MATTHEW 25

Chapter 2 (The Old Testament) has given us a large part of the answer. In Matthew 25 Jesus hammered it home and left no room for any further questions. As an interesting sidelight, Matthew places this passage at the end of a long series of teachings and then continues, "When Jesus had finished all these sayings, he said to his disciples, 'You know that after two days the

30

Passover is coming, and the Son of man will be delivered up to be crucified' "
(Matt. 26:1,2). The rest of the Gospel of Matthew is a straight narrative leading
up to the crucifixion and resurrection.

Matthew 25:31–46 is not only the end and summation of Jesus' teaching; it is
also a vision of the end of the world. In effect, it is a hellfire sermon. Hellfire
sermons are no longer popular, and perhaps this is one reason why Matthew 25
is not more frequently quoted. Actually, it is a heaven-and-hell-fire sermon,
but it is not built around the usual sins and virtues. There is nothing about sex
in it. The only questions asked are, "Did you feed the hungry, clothe the naked,
shelter the shelterless, visit those who are sick or in prison?" No questions are
really asked, of course. The Son of Man sits on his throne and separates the
sheep from the goats. He knows. He does not have to ask questions. He tells
the sheep, "I was hungry and you gave me food. . . . Inherit the kingdom
prepared for you from the foundation of the world." And to the goats, "I was
hungry and you gave me no food. . . . Depart from me, you cursed, into the
eternal fire prepared for the devil and his angels." Both groups, surprised, ask
him, "When did we do this to you?" And he responds, "Truly I say to you, as
you did it to one of the least of these my brethren, you did it to me."

Jesus' identification with the hungry, the poor, the sick, and the prisoners is
one powerful element in this passage. It is an element that Christians can never
permit themselves to forget. For the Christian socialist, however, the passage
is, or should be, the cornerstone of his or her faith.

Monsignor Joseph Gremillion, former director of the Vatican's Commission
on Justice and Peace, said something once that throws a bright beam of light on
the meaning and significance of this passage. His words were to the effect that
to feed the hungry is a simple imperative, but it is not a simple undertaking.
That is, "to feed the hungry" takes planning, and the planning will have to be
just as sophisticated, just as long-range, just as complex as the demand for
food, clothing, and shelter requires. For the demand must be met, the hungry
must be fed, the naked must be clothed, the homeless must be given a decent
roof over their heads, the sick must be cared for, the prisoners (even) must be
treated with compassion. Otherwise, hellfire.

"Hellfire." The sophisticated Christian may flinch at that expression, but
there is no escaping the fact that fear of hell and hope of heaven are essential
elements of the gospel. One count reveals forty references by Christ to hell or
damnation, most of them in terms of hellfire or some similar expression. He
refers sixty-eight times to salvation, heaven, or eternal life. Only a few of either
group are duplicates from one gospel to another.

The sophisticated Christian is embarrassed by all these references to rewards
and punishments. It seems demeaning. The unsophisticated Christian must
point out that the truth about human nature is demeaning, as well as enno-
bling, and that it seems likely that God knew exactly what he was doing when
he constructed a universe with at least one earth, one hell, and one heaven.

The defenders of capitalism like to dismiss socialism on the ground that it is
based on an unrealistic view of human nature. They insist that the average

human being can never be motivated to work, much less to make substantial sacrifices, except by hope of material reward or by fear of loss of it, failure, unemployment, starvation.

The secular socialist has some difficulty with this, because socialism does demand more sacrifices than capitalism, especially by the more talented members of society, those who are essential to its success. The Christian socialist who believes in Christ's teachings has an answer, namely, how can we compare the rewards of this life to the rewards of eternal life? How can we compare the loss and pain of this life to the loss and pain of eternal life? The argument, then, between capitalism and socialism becomes simply one between a partial realism and total realism.

The argument between socialism and communism has a similar quality. Communists share the capitalist skepticism about otherworldly incentives and base their system on a this worldly fear of the Gulag and hope of happiness through loyalty to the Party. They leave their Utopian dreams of human transformation to some distant point in time when the abolition of private property will change today's selfishness and weakness into unfailing altruism and moral strength.

How do we reconcile Matthew 25 with the passage about the lilies of the field ("Do not be anxious about your life . . . "). This does not seem difficult. Jesus is telling us, "Do not be anxious for yourself, be anxious for others. This kind of anxiety is good, this kind of anxiety is what I mean by seeking the kingdom of God and God's justice."

THE CORNERSTONE OF CHRISTIAN SOCIALISM

To call Matthew 25 the cornerstone of a Christian socialist's faith or, more accurately, of the faith of a Christian socialist who has given serious thought to the implications of the gospel, is not to say that if Matthew 25 were to be stricken from the Bible then Christian socialism would have no foundation. We still have all we need in the second great commandment, which is like unto the first, "You shall love your neighbor as yourself." This is emphasized in all the gospels, but Luke 10:25–37 answers the follow-up question "And who is my neighbor?" with the revolutionary doctrine that the neighbor includes the Samaritans of this world, all those who are most despised and rejected. (As a heretical sect the Samaritans were objects of great hostility and contempt for the ancient Jews.)

Let us proceed then to draw out the implications of Matthew 25, which is simply Jesus' further explanation of what it means to love one's neighbor as oneself. Let us combine with Monsignor Gremillion's aphorism another, more ancient one: "Feed people fish and you feed them for a day; teach them how to fish and you feed them for a lifetime." No one would deny that this is even more in keeping with the spirit of Matthew 25. Who wants a permanent population of beggars or welfare mothers? Everyone wants to see the poor working, at least those who are able to; we all agree with St. Paul (2 Thess. 3:10),

"If anyone will not work, let him not eat." All, that is, but the idle rich agree.

The unemployed are dangerous and expensive. They breed crime, physical and mental illness, loss of tax revenue, unbalanced budgets, high interest rates, recession and depression, vicious circles and spirals, Keynesian cycles of boom-and-bust. And there is the psychic element, the psychic hunger. Those who are unemployed hunger not only for food but for fulfillment, for work that will permit them to reach their potential as children of God, to share in the creative work of God, making and remaking the world.

"Teach them how to fish and you feed them for a lifetime." It is still too simple. Teaching people how to fish with a hook and line will not feed them for a lifetime. More is required. They need fishing boats that are big enough to go to sea winter and summer and are equipped with expensive gear. They need a society around them that can be counted on to pay a fair price for the fish so that they can support themselves and their dependents in what has come to be called "reasonable comfort."

Now we are really into economic and political planning. In the previous chapter I listed the various measures that the ancient Jews, moved by the spirit of God, wrote into the Mosaic Law in order to meet the problem of poverty. As befitting a time when modes and relations of production were relatively simple, these measures were simple, and not always the most practical, but they sufficed.

JESUS' COMMAND

Today they clearly do not suffice, and the problem remains. Marxist solutions have tended not to solve the problem but to spread it around among a larger percentage of the population, the number of the rich diminishing, the number of the poor or near-poor increasing. At least, the poor in this case do not suffer the extremes of poverty permitted under more capitalist societies, but the price paid is the loss of important freedoms.

What can modern Christians learn from the words of Jesus? He taught us to pray "Thy kingdom come on earth as it is in heaven." He told Pilate "My kingship is not of this world," but again and again he made it clear that the only way to enter that kingdom hereafter was to work for its realization here and now. Vertical, individual, purely spiritual religion was not the religion of Jesus Christ. The vertical relationship with God could only be found, developed, and maintained by way of a horizontal, social, material and spiritual, *loving* relationship with other human beings, *all* other human beings. The second commandment is like unto the first. In one sense that is a strange and difficult, a hard saying. Loving the neighbor is like loving God? How can that be? Neighbors are so often unlovable, especially if we take Christ's definition of the neighbor as including the most despised and rejected members of the human race.

The answer must be that God is in the neighbor, the neighbor is made in the image and likeness of God, and Christ has already told us that he *is* the neighbor. Since those who can enjoy a direct knowledge of God are relatively few, the odds are that the principal way we get to know God, or Christ, is through knowledge of the neighbor. And it should be certain by now that the only way we can prove our love of God is through love of the neighbor.

Love. An ambiguous word. The modern man or woman finds it hard to accept that love can or should be *commanded* by God. Love is not something you can command, they protest. Love must be spontaneous, voluntary, freely given, from the heart. Not in Christian theology, it mustn't. Love is an act of the will, an act of the will that is designed, according to the coolest, clearest thinking of which the lover is capable, to promote the good of the loved one.

The custom of referring to the duties imposed by Matthew 25 as "the Works of Mercy" contributed to the notion among Christians that practical, active love of the poor was not commanded, either by God or by Christ. Christians tend to think of mercy as a quality over and above justice, something like the distinction that theologians have drawn between *praecepta* and *consilia*, the precepts or commandments of God and the "counsels of perfection" that Christ outlined in the Sermon on the Mount—turning the other cheek, giving one's cloak when sued for one's coat, walking the extra mile (Matt. 5:39–41) or selling all you have, giving the proceeds to the poor and following Jesus (Matt. 19:21). The translation of the Hebrew word *sedakah*, "justice," by the Septuagint scholars as equivalent to the Greek word *eleemosyne*, "almsgiving," has sanctioned this erroneous tradition (see chapter 2).

If Christ listed these so-called works of mercy as the absolute, rock-bottom, essential condition for the salvation of one's soul, doesn't it follow that these are not works of mercy in the sense that mercy has come to be understood by the modern mind? These are works of justice. True, the mandate falls differently on those who have superfluous goods and those who do not. For the first the mandate clearly refers to works of justice, for the second works of mercy, although even for the poor there may be times when some superfluity characterizes their state of life. For them, however, most of the time it seems reasonable to interpret the mandate spiritually. There are other kinds of hunger and need besides the hunger for food and the need for clothing and shelter. Pursuing this interpretation, the church has encouraged the practice of the Spiritual Works of Mercy, telling us to instruct the ignorant, counsel the doubtful, comfort the afflicted, admonish sinners, forgive all injuries, bear wrongs patiently, and pray for the living and the dead. Perhaps the only way to dispel the ambiguity about the Works of Mercy is to rename them the Works of Justice and Mercy.

We can conclude then that without the works of justice, either performed voluntarily or enforced by the state, there can be no socialist society, or any just society. Without the spiritual works of mercy a socialist society is most improbable. The spiritual works are the oil that makes the machinery of the just society run smoothly. As St. Paul puts it, if we give away all we have to the poor and have not love, we gain nothing.

I once heard a famous economist, son of a Methodist minister, complaining to an audience of priests, ministers, and rabbis that Judeo-Christian ethics include no sanction for the state to take from the rich and give to the poor. That the son of a minister believed this is a tribute to the success of capitalism and its friends in rewriting the Bible. Jesus not only expressed no opposition to the payment of taxes, even to the Roman emperor (Matthew 22:15–22) but paid taxes himself (Matt. 17:24–27). Nothing in the Bible exempts public officials, or the state, from the obligations imposed by Matthew 25.

ON GAINING AND SAVING

I quoted John Wesley in chapter 1 to the effect that "Our Lord has given us three rules to guide us" as regards the use of money. Wesley puts two of these rules in the mouth of Jesus himself: "gain all you can" and "save all you can." Nowhere in the gospels does Christ say anything of the kind. Wesley was apparently paraphrasing what he thought Jesus *meant* to say by the Parable of the Talents. The parable appears in Matthew (25:14–30) and in Luke (19:12–27) in somewhat different form. The talent was a unit of money in ancient times. The Matthew story tells of a master who went on a journey and entrusted five talents to one servant, two to another, and one to another, "to each according to his ability." The first traded with his talents and made five more, the second two more, but the third hid his talent in the ground for fear that he might lose it. The first two were praised by the master on his return, but the third was condemned, his talent taken from him and given to the one with ten talents. The master concludes, "For to every one who has will more be given, and he will have abundance; but from him who has not, even what he has will be taken away."

How common Wesley's interpretation was I do not know. Among contemporary theologians it would be difficult to find anyone who would agree with it. The most common reading is to interpret "talent" in another meaning and draw the obvious moral that unused talents atrophy physically, mentally, and spiritually and used talents grow and become stronger.

Students of the gospel are reluctant to read this parable as a kind of pep talk for sales persons, knowing that this interpretation cannot be reconciled with other things Jesus said, things about which there is no ambiguity. For example:

Do not lay up for yourselves treasures on earth, where moth and rust consume and where thieves break in and steal, but lay up for yourselves treasures in heaven, where neither moth nor rust consumes and where thieves do not break in and steal. For where your treasure is, there will your heart be also. . . . No one can serve two masters. . . . You cannot serve God and mammon [Matt. 6:19–21,24].

What can be done with the story of the rich young man? This incident, which is reported in almost exactly the same words in Matthew, Mark, and Luke, tells of the young man who wanted to follow Christ, but, when he was urged by

Jesus to "sell what you possess and give to the poor . . . went away sorrowful, for he had great possessions." Jesus remarks, "It is easier for a camel to go through the eye of a needle than for a rich man to enter the kingdom of God." All sorts of things have been done with this parable from the discovery of a gate in Jerusalem allegedly called the Needle's Eye to the *New Yorker* cartoon of the rich man who had a needle made that was so large a camel could get through it. We should be content with Jesus' own comment, "With men this is impossible" (Matt. 19:16–26). True, he did add the words, "but with God all things are possible," presumably meaning that God can still perform miracles for saints.

In fairness one must add that Jesus' advice to "sell what you possess and give to the poor" is a counsel, not a precept. Otherwise all of us would be in trouble. His first answer to the rich young man's question "What good deed must I do to have eternal life?" was simply, "If you would enter life, keep the commandments." The young man persisted, asking "what else?" and only then did Jesus spell out what it would mean for him if he wanted to go all the way. The point of the incident for the rest of us, however, is what Jesus had to say about the extreme difficulty that the rich face in saving their immortal souls.

If any doubts remain that Jesus sharply disagreed with those before and after him who said that financial success in this world is a reliable sign of spiritual success, the story reported in Luke 12:16–21 should put them to rest. This is the story of the rich man whose barns were not big enough to hold his crops. He tore them down and built larger ones and said to himself, "Soul, you have ample goods laid up for many years; take your ease, eat, drink, be merry." But God said to him, "Fool! This night your soul is required of you." And Jesus adds, "So is he who lays up treasure for himself, and is not rich toward God."

If, after that, any doubts still linger, there is the Parable of Dives and Lazarus. Dives (Latin for "the rich one") is the name tradition has given one of the characters in this story, but Jesus said only, "There was a rich man." St. Gregory the Great makes an excellent point:

> In common life the names of the rich are better known than those of the poor. How comes it then that when our Lord has to speak of both he names the poor man and not the rich? The answer is that God knows and approves the humble but does not know the proud.[1]

Actually, this rich man does not seem to have done anything terrible except to enjoy his riches in total indifference to the poor beggar who lay at his gate, full of sores. Dives went to hell and the beggar to heaven, to the bosom of Abraham. The rich man complained to Abraham, and Abraham replied, implying that the rich man should know better than to make such an unreasonable complaint: "Son, remember that you in your lifetime received your good things, and Lazarus in like manner evil things; but now he is comforted here, and you are in anguish" (Luke 16:19–31). Another hellfire sermon. And again, in Luke 6:24, Jesus says, "But woe to you that are rich, for you have received your consolation."

Conversely, Jesus is consistently partial, even biased, toward the poor. Lazarus is one example. Jesus' quotation from Isaiah in the synagogue at Nazareth, mentioned above, is another. Matthew 25 is another. The Sermon on the Plain is another. Jesus says, "Blessed are you poor, for yours is the kingdom of God. Blessed are you that hunger now, for you shall be satisfied" (Luke 6:20, 21).

Some have interpreted these blessings as being unconditional, as a kind of sanctification of the poor, much as Marx sanctified the proletariat and endowed them with all virtue and wisdom. This would be contrary to common sense. It does not therefore follow that Jesus' blessing is limited to "the poor in spirit," a phrase that occurs in a similar passage reported by Matthew from the Sermon on the Mount (Matt. 5:3). The French theologian J. Dupont reconciles these two blessings:

Blessed are the poor, not because they are better than others, or better prepared to receive the Kingdom which is to come, but because God seeks to make his Kingdom a tangible manifestation of his justice and love for the poor, the suffering and those who live in misery.[2]

The French Dominican Pie-Raymond Régamey sees significance in the message that Jesus sends to John the Baptist: "Go and tell John what you have seen and heard: the blind receive their sight, the lame walk, lepers are cleansed, and the deaf hear, the dead are raised up, the poor have good news preached to them" (Luke 7:22). This is a list of miracles. Father Régamey notes, "The sentence clearly rises past the raising of the dead, to a climax, to a kind of miracle still more amazing than those first mentioned."[3]

Before leaving the gospels it is appropriate to quote a point made by Stephen Mott about the Good Samaritan in his excellent book *Biblical Ethics and Social Change* (New York: Oxford University Press, 1982):

If every time the Good Samaritan went down that road from Jerusalem to Jericho he found people wounded and did nothing about the bandits, would his love be perfect? Spontaneous, simple love, following the dictates of its own concern for persons in need, grows into a concern for the formal structure of society [p. 58].

THE SOCIALIST ACTS OF THE APOSTLES

To understand the meaning of a person's life and teaching, it is important to listen to those who knew him or her well and to observe the manner of their lives. This will provide clues to what such persons regarded as their most essential ideas.

In the days immediately after the ascension of Jesus we read: "And all who believed were together and had all things in common; and they sold their possessions and goods and distributed them to all, as any had need" (Acts 2:44,45).

Two chapters later we read:

> Now the company of those who believed were of one heart and soul, and no one said that any of the things which he possessed was his own, but they had everything in common. . . . There was not a needy person among them, for as many as were possessors of lands or houses sold them, and brought the proceeds of what was sold and laid it at the apostles' feet; and distribution was made to each as any had need (Acts 4:32, 34, 35).

A man named Ananias and his wife, Sapphira, sold some of their property and brought part of the proceeds to the apostles, pretending that they were contributing the entire amount. Peter angrily rebuked them, "You have not lied to men but to God," and they fell down dead. The incident is significant for several reasons. First, it underlines the importance that the early Christians attributed to the commandment "You shall not bear false witness." Some theologians have suggested in recent years that the early Christians had a free-and-easy attitude about false witness when it came to editing or revising or embroidering the accounts of what Jesus and his apostles said and did. Second, it underlines the importance of Jesus' mandate about the Works of Justice and Mercy, about feeding the hungry, clothing the naked, and so on. Third, it says something about the Christian view of property and property rights. What it says can easily be exaggerated. After all, these people were "of one heart and soul." Their socialism was voluntary. It was more akin to the socialism of monasteries than to the socialism of states. But the incident does tell us that where the spirit of Christian love predominates, there and to that extent property rights yield to the Works of Justice. The socialism of those early Christians was a kind of signpost, pointing the way to the kingdom of God on earth.

In describing this early Christian commune, writers often use the phrase "Christian communism." I prefer the word "socialism," first, because communism has come to be identified with coercion and dictatorship, and second, because these Christians were democratic, and democracy is an essential characteristic of true socialism.

To say that the early Christians were democratic does not imply that Peter was not recognized as the head of the church. His deadly rebuke to Ananias and Sapphira would certainly indicate that he was, even if we did not have Jesus' word for it. But Acts also tells us that Peter's pontificate functioned in a way very different from what we are accustomed to think of as the pontifical style. Chapter 15 of Acts gives a detailed account of the Council of Jerusalem, at which the controversial question of circumcision was discussed and resolved. We learn that "the apostles and the elders" were present. At another point "the whole church" was involved with the action taken. Even after "much debate," four additional speakers are mentioned: Peter, Barnabas,

Paul and, finally, James. There was ample opportunity for opposing viewpoints to be heard. "But some believers who belonged to the party of the Pharisees rose up and said, 'It is necessary to circumcise them, and to charge them to keep the law of Moses' " (v.5). After James's summation, "Then it seemed good to the apostles and the elders, with the whole church . . . " (v.22). If there was not an actual vote, there was clearly a consensus, a sense of virtual unanimity, but not the unanimity that is imposed from above and assented to from fear. It was rather the unanimity, the consensus, that follows full consideration of all points of view and argument based on reason and appeals to the spirit of Christian love. If it was not a meeting of Christian socialists, it was a meeting in which a Christian socialist would have felt very much at home.

PAUL, JAMES, AND JOHN

St. Paul was an intellectual. He was not a pure intellectual, or to put it better, he was not just an intellectual. He supported himself by working at a manual trade, tent making. He was a missionary and an organizer, a man of action, with the kind of physical courage that is not usually associated with intellectuals. He was a saint, an intellectual saint.

Like most intellectuals, he was interested more in the life of the mind than in the life of the body. He was keenly aware, as he warned Timothy, that nothing is more dangerous to the life of the mind and the spirit than the love of money. "If we have food and clothing, with these we shall be content" (1 Tim. 6:8). He knew the value of voluntary poverty, but the French scholar P. Seidensticker has pointed out that "analysis of the Pauline texts reveals the surprising fact that the notion of 'poverty', understood as a state of need, is almost totally absent from Paul's thinking."[4] Almost, but not totally. For Paul expresses as well or better than anyone else the election of the poor:

> For consider your call, brethren: not many of you were wise according to worldly standards, not many were powerful, not many were of noble birth; but God chose what is foolish in the world to shame the wise, God chose what is weak in the world to shame the strong, God chose what is low and despised in the world, even things that are not, to bring to nothing things that are [1 Cor. 1:26–28].

As for Paul's comparative lack of interest in material poverty, Seidensticker gives this explanation:

> Paul has sought and found his own way to define Christian life and resolve its problems. The rules of his morality arise from the paschal condition of the Christian who, in Jesus Christ, has become a "new creature" (Gal. 3:27; Col. 3:11). And from this paschal reality of Christ Paul draws the conclusions which determine the paschal life of the Christian. Faced with these "riches of Christ," all worldly realities have to a certain extent ceased to exist.[5]

For contrast and, some believe, for a view of life that is closer to the real world, there is the Epistle of James. The older tradition is that it was written by St. James the Less, son of Alpheus, a cousin of Jesus, and a leader of the church in Jerusalem as reported in Acts. Some scholars think it was more likely written by a Hellenistic Christian, which would explain its vivid use of Greek metaphor and idiom. In favor of the St. James theory, it is written with great authority, containing 60 imperatives in its 108 verses. Clearly the author was a person of highly respected position in the Christian world.

Some have claimed that James is in conflict with Paul on the question of justification by faith or works. Martin Luther thought so. Preferring Paul's emphasis on faith, he dismissed James's work as "an epistle of straw." The differences between Paul and James, however, are mainly differences of emphasis and vocabulary. Some representative quotes from James:

> Religion that is pure and undefiled before God and the Father is this: to visit orphans and widows in their affliction, and to keep oneself unstained from the world [1:27].

> For if a man with gold rings and in fine clothing comes into your assembly, and a poor man in shabby clothing also comes in, and you pay attention to the one who wears the fine clothing and say, "Have a seat here, please," while you say to the poor man, "Stand there," or, "Sit at my feet," have you not made distinctions among yourselves, and become judges with evil thoughts? Listen, my beloved brethren. Has not God chosen those who are poor in the world to be rich in faith and heirs of the kingdom which he has promised to those who love him? But you have dishonored the poor man. Is it not the rich who oppress you . . . ? [2:2–6].

> What does it profit, my brethren, if a man says he has faith but has not works? Can his faith save him? If a brother or sister is ill-clad and in lack of daily food, and one of you says to them, "Go in peace, be warmed and filled," without giving them the things needed for the body, what does it profit? So faith by itself, if it has no works, is dead [2:14–17].

And, finally, one of the more critical statements ever made about those whom we moderns regard highly:

> Come now, you rich, weep and howl for the miseries that are coming upon you. Your riches have rotted and your garments are moth-eaten. Your gold and silver have rusted, and their rust will be evidence against you and will eat your flesh like fire. You have laid up treasure for the last days. Behold, the wages of the laborers who mowed your fields, which you kept back by fraud, cry out; and the cries of the harvesters have reached the ears of the Lord of hosts. You have lived on the earth in

luxury and in pleasure; you have fattened your hearts in a day of slaughter. [5:1-6].

Paul will probably continue to be more popular with the theologians, but I find James closer to both the letter and the spirit of Christ. He may have been only an anonymous Christian from some Greek settlement in Asia Minor, but another more prestigious figure supports his position—John, "the disciple whom Jesus loved."

Writing toward the end of the first Christian century, John summed up his understanding of what Jesus expected of the true believer:

But if any one has the world's goods and sees his brother in need, yet closes his heart against him, how does God's love abide in him? Little children, let us not love in word or speech but in deed and in truth [1 John 3:17, 18].

That Jesus spelled out in the New Testament a socialist program would be a ridiculous claim. However, he did spell out certain basic principles that a conscientious Christian should look for in any economic or political system. First among these was an active, practical, effective concern for the poor. In our times the goal that seems most consistent with that concern is full employment. If it can be shown that the only way to achieve that goal is through some form of socialism (as defined in the Introduction), then it can logically and fairly be said that Jesus was a socialist, or would be a socialist if he were living in the world today.

Since in another sense, Jesus *is* living in the world today, it is interesting to speculate on the consequences if those in whom he lives were to consider, and accept, the implications of that logical probability.

CHAPTER 4

The Fathers of the Church

"The Fathers of the Church," to quote one definition, is

> a name given by the Christian Church to the writers who established Christian doctrine before the eighth century. The writings of the Fathers, or patristic literature, synthesized Christian doctrine as found in the Bible, especially the Gospels, the writings of the Apostolic Fathers, ecclesiastical dictums, and decisions of Church councils.[1]

Eight of the Fathers were also designated Doctors of the Church, four from the East and four from the West. The designations were not made until 1298 (West) and 1568 (East), so it is evident that the titles were not the fruit of hasty judgment. This chapter will call seven of them to the witness stand. (St. Athanasius, who may have been too busy battling the Arians to devote much time to the problems of poverty, will not be quoted.) Six of these seven Father-Doctors were born within twenty-five years of each other in the fourth century B.C. They lived, studied, and wrote in all the major centers of the Mediterranean world and were, most of them, familiar with both Greek and Latin literature.

It is not so surprising that these Fathers were contemporaries. In 312 Constantine was fighting for the right to be recognized as sole emperor of the Western division of the Roman Empire; he defeated Maxentius at the decisive battle at the Milvian Bridge in Rome. Just before this battle he is said to have had a vision of the Christian cross with the legend in Greek, "By this sign thou shalt conquer." He did, whether by that sign or by his own military superiority, and by 324 had defeated his Eastern rival, Licinius, established his capital at Constantinople (formerly Byzantium, subsequently Istanbul), and made Christianity the official religion of the Roman Empire.

Some say that it has been all downhill since then. That is another question. It is clear, however, that it was no longer a dangerous, unpopular thing to be a Christian. The contrary, in fact, was now true. Therefore rich Christians became numerous and the thinkers in the church were faced with the question "To what extent can the rich be Christian, and vice versa?" That is one reason why the next hundred years produced so much intellectual activity directed to these questions.

THE FATHERS OF THE EASTERN CHURCH

First, the Fathers of the East. St. Gregory of Nazianzus (c. 329–389) was born in Asia Minor, educated in Alexandria and Athens, and eventually became bishop of Constantinople. His words in this instance are a clear echo of Jesus' words in Matthew 25:

> To conclude, if you believe what I say, servants of Christ, brothers and fellow heirs, while there is still time let us visit Christ, care for Christ, feed Christ, clothe Christ, welcome Christ, honour Christ; not only by seating him at our table, as some did (Luke 7:36) nor with ointments, like Mary (John 12:3); nor only with a burial, like Joseph of Arimathea; nor with what was needed for the burial, like Nicodemus, who only half loved Christ; nor with gold, incense and myrrh, like the wise men before all the others. No, the Lord of all things wants mercy rather than sacrifice (Matt. 9:13), and he wants hearts full of compassion rather than thousands of lambs; let us give them to him, then, through the poor and those who suffer today, so that when we leave this world we shall be received in the eternal storehouses by the same Christ our Lord, to whom be the glory forever. Amen.[2]

St. Basil the Great (c. 330–379), patriarch of Eastern monks, was born in Caesarea (now Kayseri, Turkey), educated in Constantinople and Athens, and then became bishop of Caesarea, where he established a complex around the church and monastery that included hostels, almshouses, and hospitals for infectious diseases. During the great famine of 368 he preached vigorously against profiteers and the indifferent rich. He was among the first to speak and write with clarity on the subject of property rights, the question of "mine and thine," which is so essential to any discussion of either capitalism or socialism. The following excerpt from his sermon on *The Rich Fool* is perhaps his most famous statement, and again we hear echoes of Matthew 25 as well as of the confusion, or distinction, between *sedakah* (justice) and *eleemosyne* (almsgiving):

> Who is the covetous man? One for whom plenty is not enough. Who is the defrauder? One who takes away what belongs to everyone. And are not you covetous, are not you a defrauder, when you keep for private use what you were given for distribution? When some one strips a man of his clothes we call him a thief. And one who might clothe the naked and does not—should not he be given the same name? The bread in your hoard belongs to the hungry; the cloak in your wardrobe belongs to the naked; the shoes you let rot belong to the barefoot; the money in your vaults

belongs to the destitute. All you might help and do not—to all these you are doing wrong.[3]

The Latin original for the last sentence is *Quocirca tot injuriaris quot dare valeres.* An even stronger translation is "In other words, you are committing as many injustices as there are things you could give away." My own favorite summation of this passage is the formula learned by a generation of Catholic Workers from Peter Maurin, simply, "The coat that hangs in the closet belongs to the poor."

Basil returned again and again in his sermons to this theme. In the following excerpt he deals with the Christians who, like the young man in the gospel, keep all the other commandments but forget the most important one:

> Though you have not killed, like you say, nor committed adultery, nor stolen, nor borne false witness, you make all of this useless unless you add the only thing which can allow you to enter the kingdom. . . . If it is true that you have kept the law of charity from your childhood, as you claim, and that you have done as much for others as for yourself, then where does all your wealth come from? Care for the poor absorbs all available resources. . . . So whoever loves his neighbor as himself owns no more than his neighbor does. But you have a great fortune. How can this be, unless you have put your own interests before those of others? . . . I know many people who fast, pray, groan, and do any kind of pious work that doesn't affect their pockets, but at the same time they give nothing to the needy. What good are their merits? The Kingdom of heaven is closed to them. Every time I go into the home of one of these foolish rich people, resplendent with ornaments, I notice that for its owner there is nothing more precious than visible goods, which deck him out according to his pleasure, but that he despises his soul. I wonder then what great benefit this silver furniture and ivory chairs can be producing while all these hoarded riches are not passed to the poor, who in their multitudes cry in misery at the gates of rich men's houses.[4]

Basil was shrewd enough to anticipate an argument of John Maynard Keynes, the British economist:

> As a great river flows by a thousand channels through fertile country, so let your wealth run through many conduits to the homes of the poor. Wells that are drawn from flow the better; left unused, they go foul. So money kept standing still is worthless; moving and changing hands, it helps the community and brings increase.[5]

Basil was by no means a bleeding-heart liberal. Like Paul he had no sympathy for deadbeats or able-bodied beggars, unless they were unemployed through no fault of their own. "Don't go knocking on other doors," he advised.

The well of one's neighbor is always narrow. It is much better to meet your needs through your own work than to be lifted up suddenly thanks to another's support. . . . Do not submit yourself to the moneylender, who will attack you, nor let yourself be hunted and captured like prey.[6]

These Doctors were not dreamers. They were sharp, practical men who, despite their deep spirituality, had a realistic knowledge of the world.

St. John's surname, Chrysostom, was given him because it meant "golden-mouthed"; he was recognized as the greatest orator of his time (c.349–407). He devoted a large part of his talent to afflicting the comfortable: "The rich are in possession of the goods of the poor, even if they have acquired them honestly or inherited them legally."[7] If the wealthy do not share their superfluous goods with the poor, he insisted, they are "a species of bandit."[8] In pursuing this argument he followed that of Aristotle and anticipated its further development by Thomas Aquinas:

Do not say, "I am using what belongs to me." You are using what belongs to others. All the wealth of the world belongs to you and to the others in common, as the sun, air, earth, and all the rest.[9]

Using such quotations from John Chrysostom and other Fathers, José Miranda has concluded that any ownership of private property that "differentiates" the rich from the poor is condemned by the Judeo-Christian tradition.[10] What St. James had to say about the rich, what Basil had to say about the conflict between love of neighbor and the accumulation of wealth, would seem to bear this out, but many scholars disagree. R. M. Grant maintains that "only Irenaeus among the early Fathers suggested that the ownership of property was due to avarice. . . . The right to own private property was taken for granted."[11] This, of course, Miranda does not deny, but only that "differentiating ownership" was permitted. On this point some of the Fathers seem ambiguous. After all, Jesus conceded that "with God all things are possible," including the salvation of the rich. John Chrysostom himself was not ambiguous, as the following would indicate:

I am often reproached for continually attacking the rich. Yes, because the rich are continually attacking the poor. But those I attack are not the rich as such, only those who misuse their wealth. I point out constantly that those I accuse are not the rich, but the rapacious; wealth is one thing, covetousness another. Learn to distinguish.[12]

What the Fathers are agreed on, however, in their interpretations of both Old and New Testaments, is that superfluous wealth belongs to those who are truly needy.

Truly needy. Like the others, John Chrysostom had no illusions about poor people:

Enough of stealing what is not yours, both rich and poor; for now I am speaking not only to the rich but also to the poor. For the poor also rob those who are poorer than they; the richer and stronger craftsmen exploit the more needy and less well off; the tradesmen exploit other tradesmen and those who sell in the market. I want to eradicate injustice everywhere. An unjust act is not measured according to the amount defrauded or stolen, but by the intention of the one who robbed or defrauded. This is true, and I remember saying to you that the most miserly and the thieves are those who do not forgive even small amounts. . . . Let us learn not to want more than is fair and not to covet what we do not need. In the things of heaven our longing should not be limited; there, we should desire always more; but on earth each one should seek only what is necessary and sufficient and not ask for more, so that we can obtain true goods through grace.[13]

Again we see the theme that St. Paul stressed in his letter to Timothy: The Christian should be content with that modest amount of material goods that he or she really needs. This is the precise opposite of the capitalist creed preached by Adam Smith and Ben Franklin and, mistakenly, by John Wesley in his "Gain-all-you-can-Save-all-you-can" interpretation of the gospel.

THE FATHERS OF THE WESTERN CHURCH

The positions taken by the Doctors of the West are similar to those we have observed among the Doctors in the East.

St. Ambrose (c. 340–397) was born in what is now West Germany and educated in Rome. Son of the prefect of Gaul, he studied law and was appointed consular magistrate in North Italy, with headquarters at Milan. His kindness and wisdom won him the love of the people. The story goes that when he was presiding at a meeting of the people to elect a new bishop, a small boy cried out, "Let Ambrose be bishop!" and all the people took up the cry. Ambrose, who had not even been baptized, left the city to avoid the call of the people, but eventually returned, was baptized, ordained, and consecrated bishop.

In this first statement note that the words are almost identical to those employed by Basil in reminding the faithful of the true nature of property rights:

It is the bread of the poor which you are holding back; it is the clothes of the naked which you are hoarding; it is the relief and liberation of the wretched which you are thwarting by burying your money away.[14]

And again:

You are not making a gift of your possessions to the poor person. You are handing over to him what is his.[15]

The reasoning behind this view of property rights is similar to that of John Chrysostom. Ambrose puts it as follows:

God has ordered all things to be produced so that there should be food in common for all, and that the earth should be the common possession of all. Nature, therefore, has produced a common right for all, but greed has made it a right for a few.[16]

He could express the same idea with greater passion. In his commentary on the despoiling of Naboth's vineyard by the greedy Ahab (I Kings 21) Ambrose really lets go:

You rich, how far will you push your frenzied greed? "Are you alone to dwell on the earth?" (Isa. 5:8). You cast out men who are fellow-creatures and claim all creation as your own. Why? Earth at its beginning was for all in common, it was meant for rich and poor alike; what right have you to monopolize the soil?[17]

Like Basil and John Chrysostom, Ambrose was a practical man and recognized that not all the poor were deserving:

We must not confuse generosity with prodigality. The priest must be able to judge how to be liberal without exhausting the reserves on one case, but sharing them among all in need. The search for vainglory must never replace the search for justice! If this happens, he will easily fall victim to impostors and swindlers, who are legion. Many pretend to be poor. They come asking for alms which they do not need, just so they can walk the streets and do nothing. They wear ragged clothes. They disguise their true age so as to receive more. They pretend to be in debt, or claim to have been robbed. All this must be carefully checked, so that the poor man's money shall not end up in the swindler's pocket. In a word, the priest's generosity must lie exactly half way between thoughtless prodigality and meanness, which might lead him to give the money of the faithful to the undeserving.[18]

This was a somewhat different emphasis from that of St. Clement of Alexandria (c.150–220), one of the apostolic Fathers, who wrote:

You must not try to distinguish between the deserving and the undeserving. You may easily make a mistake, and as the matter is in doubt, it is better to benefit the undeserving than, in avoiding this, to miss the good. We are told not to judge.[19]

Ambrose was more practical, but it seems safe to conclude that he would agree with Clement that, *in case of doubt*, it is better to make a mistake in the direction of obedience to the commandment than to run the risk of disobedience.

St. Jerome (c. 345–420) was born in what is now Yugoslavia, lived and worked in Constantinople, Rome, and Bethlehem. His great work was translating the Bible (Vulgate). Only one quotation suits our purpose, but it is a powerful one and comes down on the side of those who maintain that to be wealthy is by definition a condition inconsistent with Christianity.

Commenting on Jesus' reference (Luke 16:9) to "the money of injustice" (also translated as "unrighteous mammon" or "mammon of wickedness"), Jerome writes:

> And he very rightly said, "money of injustice," for all riches come from injustice. Unless one person has lost, another cannot find. Therefore I believe that the popular proverb is very true: "The rich person is either an unjust person or the heir of one."[20]

Of all the Fathers and Doctors of the Church, at least before the appearance of Thomas Aquinas, the superstar was undoubtedly St. Augustine (354–430). Some prefer him to Aquinas. Reinhold Niebuhr, the great Protestant theologian, once said of him, "Augustine, whatever may be [his] defects . . . nevertheless proves himself a more reliable guide than any known thinker."[21]

Born in Tagaste in what is now Algeria, Augustine spent the first thirty-three years of his life as a free-living pagan and a Manichaean. He was converted by the prayers of his mother, Monica, and the words and example of St. Ambrose. He became a priest and then bishop of Hippo in North Africa.

One of his most significant statements was this simple Latin sentence: "*Iustitia est in subveniendo miseris*" (Assisting the needy is justice).[22] This teaching is typical of the Fathers, most of whom thought and wrote of almsgiving in terms of *iustitia* (justice) as well as *caritas* (charity). Matthew 25 was indeed for them the Works of Justice *and* Mercy.

As befits his philosophical bent, Augustine gives a philosophical answer to the question "Can human beings find happiness in riches?"

> All men do whatever good or evil they do to free themselves from the causes of their misfortune and to acquire happiness, and they always seek to live happily, whether by good or evil. However, not all of them attain what they seek. Everyone wants to be happy, but only those who act justly will be happy. I don't understand how those who do evil can hope to be happy. How? By owning money, silver and gold, land, houses and slaves, by the pomp of this world and worldly honor, which is fickle and transitory? They seek to find happiness by owning things.
>
> But what must you own to be happy? When you become happy, you say, you will become better than you are now, wretched as you are. But it is not possible for what is worse than you to make you better; you are a man, and everything you long for to make you happy is inferior to you.

Gold and silver and any material thing you long to obtain, possess and enjoy are inferior to you. You are better and are worth more, and as you wish to be happy, you want to be better than you are because you are unhappy. True, it is better to be happy than wretched. But to be better than you are, you seek what is worse than you. Everything on earth is worse than you. . . . So take my loyal advice: we all know you want to be better and we want it too; seek what is better than you, which is the only thing that can make you better.[23]

In one short sentence of Latin alliteration Augustine sums up a volume of patristic theory: "*Non sunt divitiae nec verae nec vestrae*" (Riches are neither real nor are they yours).[24] But he was not one of those who condemned the rich out of hand:

I do not say, "You are damned if you have possessions." I say, "You are damned if you presume on them, if you are puffed up by them, if you consider yourselves important because of them, if because of them you disregard the poor, if you forget your common human status because you have so much more of vanities."[25]

He did not insist that all people, or even all Christians, must live as did the first Christians in Jerusalem. He did, however, have a great love for that manner of life, promoted the patristic tradition of referring to it as "the apostolic life," and incorporated it into the Augustinian Rule for the monastic community at his own see of Hippo. This was the heart of it: "Now the company of those who believed were of one heart and soul, and no one said that any of the things which he possessed was his own, but they had everything in common" (Acts 4:32).

Father Régamey tells this story: Augustine once called his people together in his cathedral and had the deacon read the text from the Acts. He then took the book from the deacon and said, "I also want to read to you in my turn. I take more joy in reading you these words than in giving you my own." He read the text again, and then said, "This is how we want to live; pray that we may be able."[26]

In rebuking both rich and poor who neglect the Works of Justice, Augustine combines St. Paul's teaching on the Mystical Body of Christ with Matthew 25:

For consider, brethren, the love of our head. He is in heaven, yet he suffers here as long as his Church suffers here. Here Christ is hungry, here he is thirsty, is naked, is a stranger, is sick, is in prison. For whatever his body suffers here, he has said that he himself suffers.[27]

In chapter 3 I discussed the implications of Matthew 25 and suggested that full employment at decent wages is even more in keeping with the spirit of Christ's words than the individual performance of giving food to a hungry person. Conversely, the refusal to provide full employment at decent wages is even more in violation of that spirit than is individual refusal. This is the kind of point that Augustine is making in the following passage:

> A certain exploiter of the property of others says to me, "I am not like that rich man. I give love-feasts, I send food to the prisoners in jail, I clothe the naked, I take in strangers." Do you really think that you are giving? . . . You fool. . . . You must grasp the fact that when you feed a Christian, you feed Christ, and when you exploit a Christian, you exploit Christ. . . . If then he shall go into eternal fire to whom Christ will say, "When naked you did not clothe me," what place in the eternal fire is reserved for him to whom Christ shall say, "I was clothed and you stripped me bare"?[28]

Economic injustice, in Augustine's view, is therefore even worse than failure to share one's superfluous goods with the needy. This conclusion is the cornerstone of Christian socialism. Let me spell that out a little more specifically in terms of this chapter. We cannot pretend that we are Christians unless the Works of Justice are a top priority in our private morality *and* our public morality, in our economic morality *and* our political morality. We cannot pretend that we are doing the Works of Justice if we limit ourselves to individual relief of the needy or if we limit ourselves to public relief of the needy. The Works of Justice start with full employment, meaningful jobs, and living wages, assuming, that is, that we read Augustine and Jesus not simply in the light of their times but in the light of our times. To put a worker out of work is, in Augustine's phrase, to strip Christ bare.

There is one weakness, or ambiguity, in the words of Augustine quoted above, which in all honesty we cannot ignore. By use of the term "Christian" he *seems* to limit the application of Matthew 25 only to Christians. This is an ancient interpretation that has long since been abandoned. Jesus' reference to "the least of these my brethren" cannot be limited to Christians. There is no way one can reconcile the Parable of the Good Samaritan, or good sense, with such a reading.

St. Gregory the Great (c. 540–604) came to the Catholic Church by the political route. Born in Rome of a wealthy patrician family, he was named prefect of Rome by the emperor, Justin II. When his father died, his inherited wealth went to the poor and to the founding of monasteries. He retired to one of these monasteries as an ordinary monk, but was soon pressed into the service of the church by Pope Pelagius II. He became pope himself in 590. His greatest work, *Moralia*, runs to thirty-five volumes. He is the father of Gregorian chant and was largely responsible for the conversion of England. He distinguished himself by his protection of the Jews from persecution and from losing their legal privileges.

The following passage echoes the teaching of the earlier Fathers but is even more explicit in asserting that the Works of Mercy are really Works of Justice:

Those who neither make after others' goods nor bestow their own are to be admonished to take it well to heart that the earth they come from is common to all and brings forth nurture for all alike. Idly then do men hold themselves innocent when they monopolise for themselves the common gift of God. In not giving what they have received they work their neighbors' death; every day they destroy all the starving poor whose means to relief they store at home. When we furnish the destitute with any necessity we render them what is theirs, not bestow on them what is ours; *we pay the debt of justice rather than perform the works of mercy.* . . . Of Dives in the Gospel we do not read that he snatched the goods of others but that he used his own unfruitfully; and avenging hell received him at death not because he did anything unlawful but because he gave himself up utterly and inordinately to the enjoyment of what was lawful [emphasis added].[29]

Two other Fathers of the church were eventually designated as Doctors, and they should be included in this anthology.

St. Leo the Great (c. 400–461, pope from 440 to 461), an Italian, was unanimously elected pope by the Roman populace. In 452 he saved Rome from destruction by Attila the Hun when in a personal confrontation, according to one report, "he subdued the barbarian king by the majesty of his presence." I quote him at length because he deals with a question that has bothered others: why does Jesus in Matthew 25 say nothing about the other commandments?

But perhaps there are some rich men who without assisting the Church's poor by alms nevertheless keep other commandments of God; they have merits of faith and rectitude and so forth, and think it a venial matter that one virtue should be wanting. Ah, but this virtue is such that without it their other virtues—if indeed they have them—can be of no avail. Our Lord says that the merciful are blessed because on them God will have mercy. And when the Son of Man comes in his majesty and sits on the throne of his glory; when all nations are assembled and division is made between good and bad, for what will praise be given to those on the right hand? Only for the works of kindness and deeds of charity, which Jesus Christ will hold to be spent on himself; for he who made man's nature his own nature withdrew himself in nothing from human lowliness.

And what will be the reproach to those on the left hand? Only the neglect of love, the harshness of inhumanity, the denial of mercy to the poor. It is as if the first had no other virtues, the second no other sins. But at that great and supreme judgment, such value will be set on the graciousness of giving or the wickedness of withholding that this or that will stand for the fullness of all virtues or the sum of all sinning. It is by the path of that one good thing that these will pass into the kingdom, by the path of that one bad thing that those will travel to everlasting fire.

Therefore, beloved, let no man flatter himself on any merits of worthy living if he lacks the works of charity, or be confident in the purity of his body when he is not cleansed by the purification of alms. Alms blot out sins, destroy death, and quench the punishment of eternal fire.[30]

St. Isidore of Seville (c. 560–636) was the last of the Western Fathers. He became archbishop of Seville in 600 and was known as the most learned scholar of his day, author of a 20-volume encyclopedia that has the distinction of being the first work to contain a printed map of the world. He is tough on "oppressors of the poor." His treatment of the subject is unusual in that he offers arguments as to why and how God brings good out of such oppression:

> The oppressors of the poor are to know that they win a heavier sentence when they prevail against those they seek to harm. The more strongly they prove their power on the lives of the wretched here, the more terrible is the future punishment to which they must be condemned. . . .
> The wicked seek a thing in the evilness of their will but God gives them leave to accomplish it in the goodness of his, because he works much good from our evil. . . . Sometimes the wickedness of the perverse makes for the profit of the just, who are instructed by these men's malice and urged by temporal afflictions to seek the kingdom of heaven. This is proved by the example of the Israelites, who were hardest driven in Egypt when it was appointed them to be called by Moses to the land of promise, to depart from the evils they suffered in Egypt and to hasten to their own promised land.[31]

Likewise, as evil and injustice have recurred down through the centuries, men and women have been moved to depart from that evil and injustice and "to hasten to their own promised land." It is the perennial hope that both consoles and spurs us on.

One other thing should be noted in this brief summary and sample of the teachings of the Fathers and Doctors. We see here the beginnings of a theory of property rights. The development of this theory by St. Thomas Aquinas and the first challenge to that theory from within the Christian fold are the main burden of the next chapter. Both the theory and the challenge are essential to an intelligent understanding of Christian socialism, for the theory is at the opposite end of the spectrum from the theories of Adam Smith, John Locke, and most modern Christians.

CHAPTER 5

The Middle Ages
and Thomas Aquinas

During the fifth and sixth centuries, wave after wave of Germanic tribes broke through the frontier defenses of the Roman Empire. By 600 A.D. they had gained possession of most of its territory. Culture, philosophy, and theology survived mainly in the monasteries, and even there did not always thrive.

What has been called the Constantinian church reached a kind of apogee when on Christmas Day of the year 800, Pope Leo III inaugurated the Holy Roman Empire and crowned Charlemagne as Emperor of the West. Despite the mingling of spiritual and temporal power, of spiritual and temporal wealth, the tradition of Matthew 25 and its imperatives remained strong.

A significant voice was that of St. Ambrose Autpert (d. 778), who was an official of some importance under Charlemagne's father, Pepin the Short, first king of the Franks. Autpert was at one time tutor to Charlemagne, but left his courtly career to enter a Benedictine abbey. From there he warned the rich and powerful:

> Listen, you who are rich, whom greed has blinded, who judge perversely—if you scorn the poor man prostrate beneath your feet, have you no fear of his lord and yours, rising in wrath against you? . . . You who are as rich in earthly prosperity as poor in heavenly treasure, hear the words that God has for you, God who is judge of all men: "Do not rob the poor because he is poor, or crush the afflicted at the gate; for the Lord will plead their cause and despoil of life those who despoil them" [Prov. 22:22–23].[1]

Author's Note: I am indebted for much of the argument of this chapter to Sister Mary Emil Penet, IHM, "Property and Right in Representative Catholic Moralists." Ph.D. diss., St. Louis University, 1951.

Another powerful voice was that of St. Bernard of Clairvaux (1090–1153), founder of ninety Cistercian monasteries, Doctor of the Church, friend of kings and popes, preacher of the Second Crusade. He went right to the source:

> Clothe the naked, feed the poor, visit the sick, lest it befall you to hear the hard saying, the word of bitterness, the evil tidings: "Depart from me, you cursed, into the eternal fire prepared for the devil and his angels."[2]

St. Catherine of Siena (1347–1380), the Dominican mystic whose opinion was valued and followed by popes, suffered no illusions about the compatibility of riches and virtue:

> Riches impoverish and kill the soul; they make a man cruel toward himself; they make him finite and dispossess him of the dignity of the infinite, for his desire, which should be united with [the] infinite Good, has been set on a finite thing and lovingly united with that.[3]

THOMAS AQUINAS

Of all the medieval saints and sages, however, one stood far above the rest, so far above that even today, especially in the Catholic Church, his influence probably remains greater than that of any other Christian thinker since St. Paul. That one was St. Thomas Aquinas (1225–1274).

During the twelfth century a Spanish Arab named Averroës, a man so brilliant he distinguished himself in separate careers as jurist, physician, and philosopher, had revived the interest of Western Europeans in Aristotle. He maintained that there were two ways of knowing the truth: one by reason and philosophy, notably that of Aristotle, and the other by religion, which is truth in a form that the ordinary person can understand. Clearly to him religion was the inferior way.

This theory, which came to be known as the theory of "double truth," won followers in France, one of whom was Siger de Brabant (c. 1235–81). He maintained that therefore philosophy was independent of Christian revelation. The man who, before all others, met the challenge was Thomas Aquinas.

The most dramatic incident of his monastic life was the manner of his entering it at the age of eighteen. His widowed mother, determined that he should not become a Dominican monk, confined him for a year to the family castle near Aquino. At one point, the story goes, his brothers introduced a shady lady into his room with a view to weakening his monastic resolve. Brandishing a torch, Thomas drove her out and then used the torch to burn a cross on the door of his room.

Aquinas may have tenaciously resisted the wishes of his family, but he certainly was no revolutionary radical. In an early work, *De Regimine Principum* (On Princely Government), written for the king of Cyprus, he maintained that monarchy was the best form of government, but much of the work justifies the overthrow of tyrannical monarchs.[4] Later in the *Summa Theologica* he concluded that the best form of government combined elements of monarchy, aristocracy, and democracy in a manner not very different from the American arrangement of executive, judicial, and legislative branches.[5]

On the subject of property, which is central to the question of Christian socialism, Thomas took off from a principle first expressed by Aristotle, as he did in so much of his work. That principle was: "Property should be in a certain sense common, but as a general rule private."[6]

Thomas adds, "Community of goods is . . . part of the natural law,"[7] and he defines the natural law as "the participation of the eternal law in rational creatures."[8] This law implies that God made the universe and all that is in it for the use of *all* humankind.

> The distribution of property is a matter not for natural law but, rather, human agreement [*humanum condictum*]. . . . The individual holding of possessions is not, therefore, contrary to the natural law; it is what rational beings conclude as an addition to the natural law.[9]

Thomas gives three reasons to explain why rational beings have made this addition to the natural law of "community of goods." They must be considered carefully by every socialist, and especially by those who put all their confidence in public ownership.

> *First,* because each person takes more trouble to care for something that is his sole responsibility than what is held in common or by many—for in such a case each individual shirks the work and leaves the responsibility to somebody else, which is what happens when too many officials are involved. *Second,* because human affairs are more efficiently organized if each person has his own responsibility to discharge; there would be chaos if everybody cared for everything. *Third,* because men live together in greater peace where everyone is content with his task. We do, in fact, notice that quarrels often break out amongst men who hold things in common without distinction.[10]

Some of these reasons are more and some less relevant, but those who favor social ownership, whether public or cooperative, must be sure that the structural arrangements used are as consistent as possible with these common-sense principles.

But just as Thomas insists on the advantages of those *human* laws by which governments provide for private possession, so does he insist on the *natural* law of common use. There would seem to be a contradiction here, and the seeming contradiction has been the excuse for conservative Christians to neglect the natural law and concentrate exclusively on human laws. Let us, however, pursue the Thomistic resolution of the problem—and it is a genuine problem—

of reconciling private possession and common use. Thomas starts from an assumption that should be acceptable to the good pagan or humanist:

> For the well-being of the individual two things are necessary: the first and most essential is to act virtuously (it is through virtue, in fact, that we live a good life); the other, and secondary, requirement is rather a means, and lies in a sufficiency of material goods, such as are necessary to virtuous action. . . . Finally, it is necessary that there be, through the ruler's sagacity, a sufficiency of those material goods which are indispensable to well-being.[11]

In that section of the *Summa Theologica* in which Thomas explains that "if one is to speak quite strictly, it is improper to say that using somebody else's property taken out of extreme necessity is theft," he places the two aspects of his theory of property in their proper relationship and grounds them solidly in the teaching of Ambrose and Basil:

> The dictates of human law cannot derogate from natural or divine law. The natural order established by God in his providence is, however, such that lower things are meant to enable man to supply his needs. A man's needs must therefore still be met out of the world's goods, even though a certain division and apportionment of them is determined by law. And this is why according to natural law goods that are held in superabundance by some people should be used for the maintenance of the poor. This is the principle enunciated by Ambrose. . . , "It is the bread of the poor that you are holding back; it is the clothes of the naked that you are hoarding; it is the relief and liberation of the wretched that you are thwarting by burying your money away. . . ."[12]

The question then comes down to this: Can Judeo-Christian ethics justify the state in taking from the superabundance of the rich to supply the necessities of the poor? The answer is certainly implied in the passage above about the necessity for the ruler to supply "a sufficiency of those material goods which are indispensable to [individual] well-being." In listing the duties of a prince, Thomas is even stronger: "Finally, provision must be made so that no person goes in want, according to his condition and calling; otherwise neither city nor kingdom would long endure."[13]

St. Thomas is not satisfied with the idea of welfare. He wants people to support themselves—full employment.

> For the peace of the state it is necessary therefore that the legislator should think out remedies against these three reasons for injury done to others. In the case of those who are injured because they are unable to acquire what is necessary for subsistence, there will suffice the remedy of

some modest possession, so that through their own labor they can earn their keep for themselves.[14]

In all probability Thomas was thinking of land, or perhaps a sum sufficient to start a small business. The equivalent today is, of course, a job. Note that Thomas is saying that if the government does not take care of this, then there is question of injury. Justice has been violated, not just charity.

It remained for Cardinal Tommaso Cajetan (1469–1534), the Italian theologian and papal legate who was one of the greatest commentators on St. Thomas, to spell out the implications of the Thomistic theory of property most clearly:

> Now what a ruler can do in virtue of his office, so that justice may be served in the matter of riches, is to take from someone who is unwilling to dispense from what is superfluous for life or state, and to distribute it to the poor. In this way he just takes away the dispensation power of the rich man to whom the wealth has been entrusted because he is not worthy. For according to the teaching of the saints, the riches that are superfluous do not belong to the rich man as his own but rather to the one appointed by God as dispenser, so that he can have the merit of a good dispensation. The legal obligation [*legale debitum*] in this case is founded on the justice obligations of riches themselves. These belong in the classification of useful goods. And superfluity that is not given away is kept in a way that goes counter to the good of both parties. It is counter to the good of the one who hoards it, because it is his only so that he can preside at the giving away. And it is counter to the good of the indigent because someone else continues to possess what has been given for their use. And therefore, as Basil said, it belongs to the indigent, at least as owed, if not in fact. And therefore an injury is done to the poor in not dispensing the superfluous. And this injury is something that the prince, who is the guardian of the right, should set to rights by the power of his office.[15]

The paragraph you have just read is perhaps the most important paragraph of the entire book so far; it summarizes and concentrates the whole Judeo-Christian tradition as it relates to property, the distribution of wealth and income, the obligations of people and governments in regard to the same, and the whole subject matter of Christian socialism.

Another important contribution of Aquinas was his insistence on the "just price." This was a price that reflected the fair value of the thing or service sold, without fraud, and included a just wage, a wage sufficient to meet the requirements set forth in the passages above, plus a fair profit. As follows:

> Profit-making can become justifiable, provided this is not the ultimate aim and is meant to fulfill some necessary and worthy purpose. . . . This is exemplified by the man who uses moderate business profits to

provide for his household, or to help the poor; or even by the man who conducts his business for the public good in order to insure that the country does not run short of essential supplies, and who makes a profit to compensate for his work and not for its own sake.[16]

The old socialist slogan, "Production for use and not for profit," sums up this passage very well, though perhaps Thomas would like the substitution of "only secondarily for profit" in the interests of clarity.

Thomas recognized the need for inequality of income within reason, an income that might differ from others, depending on one's station in life. The following passage sums up the just wage/just profit/just price theory, which we might do well to start promoting in our graduate schools of economics. It is grounded firmly on the notion of "that which is necessary":

When we say a thing is necessary, we mean that without it a man cannot have a livelihood in keeping with his own and his dependents' social position. . . . Nobody should live unbecomingly . . . [so] that he could no longer live in decency on the residue according to his position and business commitments.[17]

AWAY FROM AQUINAS

We must now consider how the tradition of Aquinas was gradually undermined and twisted out of shape until, moving through Adam Smith to the Reverend Jerry Falwell, it became a fundamental teaching of Christianity à-la-TV-preacher that we must "get government off the back of business." This is a direct quote from a Falwell sermon.

No need to look to the Reformation or Calvinist preachers in England for an explanation. The men who began the movement away from Aquinas and Cajetan toward Smith and Falwell were not only medieval Catholics in good standing but, irony of ironies, Francisicans. St. Francis of Assisi (1182?–1226), founder of that order, was of all Christian saints the one who gave the most dramatic witness of contempt for property and material possessions. Inspired by a passage of Matthew's Gospel (10:5–14) he urged his disciples to follow his own example and Jesus' commandment to his disciples and go out into the world to preach and do good, taking "no gold, nor silver, nor copper in your belts, no bag for your journey, nor two tunics, nor sandals, nor a staff."

The men I refer to were the English theologians Duns Scotus (1265?–1308) and William of Ockham (1285?–1349?). To understand more clearly how they altered the Thomistic view of property, we must backtrack to St. Thomas and his view of what constitutes "a right." The key to this understanding lies in Thomas's steadfast refusal to separate "a right" from "*the* right," *jus* from *justum*. A key quote from the *Summa*:

The proper characteristic of justice, as compared with the other moral virtues, is to govern a man in his dealings with others. It implies a certain balance of equality, as its very name shows, for in common speech things are said to be ad*just*ed when they match evenly. Equality is relative to another. . . . With justice that which is correct is constituted by a relation to another, for a work of ours is said to be just when it meets another on the level, as with the payment of a fair wage for a service rendered. . . . We call it the just [*justum*] . . . and this indeed is a right. Clearly then, right is the objective interest of justice [*jus est objectum iustitiae*].[18]

Justice therefore, as well as the right, or a right, involves an intellectual determination, or judgment, as to equality [*aequale*] in the relations between human beings. How do we determine this equality when it comes to property rights? Under human law each individual had given up his or her claim to the free use of the material goods, property, over which God had given humankind, *all* men and women, by natural law, a common dominion, in exchange for a social arrangement of private property. This same individual gets in return the implied assurance that this arrangement will fulfill the purpose of giving him or her what property or possessions he or she needs for subsistence. The community, which thus benefits from the relinquishment of all these private claims, is obligated to assure to the individual access to those goods necessary for his or her sustenance, and if possible, for his or her "state of life."

Shortly after the death of Thomas, Duns Scotus evolved a system with a voluntarist emphasis, contrasting with the intellectualist emphasis of Thomas. In this system *dominion* (a key word from now on) is seen as a relation between a person and a thing established by an act of will (hence the term "voluntarist"). In running down a property right, therefore, what is important is not an intellectual judgment about equality but a *history* of how dominion was conferred or how it changed hands. This tradition culminated in the work of William of Ockham, who gave the world the first great presentation of a doctrine of individual rights.

In the legal sciences, that is in civil and canon law, property is generally taken as dominion over a thing, so that dominion and property are the same.[19]

Here we are in a whole new thought-world. "Right" now becomes a kind of will-force or moral impetus imparted to a claimant to dominion, without any necessary reference to an objective rightness (*justum*). Right is seen either as law or power, or as both, namely, licit power.

Because Ockham denied the metaphysical reality of relation, to him St. Thomas's *justum,* the relation of equality between persons affected by the virtue of justice, made no sense. In discussing property, Ockham found most useful not the speculations of either the philosophers or the theologians but the literal sayings of the Roman jurists and the canon lawyers. Actually, neither a unified philosophy nor theology of right was to be found here, but many and varying definitions, from which Ockham chose those that suited his purpose. The lawyers could not be blamed for neglecting to develop the Aristotelian notion of the *justum* on which St. Thomas had built his system. So it may be said that whereas *justitia* and *justum* received very little attention from Ockham, his references to rights (*jura*) and powers (*potestates*) are ubiquitous.

From this new concept of property and property rights, it followed inevitably that the sharing of superfluous goods with the poor would no longer be regarded as a matter of justice, but merely a question of charity.

Thomists like Cardinal Cajetan tried to stem the tide, but it was flowing strongly against them. It swept along not only Protestants like Locke and the Calvinist preachers, but also Catholic popes and progressive theologians. Leo XIII, for example, who is rightly honored for his pro-labor encyclical *Rerum Novarum* (1891), wrote in that encyclical, "Nature confers on man the right to possess things privately as his own" and "no one in any way should be permitted to violate his right."[20] In America one of the more progressive Catholic theologians wrote during the Depression:

> An owner who is using his own property for a foolish or a selfish purpose, e.g., lighting a cigar with a ten-dollar bill instead of giving it away to the community chest, is not failing against any acquired rights of the individual. He is not sinning against commutative justice, but he is surely sinning against charity.[21]

Only in the 1960s would the tide begin to flow in another direction and the ancient notions of Ambrose, Basil and Thomas Aquinas come once again into favor with popes and theologians. As a result, within the Catholic Church a new interest in Christian socialism will come. But that day remains far off in terms of our history.

Looking back on the Judeo-Christian tradition from 1000 B.C. to A.D. 1500, we can conclude that our economist was wrong and that there is more than sufficient justification in that tradition for the state to take from the superfluity of the rich to relieve the necessity of the poor, that this is a matter of fundamental justice and not simply of individual, voluntary charity.

We should also note the shift in Thomas Aquinas's preference for monarchy toward a preference for a combination of monarchy, aristocracy (by which he meant rule of the best), and democracy. He liked monarchy because, as long as the king was a good man, it seemed a more efficient way of providing the essentials of good government. He leaned toward democracy as he contemplated how infrequently the king was a good man and how inefficient tyrannical kings were in providing those essentials.

Similarly, Aquinas's arguments for private ownership of property are based mainly on efficiency. He did not have the experience that we have had in observing how inefficient private ownership can be in providing to every individual that "sufficiency of material goods such as are necessary to virtuous action," which his understanding of justice and Christian faith alike demanded.

If he had known what we know and seen what we see, no doubt he would have concluded that democracy in the use of productive property can be just as beneficial as he finally concluded that it was in the use of political power. For the use of power, whether it be productive power or political power, is subject to the same laws, and lawlessness, of human nature.

THE STIRRINGS OF REVOLT

Modern historians, both Marxist and non-Marxist, often give the impression that the Middle Ages was a time of static uniformity when feudal lords dominated peasant serfs in the countryside and, in the towns, master craftsmen lorded it over little groups of apprentices and journeymen.

In some areas this pattern prevailed. In others it did not. In still others the pattern progressed to greater freedom, diversity, manufacturing, and international trade. In the Flemish city of Ghent, for example, in the middle of the fourteenth century the international trade in cloth was so great that over five thousand weavers and fullers (pressers) were employed in a population of only fifty thousand. Strikes of journeymen against masters were not uncommon in such cities. In 1323 armed rebellion of the peasantry, encouraged by the craftsmen of Ypres and Bruges, broke out in western Flanders against the oppressive taxation of the nobility and lasted until the bloody battle of Mount Cassel in 1328.

In England the teachings of the pre-Reformation Protestant John Wycliffe coincided with another tax rebellion under Wat Tyler that led to the capture of London in 1381 and forced Richard II to cancel the poll tax. He was finally able to suppress the rebels.

The Hundred Years' War (1337–1453) between France and England weakened both countries and the Black Plague (1347–1350) wiped out entire cities and probably one-third of the population of Europe. Not until the revival of trade and industry in the second half of the fifteenth century, aided and inspired by the geographical discoveries of explorers and the intellectual discoveries of Renaissance humanists, did Europe begin again to think seriously about the problems of poverty, property, and economic power.[22]

CHAPTER 6

Thomas More and
the Radical Reformers

THOMAS MORE

On May 16, 1532, Thomas More resigned as Lord Chancellor of England. He had told his master, Henry VIII, that he could not agree that Henry's marriage to Catherine of Aragon was invalid and that Henry was free to marry Anne Boleyn. His disagreement, along with his refusal to recognize Henry as supreme Head of the Church, led inevitably to More's execution in 1535.

Sometime after More's refusal to agree to Henry's marriage to Anne Boleyn three of More's friends, all bishops, came to him and invited him to accompany them to Anne Boleyn's coronation. More, in declining the invitation, responded as follows:

> It putteth me in remembrance of an emperor that had ordained a law that whosoever committed a certain crime, except it were a virgin, should suffer the pains of death, such was the reverence he bare to virginity. Now so it happened that the first committer of the offense was indeed a virgin; whereof the emperor hearing was in no small perplexity, being greatly desirous to have the law put in execution and, by example of justice, terrify others. Whereupon when his council sat long, solemnly debating the matter, suddenly there arose up one of his council, a good plain man, among them, and said, "Why make you so much ado, my lords, about so small a matter? Let her first be deflowered, and then after may she be devoured."[1]

William Roper, More's son-in-law, telling the story later, adds that More then said to the bishops, "Now, my lords, it lieth not in my power but that they may devour me, but God being my good lord, I will provide that they shall never deflower me."

This story serves admirably to illustrate the life and significance of St. Thomas More (1478–1535), author of *Utopia*, inventor of that word, most prestigious, most humorous, and probably most admirable of all Christian socialists.

To begin with, the story comes from Tacitus, the Roman historian. More was, after all, one of the most learned, if not the most learned, student of the classics in Tudor England, dear friend of Erasmus, the most learned man in all Europe. His story is one of practical politicians, persons of power. Thomas More was that also, a lawyer who had risen, by dint of talent, hard work, and integrity, steadily up the ladder of political advancement, from under-sheriff of London to judge to ambassador to speaker of Parliament to under-treasurer of England to Lord Chancellor, the equivalent of today's prime minister.

The story involves the bishops of England, most of whom gave in to Henry, but who were also good friends and admirers of More. In fact, they took up a collection, estimated to be the equivalent of several hundred thousand dollars, to give to More as an expression of their gratitude for his writings in defense of their faith and their church. He steadfastly refused the gift, saying, "Not so, my lords, I had liefer see it all cast into the Thames than I, or any of mine, should have thereof the worth of one penny."[2]

It is a story of wit, somewhat earthy, with a touch of gallows humor. All these characteristics marked that complex man, St. Thomas More. Frank and Fritzie Manuel, authors of *Utopian Thought in the Western World*, have written well about this aspect of his personality:

> With gallows humor he was able to annihilate reality. . . . It is easy to discover in later utopians of stature ambiguities . . . akin to Thomas More's. There are martyrs among them. But none to our knowledge achieved his transcendent humor. . . . The utopia of Christian humanism could still ridicule itself as the miserable real world in which the colloquy took place. In later utopias there are no jokes worth telling, no absurd scenes to narrate.[3]

More's is the story of a person who placed loyalty to God clearly and cleanly above loyalty to the state. Just before More was to leave his prison cell in the Tower of London for the scaffold, a messenger came from Henry to tell him, "The King's pleasure is further that at your execution you shall not use many words."[4]

Perhaps because More knew that Henry could still make things difficult for his family, he agreed to this request, although it was customary to permit the victim of Tudor executions to speak at length if he or she so desired. More therefore set his bright mind to say much in a few words. An eyewitness reported them as follows:

> He spoke little before his execution. Only he asked the bystanders to pray for him in this world, and he would pray for them elsewhere. He then begged them earnestly to pray for the King, that it might please God to give him good counsel, protesting that he died the King's good servant but God's first.[5]

"The King's good servant but God's first." Not since Peter stood before the Sanhedrin and rejected the high priest's command to cease and desist in his preaching with the words, "We must obey God rather than men,"[6] had so much been said so briefly.

With his words More underlined the basic difference between religious socialism and all secular socialisms. The religious socialist is God's servant first and only then, within the limits set by that service, the good servant of the state.

More's application to himself of the story of the Emperor and the Virgin demonstrates and foreshadows his willingness to die for his loyalty to God. The final test of the word is the act. In this More reminds one of Marx's eleventh thesis on Feuerbach: "The philosophers have only *interpreted* the world, in various ways; the point, however, is to *change* it" [emphasis in the original].[7] More knew all there was to know about interpretations of the world of his time. He had read them and written them. He had also written much about how the world should be changed and he knew that the ultimate challenge was in the question, "What are you going to do about it?" Having failed to change the world as good servant to the king, he was willing to die for his faith in how it should be changed and for his faith in how it should *not* be changed. No act of faith is more final, more total than this.

Was Thomas More an authentic socialist? Marx and Engels certainly thought he was an authentic precursor of socialism.[8] Karl Kautsky, the foremost Marxist of the period immediately following Engels's death, devoted a whole book to More and his *Utopia*. He described More as "a man of genius who understood the problems of his age before the conditions existed for their solution," a man who "championed the oppressed classes even when he stood alone." Kautsky added:

> And nothing speaks more eloquently for the greatness of the man, nothing shows more clearly how, like a giant, he towered over his contemporaries, than the fact that it needed more than three hundred years before the conditions have come about which show us that the aims which More set before himself are not the fancies of an idle hour, but the result of a deep insight into the actual economic tendencies of his age. Already More's four hundredth birthday is past. *Utopia* will soon be four hundred years old, but still his ideals are not defeated, still they lie before struggling mankind.[9]

Kautsky's tribute is significant, and basically correct, but at the same time one cannot accept uncritically his attempt to claim More as a kind of pre-Marxian Marxist.

UTOPIA

The story of *Utopia* (a made-up word meaning "No Place" in Greek) is told by a fictional character named Hythloday, a Portuguese adventurer who had sailed with Amerigo Vespucci on voyages to the other side of the world. The publication of *Utopia* in 1516 came only twenty-four years after Christopher Columbus landed in America. The discovery of new lands was a common news item in More's England. In fact, one English bishop took More's story as bonafide news and volunteered to serve as a missionary bishop in Utopia. For Utopia was not a Christian country. It was a country of virtuous pagans who were ruled primarily by reason and by faith in a just and benevolent God.

More himself was a character in the story, who met Hythloday in the course of his service as one of Henry's ambassadors to Flanders, where he had in fact served in 1515. More was then thirty-seven years old, his feet already planted on the ladder of advancement, but still young enough and free enough from major responsibility to indulge his liking for playing fanciful variations on serious themes. He was too shrewd, however, to commit himself to agreement with all the customs of the Utopians or all the opinions of Hythloday, the narrator of the story.

For example, on several occasions in the early pages Hythloday expresses the view that "unless private property is entirely done away with, there can be no fair distribution of goods nor can the world be happily governed."[10] More disagrees. " 'On the contrary,' I replied, 'it seems to me that men cannot live well where all things are in common. . . . The hope of gain will not drive them; they will rely on others and become lazy."[11]

We might note here a replay of the built-in tension that exists in the views of Aristotle and Aquinas as regards the conflicting claims of the communal and the private in the institution of private property. Hythloday appeals to the actual experience of the Utopians to prove his point, but since we know that there was no such experience, the conflict and the tension remain. At the end of the book More again inserts a disclaimer:

> I admit that not a few things in the manners and laws of the Utopians seemed very absurd to me: their way of waging war, their religious customs, as well as other matters, but especially the keystone of their entire system, namely, their communal living without the use of money.[12]

The Utopians used gold to make chamber pots, one way of demonstrating their contempt for it. Their clothing was as simple and uniform as that of Franciscan monks. In real life More could dress in purple velvet and wear a gold chain around his neck.[13]

The contradictions are not so difficult to understand if we remember that as a younger man More had hoped for several years to join either the Carthusians or the Franciscans. He lived for some time in a Carthusian monastery, but eventually chose, as Erasmus put it to a mutual friend, "to be a chaste husband rather than a licentious priest."[14]

At one point in *Utopia* More writes, "Christ instituted community of goods and this custom is still in practice among the most sincere of the Christians."[15] Clearly he is referring to monasticism, and probably also to the socialism of the early Christians in the Acts of the Apostles.[16] *Utopia* makes more sense if we think of it as More's idea of a monasticism for married people based on the assumption that most people were motivated by faith in a religion based on reason, what is sometimes called natural religion. He is saying, "This is how people would act if they were really ruled by reason and faith in a God who rewards the good and punishes the wicked." He knows that a large number of people are not so ruled. He adds to his disclaimer at the end of the book, "Yet I must confess that there are many things in the Utopian Commonwealth that I wish rather than expect to see followed among our citizens."[17]

This does not mean that we should not take *Utopia* seriously or that More did not write it with serious intent as a model of a good society. It means only that More was realistic enough to know that models have to be used with discretion and intelligence, making allowance at every moment for what is possible as well as what is desirable.

With this introduction let us consider what Utopian society was really like. To begin with, it was *unlike* much of English society. More was particularly incensed at the way the nobility, and even some of the abbeys, were driving the peasants off their land to make room for more and more pasture for sheep, whose wool was becoming a major source of cash income. He quotes Hythloday:

> Your sheep, that used to be so gentle and eat so little, now are becoming so greedy and so fierce that they devour the men themselves, so to speak. They lay waste and pillage fields, homes and towns. For wherever the sheep yield a softer and richer wool than ordinary, there the nobility and gentlemen, yea even the holy men and abbots, are not content with the old rents which their lands yielded. They are no longer satisfied to live in idleness and luxury without benefiting society. . . . They leave no land for cultivation, they enclose all the land for pastures, they destroy houses and demolish towns. . . . The tenants are turned out, and by trickery or main force, or by being worn out through ill usage, are compelled to sell their possessions. . . . When that little money is gone, what is left for them to do but steal and so be hanged? . . . If you do not find a remedy for these evils, it is idle to boast of your severity in punishing theft. Your policy may have the appearance of justice, but it is neither just nor expedient. . . . What else is this, I ask, but first making [these people] thieves and then punishing them for it?[18]

More, despite what Erasmus called "his rare affability and sweetness of manner,"[19] could be savage in denouncing the idle rich and their treatment of the poor:

> Is not a government unjust and ungrateful that squanders rich rewards on noblemen (as they are called), goldsmiths, and others that do no work

but live only by flattery or by catering to useless pleasures? And is it just for a government to ignore the welfare of farmers, charcoal burners, servants, drivers and blacksmiths, without whom the commonwealth could not exist at all? After their best years have been consumed by labor and they are worn out by age and sickness, they are still penniless, and the thankless state, unmindful of their many great services, rewards them with nothing but a miserable death. Furthermore the rich constantly try to whittle away something from the pitiful wages of the poor by private fraud and even by public laws. To pay so little to men who deserve the best from the state is in itself unjust, yet it is made "just" legally by passing a law.[20]

Hythloday concludes, and here he is clearly speaking for More:

So when I weigh in my mind all the other states which flourish today, so help me God, I can discover nothing but a conspiracy of the rich, who pursue their own aggrandizement under the name and title of the Commonwealth. They devise ways and means to keep safely what they have unjustly acquired, and to buy up the toil and labor of the poor as cheaply as possible and oppress them. When these schemes of the rich become established by the government, which is meant to protect the poor as well as the rich, then they are law. With insatiable greed these wicked men divide among themselves the goods which would have been enough for all.[21]

These phrases, "the sheep that devour men" and "a conspiracy of the rich," have echoed and re-echoed down the ages and done much to establish Thomas More's reputation as a social revolutionary.

In Utopia there is complete equality, even in clothing.

All the Utopians, men and women alike, work at agriculture. . . . Besides sharing in the farmwork, every person has some particular trade of his own, such as the manufacture of wool or linen, masonry, metal work, or carpentry.[22]

But the workday is only six hours long, for

you can easily imagine how little time would be enough to produce the goods that man's needs and convenience demand (and his pleasure too if it were true and natural pleasure) if only the workers in useless trades were placed in worthwhile occupations and all the idlers who languish in sloth but eat twice as much as laborers were put to work on useful tasks.[23]

The workday is also short because

the chief aim of their institutions and government, above all else, is to give all citizens as much time as public needs permit for freeing and developing their minds. In this they suppose the felicity of man's life to consist.[24]

The countryside, all common land, is dotted with houses—apartment houses really—containing rooms for forty men and women and their children, and these work on the farms for two years, twenty persons being replaced each year so that the new arrivals can learn from the one-year veterans. As with Socrates and Marx, city life is preferred to rural life, so no one is compelled to "do this hard work against his will for more than two years, but many of them ask to stay longer because they take a natural delight in farm life."[25] In these respects Utopia is both like and unlike Mao's China, like in that city dwellers are compelled to do time on communal farms, unlike in that it is easier to get back to the city than was the case in Mao's China.

In the city, groups of ten to sixteen adults, preferably of one family, have their own houses and gardens, but "every ten years they change houses by lot."[26] They have their meals in common halls, the women taking turns in preparing them. "While it is not forbidden to eat at home, it is not thought proper. Besides no one would be so foolish as to prepare a poor meal at home when there is a sumptuous one ready for him so near at hand."[27]

Was More's Utopia democratic? In some respects very much so, in others not so much so. As with Aquinas, More seems to prefer a combination of monarchic, aristocratic, and democratic elements. The restrictions on freedom of speech and religion are the weakest feature of his model.

Each year thirty households choose a magistrate, called the syphogrant. . . . All the syphogrants, two hundred in number, choose the prince by secret vote. . . . The prince is chosen for life, unless he is suspected of trying to become a dictator. . . . The tranibors [one for every ten syphogrants] meet every third day, and more often if necessary, to consult with the prince on affairs of state. . . . No decision on public business can be made unless the matter had been considered on three different days in the senate.[28]

The manner of electing the senate is not clear from the text. One passage indicates that the senate consists of the twenty tranibors, each of whom is elected by ten syphogrants.[29] Another passage speaks of "the annual senate . . . made up of three representatives from each city."[30] Another speaks of "the people's assembly."[31]

Economic planning in Utopia is both centralized and democratic: "In the annual senate at Amaurot [the capital] . . . they find out what surpluses and shortages there are, and promptly assign the surplus of one place to supply the needs of another."[32] More's faith in the Utopians' ability to accomplish this task in one annual meeting seems a little on the sanguine side, but then the Utopians were very bright people.

The selection of work supervisors is also democratic: "The chief and almost the only business of the syphogrants [elected annually, one by every thirty households] is to see that no one sits around in idleness, and that everyone works hard at his trade."[33]

The most repressive aspect of the political organization of Utopia appears in the sentence, "It is a capital offense to consult together on public affairs outside the senate or the people's assembly."[34] In other words, if two critics of public policy have a private conversation on how to get that policy changed, this is a crime punishable by death. Perhaps we should not expect a man like More, a product of a repressive, monarchical society, to understand how such a law must inevitably become a bad law in any time or place. Subsequent human experience with political process has by now convinced most students of government that consultation outside of public bodies is not only impossible to prevent but absolutely essential to free and effective consultation inside such bodies.

A similar weakness appears in Utopia's treatment of religion. There are democratic elements: "The priests are chosen by secret, popular vote, as are the other magistrates, in order to avoid strife." And, of significant interest to religious feminists, "women are not excluded from the priesthood" but, of less interest, "are chosen less often, and only if they are elderly widows."[35]

Also, the Utopians "count it among their oldest institutions that no man shall be made to suffer for his religion." Freedom of speech is permitted in matters of religion but only up to a point:

> The Utopians believe that after this life there are punishments for wickedness and rewards for virtue. They consider one who thinks otherwise as hardly a man, since he has degraded the human soul to the low level of a beast's body. Such a man they do not count fit for human society, for if he dares, he will scorn all its laws and customs. Who can doubt that a man who fears nothing but the law and apprehends nothing after death would secretly flout his country's laws or break them by force to satisfy his greed? Therefore no preferment is awarded to one with such views, and no magistracy or any public responsibility is entrusted to him. Instead, he is generally looked down upon as a man of worthless and sordid nature. Yet they do not punish such a man further, for they are persuaded that no one can make himself believe anything at will. Nor do they force him by threats to conceal his thoughts, and so open the door to deceit and lying, which they detest as the next thing to fraud. But they take care that he does not argue for his opinions, especially before the common people. They permit and even encourage him to discuss these matters with their priests and other serious men, in full confidence that finally his mad opinions will yield to reason.[36]

More, like virtually all other "serious men" of his time, both Protestant and Catholic, believed that a common religious faith was the only sure foundation of a secure, peaceful, and successful society. Therefore the preaching of heresy was tantamount to sedition and treason against the state. This kind of reasoning survived in some circles even into the twentieth century, even up to Vatican Council II. Although More as chancellor was not as harsh with heretical preachers as hostile historians like John Foxe have charged, nevertheless, he was a product of his time and should not be expected to appreciate all the contradictions and inconsistencies contained in the passage quoted above.

Frank and Fritzie Manuel, perhaps the world's most knowledgeable students on utopias, have written that "of the thousands of paradisaical settlements that have been founded in Europe and America since the seventeenth century, only the religious ones . . . have exhibited any signs of longevity."[37] The Manuels might well have gone back a few millennia. A monastery, after all, is a kind of "paradisaical settlement."

Why this is so, this need for religious content, we can learn from the concluding pages of *Utopia*:

> If that one monster pride, the first and foremost of all evils, did not forbid it, the whole world would doubtless have adopted the laws of the Utopians long before this, drawn on by a rational perception of what each man's true interest is or else by the authority of Christ our Saviour, who in His great wisdom knows what is best and in His loving kindness bids us do it. Pride measures her prosperity not by her own goods but by others' wants. Pride would not deign to be a goddess, if there were no inferiors she could rule and triumph over. Her happiness shines brightly only in comparison to others' misery, and their poverty binds them and hurts them the more as her wealth is displayed. Pride is the infernal serpent that steals into the hearts of men, thwarting and holding them back from choosing the better way of life.
>
> Pride is far too deeply rooted in men's hearts to be easily torn out. I am glad, therefore, that the Utopians have achieved their social organization, which I wish all mankind would imitate. Their institutions give their commonwealth a moral and social foundation for living happy lives, and as far as man can predict, these institutions will last forever.[38]

What are we to make of these words? We know that the institutions of Utopia did not last for five minutes. Does this mean, for example, that "pride is far too deeply rooted in men's hearts" to make possible a more equitable distribution of income, to make possible any public ownership of productive property or any cooperative ownership of productive property that has a hope of permanent success *unless* the vast majority of the people involved are either ruled by reason or by obedience to Christ our Savior and have thereby conquered their own pride?

Such a conclusion seems unwarranted. A more reasonable multiform conclusion would be this: (1) pride is a mortal enemy of social justice; (2) any exercise of reason or of religious faith that can tame human pride will make social justice more easily attainable; (3) pride and selfishness are too deeply rooted in human nature to be ignored and must be given serious consideration in the determination of what is possible in the planning of political and economic structures, especially in a society that is not, like monasteries, based on a voluntary commitment of obedience to "the authority of Christ our Saviour"; (4) Thomas More earnestly wished that "all mankind would imitate" the institutions of Utopia and believed that it was possible, not to imitate them perfectly, but to come much closer to imitating them than "mankind" had done up to that time.

With that we might well leave this most prestigious, most humorous, and most admirable of all Christian socialists.

ANOTHER THOMAS, ANOTHER MARTYR

Thomas More was not the only one in Europe who was reading Plato's *Republic* and phantasizing about a more perfect life on earth. In Italy a veritable rash of utopian literature appeared both before and after the first Italian translation of More's book in 1546. Most of this literature, especially before *Utopia*, was produced and illustrated by architects who shared Plato's elitist prejudices but not his penchant for common ownership of property. One of the more extreme examples was the plan developed by Leonardo da Vinci (1452–1519), who designed a two-level city, "the nobles on the elevated platform in the sun, and the common people down below with the canals, sewers and carts."[39]

An exception to the aristocratic bent of this literature was the work of Ludovico Agostini, a Christian mystic who had made a pilgrimage to the Holy Land. His denunciations of "the inhuman rich" were as strong as anything in *Utopia*: "Contrary to human piety and Christian charity they traffic in the blood of the poor without any feeling of pity."[40]

Agostini's *Repubblica Immaginaria* was even stricter in religious matters than *Utopia* had been and featured a kind of daily compulsory chapel:

Since the most important part of a Christian (or civilized person) is religion, I do not intend to open the businesses of my city until the whole people . . . has heard and seen the sacred mystery of the Altar, and the priest has exhorted them in a brief sermon to carry out the doctrine of the Gospel that has been read, and they have been dismissed with his blessing.[41]

In the rugged regions of the North another man had read Plato's *Republic* and probably More's *Utopia* as well. He was Thomas Müntzer (1488?–1525), a radical reformer who became the prototype of the violent revolutionary, just as

More has been the model of the Christian humanist dedicated to peaceful reform. Friedrich Engels saw in Müntzer's impoverished artisans and landless peasants

> an outburst of that class which was the forerunner, more or less developed, of the modern proletariat . . . red flag in hand and the community of property on their lips.[42]

Müntzer can only be understood against the background of Luther's rebellion against the papacy and the chiliastic Anabaptists' rebellion against Luther.

Chiliasm holds that Christ will reign on earth for a thousand years, a period often referred to as the Millennium. The belief is based on Revelation 20:1–7. The Anabaptists (literally, those who "baptize again") were not a strictly defined sect but included a number of Protestant groups who believed in adult baptism, the establishment of egalitarian and communal Christian communities, nonparticipation in civil government, and opposition to state churches, which could mean either Catholic, Lutheran, or Calvinist churches. They were therefore unpopular with both political and ecclesiastical authority, especially in Switzerland, Germany, and Austria, where they were most numerous.

Müntzer was not typical of the itinerant preachers who ranted about "monkery" and named specific dates when the millennium would commence, only to have to revise the date or lapse into obscurity, or both. He was a learned man and spoke and wrote of the millenium as in *process* of commencing. At first supporting Luther and supported by him, he soon gravitated to the more radical Hussites, Taborites, and Anabaptists and began to attack Luther, whom he called Doctor Liar (*Doktor Luegner*) and whose devotion to the literal meaning of the Bible he ridiculed as *"Bibel Babel Bubel."* Müntzer was very free in his reading of the Bible and, in fact, was a pioneer in proclaiming that the Holy Spirit, "the inner word," might dwell within the hearts and minds of the illiterate weavers and peasants far sooner than in the learned Lutheran pastors and their rich and powerful patrons:

> Well, perhaps you inquire how the Word gets into the heart? Answer: it gets down from God above when you are in a high state of wonderment. . . . And any man who has not become aware and receptive through the living witness of God (Romans 8) really has nothing to say, even if he stuffed himself with a hundred thousand Bibles.[43]

Both in spiritual and political matters Müntzer gave priority to the poor and the oppressed, a reversal of the later Calvinist preference for those whose prosperity proved their divine election:

> According to the seventh chapter of Daniel and Revelation 18 and 19, authority should be vested in the common people. Virtually all judg-

ments in the Bible bear witness that the creatures must be free, otherwise the pure word of God will be undone.[44]

As time went on Müntzer's language became more violent and his challenges to secular authority more bold. When Duke George of Saxony and Count Ernst von Mansfeld forbade their subjects to attend his services, he wrote to the count:

> And you should know that in such mighty and righteous matters I am not afraid of the whole world. But you want to be feared more than God himself. . . . I'll deal with you a hundred thousand times worse than Luther did with the Pope.[45]

He signed himself "Thomas Müntzer, a Destroyer of the Unbelievers." In a sermon at Allstedt in 1524 he thundered at Duke Johann of Saxony, who was sitting in the congregation: "For the stone, torn from the mountain without hands, has become mighty. The poor laymen and peasants see it more sharply than you do."[46]

Thousands crowded the churches where he preached. At Mallerbach he inflamed the crowd with a sermon calling attention to a Catholic chapel at the gate of the city where, he said, the devil was being worshiped under the name of Mary. He urged the people to end this shameless blasphemy and then watched with righteous pleasure as they set fire to the chapel.

During the peasant uprising of 1524 Müntzer applauded those who sacked forty monasteries in Thuringia and the Harz region of Germany within a two-week period. When Luther rebuked the plundering by the peasants and called for armed reprisals, Müntzer counterattacked:

> And so they let God's commandment be spread among the poor and they proclaim, God has commanded, Thou shalt not steal. But it does not work. Since they cause any man who lives, the poor ploughman, the handworker, everyone, to shove and scrape (Micah chapter 3), so as soon as he does the least thing wrong, so he must hang. Whereupon Doctor Liar says Amen. The lords are themselves to blame that the poor man is their enemy. They do not want to do away with the cause of the uproar. How can it ever be good in the long run?[47]

Note here the echoes of the Fathers and of Thomas Aquinas on the morality of stealing in cases of necessity (expressed with less precision) and of Thomas More's Hythloday in the first book of *Utopia*: "If you do not find a remedy for these evils, it is idle to boast of your severity in punishing theft."

By April 1525, Müntzer had committed himself to armed rebellion in support of the peasants' demands, which were an interesting mix of religious, economic, and political grievances: the right to choose their own priests and burgomasters, the abolition of serfdom (because Christ has freed all), the right to fish and kill wild game, the abolition of certain feudal taxes, a guarantee of fair treatment in the nobles' courts, and an end to the appropriation by nobles and clergy of peasant lands or lands held traditionally in common. They added a provision that if the nobles could show that any demand was contrary to the word of God it would be withdrawn.

Müntzer wrote with some exaggeration to the people of Allstedt:

> All the German, French and Italian lands are wakeful. . . . If you were only three who with faith seek His name and glory, you need not fear a hundred thousand. Go to it, go to it, go to it! Pay no attention to the howling of the godless. They will entreat you so gently, they will whimper, they will implore you like children. Show no pity, as God has commanded through Moses.

He urged them to rally the people in the surrounding towns and villages and concluded: "Do not let your sword grow cold. Strike the anvil with the hammer—*pinkepanke*.[48]" (It does seem that Müntzer could have built to a stronger climax than "*pinkepanke*," but perhaps it sounds more formidable in German.)

The Peasants' War, on the basis of grievances, could certainly qualify as a just war, but it did not really have a reasonable chance of success. The immediate cause of hostilities was a demand by the countess of Lüpfen-Stühlingen that her peasants gather snails for her table at a time when they were concerned to get in their hay. Supported and led by a few dissident, idealistic knights and joined by rebellious workers in some of the middle European towns, the peasants won a few minor skirmishes and concessions from the more reasonable nobles and clergy.

At the climactic battle of Frankenhausen in June 1525, however, their little army's pikes and clubs were no match for the cannon and cavalry of the nobles. Müntzer escaped, but was found hiding in a cellar and carried off to the castle of Count Ernst von Mansfeld, the same count whom he had once threatened so boldly. There the torturers extracted a lengthy confession from Müntzer, which under the circumstances has to be regarded with the utmost skepticism. The confession is significant largely because it contained a Latin phrase that forms the major basis for the claim that Müntzer was a Christian communist. One report of this interrogation on May 16, 1525, described as follows the purpose of the Allstedt Union organized by Müntzer:

> This was their belief and what they wanted to put into practice: *Omnia sunt communia* [All things are common]. Each and every one should be given what he needs when he needs it. If any Prince, Count or Lord did not want to do this, and had been warned, he should have his head chopped off or be hanged.[49]

Another report gives the key phrase as *Omnia simul communia* (Everything should be as if it were held in common). The Manuels conclude from their study of the literature:

> Müntzer evidently had some notion of a *communio rerum*, as one contemporary report has it, and he made a distinction between *Gemein-nutz* [common use] and *Eigen-nutz* [private use]. But this does not equate his views with a Platonic holding of all things in common. Müntzer still thought primarily in terms of the peasant "commons" that were being expropriated by the lords, and he was far more concerned with the souls of the victorious elect and their hard-won religious belief than with material goods and their equitable distribution.[50]

Eleven days after the extraction of his confession Müntzer was executed and his head exposed to public view. So many people came to visit the spot that his enemies feared they had created a saint.

Thomas Müntzer by no means fits neatly into the mold of a pre-Marxian revolutionary. His interests were far too religious for that. But he does seem to fit the role of prototype for all the religious zealots who have ever been tempted by the vision of a quick and bloody victory over the oppressors of the poor. The victory was quick and bloody, but it turned the wrong way and served only to warn those who are willing to listen to the lessons of history that such victories go the wrong way more often than not. Listening to the lessons of history, unfortunately, has never been a strong point among religious zealots.

THE IRONY OF JAKOB HUTTER

There is an irony in both the history of Christianity and the history of socialism in that for every ten who have heard of Thomas Müntzer one at most has heard of Jakob Hutter. Yet the revolutionary Anabaptists led by Müntzer were wiped out at Frankenhausen; whereas the pacifist Anabaptists led by Jakob Hutter, a contemporary of Müntzer, today boast some twenty-two thousand followers in two hundred sixty socialist colonies in Canada, in the American Northwest and in New York, Connecticut, Pennsylvania, England, and, since 1982, Japan.

The pacifist Anabaptists originated in Zurich, Switzerland, but were driven out when the Swiss reformer Ulrich Zwingli (1484–1531) took control of the city. Zwingli himself was fairly radical on the subject of private property. He once wrote: "Even if we were not sinful by nature, the sin of having private property would suffice to condemn us before God; for that which he gave us freely we appropriate to ourselves."[51] If Zwingli had not been killed by the Swiss Catholics in 1531 and his influence taken over a few years later by John Calvin, the Swiss Reformation might have developed differently.

Expelled from Zurich in 1525, the pacifist Anabaptists spread over Central

Europe and divided into Mennonites and Hutterites. Both of these groups eventually emigrated to North America.

Jakob Hutter became the undisputed leader of the Anabaptists in Moravia by reason of h's eloquence as a preacher, his selfless dedication, and a dramatic replay of St. Peter's confrontation with Ananias and Sapphira that eliminated Hutter's two principal rivals. Within three years, however, he was dead. In 1536 he was burned at the stake. The tortures employed to persuade him, unsuccessfully, to name his associates included immersion in freezing water and pouring brandy on his lacerated flesh and setting it aflame.

Eventually, in part because of their industry in agriculture and various crafts, the Hutterites won tolerance from the nobles of Moravia and were able to establish over a hundred communal colonies (*bruderhof*) as their numbers grew to twenty-five thousand. In a typical *bruderhof*, forty or more buildings might be arranged around a village common or square. Families lived on the top floors and workshops for the various crafts were located on the ground floor. One writer of the time described one of these colonies as "a big beehive where all the busy bees work together to a common end, the one doing this and the other that, not for their own needs but for the good of all."[52] The result was a kind of rationalized form of production on a scale that was unheard of until the Industrial Revolution.

Peter Rideman, one of the early leaders of the group, explained the theology behind their lifestyle:

> Now, since all God's gifts—not only spiritual, but also material things—are given to man, not that he should have them for himself alone but with all his fellows, therefore the communion of saints itself must show itself not only in spiritual but also in temporal things, that as Paul saith, one might not have abundance and another suffer want, but that there may be equality. This he showeth from the law touching manna, in that he who gathered much had nothing over, whereas he who gathered little had no less, since each was given what he needed according to the measure.[53]

On the basis of such quotes Karl Kautsky included the Hutterites among the forerunners of modern socialism, but Rideman makes it clear that his notion of *Gutergemeinschaft* (community of goods) was based on early Christian socialism as expressed in Acts 2:44–45 and 4:32.

A Hutterite tract written in 1593 by Colman Rorer nicely rebukes a hostile critic:

> The Christian community of goods is for the purpose of providing for the needy believers who may be old, sick, crippled and unable to provide for themselves, so that they be furnished with the necessaries of life the same as the others. But you say there can be no community of goods if such are present. *You understand the Christian principle of community of goods about as well as a blind man appreciates colors* [emphasis added].[54]

The Hutterites' sharing of material goods was not simply that required by Jesus in Matthew 25, but the kind of total surrender of possessions that he suggested to the rich young man who went away sad. This note was struck by Joseph Hausser in 1606:

> By community of goods I understand not that one gives only something of that which is superfluous and keeps the most for himself, as was the case under the law and is today the common custom the world over. But the community of goods of which we speak means that all that one possesses is surrendered, the heart is freed from it, and it is gladly and voluntarily given over, as the spirit of the Gospel requires and as the saints in Jerusalem did.[55]

Regarded by both Catholic and Protestant princes as heretics, the Hutterites created further difficulties for themselves by reason of their pacifism. They refused to serve as soldiers in the war against the Turks; they refused to pay taxes to finance the war. Their lands and goods were confiscated, their leaders killed or jailed. By 1767 they were almost wiped out in Central Europe, but sixty-seven escaped from house arrest in Transylvania and fled to Wallachia (near Bucharest). For seventy years no *bruderhof*, no communal living existed, but this group revived it in 1765, tried it briefly in Wallachia, then, having suffered plunder by marauding soldiers in the Russo-Turkish War, moved on to Russia, where a noble Russian general had offered them refuge.

From 1819 to 1859 the Hutterites again abandoned communal living and joined a Mennonite settlement. By 1859 a visionary leader named Michael Waldner revived the communal way of life. However, by this time nationalism had swept Russia and they could obtain no commitment from the Russian government to exempt them from conscription. Therefore, starting in 1874, 1,265 Hutterites emigrated to South Dakota, the first group purchasing 2,500 acres for $25,000. By 1874 eight communal societies were established in the United States: Harmony, Oneida, Shakers, Amana, Bethel, Zoar, St. Nazianz, and Ephrata. The original social systems in these places have vanished, but the Hutterites have steadily increased, even though only about fifty adult outsiders have been converted.

In over four hundred years there has never been a homicide in any of their colonies and only one suicide. Only one in forty-three Hutterites suffers from psychosis as compared with one in ten among the general U.S. population. From 1918 to 1950 only one hundred six men and seven women left the Hutterite community.

During World War I, young Hutterite men were of course conscientious objectors. They were so badly mistreated (two died in military prison) that the Hutterites sold eleven of their fifteen colonies in South Dakota, at severe loss, and moved to Canada. Although they eventually resettled all but three of their U.S. colonies, about seventy percent of the current population is in the Canadian provinces of Saskatchewan, Alberta, and Manitoba.

The *bruderhof* consists of a clustered group of buildings—church, dining hall, apartments, barns, workshops—in the midst of carefully cultivated and fertile fields. Unlike the Amish farmers of Pennsylvania, the Hutterites use mechanized equipment.

Baptism takes place when the applicant is mature enough to decide freely to "establish a covenant with God and all his people to give self, soul and body, with all possessions, to the Lord in Heaven."⁵⁶ This is usually about the age of twenty for women, later for men. All baptized members make up the church (*gemein*), but only men have voice and vote. They elect the Council, which usually consists of First Preacher, Second Preacher, Steward, Field Manager, and German Teacher (they still speak Hutterische, a German dialect with some Slavic variations picked up during their time in Moravia, Rumania, and Russia). A few elders fill out the Council membership, and this group makes all the major decisions.

The women do not seem to have accepted their subordinate role entirely without resistance. They usually show "strong loyalty toward their families and children and are therefore more difficult for the colony to manage and integrate." One preacher has complained, "Our colony troubles would amount to very little if it were not for the women."⁵⁷ This view is not necessarily typical of other *bruderhofs*, particularly the newer ones in the eastern United States, where women take an active role in community meetings.

Nevertheless, as indicated, very few have left the community. Between 1874 and 1950 only one divorce and four desertions were recorded. Only 2 percent of the men and 5.4 percent of the women never marry. Birth control is not practiced and the median family has 10.4 children. Small wonder that their colonies increase in number.

According to their rule, every member "shall give and devote all his or her time, labor, services, earning and energies . . . [to] the community freely and without compensation." In return, the individual, together with his or her dependents, will be "supported, instructed and educated by the community."⁵⁸ One colony gave the men $1 a month for spending money, the women $1 every six months, but then gave it up and handed out only enough money for necessary purchases on the rare visits permitted to the local town.

The colonies are almost entirely agricultural, crafts being limited to making those things necessary for the colony. One typical colony in Alberta consisted of 78 persons, 8,300 acres, an annual income of $230,000 from the sale of cattle, milk, pigs, eggs, grain, honey, geese, turkeys, and sheep (in that order), and expenditures of $190,000 for machinery, gas, feed, fertilizer, pesticides. Net profit: $40,000. When an agricultural colony accumulates about $200,000 and a population of about 140, at which point there is more labor than needed for the available land, the colony is split in two, and one half, chosen by lot, goes off to start another colony. In non-agricultural *bruderhofs*, as in the eastern United States, where crafts and manufactures provide income, populations of four or five hundred are possible.

According to observers, the integration and unity of the Hutterite communities is achieved mainly by song, prayer, and communal worship, which occurs every day before supper and twice on Sundays, and, of course, perhaps mainly, by reason of the strong religious faith their liturgy expresses. The preacher reads the sermons, which were mostly composed in the seventeenth century. He makes virtually no application to the current life of the community. The songs consist mainly of forty melodies composed in the sixteenth century. Private interpretation of the Bible yields to what one Hutterian elder has defined as "a common interpretation, not according to the letter but the spirit."

A RESEMBLANCE TO UTOPIA

Anyone who has read *Utopia* must be struck by the similarities between Thomas More's imaginary island and the real-life colonies maintained so successfully by the American and Canadian Hutterites. The Utopians were clearly more interested in intellectual pursuits and they did not share the Hutterites' pacifism, but many aspects, good and bad, are remarkably similar.

The Hutterites have proven, at least, that where Christian faith and discipline are strong enough, a monastery for married people can be successful, that it is possible to eliminate almost every vestige of private property, including the use of money, except for purposes of exchange with the outside world.

This model cannot, practically speaking, serve as a pattern for a socialist state or even a socialist community where there is any kind of cultural pluralism or diversity of religious faith. Although democratic elements play a part in the manner of electing leaders (on a sexist basis), freedom of expression or belief is clearly limited. The principal freedom seems to be the freedom to leave. That so few have left, that so few appear to be unhappy or maladjusted, does give one pause and make one appreciate the power and value of those positive qualities that the Hutterite colonies embody.

Another offshoot, or reincarnation, of Hutter's movement arrived on the East Coast of the United States in 1954 and established English-speaking *bruderhofs* in Rifton, N.Y., Farmington, Pa., and Norfolk, Ct.

The founder of this branch was Eberhard Arnold (1883–1935), a dynamic Protestant who came out of the "religious-social" movement in Germany and was, in fact, the speaker who responded to Karl Barth at the Tambach conference in 1919 (see chapter 9). He founded, with his wife, Emmy, a Christian commune in 1920 and joined the Hutterian church in 1930 after visiting *bruderhofs* in the United States and Canada. The colony he founded was dissolved by Hitler in 1937, two years after Arnold's death, its property confiscated, and its members driven from Germany. They held together, however, through migrations to Liechtenstein, England, and Paraguay until they arrived in the United States.

Like their Hutterish brethren, the Hutterians of the East Coast are conservative in theology, discipline, and dress, but more sophisticated in their outreach, producing attractive literature and winning plaudits from such diverse personalities as Malcolm Muggeridge, Jim Wallis of *Sojourners*, and Senator Mark Hatfield of Oregon.

A HALF DOZEN CHRISTIAN UTOPIANS

During the latter part of the sixteenth century and all of the seventeenth century, Plato's *Republic* and More's *Utopia* continued to inspire Christians. These utopias, however, came to reflect the contemporary fascination with scientific discovery. Francis Bacon (1561-1626), the English philosopher-statesman and author of *The New Atlantis*, put it this way: "The end of our foundation is the knowledge of causes, and secret motion of things; and the enlarging of the human empire, to the effecting of all things possible."[59]

These utopias did not thereby slight religion, though several were badly treated by it. Bacon himself, a somewhat corrupt courtier, warned that "divers great learned men have been heretical, whilst they have sought to fly up to the secrets of the Deity by the waxen wings of the senses."[60]

Giordano Bruno (1548?-1600), an Italian Dominican and a victim of the Inquisition burned at the stake, held the institutional forms of Christianity in contempt, but considered himself inspired by the true God. In his book *The Heroic Frenzies* (a title that seems also to describe the author) Bruno wrote this eloquent tribute to his own death:

A heroic mind will prefer falling or missing the mark nobly in a lofty enterprise, whereby he manifests the dignity of his mind, to obtaining perfection in things less noble, if not base. . . . Certainly a worthy and heroic death is preferable to an unworthy and vile triumph. . . . Fear not noble destruction, burst boldly through the clouds, and die content, if heaven destines us to so illustrious a death.[61]

That could serve as a comment on the death of Christ himself.

Tommaso Campanella (1568-1639) another Italian Dominican, created a utopia in his book *City of the Sun*. He spent nearly thirty years in prison, charged with heresy and conspiracy against the kingdom of Naples. Three hundred years later Maxim Gorki read his book, and told Lenin about him; his name is now on a monument in Red Square, honoring him as one of the fathers of the Russian Revolution.

Johann Andreae (1586-1654), a German pastor portrayed in *Christianopolis* an ideal Christian society in which science and orthodox Lutheran religion were completely integrated. Jan Amos Comenius (1592-1670), a Moravian bishop, wrote works that have been described as combining

insights of genius, practical educational plans of immediate applicability that reveal a knowledge of children and men, but also much sheer nonsense and a great utopian's jungle profusion of plans whose density would not be equaled again until the nineteenth century.[62]

Finally, there was Gottfried von Leibniz (1646-1716), German philosopher-mathematician-statesman, whose work has been described as "the last great utopian vision that derived its meaning from the love of God and the exploration of His world in all its dimensions—geographical, historical, theological and scientific."[63]

These are all fascinating characters. To know more about them, read the magnificently comprehensive and readable *Utopian Thought in the Modern World* (Manuel and Manuel).

PART II

THE DEVELOPMENT OF CHRISTIAN SOCIALISM IN EUROPE AND THE WESTERN HEMISPHERE

Being a more Explicit Study of Christian Socialism as Elucidated in Europe and the Americas during the Nineteenth and Twentieth Centuries, and as Practiced by Some, with Consideration of the Action and Reaction of Same with Marxism and Capitalism in both Protestant and Catholic Thought

Introduction

The burden of Part I was to show the development of Judeo-Christian thought from Moses through Jesus, the Fathers and Doctors of the Church, Thomas Aquinas, and various utopians and Protestant reformers, especially as that thought impacted on the concerns of Christian socialism.

Chapter 1 discussed various challenges to the ancient tradition by various religious and irreligious thinkers, culminating in the publication of what might be called capitalism's Bible, Adam Smith's *The Wealth of Nations*. We then moved back to Moses and attempted to show how profoundly the more ancient tradition differed and differs from Smith's ideas, even when those ideas were, as they still are, concealed behind the slippery reasoning of Christian theologians, starting with Duns Scotus and William of Ockham.

The gist of the tradition, or the ultimate expression of it, is found in its clearest form in the commentary of Cardinal Tommaso Cajetan on Thomas Aquinas's concept of property. The cardinal wrote:

> Now what a ruler can do in virtue of his office, so that justice may be served in the matter of riches, is to take from someone who is unwilling to dispense from what is superfluous for life or state, and to distribute it to the poor . . . [for], as Basil said, it belongs to the indigent, at least as owed, if not in fact.[1]

Few intelligent Christians still believe Adam Smith's Gospel to the effect that private greed will inevitably work public good. However, many intelligent Christians do still believe the notions about property and government's relation to it contained in the work of the English thinker John Locke (1632–1704).

Those notions are summed up in a sentence from Locke's *Second Treatise of Government,* written around the time of the Glorious Revolution of 1689. The *First Treatise* was intended to explode the idea of the divine right of kings, establishing in its place the idea of popular sovereignty, and defending the right, if not the obligation, of the people to overthrow tyrannical rulers.

The progressive thrust of the *First Treatise* made all the more persuasive the conservative thrust of the *Second.* This is the key sentence:

> The great and *chief end* therefore of Men's uniting into Commonwealths, and putting themselves under Government, is the *Preservation of their Property* [emphasis in the original].[2]

Unlike Smith and Franklin, who were typical products of the skeptical eighteenth century, Locke was a product of the more religious seventeenth century. So he begins his chapter on property with a reminder that both reason and revelation tell us that God has "given the earth . . . to mankind in common."[3] This thinking Locke shares with Aquinas and Cajetan. He also acknowledges that "every Man has a Property in his own Person," which "no Body has any Right to but himself."[4] He even introduces a radical labor theory of property that Aquinas and Cajetan might have found congenial:

> Labour being the unquestionable Property of the Labourer, no Man but he can have a right to what that is once joyned to, at least where there is enough, and as good left in common for others.[5]

The assumption here is that labor is not only the basis and justification for a property right, but that such a right does not exist where property is not used or *labored* over and then only "where there is enough and as good left in common for others."

But if there is *not* "enough or as good left in common for others," what then? Aquinas and Cajetan say that the prince, or the government, must see to it that "the others" get a sufficiency of this world's goods, even if it must be taken from those who have more than they need. Locke, by contrast, insists that "the Supream Power cannot take from any man any part of his Property without his own consent."[6] True, Locke provides for consent by a majority of the people's representatives, but only for taxes for government expenses, not for transfer to the poor, and there lies the profound difference.

So, though there may be some theoretical comfort for the radical in Locke's labor theory of property rights, there is far more comfort for the conservative in Locke's raising of government's obligation to protect property—no matter how acquired—to the rank of an absolute value and government's "great and chief end." There is not only comfort, there is the ideological weapon that can be used to resist every effort by government since then to do something about the maldistribution of wealth and income that has flowed from the Gospel according to Adam Smith.

We shall now proceed to relate the fortunes of those Christians who in turn fought, in various and often confused and confusing ways, to defend the ancient traditions against the newer heresies. We shall do this on a country, language, and ethnic basis, starting with France.

CHAPTER 7

France

Much could be said for the idea that France, over the period from 800 to 1850, influenced the western world more profoundly than any other country.

Consider Charlemagne, crowned by Pope Leo III in 800 as head of the Holy Roman Empire (thus confirming the creation of the papal states); Thomas Aquinas (granted he was Italian) teaching at the University of Paris; Louis IX, king and saint, leading the last two crusades; Louis XIV, the Sun King, dazzling the world with his arrogant splendor; Voltaire and Rousseau, pricking the bubbles of royal and ecclesiastical complacence; the French Revolution; Napoleon.

There was much justice in the claim that "a dangerous work written in French is a declaration of war on the whole of Europe." Almost everywhere in Europe, even in distant Russia, rulers, aristocrats, and intellectuals preferred French to their native tongues.[1]

Leader in the intellectual and political realms, France also led the way in the development of modern socialism. G. D. H. Cole reminds us that up to 1848 "the only great socialist thinker before Marx who was not a Frenchman was Owen: Babeuf, Saint-Simon, Fourier, Enfantin, Leroux, Cabet, Blanqui, Blanc, Buchez, Proudhon were all Frenchmen."[2] He could have added Lamennais and Considérant. Most of those named above were Christian socialists.

Arnold Ruge failed to find any French socialists to collaborate with him and Marx on the *Franco-German Annals* only because the French socialists rejected the atheism of the Germans, and Marx had little use for the more secular types like Blanqui and Proudhon.

Yet, by the end of the nineteenth century, Marxism and the atheism of the Germans had clearly won a dominant position in the socialist and working-class movements of France and the rest of Europe. Looking back from the 1920s, Pope Pius XI lamented that "the great scandal of the nineteenth century was that the Church lost the workingclass."[3] What happened?

87

A TURNING POINT

Historians are reluctant to identify any one event as a turning point. History is more complicated than that. But some events are pivotal. One of these occurred on the evening of June 25, 1848. The Industrial Revolution, starting later in France than in England, had created a proletariat that was concentrated in Paris. Crop failures in 1845 and 1846, added to the collapse of the railroad-building boom in 1847, had produced inflation, unemployment, and a depression that was fueling revolutions throughout Western Europe. As Francis Bacon said, "The rebellions of the belly are the worst." In London, Marx and Engels had already published *The Communist Manifesto,* but the document was not yet well known, much less taken seriously, by French workers.

In February of 1848 the bourgeois monarchy of Louis Philippe fell with scarcely a shot fired, and the Second Republic, using universal manhood suffrage for the first time, elected a national assembly that chose one Christian socialist, Philippe Buchez (1796–1865), for president and another, Anthime Corbon, as vice-president. By June the conservative majority, now less frightened by worker discontent, asserted itself and suspended the work-relief projects that had kept large numbers of unemployed in a state of relative submission.

The workers, led by followers of Auguste Blanqui (1805–1881), one of the few revolutionary socialists in France, joined a riotous demonstration on June 23. The government gave General Louis Cavaignac dictatorial powers. By June 25 thousands had been killed in bloody fighting in the streets of Paris. That evening Frédéric Ozanam (1813–1853), the elegant intellectual who founded the St. Vincent de Paul Society, went to see Denis-Auguste Affre, the Archbishop of Paris, and pleaded with him to do something to stop the slaughter. The archbishop was a brave man, in sympathy with the workers' grievances, and he set out to parley with the rebels, hoping to negotiate a truce. Preceded by a worker waving a green branch, he crossed the Place de la Bastille calling, "My friends, my friends!" The insurgents recognized and welcomed him. The Catholic historian Henri Daniel-Rops has given us a vivid account of what followed:

> With their help he climbed the first barricade and walked on toward the second in impressive silence. Some militiamen, however, tried to follow him. A short scuffle ensued and a few shots rang out. Suddenly Archbishop Affre collapsed. A bullet, doubtless not intended for him, had broken his spinal column. The rebels on the barricades were horrified; they rushed forward and carried him into the presbytery of St. Antoine, where he died thirty-six hours later, murmuring, "May my blood be the last."[4]

The blood of martyrs is not always the seed of faith. The archbishop's death set off a violent reaction among Catholics against the workers and against the ancient belief that fidelity to Christ could only be proven by fidelity to the cause of the poor. In vain Bishop Parisis tried to read a statement in the National Assembly that the fatal bullet had not been fired by the workers. He was drowned out by the boos of the deputies, most of whom were either Catholics or owed their seats to Catholics. Even liberal churchmen like Lacordaire and Montalembert swung over to the conservatives. The workers' revolt was mercilessly suppressed and a few years later, with Catholic support, Louis-Napoleon suppressed the Second Republic and imposed the dictatorship of the Second Empire.

Ozanam, in the dark days of June 1848, warned his fellow Catholics, "You have crushed the revolt, but another enemy, poverty, remains."[5] Pius XI might more accurately have said, "The great scandal of the nineteenth century was that the Church *abandoned* the workingclass." What happened in France set the tone and pattern for all of Europe.

All this need not have happened. Before 1848 Christians and Catholics were among the most articulate and influential of the advocates and defenders of the poor. They were not always orthodox in theology, they were not all practicing Christians, but they all based their social concerns on the example and the teachings of Jesus Christ.

Historical accuracy compels one to concede that, though it need not have happened, the momentum of Catholic conservatism and blind reaction was too strong to make any other outcome likely. Some would say it all started with Constantine and the establishment of Christianity as the state religion, the foundation and underpinning of royal power, the beneficiary of royal power, the weaker bedfellow in the marriage of "crown and altar."

THE SEVENTEENTH CENTURY

As previous chapters have indicated, the church did not go quietly to that bedchamber, nor was it always a meek, submissive bride. There were times when it proved itself the stronger partner. There were also isolated examples, in France as elsewhere, of brave and articulate church leaders who spoke out against the rich and the powerful, against kings themselves, in defense of the poor.

There was François Fénelon (1651–1715), archbishop and duke of Cambrai, who became tutor to the grandson of Louis XIV. For the edification of his royal pupil he wrote *Télémaque,* a work that greatly irritated the grandfather. *Télémaque* was an adventure story, the adventurer being Telemachus, son of Ulysses, who, privileged to visit Hell,

espied there those kings that were punished for having abused their power . . . for their dread to hear the truth, their love of base men and flatterers, their pride, their excessive pomp built upon the ruin of their people, their ambition to purchase a little vainglory with the blood of their subjects.[6]

Like Thomas More, Fénelon used a traveler, Adoam, to describe a utopian country, Boetia, where "they live all together, without dividing their lands. . . . All their goods are in common . . . so that having no private interests to maintain one against another, they all love one another with brotherly affection."[7] Fénelon covered himself by presenting another model society in Salentum. There the wise Mentor advises the ruler, Idumeneus:

You must limit the amount of land that each family may possess . . . [to] only that land absolutely necessary to support the number of persons in that family. All should have land, but each relatively little and each therefore will be concerned to cultivate it well.[8]

So in the end we see a touch of communism, mixed with the notion of family farms, that could not have been very pleasing to the noble landowners of "the old regime" with their vast estates.

Even Bishop Jacques Bossuet (1627–1704), great preacher at the court of Louis XIV, tutor of his son, and supporter of Louis's claims against Innocent XII, did not hesitate to remind his sovereign lord that "the true character of the prince is to provide for the needs of the people, as that of the tyrant is to think only of himself."[9]

JEAN JACQUES ROUSSEAU

A series of eccentric monks and abbés, some of them anticlerical, men like Dom Leger Deschamps, Jean Meslier ("The powerful of the earth should be strangled with the guts of priests because they live in pleasure while the people suffer"[10]), and Gabriel Mably enlivened the eighteenth century with tales and theories of communist utopias, but the great theorist of revolution, and in some sense a precursor of Christian socialism, was Jean Jacques Rousseau (1712–1778). Philippe Buchez, the most prominent leader of the Christian socialists of the nineteenth century, was an admirer of Rousseau. In his history of the French Revolution he points out that of the members of the Third Estate in the Constituent Assembly of 1789 "The serious men were nourished on the reading of Rousseau's *Social Contract* and the less serious on Voltaire."[11]

Rousseau was a most unorthodox Christian, who fathered (and abandoned) five illegitimate children, was converted to Catholicism, then returned to the Protestant Church, and finally arrived at a kind of free-floating Christianity of his own invention. "I am attached to the Gospel," he protested, "with all the zeal of my heart." He called himself "the only man in France who believes in God" and reminded his readers that he had read the Bible through five or six times.[12] In works of literary and emotional power he did propel some basic Christian concepts onto the center stage of French intellectual and political life—the concepts that were translated into the Revolution's slogan of "Liberty, Equality, Fraternity."

In his essay *Discourse on the Origins of Inequality* (1754), he set out to prove that human nature is naturally good but has been corrupted by civilization ("It was iron and corn that first civilized men and ruined humanity"[13]). In the course of this dubious exercise he did strike some telling blows at the particular corruptions of French royalty and aristocracy. One example:

> It is plainly contrary to the law of nature, however defined, that children should command old men, fools wise men, and that the privileged few should gorge themselves with superfluities, while the starving multitude are in want of the bare necessities of life.[14]

The first sentence of *The Social Contract* (1762) strikes a revolutionary tone: "Man is born free, and yet we see him everywhere in chains."[15] Charles Frankel has made the excellent point that

> *The Social Contract* was an incitement to revolution because it did what a revolutionary book has to do: it joined justice and utility, and showed men that their interest and their duty were on the same side. *The Social Contract* made social change not only a matter of self-interest but a moral obligation incumbent upon all.[16]

Rousseau put it simply, "I shall endeavor to unite what right permits with what interest prescribes, that justice and utility may not be separated."[17]

It is impossible to construct a logical, consistent system out of Rousseau's thought. Voltaire (1694–1778) was contemptuous of it, sometimes for good reasons, sometimes for reasons that revealed his own bourgeois, elitist prejudices. Rousseau's notion of the general will, which is always right, as distinguished from the will of the majority, which is often wrong, has been used to justify rule by a dictator who knows better than the people what is good for them.

The Social Contract contains passages that are anti-property and passages that are pro-property, anti-religion and pro-religion, anti-democracy and pro-democracy. As Frankel put it, "Rousseau's doctrine seems to warrant almost anything from complete justificiation of the status quo to a state of permanent revolution."[18]

But the passages that people remembered were more often the revolutionary ones. When the people meet in public assemblies, Rousseau insisted,

> two questions should always be proposed . . . and the votes should be taken separately on each. The first should be: "Does it please the Sovereign [the people] to preserve the present form of government?" And the second: "Does it please the people to leave the administration with those who are at present charged with it."[19]

This passage was the main reason for the condemnation of *The Social Contract* by the government of Geneva, Rousseau's home city. Also: "We are told that a despot ensures civil tranquillity. . . . We find tranquillity also in dungeons; but is that enough to make them enjoyable?"[20]

In one passage Rousseau equates the beginnings of human strife and dissension with the institution of private property. In other passages he defends the right to private property, and his reasons are an interesting echo of Thomas Aquinas. He does not concede that property is a natural right: "It does not become a real right until after the right of property is established" by civil society. Property rights in land are valid when the holder does not

occupy more land than is sufficient to supply him with subsistence. . . . He must take possession, not by a vain ceremony, but by labor and cultivation, as they are the only proofs of a man's being a proprietor which, in default of a legal title, deserve to be respected by others.[21]

This last sentence echoes Locke, and both the passages quoted anticipate Marx's theory of labor value.

Marxists have also admired in Rousseau's *Social Contract* a footnote he added to a passage on the moral and legal equality that convention and law should substitute for inequality "in strength or in genius":

Under bad governments this equality is but an illusive appearance which only serves to keep the poor in misery and support the rich in their usurpation. In fact, laws are always useful to those who have abundance and injurious to those who have nothing; from whence it follows that the social state is only advantageous to men when every individual has some property, and no one has too much.[22]

Marxists may admire this passage, but it is actually as much a critique of excessive nationalization as it is of government by and for the rich.

Rousseau distinguished three different varieties of religion, two of which he favored. One of these was his own invention, "the pure and simple religion of the Gospel . . . without temples, altars or rites." The other was civil religion,

the religion of the citizen . . . the articles of which it is the business of the Sovereign to arrange . . . [and] without which it is impossible to be either a good citizen or a faithful subject. . . . The existence of a powerful, wise and benevolent Divinity, who foresees and provides the life to come, the happiness of the just, the punishment of the wicked, the sanctity of the social contract and the laws. These are the positive dogmas. The negative dogmas I would confine to one: intolerance.

The context indicates that Rousseau means intolerance would be condemned. However, atheists are to be banished from the state, and "if any one, after he has publicly subscribed to these dogmas, shall conduct himself as if he did not believe them, he is to be punished by death."[23]

Rousseau's peculiar notion of religious toleration was limited mainly to those who rebelled against institutional religion and particularly against what he defined as

> a third and more bizarre kind of religion, which gives to humanity two codes of legislation, two chiefs, and two countries, requires from them contradictory duties, and prevents their being devout men and citizens at the same time. . . . Such as Roman [Catholic] Christianity, [which] may be called the religion of the priest. . . . [It] is so evidently bad that it would be wasting time to demonstrate its evils. Whatever breaks social unity is worthless; all institutions that set man in contradiction with himself are worthless.[24]

In Rousseau's France the average person's reading of this was, "You cannot serve the pope and the state." Loyal Catholics were more likely to read it, "You cannot serve God and Rousseau's notion of the state."

I have devoted more space to Rousseau than might seem appropriate in a history of Christian socialism, since he was neither a socialist nor a Christian, really, in any traditional sense. He was important, however, because he set the intellectual tone and agenda for the nineteenth century. In his ambiguities and contradictions he was not typically French. We are still wrestling with the job of sorting out the sense and the nonsense in what he wrote. In 1794 the French Republic honored Rousseau as a national hero. When Gregory XVI and Pius IX condemned "liberalism," and with it those who defended democracy, freedom of religion, free speech and socialism, it was mainly from Rousseau that they got their idea, their vague, undefined impressions and feelings, about what most of these terms meant. And that was, mostly, a declaration of war on the Catholic Church.

THE FRENCH REVOLUTION

The French Revolution (1789) carried out that declaration of war. It is impossible to exaggerate the effects of that war and the resulting trauma upon the Catholic Church, whether we think of that church in terms of the papacy, the French clergy, or the loyal laity.

Of the estimated seventeen thousand persons executed during the Reign of Terror and the twenty-three thousand more who died in overcrowded, disease-ridden prisons or on the field of battle, it is probable that the great majority were Catholic; over one thousand were priests.

The Paris Commune closed all Paris churches in 1793, as did many of the provincial authorities, and sponsored a revolutionary religion called the Cult of Reason. This did not last, but the Civil Constitution of the Clergy, approved in 1791 while Louis XVI was still on the throne, had already stripped the church of its land and set up a priesthood and episcopacy independent of the pope and subject to election by all French citizens, whether Catholic or not.

Most of the land, including that of the king and the nobles, was distributed to the peasants and, ironically, these peasants, who were mainly loyal Catholics, became during the nineteenth century the mainstay of Catholic power and influence and a major source of antisocialist opinion.

The Revolution was the occasion for violent conflict over and between different theories of property and property rights, as well as of the duties of government toward the poor. The preamble of the Constitution, for example, known as the Declaration of the Rights of Man, in Article 21 incorporates the ancient Judeo-Christian principle dear to the Fathers and Thomas Aquinas: "Public relief is a sacred duty; society owes a living to its less fortunate members, either by procuring them employment or by assuring the means of sustenance to all those who are unfit for work." At the same time, the Constitution repudiated the more ancient Christian notion of property rights represented by Thomas in favor of that promoted by Ockham and Scotus, which was a repeat, actually, of the total, unlimited dominion enshrined in Roman Law.

It is an irony of history that Maximilien Robespierre (1758–1794), the man who presided over the Reign of Terror until he himself fell victim to it, was the major spokesperson for the Christian view. Article 6 of his version of the Declaration reads: "The right of property is the right that each citizen has of enjoying and disposing at his pleasure of that portion of goods that is guaranteed him by the law." In other words, property rights are not absolute but are limited by some notion of the common good, which is determined by society and incorporated in the law.

This wording was rejected, however, by the National Convention in 1793. Article 2 of the approved Constitution included property among the natural and imprescriptible rights of man along with liberty, equality, and security. Article 16 deleted Robespierre's reference to "that portion of goods that is guaranteed him by the law," Aquinas's *humanum condictum* (see chapter 5 above), and substituted "his goods, his revenues, the fruit of his labor and his industry" (period). In short, no limitation on property rights. You have every right to light your cigar with a ten dollar bill, every right to enjoy your superfluous goods while Lazarus lies starving at the gate.

The peasants got land and freedom from feudal taxes, but the workers wound up with nothing. Universal *manhood* suffrage was part of the Constitution of 1793, but in 1795 this was replaced by property qualifications. The French Revolution, in the final analysis, was a bourgeois revolution, a revolution of property-holders, by property-holders, for property-holders—anticlerical property-holders. Even the right to organize was denied the workers. Unions and collective bargaining remained illegal until 1884.

There was rebellion on the left. Gracchus Babeuf (1760–1797) organized a Conspiracy of the Equals, protesting that the Revolution had been betrayed and must be "replayed." Their manifesto incorporated the first revolutionary communist program: all property held in common, elimination of the right of inheritance, seizure of the state by a disciplined minority, and a dictatorship to weed out the more hopeless dissidents before a return to universal manhood suffrage. "We are equal, is it not so?" the Manifesto asked. "Well, henceforth we intend to live and to die equal. . . . We want real equality or death, no matter what the price."[25] What they got was death. The Conspiracy was discovered and Babeuf executed in 1797.

Karl Marx remembered, however, and in the *Communist Manifesto* saluted Babeuf as one of the first who had "given voice to the demands of the proletariat."[26] This trial run à la Marx did nothing to prevent the word "communism" from becoming the bugaboo of most Christians in the nineteenth and twentieth centuries.

HENRI DE SAINT-SIMON

Even before Adam Smith's "invisible hand" began to write large on the pages of world history, men in France were promoting ideas like his. They were the physiocrats. Led by François Quesnay (1694–1774), physician to Louis XV, and Vincent de Gournay (1712–1759), who invented the phrase *Laissez faire et laissez passer,* they were reacting against the restrictive government policies of mercantilism. In their reaction they wrote things that were just as contrary to Christianity and common sense as anything Smith would write. For example, in 1767 the physiocrat Mercier de la Rivière wrote:

We have seen that it is of the essence of order that the private interest of an individual can never be separated from the common interest of all. . . . Society then runs itself; the desire of wealth and the liberty of possession incessantly promote the multiplication of production and the expansion of industry, and impart to society entire a movement which becomes a perpetual tendency toward the best possible condition.[27]

Another physiocrat, Pierre Du Pont de Nemours (1739–1817), president of the Constituent Assembly of 1790 and founder of the Du Pont dynasty in America, insisted that the main function of government was not to obstruct the automatic and beneficent operation of economic laws, but to "punish the small number of people who attack the property of others,"[28] for "the social laws established by the Supreme Being prescribe solely the conservation of the right of property and of the liberty which is inseparable from it."[29]

And so it logically followed that, when the bourgeoisie, fed and fattened on such ideas, came after the Revolution and Napoleon to dominate the governments of France, the workers in their factories had to put in fifteen to seventeen hours a day for a wage of one franc, 50 centimes. In 1832 the Baron de Morogues estimated that an industrial worker who worked steadily might make 450 francs a year. Since the minimum cost of supporting a family with three children was 860 francs, this meant that husband, wife, and children would all have to work to stay alive. Four-year-old children could be found working in factories. Older children might make as much as 75 centimes a day.[30] These children, wrote Villermé, who did a careful survey for the Academy of Moral and Political Sciences,

> remain on their feet sixteen to seventeen hours a day, thirteen hours of which are spent in a closed room, with hardly a change of station or attitude. That is not work, a task, it is torture; and it is inflicted upon children from six to eight years, underfed, poorly clad, obliged to walk, at five in the morning, the long distance to the factories and then to walk back at night, exhausted.[31]

The first voice raised in protest that caught the attention of France, and the world beyond, was that of Henri de Saint-Simon (1760–1825). Although he died before the word "socialism" had been invented and his ideas fit poorly into any socialist framework, he is included in every history of socialism. His writings influenced all the early champions of that movement, as well as its enemies. Although he was not a Christian in any traditional sense, he wrote an important book called *The New Christianity (Le nouveau Christianisme)*, which was widely read and widely disputed. A romantic figure, he fought in the American Revolution at the age of nineteen, giving up his title to become plain Citizen Bonhomme. He barely escaped the guillotine under Robespierre, became very rich speculating in the property of fleeing fellow aristocrats, became very poor living it up in Paris and Geneva, became very serious in his poverty and poured out a series of books on science, history, and economics that Émile Durkheim claims did more than Saint-Simon's one-time disciple Auguste Comte to launch the intellectual movements that evolved into positivism and sociology.[32] He became very sick both physically and mentally, and at one point was a fellow resident with the Marquis de Sade in the insane asylum. He died in 1825, surrounded by disciples, murmuring, "Religion cannot disappear from the world. It can only be changed. . . . The workers' party will soon be formed. The future is ours."[33]

The New Christianity did not appear until a month before Saint-Simon's death, but already in 1807 he had been trying to change Christianity:

> The most generally taught moral principle is that of the Gospel: "Do unto others as you would have others do unto you." . . . I propose to substitute the following principle for that of the Gospel: "Man must work."[34]

Belief in the universal obligation to work and St. Paul's principle, "If any one will not work, let him not eat,"[35] was common to the thought of all French Christian socialists.

By the end of his life, however, Saint-Simon had come around to the conviction that the principle "Do unto others . . . " was the essential one. The following quotes from *The New Christianity* will give an idea both of the peculiarities of his religious faith and of his socialism:

> God has said, "Men should treat one another as brothers." This sublime principle includes all that is divine in the Christian religion. . . . Now, according to this principle, which God has given us as a rule for our conduct, we should organize our society in a way that will be the most advantageous for the greatest number; we must direct all our work and all our activity toward the end of improving as quickly and completely as possible the moral and physical existence of the most numerous class. I say that it is this, and this alone, that is the divine part of the Christian religion.[36]

A short book of a hundred pages, *The New Christianity* consists of a dialogue between a Conservative and an Innovator.

Conservative: "Do you recognize the Church as a divine institution?"

Innovator: "I have the greatest respect and admiration for the Fathers of the Church. . . . To the men of power they declared positively and most vigorously that their first duty should be to employ all their resources for the quickest possible improvement in the moral and physical condition of the poor."[37] In other words, No.

Like St. Basil, Saint-Simon was wise enough to see that more money in the hands of the poor and less lying idle in the hands of the rich would mean a more efficient and prosperous economy for all:

> If all institutions were directed toward the end of improving the moral and physical well-being of the poorest class, they would bring prosperity to all classes of society and all nations with the greatest possible speed.[38]

Liturgy and dogma were for Saint-Simon only window-dressing to show off and accent the morality summed up in Jesus' Second Commandment, "Thou shalt love thy neighbor as thyself."

Innovator: "The doctrine of morality will be considered by the new Christians as the most important; cult and dogma will be regarded by them only as accessories . . . to fix the attention of the faithful of all classes on morality."[39] Other opinions of the Innovator:

"The Jesuits [dominate] all humankind by an odious system of mystical tricks."[40]

The pope and his church are heretical because—

1. The teaching given to the laity is designed only to convince them that they are "absolutely dependent on the clergy."

2. They give "bad instruction to the seminarians." Before the time of Leo X (1513–1521) the clergy were orthodox "because they were superior to the laity in all the sciences whose progress contributed to the well-being of the poorest

class." Since Leo X they have become heretical "because they have only pursued theology and allowed the laity to surpass them in the fine arts, the exact sciences, and industrial technology." This is a peculiar notion of heresy, but as a judgment on the church's neglect of science, scholarship, economics, social justice, and the practical arts, it makes some sense.

3. The pope's administration of the Papal States is "more opposed to the moral and physical interests of the temporal subjects belonging to the destitute class" than that of any lay prince, because (a) large tracts of land lie fallow; (b) "There is no manufacturing . . . every branch of industry is paralyzed"; and (c) the poor are therefore unemployed and dependent on charity.

4. "I accuse them of having consented to the formation of two institutions diametrically opposed to the spirit of Christianity: the Inquisition and the Jesuits."[41]

"At the end of the fifteenth century the sacred college [of cardinals] changed completely. . . . It no longer identified with the lowest class of society."[42]

But if Saint-Simon had little use for the Catholic Church, he had even less for Luther and the Protestants. He judged the Lutherans heretical for several reasons.

They have not wrenched the church's attention away from dogma and liturgy, the saying of prayers, abstinence and the doing of penance, to an effective use of art, science, and industry to improve the lot of "the poorest and most numerous class." "Certainly all Christians aspire to eternal life, but the only way of obtaining it consists of working in this life for the increase of the wellbeing of humanity."[43] A good point, and not a bad statement of Jesus' meaning in Matthew 25, but how can the poor weak Christians be motivated to do this without the theology, dogma, and liturgy that establish and express and transmit the living power and truth of that figure Jesus Christ, who gave the commandment and will dispense the rewards and the punishments to those who do and who do not obey? Saint-Simon ignored that question, and it was his ignoring it—rather, his dismissal of the question as irrelevant—that weakened the appeal of his "new Christianity" to believing Catholics and Protestants.

Luther, Saint-Simon argued, had

ignored the immense progress that the priests had made in civilization and the great social importance that they helped peaceful workers to acquire by diminishing the strength and status of temporal power, that unholy power whose natural tendency is to subject men to the rule of physical force.[44]

Neither one [Catholicism] nor the other [Protestantism] is the Christian religion. . . . Since the fifteenth century Christianity has been abandoned. My purpose is to strip [Christianity] of all its superstitious or useless beliefs and practices . . . to bring together the scholars, artists and industrial leaders and to make them the directors general of the human race . . . to place the fine arts, sciences and industry at the head of the sacred teachings . . . to pronounce anathema on theology.[45]

A peculiar kind of Christian, Saint-Simon was also a peculiar kind of socialist. In some ways he was a prophet of big-business-with-a-sense-of-social-responsibility. In others he anticipated the Marxian emphasis on top-down state control. He was no democrat. He wanted the vote restricted to property holders and men of distinction in the arts, the sciences, and industry. He was perhaps the first technocrat, the first apostle of the managerial revolution, and one of the first among the French to understand the significance of the Industrial Revolution, which, well behind England, had produced only 200 steam engines by 1820 (but would produce 18,700 by 1860).

Saint-Simon was closer to the Christian tradition on the question of property rights than he was on questions theological. "What is necessary," he wrote,

is a law that establishes the right of property and not a law that establishes it in any particular way. . . . These questions follow: what are those goods that are suitable to become private property? By what means can individuals acquire property? In what ways have they the right to use property once they have acquired it? These are the questions with which legislators of every country and every time have the right to deal whenever they find it necessary, for the individual right to property can be founded only on the common and general good (*utilité*) of the exercise of that right, a good that can vary according to the times.[46]

THE SAINT-SIMONIANS

The followers of Saint-Simon, who at his death included some of the brightest and most dedicated young men in France, took the master seriously and tried to make a religion out of his New Christianity. Their high priest was Barthélemy-Prosper Enfantin (1796–1864). He had seen Saint-Simon only once (Saint-Simon's dog, Presto, is said to have barked his disapproval). G. D. H. Cole concluded that Enfantin, a handsome, charismatic leader,

had an astonishing capacity for inspiring love and veneration and for getting people to listen respectfully to absolute nonsense. . . . He was no doubt mad, and he buried the fruitful ideas of Saint-Simon under the mass of rubbish he erected on them.[47]

The feverish goings on are reminiscent of a twentieth-century cult devoted to the use of drugs and the veneration of a guru. Enfantin, who assigned Saint-Simon "a rank higher than the son of God," encouraged his followers to place him (Enfantin) on a similar level. At one of the initiation ceremonies at their retreat in Ménilmontant, a Paris suburb, a man named Retouret responded, "Father, once I told you that I saw in you the majesty of an emperor . . . the goodness of a Messiah. You appeared formidable to me. Today I have felt how profoundly tender and gentle you are. Father, I am ready."[48] Father Enfantin journeyed to Egypt in search of a holy Mother whom he might marry, but without success. He inveighed against the hypocritical and adulterous marriages of the Parisian upper classes and preached the virtues of free and honest love.

For a time the people of Paris were fascinated—and shocked. As many as ten thousand at a time journeyed to Ménilmontant on holidays to watch the Saint-Simonian priests and priestesses laboring in their gardens and celebrating their original liturgies. Maxime du Camp has described their costumes: "The trouser was white, the vest red, and the tunic blue-violet. White is the color of love, red that of labor, and blue that of faith."[49] The tunics were buttoned in the back to emphasize mutual dependence (somebody other than the wearer had to button it).

Eventually the more sober apostles departed. But before they did they left a body of doctrine that went a good deal further than Saint-Simon himself had gone toward collectivism in the ownership and control of the means of production. The doctrine also contained some ambiguity. The Saint-Simonians

> reject the system of community of goods; for that community would be a clear violation of the first of all moral laws: . . . each should be employed according to his [or her] capacity and rewarded according to his [or her] works. But in virtue of this law they demand the abolition of all privileges of birth without exception, and consequently the elimination of inheritance. . . . All instruments of labor, land and capital [should be placed] in a social pool . . . [and] exploited by association and hierarchically.[50]

In other words, with inheritance abolished, the state would eventually own and control everything; but the state would be controlled by an elite hierarchy that would reward everyone, not according to their needs, but according to their works.

Another French socialist, Louis Blanc (1811–1882) was to revise this doctrine in favor of needs, a phrasing that was adopted by Marx in his *Critique of the Gotha Program* as a characteristic of the perfect communist society.[51] By that time (1875) most French socialists, Christian or not, had been pushing or criticizing one form or another of the formula. In this debate the Christians tended to quote the Bible. If they favored rewards according to works, they would quote St. Paul's "If anyone will not work, let him not eat" or the many passages in Old and New Testaments that remind us that God will reward every person "according to his works." If they favored needs, they would quote passages like Matthew 25 that emphasize the obligation to provide for the needs of others. No one thought of phrasing it, "In this life from each according to his ability, to each according to his needs; in the next life to each according to his works." Too complicated.

Another key word in the Saint-Simonian statement was the French word *"association."* This word, already introduced by the Owenites in England, appears again and again in the writing of French socialists. Its closest equivalent in modern English would be "cooperation" or "cooperative society." Its use by the Saint-Simonians exposes their most serious ambiguity, since the sentence in which the word appears favors state ownership and control. So the one sentence contains expressions of the two conflicting tendencies that have marked the socialist movement from its beginning to the present, namely, social ownership and control by way of worker ownership as against social ownership and control by way of state ownership. The conflict was particularly prominent in the first two-thirds of the nineteenth century. By the last third of that century the Marxists were beginning to win the battle in favor of state ownership, a battle much influenced by the natural human tendency toward impatience. By the second half of the twentieth century, when the dangers of state ownership and control had been amply demonstrated, the pendulum was swinging back either to worker ownership and control or to some blend of worker ownership, private ownership, state ownership, and worker control.

Here we are speaking about the means of production: land, factories, capital investment. Writing at the end of the nineteenth century, Émile Durkheim, the French sociologist, defined French communism in terms of private production and common consumption, as in the *phalanstère* of Charles Fourier (1772–1837), and socialism in terms of common production and private consumption, as in Louis Blanc's plans for "national workshops" or what Durkheim understood Marx to favor.[52] Here again we see some confusion and ambiguity. Most critics, like Pius IX, simply combined the two movements as one word in one anathema, "socialism-and-communism."

At any rate, the Saint-Simonians had been clear enough to scare the bourgeoisie and the bourgeois king, Louis Philippe, who had just taken over the French government from the pious Bourbon Charles X after the almost bloodless revolution of July 1830. The Saint-Simonians stated their proposals in a letter to the Chamber of Deputies on October 1, 1830.

It was not, however, until later, November 12, 1831, that Alexandre Vinet, a contributor to the Protestant newspaper *Le Semeur,* wrote an article in which the word *"socialisme"* appeared for the first time in France. He used it to designate the opposite of "individualism." By this time Enfantin had set the movement firmly in the direction of free love and the emancipation of women from their adulterous husbands. That, plus some suspicion of embezzlement, was enough for the authorities. They put Enfantin and a score or more of his apostles on trial in August 1832. It was the social, political, and theatrical event of the year. Enfantin insisted on providing his own defense and proved once again the old adage, "He who insists on trying his own case has a fool for a client." In effect, he pleaded guilty to the charge of "outrages against public morals" but innocent by reason of his countercharge that the public morals were immoral.

The jury declared Enfantin and all his followers guilty and they were sentenced to one year in prison, a sentence that Louis Philippe commuted after seven and a half months. But the movement was dead. What the trial and sentence had not killed was killed by the ridicule of Parisian wits. Enfantin and many of his followers eventually became business executives.

And the infant Socialism, barely out of the cradle, was the victim of what American slang has succinctly defined as "a bum rap."

HUGUES-FÉLICITÉ ROBERT DE LA MENNAIS

The next Frenchman to champion the socialist cause was, at the beginning of his career, as orthodox a Christian and Catholic as Saint-Simon and Enfantin were unorthodox. Hugues-Félicité Robert de la Mennais, or Lamennais (1782–1854), known to his friends and family as Féli, was the son of a Breton merchant and shipowner whose surname was Robert de la Mennais. The son changed his name to Félicité Lamennais in middle age, when he had identified himself with the democratic cause. He became a priest and, in the opinion of many, the most eloquent advocate of Christianity in the nineteenth century.

Socialist historians differ as to whether Lamennais was a socialist. G. D. H. Cole says he was not, but classifies him as an important ally of socialism and devotes a sympathetic chapter of his book to Lamennais's ideas and career.[53] Jacques Droz's history lets Lamennais speak largely for himself and notes that he described himself as a socialist

> if one understands by socialism the principle of association as one of the essential foundations of the order to be established . . . if one understands by socialism one of the systems which, since Saint-Simon and Fourier, have multiplied [*pullulé*] everywhere and whose general character, explicit or implicit, is the negation of property and the family, no, we are not socialist.

He opposed communism as "forced labor paid at the pleasure of the state."[54]

Lamennais was slow in accepting the Catholic faith; he did not receive his first communion until he was twenty-two years old and he was ordained at thirty-four. His home at La Chesnaye in Brittany became the center of a dynamic movement of "liberal Catholics" that included brilliant men such as Henri Lacordaire (1802–1861), who later headed the Dominican Order in France, and the aristocratic Charles de Montalembert (1810–1870).

In 1817 Lamennais published a book with the churchy title *Essay on Indifference in Matters of Religion*. Much to his surprise the book catapulted him into the center of the literary and ecclesiastical world. He was hailed as the new Pascal, the new Bossuet. Lamartine, the popular poet-politician, was enthusiastic: "It is magnificent. Reasoned like de Maistre, written like Rousseau, strong, true, lofty, picturesque, convincing, novel, it is everything."[55] Even the cynics in the fashionable salons were reading it. It was soon being read by all Europe. Over the next six years three more volumes appeared, and with them new ideas and controversy. Even royalist Catholics had liked the first volume, whose main target was the notion, beloved of Saint-Simon and Rousseau, that one could accept and *use* the morality of Christianity but discard its dogma and theology.

The later volumes put forth philosophical novelties based on the notion of *sensus communis* (the common consent of humanity as a basis for religious faith), emphasized political and religious liberty as necessary to the independence of the Catholic Church from state domination, and defended papal authority as a bulwark against nationalism in religion.

There was something here to worry everybody. The conservative theologians worried about *sensus communis,* the pope about political and religious liberty, the Gallican bishops about Lamennais's ultramontanism. (*Ultramontane*, literally "beyond the mountains," signified a preference for the pope's authority to that of national hierarchies, which tended to be more subservient to the king.)

Meanwhile Lamennais, in his writing for various journals, had revealed a sharp polemical style that could not disagree without being disagreeable. He had made enemies.

In 1824 Lamennais went to Rome and was received with cordiality by Leo XII (1823–1829), a shrewd and kindly man, who recognized in Lamennais both an ally armed with a powerful pen and a sensitive, prickly personality who had to be handled with tact. The story that Leo XII offered Lamennais a cardinal's hat, which Lamennais refused, seems to be unfounded. There is evidence for the belief that the pope wanted to make Lamennais a bishop assigned to Rome, where he could be kept on a shorter rein.

The unconventional George Sand is quoted by an English historian as describing the personality of Lamennais. She

> speaks of the "austere and terrible face of the great Lamennais" with his brow like that of an unbroken wall, "a brass tablet—the seal of indomitable vigor" upon it. She compares the stiff and rigid inclination of his profile and the angular narrowness of his face with his inflexible probity, hermit-like austerity and incessant toil of thought, ardent and vast as heaven. But, she adds, "the smile which comes suddenly to humanize this countenance changes my terror into confidence, my respect into admiration."[56]

Victor Hugo, Alfred de Musset, and Charles Sainte-Beuve, other literary figures, were personal friends of Lamennais and were moved by his writing to take a more positive view of Christianity.

But meanwhile he made enemies. And he moved further to the left. His appeals for political and religious liberty, freedom of conscience, and separation of church and state grew stronger. When Hyacinthe de Quélen, the royalist archbishop of Paris, described him as a man so rash "as to set up his personal opinions as articles of faith," Lamennais counterattacked with intemperate invective, calling most of the French hierarchy "a disgusting hotchpotch of stupidity and arrogance, tomfoolery, besotted smugness, petty intrigue, petty ambitions and absolute intellectual impotence."[57]

The July Revolution of 1830, bringing to power an anticlerical bourgeoisie who favored the relaxation of press censorship, gave Lamennais and his friends both cause and opportunity to start their own daily newspaper, *L'Avenir* (The Future), flaunting the banner "God and Liberty" on its masthead. They claimed *L'Avenir* was the first daily paper founded in Europe in the interests of Catholicism.

The prospectus, borrowed in part from Louis de Potter (1786–1859), leader of the Belgian liberals, announced that there were now two liberalisms: the old liberalism, "inheritor of the destructive doctrines of the philosophy of the eighteenth century, and in particular its hatred of Christianity . . . exhales intolerance and oppression," whereas the young liberalism, "which is growing and will finish by supplanting the other, confines itself, in regard to religion, to demanding the separation of church and state, which is necessary for the liberty of the church." The paper's goal was to effect a rapprochement between the young liberals and "enlightened Catholics."[58]

The paper lasted from October 16, 1830, to November 15, 1831. Its editors were unaware of the expense of publishing a daily newspaper. There were simply not enough enlightened Catholics in Paris to support it, and though it created a sensation and its influence was profound, subscribers never numbered more than a few thousand. The opposition of most of the bishops was also a formidable obstacle. Lacordaire persuaded Lamennais to appeal to Rome for support. The two communicated their decision to Montalembert who, alarmed, cried, "And what if we are condemned?" To which Lamennais replied, "It is impossible, Charles. We cannot be condemned."[59]

And so the three friends set out for Rome, having announced that the paper would suspend publication until Rome gave a decision. They arrived there December 30, 1831, and were kept waiting until March 13, 1832, when they were finally allowed to see the pope. By then Lacordaire had given up and returned to France.

The pope was no longer the kindly Leo XII, but a different man, Gregory XVI (1831–1846). Montalembert described the long-awaited audience:

> For a quarter of an hour he talked to us very pleasantly and affably. . . .
> He recalled the saying of some cardinal, that the French would all go to hell or paradise, but there would be no purgatory for them. . . . The pope then . . . dismissed us very graciously, without having uttered a single word that had the least bearing on our mission or on the fortunes of the church.[60]

Even before the trusting pilgrims had arrrived in Rome, the French government had instructed its ambassador to make sure the pope realized that any encouragement would have an adverse effect on the relations of church and state in France. The government received an assurance from the ambassador that he had seen the pope, whose disposition left nothing to be desired. Prince Metternich (1773–1859), foreign minister of Austria, sent and received similar instructions and assurances to and from his ambassador in Rome.

Apparently Gregory XVI, when he received Lamennais and Montalembert so affably, had already decided that these particular Frenchmen were on the way to hell, not paradise. His encyclical *Mirari vos,* published on August 15, 1832, is worth quoting at length as an example of the vehemence with which nineteeth-century popes condemned ideas and movements that have been explicitly approved by twentieth-century popes and by the Second Vatican Council.

The opening pages of the encyclical are one long complaint about the recent persecution of the church and, though Lamennais and *L'Avenir* are never mentioned, it is evident—and all parties were so informed—that they were, in the pope's mind, the principal culprits.

> The divine authority of the Church is opposed and her rights shorn off. She is subjected to human reason [*terrenis rationibus*] and with the greatest injustice exposed to the hatred of the people and reduced to vile servitude.[61]

Others have translated "human reason" as "earthly considerations," but either way the phrase reveals the peculiar reluctance of the church in the nineteenth century to recognize that no human institution, however divinely ordained, is or can be free from testing by "human reason" and "earthly considerations."

Lamennais and his followers had frequently called for "a restoration and regeneration" of the Catholic Church. Gregory's response:

> It is obviously absurd and injurious to propose a certain "restoration and regeneration" for [the Church] as though necessary for her safety and growth, as if she could be subject to defect or obscuration or other misfortune.[62]

Anything less than perfection was clearly unthinkable.

> This shameful font of indifferentism gives rise to that absurd and erroneous proposition which claims that liberty of conscience must be maintained for everyone.[63]

Contrast this statement from the Second Vatican Council:

> This Vatican Synod declares that the human person has a right to religious freedom. . . . In all his activity a man is bound to follow his conscience faithfully, in order that he may come to God, for whom he

was created. It follows that he is not to be forced to act in a manner contrary to his conscience.[64]

Gregory again:

Certain teachings are being spread among the common people that attack the trust and submission due to princes. [Gregory quotes St. Paul: "Let every person be subject to the governing authorities. For there is no authority except from God" (Romans 13:2).] Therefore both divine and human laws cry out against those who strive by treason and sedition to drive the people from confidence in their princes and force them [the princes] from their government.

He condemns "the detestable insolence and improbity" of those who

feign piety for religion, but are driven by a passion for promoting novelties and sedition everywhere. . . . They preach liberty of every sort; they stir up disturbances in sacred and civil affairs, and pluck authority to pieces [emphasis added].[65]

Even Lamennais's sincerity is denied.

It is noteworthy that nineteenth-century popes often quoted Romans 13:2 and 1 Peter 2:13–15, but they rarely, if ever, quoted the same Peter in Acts 5:29: "We must obey God rather than men." Only two months before *Mirari vos,* Gregory XVI acknowledged in his encyclical *Cum primum* that obedience was *not* due civil authority "if by chance something is commanded which runs counter to the law of God or of the Church."[66]

The popes have usually been quick to protest and disobey civil authority if their own rights were at stake, but the implications of "we must obey God rather than men" for the laity have rarely been explored. Thomas Aquinas justified rebellion against tyranny as a last resort, but in modern times it was not until 1967 that a pope, Paul VI, acknowledged that a revolution might be justified "where there is manifest, long-standing tyranny which would do great damage to fundamental personal rights and dangerous harm to the common good of the country."[67]

At the end of *Mirari vos* Gregory concludes, "May our dear sons in Christ, the princes, support these Our desires for the welfare of Church and State with their resources and authority."[68] Of course the principal "dear son in Christ" that Gregory had in mind was King Louis Philippe, who himself had been the accomplice of those who had "by treason and sedition driven the people from confidence" in Charles X and forced that loyal Catholic "from his government."

If ever the expression "hoist by one's own petard" applied, it applied to that poor trusting band of French ultramontanes known as the Mennaisians. For fifteen years Lamennais had extolled the popes and had built up papal authority as a countervailing force to the Gallican bishops and the governments of Louis XVIII, Charles X, and Louis Philippe. And what was his reward? Total condemnation. Not one word of defense or extenuation. Granted the man's language was intemperate, but *Mirari vos,* all in all, could only strike the more impartial Europeans as an act of intellectual bankruptcy and hopeless reaction.

Lamennais had promised that he would submit to the pope's decision, and he did so. But his proud spirit and his faith were deeply wounded, particularly his faith in the Holy See. For two years the wound festered, and then Lamennais cauterized it with the publication of *Paroles d'un croyant* (Words of a Believer). The sensation it caused was far greater than that caused by the first volume of *Essai sur l'indifference.* Vidler describes it:

> People waited in queues at reading rooms and paid so much an hour to read it; a group of students in the Jardin de Luxembourg was seen listening with enthusiasm to its being read aloud. Here are some of the epigrams that were coined at the time to describe it: "A red bonnet planted on a crucifix" [the red bonnet was a symbol of revolution]; "1793 making its Easter duty"; "Robespierre in a surplice"; "a conspiracy in a steeple"; "the apocalypse of Satan."[69]

The style was apocalyptic, and the content as well. Gregory XVI was not pleased. His encyclical *Singulari nos* (June 25, 1834) may have been the only encyclical written for the sole purpose of condemning one book.

> Though small in size, it is enormous in wickedness. . . . He cloaked Catholic teaching in enticing verbal artifice, in order ultimately to oppose and overthrow it . . . depraved ravings. . . . By Our apostolic power we condemn the book; furthermore We decree that it be perpetually condemned. It arouses, fosters, and strengthens seditions, riots and rebellions in the empires. . . . It contains false, calumnious and rash propositions which lead to anarchy, and are contrary to the word of God.[70]

I read *Paroles d'un croyant* very carefully, looking for the "false, calumnious and rash propositions," and asked myself, "Is there anything here that a modern pope might be moved to condemn?" I had to answer, "Nothing at all." First, it should be noted that seven verses in chapter 33, which made veiled reference to an agreement that Gregory XVI allegedly made with Czar Nicholas I to abandon the Catholic Poles, were deleted by Lamennais and only added three years later to subsequent editions. Lamennais and *L'Avenir* had been outspoken in their support of the Polish rebellion against the Czar, as they had been of Irish Catholics against the English and Belgian Catholics against their Dutch overlords. Gregory's encyclical *Cum primum* had outraged the Mennaisians with its demands for Polish submission and its assurances to the Polish bishops, quickly revealed as worthless, that "your emperor will act kindly toward you; at no time will he deny his patronage for the good of the Catholic religion, and he will always listen patiently to your requests."[71]

Paroles d'un croyant does not yield an inch on liberty of conscience:

> What more insane than to say to men, "Believe or die". . . . Woe unto him who writes the good tidings upon a bloody leaf. . . . When, even deceiving themselves in their belief, others shall claim from you this sacred right, respect it in them, as you required the heathen to respect it in you.[72]

Paroles d'un croyant does not yield an inch on popular sovereignty, the right of rebellion against tyranny, the duty to relieve and fight for the poor:

> Young soldier, whither goest thou? . . . I go to fight for the poor, that he may not forever be robbed of his portion of the common heritage. . . . May thine arms be blessed, young soldier. . . . The law of justice teaches that all are equal before their father, who is God, and before their only master, who is Christ. . . . And then they are free, because no one rules over the others, if he have not been freely chosen by all to rule over them.[73]

In order to illustrate how orthodox Lamennais was in his views and how effective his style, I quote here chapter 9 in its entirety:

> You are in this world as strangers.
>
> Go to the north and the south, to the east and the west, and wherever you may stop you will find a man who will chase you away, saying, "This field is mine."
>
> And after traveling through every country you will return knowing that there is nowhere a poor little corner of earth where your wife in labor can give birth to her first-born, where you can rest after your labor, where, come to your last hour, your children can bury your bones, as in a place that is yours.
>
> Certainly this is a great misfortune.
>
> And yet, you ought not be too much afflicted, for it is written of him who saved the human race:
>
> "The fox has his lair, the birds of the air their nest, but the Son of Man has nowhere to lay his head."
>
> For he made himself poor in order to teach you how to endure poverty.
>
> It is not that poverty comes from God, but it is a consequence of the corruption and the wicked lusts of men, and that is why there will always be poor people.
>
> Poverty is the daughter of the sin whose germ is found in every man, and of the servitude whose germ is found in every society.
>
> There will always be poor people, because man will never destroy completely the sin in himself.

There will always be less poor, because little by little servitude will disappear from society.

If you want to work to destroy poverty, work to destroy sin, in yourselves first, then in others, and servitude in society.

It is not by taking what belongs to others that one can destroy poverty, for how, by making others poor, will we diminish the number of poor people?

Each has the right to keep what he has, without which no one could possess anything.

But each has the right to acquire by his labor what he has not, without which poverty would be eternal.

Therefore free your labor from servitude, free your arms, and poverty will exist among men only as an exception permitted by God to remind them of the weakness of their nature, and of the mutual help and love that they owe one to the other.[74]

A rather conservative statement, one might even say.

Alexander Vidler, a fair-minded Anglican who has studied the subject thoroughly, concludes that Gregory XVI was a good priest, acting in good faith out of a limited understanding of Christian tradition.[75] Henri Daniel-Rops has a similar view.[76] I cannot accept that judgment, but fairness to the reader dictates a reminder that there are more charitable opinions.

Singulari nos did succeed in driving Lamennais out of the Catholic Church. He gave up his priestly functions and in the end left firm instructions that he should be buried in an unmarked grave among paupers, without benefit of Christian service. Thousands lined the streets of Paris as his body was carried to the cemetery. His beloved brother Jean-Marie, a priest like himself, said a Mass for him in the chapel of their retreat at La Chesnaye. Then he went out on the terrace, cried aloud in anguish, "Féli, Féli, where are you?" and fell unconscious to the ground.[77]

And yet Kaufman reports on Féli's last days,

His whole mind, we are told, during his illness, was absorbed in thoughts of God. The night before his death, he had, as it were, a vision of beatitude, of which he speaks to Barbet, "These were happy moments."[78]

And Père Gratry, his friend and a friend of the poor, preaching in the Oratory of Saint-Sulpice on the Sunday after the burial, had these final words:

Must we despair of this poor soul's salvation? No. That this great example might serve as a lesson, God has allowed this ending to be stripped of hope. But this soul had helped to revive religious feeling in our country. May we not think there was a turning hidden from our eyes and that it obtained mercy?[79]

Some final thoughts from Lamennais:

What must we do? We must assure to labor that fair share of the products of labor that belongs to it; it is a question not of despoiling those who possess property already, but of creating property for those who are now deprived of all property.

Now, how do we accomplish this? By two means: the abolition of the laws of privilege and monopoly; the diffusion of capital by making credit easily available, or making the means of production [*instruments de travail*] available to all.

The effect of these two measures, combined with the immeasurable power of *association,* would be to re-establish little by little the natural development of wealth, now artifically concentrated in a few hands, to provide for its distribution in a more equal and fairer way, and to increase it indefinitely.[80]

In 1840 Lamennais had been imprisoned after he supported a strike of Parisian workers by writing a pamphlet entitled *The Country and the Government.* It included this great protest of the law forbidding labor the right to organize:

For finally, people, you must know: the workers do not have the right to act in concert even to improve their lot. One can, in the infamous gambling den of the Stock Exchange, act in concert to despoil the ignorant stockholders. . . . That is highly legal. . . . But that workers act in concert, not to steal, not to despoil, but to concern themselves with their most pressing interests, to discuss them with those who have related interests, what an abominable crime! Nothing but prison could expiate such a thing.[81]

Lamennais's interests were not primarily economic, but his passionate and highly Christian defense of democracy and *association* both in political and economic life mark him as one of the first and most persuasive apostles of Christian socialism in the modern era.

PIERRE LEROUX

Pierre Leroux (1797–1871) claimed to have used the word "socialism" for the first time in France, in an article in the Saint-Simonian journal *Le Globe* on February 13, 1832. It now appears that Vinet and *Le Semeur* were ahead of him by three months.

Leroux was one of the few French socialists who could accurately claim to be, or at least to have been, a manual worker, first a mason and then a typesetter. He was, with Buchez, one of the organizers, around 1820, of the French branch of the Italian revolutionary organization known as the Carbonari, in France *la Charbonnerie,* whose purpose was to overthrow the Bourbons. Though he joined the Saint-Simonians and became an editor of *Le Globe,* the vagaries of Enfantin drove him away. He was more attached to true Christianity than New Christianity. He was elected a member of the Constituent Assembly in 1848, but the dictatorship of Napoleon III forced him into exile in 1851. He returned nine years later and lived a peaceful existence until his death in 1871.

Leroux was an all-purpose writer, turning out plays like *Job,* semimetaphysical works like *De l'humanité,* economic studies like *Malthus et les économistes,* religious-political books like *Du christianisme et de ses origines democratiques,* and newspaper articles without number.

"The greatest economist" was the title he gave Jesus in 1848 and added, "The reign of Christ has been promised here on earth. That is what the Gospel announces in the most positive fashion."[82]

This faith in the coming of the kingdom on earth as it is in heaven was at the base of Leroux's faith-in-progress. He also detected progress in pre-Christian eras: "from Epicureanism to Stoicism to Platonism to Christianity we have distanced ourselves profoundly from the condition of animals."[83]

The goal of all politics, he maintained,

is to make it possible for all members of society to enjoy the results of common labor, each according to their needs, their capacity and their works, whether that labor be an idea, a work of art or a material product.[84]

Note Leroux's resolution of the argument about needs versus capacity versus works. He includes all three—not a bad solution.

A Leroux insight: "We are between two worlds: an inegalitarian world that is finishing and an egalitarian world that is beginning."[85]

And three quotes:

The modern era adores industry. It seems that the Bastille was taken so that a great number of men might buy and sell textiles. Before that supreme illumination that inspired his "new Christianity" Saint-Simon was wrong to immortalize industry, to make it the object of a cult. This reformer did not understand, when he attacked the feudal spirit, the spirit of conquest, that the industrial spirit was also a spirit of conquest, that under the Empire of Money we remained under the Empire of Force. Industry, the capitalist regime, economic competition—it is still war. Who says competitor, says conqueror [*Malthus and the Economists,* 1848].

France is in reality a house of commerce directed by 196,000 employers, employing 30,000,000 workers, a house of commerce returning to the employers, all expenses paid, a profit of four or five billion. That is to say that our society has for its god Pluto and not the proletarian Jesus [*Of Plutocracy and the Government of the Rich,* 1848].

Consult statistics. They will tell you what classes pay tribute to the prisons, to penal servitude, to the scaffolds. There is a society where it is impossible to be criminal without falling under the sway of the penal code and the grip of the police. These are the poor classes. There is another where you can commit almost any crime without being subject to the penal code, or at least without having to fear it. These are the rich classes. . . .

A rich thief, a thief of the upper classes . . . exercises his craft quite at his ease. He steals 100,000 francs more easily than the other a loaf of bread. . . . In our day they have invented the epithet "profiteer" for certain capitalists; but from the small to the great, in that dark forest where men today struggle one against the other to snatch riches, every capitalist is a profiteer [*Of Equality,* 1848].[86]

THE SCHOOL OF PHILIPPE BUCHEZ

Victor Considérant, about whom more later, has left us a revealing profile of Philippe Buchez (1796–1865) in his book *Le Socialisme devant le vieux monde* (Socialism Confronts the Old World). Considérant wrote the book toward the end of 1848, after Buchez had completed his brief term as first president of the National Assembly. Considérant was himself a member of the Assembly and the head of a rival school of socialism.

He refers first to "a socialist with a face as rosy, a colleague as stout and honest as the first president of the National Assembly," and continues:

Buchez is a man of sincere devotion. His life, like that of most of the socialists, has been entirely sacrificed to his ideas, to his faith and to humanity. He has the air today of capitulating a little. He may, in the corridors of the Assembly or between two chops while lunching with So-and-So, exchange some bits of gossip about his socialist brethren, even about those who are far from ever having been as revolutionary as he or, like him, anti-property. To make you forget that he is a socialist, he gives the impression that he has forgotten it himself. I am however sure that, at heart, he retains all his original ideas, although he can without serious inconvenience exchange some of them and take them back again. He is, besides, a little grouchy, but kind.

A former atheist and *carbonaro,* Saint-Simonian socialism led him back to God, to whom he had never, although a materialist, ceased to render the worship that God prefers in doing good without relaxation to his fellows. He was of the first batch of Saint-Simonians. When he saw Saint-Simonism inclining toward the establishment of a new religion and M. Enfantin preparing himself for the rank of Living Law in order to pass himself off as God, he left the new church, thinking rightly that Christianity, whose original sources he had begun to study, was not as done for as we all thought, we other socialists of Saint-Simon and the *Phalanstère* [Fourierists], at that period of the first flowering of our ideas.

Buchez was right, I repeat, and he was right on this point before most of us. When a religion has been formulated on this fundamental dogma, "Love each other, and love God above all things," one can be sure that the definitive religious formula of humanity has been revealed, and that with all the intelligence and the best will in the world you will not find anything that is more human and divine at the same time.[87]

Buchez was born in what is now Belgium. His father was a great admirer of Rousseau and of the French Revolution, and this admiration he bequeathed to his son. The first words of Buchez's 40-volume history of the Revolution are: "The French Revolution is the last and most advanced consequence of modern civilization, and modern civilization has come entirely out of the Gospel."[88]

His mother raised him as a Catholic, but as he grew older and studied to be a doctor, his faith faded into atheism. He was a leader of the French Carbonari and narrowly escaped imprisonment when its leaders were tried for treason. With Enfantin, Saint-Armand Bazard, and Olinde Rodriguez, he promoted the Saint-Simonian movement, but left it in 1829, when Enfantin and Bazard proclaimed themselves "Supreme Fathers."

In the July Revolution of 1830 Buchez gave medical assistance to the wounded among the rebels, but a letter that he and friends wrote asking for a meeting with General Lafayette, a leader of the Revolution, indicates that he also took a more active role. The letter notes that "having done their duty as soldiers [in the Revolution, they had] acquired some influence over the workers."[89]

In 1830 Buchez and the incendiary Blanqui were on the same side. An amusing footnote to that revolution: At the height of the street fighting, Blanqui, covered with blood, burst into Mademoiselle de Montgolfier's salon, banged his rifle on the floor and shouted, "The Romantics are finished!"[90] It is certain that among Romantics, Blanqui included those who had been responsible for a revival of religious faith such as Chateaubriand, Lamartine, and Lamennais. But these Romantics, some of whom were equally opposed to Charles X, were not so easily finished.

Buchez was one of them. He remained "on the threshold of the Catholic Church" until a few hours before his death when he "accepted very gladly the consolations of religion" from the Abbé Gaillouste.[91] In one of his books he protests that "if anything in this work were to constitute the least opposition to the truths sanctioned by the Church, we would renounce it as soon as we were warned."[92] This is a bit hard to understand since he had lashed out at Gregory XVI on the publication of *Mirari vos* only a few years before, calling him "a perjured pope" who has "attached himself to the wagon of civilization in order to retard its progress." This is his comment on Gregory's condemnation of the "three pilgrims of God and liberty":

> It is in vain that one looks for a Christian thought in the midst of this boastful and insipid Italian prattle, which knows only how to repeat the eternal declamations of reactionaries on liberty, the press and revolutions. . . . Not one word of good will, not a word of pity for those who suffer; all the solicitude for princes and the powerful, as if Jesus Christ had been executed in order to confirm in the right of force the Patricians who condemned Him.[93]

Buchez distinguished between Christianity, which he identified with Catholicism, and the human institution of the Catholic Church. (Protestantism he rejected as "the sovereignty of the ego.") For example:

> In praising Christianity we do not mean to praise the institution by which they have thought to replace it: police on a large scale at the service of egoism and of the aristocracy which, occupied only with sordid interests, lets the privileged enjoy superfluities while it preaches the hardships of penance to the unfortunate who are in need of bread.[94]

Buchez's position, rejecting Protestantism and the Catholic Church, but loving Christianity and Catholicism, was understandably a lonely and difficult one. Strangely enough, his influence on the faith of his contemporaries was considerable. A number of his disciples became Dominican priests. Charles Chevé, a veteran of the 1830 Revolution and one of the more talented students of the Buchez school, testified that "Buchez was for a very great number of young people imbued with democratic ideas the providential instrument and medium of their conversion to Catholicism."[95]

Like Lamennais, Buchez took advantage of the 1830 Revolution to promote his ideas. He organized public lectures and conferences, started a weekly newspaper, *L'Européen,* and founded the Association for the Instruction of the People to spread the gospel of *Association* among the workers. "We have talked with these men" he wrote,

> in their ragged jackets and iron-shod shoes, with their rough language and simple vocabulary, of things that would be unintelligible to many of the salon folks. Better than that, we have received from several of them memoranda written in bad French no doubt, but full of ideas that would make the fortune of an economist.[96]

As a result of these conversations and of his own reflection on the ideas of Saint-Simon and the Saint-Simonians, Buchez launched a new school of socialism, reacting against the statist, top-down theories of his former friends and emphasizing a voluntary approach of worker-owned-and-operated producer cooperatives, which he called *associations*. He drew up a charter for a carpenters' association in 1831, but it never functioned. In 1834, however, he wrote out an association prospectus and at night slid copies of it under the doors of a number of Paris workshops. A jeweler named J.-M. Leroy read it and that reading led to the formation of a Gilt Jewelers Association that lasted until 1873 and that at one time included eight successful shops in Paris. Other associations followed, but most of them failed after a few years. The team of editors and typographers that published *L'Atelier* formed another successful association, but it closed after ten years.

L'Européen lasted about a year, closed for lack of funds, was revived in 1835, appeared irregularly until 1838, closed again and reappeared in 1847 with a new title, *Revue nationale*. It closed for good in the wake of the reaction that followed the Revolution of 1848.

Buchez also inspired the publication of a more lasting weekly newspaper, *L'Atelier* (The Workshop), the first newspaper of any consequence in Europe that was edited by and for workers. It began publication in 1840 and appeared more or less regularly until closed by the government in 1850.

Meanwhile Buchez, with Roux-Lavergne, wrote a 40-volume history of the French Revolution. Buchez also produced books on history, philosophy, political economy, and religion. In 1846, Pius IX began his reign with reforms liberal enough to earn him the title in conservative Paris salons of "Robespierre in a mitre." Buchez hailed the new pope as "the regenerator of Italy." He also met with Archbishop Affre, who praised his work. Some reconciliation with the church seemed imminent.

When the Revolution came in February 1848, Buchez, a captain in the National Guard, led a detachment of his troops in the rebellion. They were the first to penetrate the inner court of the Tuileries, the royal palace, as Louis Philippe fled by way of another exit.

For his services Buchez was appointed one of the two deputy mayors of Paris. In the chaos that followed the revolution, Buchez was a dynamo in a tower of strength, working fourteen hours a day to restore order, to organize workshops to put the unemployed to work, to reorganize the national guard, to raise money—and all for no remuneration but his meals.

Meanwhile, Blanqui and friends were busy organizing a second revolution to take over City Hall for the far left. Through his contacts among the workers Buchez got wind of the plot and on April 17 stopped it by massing government supporters in all the approaches to City Hall. A few days later, in the first election in France by universal manhood suffrage, Buchez was elected deputy to the National Assembly. On May 4, recognizing him as a man of sense and moderation, strategically positioned between the rebellious workers, the "demo-socialists," and the religious elements, the Assembly chose him as its first president and the de facto head of the government. It also named a Buchezian, Anthime Corbon, an editor of *L'Atelier,* as vice-president.

In his inaugural address Buchez said,

Never in any assembly has there been a greater authority than in this. . . . You represent all of France. But we who have been elected by all, we are pledged to concern ourselves with all, and particularly with that class, that poor unfortunate part of the population with which no one has ever before been concerned.[97]

But Blanqui and friends were not through. On May 15, having spread the word that Buchez had sold out, that he was "a tool of Austria and the Jesuits," they incited a mob to invade and take over the Assembly. Buchez got wind of the plan and gave orders to General Courtais of the National Guard and Caussidière, prefect of the Paris police, to mass their forces around the Assembly. Because of either treachery, cowardice, incompetence, or all three, these gentlemen ignored the orders and left the way clear for the mob to invade the Assembly. To avoid bloodshed Buchez delayed until troops could arrive and oust the mob, but his behavior was seen by some (notably de Tocqueville) as weak and vacillating and his authority was damaged. For this reason and for reasons of health he declined re-election as president on June 4. The Assembly, a majority of whose members were conservative Catholics from the provinces, had been badly shaken by the invasion of May 15 and alienated from any concern for "the poorest and most numerous class." They voted to close the national workshops, the poor responded with the riots of June 23, and General Cavaignac responded with the bloody suppression of those riots over the next few days, as detailed at the beginning of this chapter.

On June 13 Buchez had stood alone in the Assembly to oppose the seating of Louis Napoleon (Napoleon III), who was already being hailed by the conservatives as a champion of law and order against the unruly mob. For this reason he was not re-elected a deputy, and so, when Louis Napoleon seized power on December 2, 1951, destroyed the Second Republic and re-established the Empire, Buchez was arrested and only escaped worse trouble through the intervention of a friendly marshall.

Most of the associations he had helped start were crushed, and Buchez retired to a quiet life of study and writing until his death in 1865.

THE IDEAS OF BUCHEZ

One of the first acts of the provisional government after the Revolution of 1848 was to set up what was called the Luxembourg Commission (because it met in the Luxembourg Palace). Its purpose was to inquire into the causes of labor unrest and to propose reforms. Louis Blanc (1811–1882), a socialist whose ideas on workers' associations bore some resemblance to Buchez's, was the head of the commission. It had no money and no power, but for a few months it was the center for a lively discussion of socialism, communism, and other varieties of social reform. These debates were echoed in the Assembly, which rapidly deteriorated to a state of panic over what they thought, or imagined, the various reformers were proposing. The ones who inspired the most panic were probably Blanqui (see above), Cabet (see below)—to whose utopian ideas the name of "communism" became affixed—and Pierre Joseph Proudhon (1809–1865), who had scared the bourgeoisie and the peasants half to death with his answer to the question "What is property?" (the title of a book he wrote in 1840). The answer was, "Property is theft." Proudhon added qualifiers, such as property is theft unless properly used, but nobody remembered the qualifiers.

The intellectual quality of these debates is admirably described by Considérant in a passage that reminds one of the atmosphere during the Joseph McCarthy era in American history:

> However invincible may be these words, "Communism! It is Communism! It is Communistic! That leads straight to Communism!" (our great orators have had the wit already to find these four variations on that all-conquering argument), however convincing, however irresistible may be these words in a speech, that kind of logic has gone decidedly stale, and the masters of the art have nearly abandoned it for the hobgoblin of Proudhon. Proudhon is the great sea serpent, the dragon, the pterodactyl, the beast of Gévaudan, the Ouivre! The simple apparition of his name is all-sufficient, answers all, defeats all. All you have to do is to pronounce from the rostrum, at the right moment, these two syllables—*Prou-dhon*—and you have secured the same effect as the head of Medusa: the entire audience is struck dumb. It is magical. And often the speaker finds himself in the same condition as the audience.[98]

Proudhon, Blanc, and Considérant were all better writers than Buchez and their works better remembered. One critic described Buchez's style, unfairly, as "that strange language of which one cannot say if it makes stickier the mouth that wants to express it, or the thought that it wants to express."[99] It *was* on the heavy side.

Buchez's written thought was clear enough, however, to give no excuse to Considérant when he, ironically, called Buchez's proposals "communism."[100] He also, as quoted above, called Buchez "anti-property." On this subject Buchez's thought was stickier.

He distinguished between the right of property, which was the fruit of labor, and the power of possession, which frequently characterizes those who have contributed no labor to what they possess.

> One cannot say that one possesses [land] by the same title and by virtue of the same principle as the thing that is the work of our hands and our intelligence. One occupies it only. . . . Land is therefore a common domain that can belong, in principle, only to the community itself, to society.[101]

Buchez quoted a Thomistic principle he found in a speech of Mirabeau, one of the first and more moderate leaders of the French Revolution: "Law alone establishes property because it is only the public will that can authorize the renunciation by all and bestow a title, a guarantee for the enjoyment of one alone."[102]

For these reasons Buchez opposed not the right of leaving property to children, as had the Saint-Simonians, but the custom of leaving it to collateral relatives when no children existed.

> The right of property cannot be transmitted by inheritance, for it is not the inheritor who has created what he inherits. . . . These are only possessions. . . . When one permits the power of possession to go beyond certain limits, it inevitably . . . violates the right of property. For example, under the form of leasing or hiring, it can force the worker to give to the possessor a usurious part of his product . . . more than half . . . two-thirds, and even three-quarters, and under the form of inheritance [it] immobilizes him in misery.[103]

Obviously, this line went over better with the wage workers in Paris than with the peasants in the provinces, who simply identified property with possession. In modern America, on the other hand, less than 5 percent of the population live on farms and the overwhelming majority work for wages. Here Buchez's emphasis should be more popular. It certainly dovetailed with his theory of *association*. Fifteen years before the *Communist Manifesto* Buchez emphasized the reality of class conflict:

> Today European society is, with regard to material interests, split into two classes which must be examined separately. This division is striking in all the countries under the rule of charters; it will become so in the rest of Europe when this rule extends itself; it will become so in America when its deserts are peopled. Of these two classes, one is in possession of all the instruments of labor: land, factories, houses, capital. The other has nothing. It works for the former.[104]

The heads of industry are "intermediaries between the happy idlers and the poor who work."[105] Buchez proposed

> an industrial organization . . . in which the greatest rewards would go to those who do the most productive work. . . . We see the land covered with agricultural and manufacturing communities where all the members would be associated and cooperating in a common effort and using for this end the capital of the community.[106]

It was probably this kind of language that moved Considérant to call Buchez "communist," but Buchez's associations were entirely voluntary. Buchez was leery of Blanc's national associations, or workshops, although Blanc had borrowed the idea of the association from Buchez. He thought Blanc's proposals were too statist, though Blanc insisted that the state should merely initiate the workshops, appoint managers for the first year and then give them over to democratic control by the workers.

Like Blanc and Proudhon and most of the French socialists Buchez emphasized the need for easy credit provided by the state, or, as Buchez proposed, by a bank independent of the state except for "a council of auditors."

An unpublished manuscript of 1830 reveals Buchez's reasoning together with a hint of Marx's theory of surplus value:

> The lack of capital puts the workers at the mercy of the entrepreneurs, and the latter profit from the worker's labor beyond the cost of their employment. [The goal of the workers' association is that] of acquiring an amount of common capital that will permit them, and all the workers who will follow them in the association, to undertake directly the enterprise.[107]

Like all sound cooperatives, Buchez's associations did not permit members to withdraw the common capital:

> This inalienable capital [deducted from the profits] will belong to the entire association. . . . Neither those who resign nor the heirs of those who die will have any right to it.[108]

Buchez said, "The association must be founded on the spirit of dedication and sacrifice."[109] If anything, there was too much emphasis on sacrifice and not enough on self-interest, which is a perfectly legitimate motive for worker cooperation. Another problem was the law against worker organizations which could, when authorities were unfavorable, be applied to the associations as well as to employee unions. This law, of course, had to be repealed.

Though he had reservations, Buchez supported Blanc's proposals for national workshops, and the National Assembly actually appropriated money to finance them. Some of the money went to productive enterprises, such as making army uniforms, but the manager was basically hostile to the idea of workers' associations. Most of the money was spent on public works and even make-work projects, with wages as low as one franc per day. General dissatisfaction with the whole program encouraged the public impression that workers' associations were impractical. In any case, little could be accomplished in the four months before the Assembly killed the workshop project.

Buchez has been called "the father of the French cooperative movement," but it is important to remember that his cooperation was not consumer cooperation (in which he had little interest) but producer cooperation. He was thus in the mainstream of early socialism, before the Marxists shifted the emphasis to state ownership and control. It is fair to say that Buchez was, with Owen, one of the first to define the breadth and depth of that mainstream, and to swim in it as well. He was not content merely to preach socialism; he practiced it. He went out and helped workers to organize their own cooperatives. He gave his talents and risked life and health to overcome tyranny and establish a democratic form of government.

What kind of Christian was Buchez, really? Barbara Petri has doubts about the orthodoxy of his Christianity:

> To approach Christianity primarily from the viewpoint of its social and political utility, as does Buchez, is to depart from strict orthodoxy, since religious dogma is the keynote of the entire religion.[110]

Yes and no. In fact, it may be that Petri shares a bit of the same misunderstanding of Christianity that characterized the nineteenth century and too much of the twentieth. In any case, forty-seven pages before this sentence she quotes a passages from Buchez's preface to the thirty-third volume of his history of the French Revolution that should have convinced her that Buchez regarded religious dogma as all-important:

> Had Robespierre and his friends been Christians instead of being simple Deists, or rather neo-Arians, considering Jesus Christ as a philosopher who had only given good example and good counsel; if they had believed that *the Gospel was the absolute code of moral obligations,* they would never have been embarrassed in distinguishing vice from virtue, in recognizing and pointing it out to others; they would not have been obliged to resort to lying in order to strike out at those whose conduct wounded their sympathies and their honest habits. . . .
>
> But Robespierre believed in the *Social Contract* of Rousseau, and above all in the Convention; that was his Gospel; and according to us, his conduct, his failure, his frightful reputation, are the greatest proof that honest habits, a devoted and energetic will, are powerless and incapable of good when they are not directed by *an absolutely obligatory moral belief, before which all calculations are reduced to silence, and only the practice of truth is accepted* [emphasis added].[111]

And where did Buchez place the foundation for that "absolutely obligatory" quality of the gospel? Armand Cuvillier, one of the most knowledgeable historians of the Buchez school, supplies a key quote. Contrasting Buchez's faith with the utilitarian Christianity of Saint-Simon and Cabet, Cuvillier quotes Buchez: "All must be positive; now this positive quality one finds nowhere else but in revelation."[112]

Buchez certainly emphasized the social and political *implications* of Christ's teaching. We need look no further than Matthew 25 to find the basis for that emphasis in the most authentic religious dogma.

THE OTHER BUCHEZIANS

Saint-Simon, Lamennais, Leroux, Cabet, Considérant—all were Christian socialists of a sort. But Buchez surpassed them all in fidelity to each of the words of that phrase. One of the proofs of his preeminence is the large number of French—some more radical, some more conservative—whom he influenced to the point that they wrote books, edited newspapers, and devoted large parts of their lives to the propagation of his ideas, or their particular refinement of his ideas. Among them, with representative quotes, are the following.

Frédéric Arnaud de L'Ariège was the last Christian socialist to sit in the National Assembly during the Second Republic. Alone among Catholic deputies, in a famous speech on September 13, 1848, he spoke in favor of an unsuccessful resolution to make "the right to work" a fundamental obligation of the state. More attached than others to the doctrine of original sin, he believed that both the intervention of the state and the institution of private property were necessary to curb the human tendency toward evil.

He argued, like Lamennais, for separation of church and state. "Modern history," he wrote in his book *La Révolution et l'Église,*

> offers to us many sad examples of what becomes even of Christian peoples when alliances of religion and politics deliver them to the double influence of fanatical princes and priests transformed into Inquisitors.[113]

Auguste Boulland, friend and fellow doctor, left the Saint-Simonians together with Buchez in 1829 when that group began getting delusions of religious grandeur. He wrote a half dozen books, of which the most significant is probably *Doctrine politique du christianisme*. This quotation from that work illustrates the Buchezian conviction that the French Revolution, despite its excesses, was the product of political virtues that had their roots in Christianity:

> It is time to recognize that the French Revolution has, in our time, provided the foundation for Christian politics. . . . The great men of the Revolution denied their origins in Catholic dogma only out of hatred for those clergy who allied themselves with the enemies of the people's liberation. . . . Fifteen centuries of Catholic sacraments had so deeply incarnated in the French people the moral law of Christianity that they rose up as one to proclaim their political faith, and have gone forth to spread that faith over all the nations of Europe and the Orient.[114]

Repeatedly Boulland strikes out at the idle rich and the atheistic bourgeoisie:

> It is the *people* who remain honest and patient, who alone retain devotion to Christianity . . . who endure without complaint the pain of labor, and

all the sorrows that are born of poverty and want, in order not to disturb the idle pleasures of the aristocracy of wealth, of birth and of all those exploiting classes that steal from them even a fair wage and kill them when they cry for bread.[115]

Charles-François Chevé, one of Buchez's more articulate converts to Catholicism, played an active role in the Revolution of 1830, was an editor of *L'Atelier,* contributor to numerous intellectual and socialist journals, and author of five books, including *Catholicism and Democracy, or the Reign of Christ.* He was especially hard on those members of the clergy who thought that personal charity would cure the evils of social injustice: Charity, Chevé insists, "cannot close the wound. It humiliates those who receive it and degrades those who become accustomed to receiving it." And again:

It is not with alms that they put an end to the slavery of the ancient world. It was not with alms that they put an end to the serfdom of the Middle Ages. Nor is it now with alms that we will free the workers from industrial serfdom. And that is why we detest that organized charity whose purpose, well-known and almost admitted, is to make the workers endure their inferior condition for as long as possible.[116]

Chevé laments the fact that those who should be friends and allies, the church and the poor, the church and the revolutionaries, have become enemies:

They have ignored each other, they have cursed each other, they have slaughtered each other. The people have cursed the Church in the name of democracy, and it is the Church who, in her councils, was the first Christian democracy. They have cursed her in the name of the poor, and it was she who made of poverty a religion and the community of goods a law for her elect. [On the other hand, the clergy] rejected liberty in the name of a religion that said, "Wherever is the spirit of the Lord, there also is liberty." They have commanded blind obedience to the will of earthly masters in the name of a Gospel in which it is written, "You have only one master who is God, and you are all brothers." They have fought those who wanted to make labor the only source of property, and the greatest of their apostles said, "He who will not work, neither let him eat."[117]

Anthime Corbon rose from the ranks of the workers, became an editor of *L'Atelier,* was elected member and then vice-president of the National Assembly after the Revolution of 1848, was elected a permanent Senator under the Third Republic, wrote several books and in 1877 an open letter to Felix Dupanloup, bishop of Orleans and a fellow senator, challenging him to explain why the workers were leaving the church. By that time Boulland's claim was no longer true; the workers *were* leaving. "When I say," Corbon wrote the bishop, "that you have abandoned us, I mean that for centuries you have abandoned our temporal cause, your influence being used even to prevent rather than to support our social liberation."[118]

Corbon drew a powerful lesson in Christian democracy for the French from the facade of the Cathedral of Notre Dame, where the great bas-relief depicts the Last Judgment, the elect on the right and the damned on the left:

> To what class belong the elect? No distinctions mark them: they are the common people.
> To what class belong the damned? Certain signs identify them: they are all—all!—the powerful of the earth. There is a pope, there is a king, a bishop, an abbot, an abbess; that is to say, all those who . . . have exercised power and abused it.[119]

Henri Feugueray was a journalist and writer, a member of the National Assembly in 1848, a contributor to the Mennaisian paper *L'Ère Nouvelle,* and author of five books, including essays on the political theory of Thomas Aquinas and on workers' associations. In the preface to this essay he noted,

> Long before the February Revolution [1848] I cooperated in the organization of several associations [and] participated in drawing up the constitution of the oldest of those that exist today. Those are the titles of my socialism.[120]

Feugueray distinguished Buchezian socialism from other brands, pointing out that they were not socialists

> in the fashion of M. Cabet, nor of M. Louis Blanc, nor of M. Considérant: we do not want to suppress property, which is an essential condition of human liberty [Cabet]; we do not want to monopolise all industry in the hands of government [Blanc]; we do not complicate the idea of association with the phantasies of Fourierism [Considérant].[121]

Like Lamennais, Chevé and other Buchezians, Feugueray emphasized what might be called demand-side economics. When money, which is demand, is concentrated in the hands of the rich, production tends toward luxury goods rather than necessities. "Suppose," he wrote,

> that the revenues of the national labor were more equitably distributed, demand would be immediately corrected. We would have fewer jewels, diamonds, costly laces, and more sturdy cloth, more shoes, more linens; fewer fine carriages and more public coaches; fewer luxury editions and more books.

And he might have added, "Fewer paupers and more jobs."[122]

Désiré Laverdant, a convert to Christian socialism from the school of

Fourier, wrote a book called *Socialisme catholique: la Déroute des Césars* (Catholic Socialism: The Overthrow of the Caesars) in 1851. Like Feugueray he was concerned to distinguish Buchez-style socialism from that of other schools. In this he revealed a gift that stands out, even in the internecine cockpit of socialist polemic:

> First we must put an end to a bad joke, much too prolonged, which consists of incarnating Socialism in Louis Blanc and especially in Proudhon, who has become, in the temple of our confusions, the high priest, the one and only God.
>
> Louis Blanc, indifferent in matters of religion, has done nothing but repeat eloquently the words "organization of labor" [the title of Blanc's most famous book] and "association" without understanding the complex terms of the problem.
>
> Proudhon, repeating harshly the message of Positivism against Theology, Proudhon, this last and tumultuous echo of philosophic negation, has known only how to defend, in his stormy voice, the rights of individual liberty, summarizing his frenzied cult of individualism in the shocking paradox of *an-archy*.
>
> Now socialism is no better represented by these two men than Catholicism would be by Manes and Arius. These are men of lively mind, but concerned to agitate, not to resolve, to shake up, not to build. I do not stop to discuss the calumnious criticism that pretends to make the socialist schools responsible for the terrorist ideas held by a few bitter or corrupt individuals. It is as if we were to judge Catholicism by the acts of Torquemada and Ravaillac, or by the spirit of *Tartuffe*.[123]

Laverdant was good at the negative critique, but he could also draw a more positive, and authentically Christian, picture. He insisted that the hope of a socialism that is properly understood is "the idea of a Kingdom of God on earth." "Socialists in general," he wrote, "flatter themselves that they have found this hope outside the Church and venture to take up weapons of war against the Catholics." But this vision, he maintained,

> of an earthly Kingdom where justice reigns, where humanity will prepare itself, in dignity and peace, for that more perfect glory and those more innocent joys of the Kingdom of Heaven, this is an idea that is essentially Judeo-Christian and Catholic.[124]

Auguste Ott, good friend and literary executor of Buchez, member of the National Assembly, published a dozen books on such varied subjects as the philosophies of Hegel and Kant, workers' associations, history, politics, and economics. He was concerned to relate socialism not only to Christian tradition but to the ideas of the Enlightenment in response to the Industrial Revolution.

If the word *socialism* is very recent . . . the idea that this word represents has been present in the tendencies of French society since the end of the last century. It is today the idea of all people of good will who believe that the iniquities of the present economic condition must come to an end. It is the great problem of the liberation of the workers. It is the search for laws that will make *real* justice and charity in the economic order. In this sense the School of which this paper is the organ [*Revue nationale*] has always been socialist.[125]

In the *Revue* Ott made some important distinctions between property as "instruments of labor" ("means of production" in Marxist terminology) and "products of labor" (consumer goods). "Instruments of labor" should be entrusted to producers united in associations.

The instruments of labor would not be the property of the State; they should always be private property, except that most of this property would be in the hands of Associations of workers.[126]

He had no objections to property as products of labor (consumer goods), belonging to individuals. This notion of private property, means of production, that is also socialized or cooperative property, was common to the early history of socialism but has only recently begun to be recognized again as an authentically socialist idea. So strong has been the Marxist influence (and in Great Britain, the influence of the Fabian Society) in the direction of defining socialism in terms of nationalized, or state-owned and operated, means of production.

The statement by Ott, trusted friend and collaborator of Buchez, proves again how wrong Considérant was to identify the School of Buchez as being against private property.

VICTOR CONSIDÉRANT

As a young man Victor Considérant (1808–1893) became a disciple of Charles Fourier (1772–1837), the most eccentric of all French socialists, perhaps of all socialists. Alexander Gray, an antisocialist historian of socialism, after describing Fourier's peculiar notions of God and religion, sums them up: "His is a heaven securely based on copulation and cookery."[127] The rationale in Fourier's words: "As soon as we wish to repress a single passion we are engaged in an act of insurrection against God. By that very act we accuse Him of stupidity in having created it."[128]

But Gray does grant some "positive facets" to Fourier: his critique of the waste and inefficiency of "unrestrained individualism"; the boost he gave the cooperative movement; his ideas for eliminating class conflict; the notion of "garden cities"; and his emphasis on making work attractive. The American social theorist Albert Brisbane (1809–1890) took him seriously. By 1850 more than forty "phalanxes" (Fourier's name for his communes) were founded in

America, of which the most famous was Brook Farm, for a few years the preoccupation of such literary lights as Emerson and Hawthorne.

When Fourier died in 1837, Considérant became the leader of his movement and winnowed out some of its more absurd characteristics. He edited *La Phalange* (1836–1843) and a daily newspaper, *La Démocratie Pacifique* (1843–1850). Elected a deputy of the National Assembly in 1848, he joined Proudhon and Ledru-Rollin in organizing a Democratic and Socialist coalition which, contrary to Considérant's pacifist tendencies, called for insurrection in 1849. For this and other "indiscreet acts," he was forced into exile, went to Texas, founded a phalanx that failed, became a U. S. citizen, returned to Paris in 1869, and died there in 1893.

Perhaps those "indiscreet acts" are responsible for the fact that Biéler does not include Considérant on his roster of Christian socialists. But for eloquence, humor, and passionate expression of Christian principles, Considérant is hard to beat. Lichtheim quotes a passage that is as relevant today as it was then:

> Make revolutions, pass decrees, promulgate constitutions, proclaim any number or kinds of republics, nominate whomever you wish for president or consul: you have done nothing for the real freedom of the masses so long as society has not guaranteed to every man, woman and child a minimum necessary for existence.[129]

Considérant made one of the most powerful pleas of any of his contemporaries for the right to work, "that first social right of humanity, the one that safeguards and carries with it all others." He added:

> Those individuals and classes who own nothing, have no capital, no instruments of labor . . . are necessarily—whatever the political system they live under—reduced to a state of dependence and helotry, sometimes called slavery, sometimes serfdom, at other times the proletariat.[130]

The Fourier-Considérant solution, the phalanx, was a strange mixture of private property and communal production and consumption. It promised dividends to those who would purchase stock, favored unequal rewards according to work and ability, and garnished all with guarantees of joy beyond compare.

On the subject of property, Considérant's insight has eluded too many socialists of every school: "The principle of Property is too human and of too general an interest and is today, in practice, too extensive to be thrown aside."[131]

He added to this, however, a warning to property-holders that has been ignored by too many of them, of every school:

> There is only one way of saving [property] from a great war of ideas first, and of deeds afterwards, and that is learning how to make a great many people property-holders, and quickly.[132]

The first paragraph of Considérant's fascinating book *Le Socialisme devant le vieux monde* strikes the same note that Buchez struck in the first paragraph of his history of the French Revolution, but with greater power and a less flattering view of contemporary life.

> Modern society is in a definite state of decomposition. The old world, the world of slavery, of feudalism, of the proletariat, the pagan world, attacked at its base 1800 years ago by the great explosion of the doctrine of Liberty, Equality and Fraternity that Christ brought to earth, the world of misery, of struggle, of exploitation of man by man, has been shaken to its very foundations: it is cracking in every part of its worm-eaten timbers.[133]

The "old world" was not as close to collapse as he thought. The passage reflects Considérant's capacity for exaggeration and optimistic prediction. The following passage is also typical of this tendency in Considérant and of his eloquent appeals to the figure and authority of Jesus Christ:

> Representatives of Caesar, scribes, pharisees, priests and princes of priests, men of the past under all robes and all habits, and you atheists and sceptics, and you worshipers of false gods, you must play your part. The glorious Christ has risen and you cannot kill him again! You cannot kill him again because he is spirit. This Christ is an idea; and this idea has taken possession of the conscience of the peoples, and it grows in proportion to your efforts to smother it. . . . This idea is the invincible demand for a society that is just, free and happy, a society that is human and Christian, made in the opposite image from that selfish, barbarous and pagan society that you want to preserve and which you will not preserve. This idea, which like the armed man of scripture has captured souls and taken possession of this century, is socialism.[134]

Considérant's socialism was not doctrinaire. It was "not a determined doctrine," but

> an aspiration toward a social order that will resolve these two problems: (1) the transformation of the wage relationship, the last form of dependence, [into] the final emancipation of industrial workers; (2) the establishment of a society of concord, peace, free and attractive labor.[135]

Considérant pleaded with his fellow socialists to unite on the basis of

> agreement on what is common, distinction in what is different, full liberty but propriety and fraternity in discussion . . . each maintaining what he believes true and rejecting what he believes false . . . in an

intelligent exchange, as brothers who wish to enlighten humanity and each other, not as savages, furious, jealous, domineering, foolish.[136]

Anyone who has read the history of socialism can appreciate the relevance of that plea.

And yet Considérant was not above criticizing his fellow socialists:

The mistake of Louis Blanc: he frightened society by giving the impression he wanted to impose on it his egalitarian socialism by authority and by surprise.[137]

The power of Proudhon, and it is great, is entirely in his negations . . . he is negation incarnate.[138]

Considérant could label Buchez with "communism" and charge him with being "anti-property," but he usually took pains to say something good about his rivals: "What Proudhon wants, the only thing he wants, is that idle capital should no longer be rewarded."[139] And: "Buchez . . . has an exaggerated fear of Satan, his pomps and his works." But:

The School of Buchez deserves a sincere esteem. It has strengthened the soul of the people. Its austerity is good for a time of struggle, its devotion appropriate for a militant socialism. . . . Also the people cannot confuse them with those sceptics, those atheists, those economists and those smug ones who preach to the people the morality of resignation so that they may digest them in quiet and comfort.[140]

The man who above all filled Considérant with fear and loathing was Louis Adolphe Thiers (1797–1877), French historian and politician, an anticlerical atheist of such dexterity that he was able to achieve the highest offices under Louis Philippe, Louis Napoleon *and* the Third Republic. When confronted with the threat posed by socialists and rebellious workers, Thiers turned quickly from anticlerical to proclerical: "I count heavily on [the clergy] to propagate that good philosophy that teaches man that he is here below to suffer."[141] All men, that is, but Thiers and his wealthy friends. This is what the Christian socialists called "clericalism without God."

Considérant summed up Thiers's philosophy as "the absolute negation of the ideal . . . each one for himself and God for the clever ones."[142] It was to Thiers and others like him that Considérant referred in the following bitter passage:

All our bourgeois reactionaries still have busts of Voltaire and Rousseau in their studies. That does not prevent them, however, from doing an about-face and invoking, atheists and pagans that they are, not the

Gospel, which they regard with horror, but that artificial religion, under the name of Christianity, to put the people to sleep, to subdue them, to teach them that they must kill themselves with work, must suffer, work, suffer again, work always, and that they cannot be happy in this world because God does not wish it. . . . Our century will not be deceived in this matter as it was permitted to the last one to be deceived. Our century goes back to the sources of Christianity, and, far from attacking Christianity, it is with Christianity that it has learned how to crush you, pharisaical hypocrites.[143]

Considérant was deceived by his own optimism. The nineteenth century did not learn, by using Christianity, how to crush the hypocrites. The Catholic Church of the nineteenth century—or at least most of its ecclesiastical representatives—had forgotten too much of Christianity and Buchez's Catholicism to reveal to the French masses the true face of Christ. And so the masses turned away from that face.

Considérant sensed that his hopeful prophecies rested on fragile foundations. But he continued to exhort his compatriots and to appeal to their faith in Christ:

In France we have nothing more to destroy. We must construct. To construct we must know. . . . Study, study, study. . . . In the last analysis, the only problem to resolve is this: how to establish among the elements of production—capital, labor and talent—relations that are right, just and fraternal, capable of multiplying public wealth and distributing it equitably among all. There is no violence or ignorance that will ever resolve that problem.

And that is not all we must learn. To the light of science we must add the warmth of love. Today, as in the time of Christ, it is always a question of freeing the slaves, and of replacing an old society of misery, deceit and oppression with a society of brotherhood. You will not do that with a party of violence, hate, envy and anger. We need a new explosion of Gospel feeling in order to save the old world. If you are not religious, you may someday have the force of the hurricane to uproot and overturn, but you will never have that of nature, which prepares the seeds, and the sun to make them grow. Let us place ourselves sincerely under the inspiration of the Gospel.[144]

It is tempting to quote Considérant at length, but space requires that the temptation be resisted. Considérant ends his book with one last lovely metaphor of optimism:

God sometimes punishes humanity, but he never abandons it. We shall see again, as in the time of the first flood, the Ark, enclosing in its hold every kind of life, brave the winds and sail over the waters.[145]

ÉTIENNE CABET

Étienne Cabet (1788–1856) was eccentric both in his Christianity and in his socialism. However, he does not seem to have been so eccentric as to justify Biéler's not only excluding him from the pantheon of "Christians and socialists before Marx" but even accusing him of wanting "to abolish Christianity."[146]

How does one reconcile a desire to abolish Christianity with writing a 636-page book full of praise for Christ and quotations from the Bible and the Fathers of the church? True, he wanted a Christianity without churches, without priests, without sacraments, without liturgy or divine service—"only the love of God, his worship in spirit and in truth, and especially the practice of Fraternity."[147] True, he dismissed some of Jesus' miracles as parables invented by the evangelists. But on both scores he was not the first or last such Christian.

Cabet, like Buchez and Leroux, began his public career as a member of the Carbonari, was tried in 1839, and condemned for revolutionary activity. He fled to England, where he was much influenced by Robert Owen and by Thomas More's *Utopia*.

Under this influence he wrote *Voyage en Icarie* in 1840, a book that went into five editions over the next eight years and was read throughout Europe. In 1847 he published *Le Vrai Christianisme suivant Jésus Christ* (The True Christianity according to Jesus Christ), which was also widely read and reprinted twice. Taking a swipe at Saint-Simon he declared,

> It is not a New Christianity that we wish to imagine; it is the True Christianity that we want to expose. . . . We will admit, without discussion, the divinity of Jesus, and we will set forth the doctrine, system, precepts and actions of this Man-God.[148]

With money from the sale of his books and donations from wealthy admirers, Cabet in 1848 bought a vast tract of land in Texas, and persuaded several hundred followers to establish an Icarian Community on it, but fever and general problems plagued the experiment. With two hundred eighty of the remnant Cabet moved in 1849 to a healthier spot at Nauvoo, Illinois, a former Mormon center, and founded Icaria, which by 1855 numbered six hundred residents. Executive officers were elected every year but they had little authority and were subject to continual approval. The constitution of the group included this sentence: "The Icarian Community adopts as its religion the religion of Christianity in its primitive purity and its fundamental principle of fraternity of men and of peoples."[149] But no Christian services were held. As an expression of their belief in the equality of men and women, to make up for lost time, as it were, husbands were required to render special acts of homage to their wives. A visitor reported, "They lived in little houses on plots of ground bright with flowers around a central house, where they had their meals in common."[150]

Dissension split the community and two hundred of them left with Cabet for Saint Louis, where he died in 1856. Icaria continued until 1895.

In one of his first essays, *For a Ruthless Criticism of Everything Existing,* the young Marx dismissed Cabet's "communism" as "a dogmatic abstraction." A major reason given was Cabet's failure to critique religion in the "ruthless" manner that Marx believed religion should be critiqued.[151] Whenever Marx, in later writings, referred with contempt to "utopian socialists," it was mainly Cabet and Fourier that he had in mind. The idea of going off somewhere to establish Icarias and phalanxes did not appeal to Marx. He was more interested in the organization of the workers, political action, and revolution.

Cabet did not believe in revolution. He and Blanqui both called themselves communists, but they were of very different varieties. Cabet once wrote, "If I held a revolution in my hand, I would keep it closed, even though I must die in exile."[152] There are totalitarian elements in Cabet's communism. In his fictional country of *Icarie* all children over five were to be educated by the state, there was to be no freedom of opinion and only one official newspaper. But *Icarie* anticipated such future reforms as progressive income taxes, a minimum wage law, and old-age pensions. The actual community of Icaria, as noted, was a very democratic society, entirely voluntary. In effect, it was another form of vaguely Christian monasticism for married idealists.

"Respect and defend women" was one of Cabet's major principles, and it is significant that he cited Jesus' strictures against adultery and remarriage as evidence of Christ's concern for the protection of women against their husbands and his intention that they be "treated as the equal of men."[153] In the home, however, he gave the father first place. He also quoted St. Paul's "There is neither Jew nor Greek, slave nor free, male nor female, for you are all one in Christ Jesus" (Gal. 3:28) as support for his demand that there be "no more inequality between women and men,"[154] but "the liberation of women, the recognition of their rights, their equality, their education."[155]

Cabet's Christianity was unorthodox, but as with Considérant, certain passages in his writings ring with the sound and feeling of "true Christianity."

"Love your neighbor as yourself" (Lev. 19:18), Cabet points out, was

an idea buried in a mass of other ideas, obscured and, in effect, smothered and drowned. Jesus took it out of obscurity and placed it in the limelight, to make of it a sun that will illuminate everything, to inscribe it as the head of the law, the generative principle of all the rest . . . like unto the commandment, Thou shalt love God. . . . That is the great, immense innovation, the incalculable reform introduced by Jesus.[156]

He closes *Le Vrai Christianisme* with this appeal:

Nourished and inspired by [Jesus'] Gospel, illuminated by his light, guided by his commandments, embraced by his love, and seeking to imitate him in all things, let us go forward.[157]

THE CLERGY AND THE POPES

Socialism in the first half of the nineteenth century was mainly an ideological movement, a movement dominated by thinkers, writers, and utopian dreamers, with occasional outbursts of revolutionary violence and small bands of "associationists" who either organized their own workshops or marched off into the wilderness to see if they could persuade Utopia to fly. The second half of the nineteenth century brought the organizers to the foreground, and socialism became a workers' movement, a union movement, an organized political movement.

In 1864 a number of socialists met in London to organize the International Workingmen's Association (1864–1876). The group was mostly from France and England, but it also included workers from Germany and Poland and some Italian intellectuals. The organizers met in a hall named for the fourth-century Saint Martin, a bishop and former soldier who gave half his cloak to a naked beggar in whom he recognized Christ. As far as we know, no Christian socialists were present.

Karl Marx (1818–1883) was present and gave the inaugural address, which he put in written form a few days later as a charter document and program. It was not one of his best efforts, but it still revealed those qualities that made him the most influential theoretician of the socialist movement from that time onward. Those qualities were a powerful intellect, detailed knowledge of economics and the conditions of industrial workers, a firm grasp of the need for organization and political action, a passionate feeling for the injustices of contemporary life, a flair for the sharp and colorful phrase and, finally, a willingness, on occasion at least, to compromise and trim his ideological sails to the prevailing wind.

For example, on this occasion, he urged "the proletarians of all countries" to "vindicate the simple laws of morality and justice."[158] Afterwards, G. D. H. Cole relates, "he told Engels, in half-jesting regret, that he had been compelled to introduce into the International's Inaugural Address some phrases about right and justice, which would do no harm."[159] Apparently some of the old-fashioned type were present. Marx, of course, did not believe in "laws of morality and justice," at least not in his head. In his head he believed that morality was determined by historical materialism, that is, by modes and relations of production, and capitalists were as much victims of that conditioning as proletarians.[160] In his viscera he was outraged by injustice and regularly referred to capitalists as "vultures" and "blood-suckers."[161] If there was a law by which right and wrong might by measured, it was Marx's *intellectual* judgment that that law was the inevitable appropriation by the working class of the means of production, and that whatever hastened that appropriation was right and whatever delayed it was wrong.

Another example of compromise in Marx's address appears in his fulsome praise for workers' associations or producer cooperatives. Owenite influence was strong among the English delegates, and the French delegates were *mutuellistes,* followers of Proudhon. Cole writes:

> The society to which they looked forward was one in which every man would own property and receive the full fruit of his own labor, either individually or as a member of a cooperative producing group.[162]

The farthest Marx felt he could go in the direction of his own preference for nationalization was to urge that "cooperative labor ought to be developed to national dimensions, and consequently to be fostered by national means."[163]

However, when the German Social Democrats, following the preference of their dead leader and Marx's rival Ferdinand Lassalle, tried to take Marx's advice at Gotha in 1875, Marx heaped contempt and ridicule all over the very idea he had proposed in 1864. In doing so he identified it with "the recipe prescribed by Buchez in the reign of Louis Philippe in *opposition* to the French socialists and accepted by the reactionary workers of the *Atelier*" (emphasis in the original).[164] Marx insists that cooperative societies are of value "only in so far as they are the independent creations of the workers and not protegés either of the government or of the bourgeois."[165] Ironically, this was precisely the position of Buchez and *L'Atelier* as opposed to the state-supported cooperatives proposed by Blanc, Lassalle, and the German Social Democrats, as well as by Marx in 1864. Marx was wrong in stating that Buchez was in opposition to the "French socialists." Anyone who has read this far will know that French socialists were all over the lot on this and most other questions and Buchez had as good a claim to represent the French socialists as anybody else.

The reader may well wonder why a section on "The Clergy and the Popes" begins with several pages about Marx and the dispute about producer cooperatives. It does so to underline the fact that as late as 1875, forty-odd years after "socialism" appeared on the French and European landscape, it was, as Considérant had insisted, "not a determined doctrine." It consisted of elements that were clearly consistent with Christian tradition, elements that were clearly inconsistent, and elements that were somewhere between and subject to dispute. There were about a dozen different "socialisms." This fact is relevant to the clergy and the popes, who as a general rule not only spoke and wrote about socialism as though it were one clearly defined doctrine but also defined it in terms of its most extreme or dubious notions. They did not do their homework.

The February Revolution of 1848 was followed by a kind of honeymoon between the Catholic clergy and the revolutionaries, democrats, socialists, and assorted rebels against the rich and anticlerical bourgeoisie who had dominated the government of Louis Philippe. Even a bishop like Pierre-Louis Parisis, who was later to be a leader of the conservative ultramontanes, was saying things that might have come from the mouth of Buchez or Considérant:

There is nothing more profoundly—indeed, I would say more exclusively—Christian than these three words that are inscribed on the national flag: LIBERTY, EQUALITY, FRATERNITY [emphasis in the original].[166]

Also, there were always French clergy, both Catholic and Protestant, who were true friends of the poor and true friends of democracy. Denis Affre, archbishop of Paris, was one of these. It was probably his influence, up to the moment of his tragic death in June 1848, that made it possible for the Christian socialists and the Christian democrats to speak and write so freely and to hail the Second Republic, at least in its hopeful beginnings, as a Christian step forward on the path of progress.

And there were others: Père Gratry, l'Abbé Gerbet, l'Abbé Maret, and Pierre Giraud, cardinal archbishop of Cambrai (Fénelon's old see), who urged the church to show that it opposed every "oppression of weakness," that it condemned every "exploitation of man by man."[167] This in 1845. In the same year Mgr. Rendu, bishop of Annecy, went further by insisting that the church must condemn capitalism, which was guilty of "such odious abuses that, as all know, it would be impossible to discover anything similar in the centuries of barbarism." He predicted that if governments did nothing to correct this situation, the workers would revolt and then, "flattered by theorists and self-seekers," they would "want to take everything" because they had been denied "a fair helping at the banquet of life."[168]

Even before 1848, however, these were exceptional voices. After 1848, as the Catholics fled pell-mell toward the promises of law and order held out by Louis Napoleon, such voices became even more exceptional and in some cases were muted or reduced to silence by the prevailing reaction. Even Lacordaire, elected to the National Assembly, had barely taken his seat with "the Mountain," the far left, when the Blanqui invasion of May 15 "insulted his Dominican habit" and moved him to resign and join the ranks of the conservatives, though he never moved as far to the right as his former colleague, Montalembert.

Much more typical of the French episcopacy than Affre, Giraud, or Rendu was Bishop Clausel de Montals of Chartres. In his pastoral of November 25, 1848, he protested,

They say that the Republic dates from Calvary, and the Revolution is Christianity. No, Jesus Christ never mentioned political liberty in his discourses. . . . When St. Paul said, "My brethren, you are called to liberty," he meant liberty from the passions, not this unbridled liberty of the revolutionaries who, it seems, would like to see the terrible days of 1793 again, and who dare to say, "Property is theft.". . . God will not allow [France] to be handed over defenceless and forever to a horde of criminals and to myriads of hangmen's assistants.[169]

Mgr. Gousset, archbishop of Rheims, was briefer: "Democracy is the heresy of our times."[170]

Thirty-three priests attended a Christian socialist dinner in Paris on April 29, 1849, and drank toasts with six-hundred diners, mostly workers, to "Jesus of Nazareth, the father of socialism" and to "the union of democracy and Christianity."[171] They were all silenced by their bishops in one way or another. Virtually all the voices of Christian socialists and Christian democrats, lay or clerical, were reduced to silence within months after the coup d'état of Louis Napoleon.

But it was not Louis Napoleon who was primarily responsible for the suppression of Christian socialism among the Catholic laity and lower clergy of France. The man who stiffened the opposition of the bishops and thereby killed a movement that was not to surface again in the Catholic Church (in any significant form) for over a hundred years was undoubtedly Pius IX.

He was a charming man, charming and impressive. Even a critic like Cardinal Newman conceded. "The main cause of his popularity was the magic of his presence."[172] However, even a supporter like Metternich concluded that he was "warm-hearted but of poor intelligence." He wrote, over a long reign of thirty-two years (1846–1878), thirty-seven encyclicals and scores of lesser allocutions. In these he condemned "socialism and communism" about ten times.

A typical condemnation appears in *Nostis et nobiscum* (December 8, 1849) in which he takes special aim at the Christian radicals whose goal is

> to drive people to overthrow the entire order of human affairs and to draw them over to the wicked theories of *socialism* and *communism*. . . . They are confident that they can first misuse the holy scriptures by wrong interpretation to spread their errors and claim God's authority while doing it" [emphasis in original].[173]

He warns the faithful to beware of following these "wicked theories of *socialism* and *communism*" and adds,

> The Divine Judge will seek vengeance on the day of wrath. Until then no temporal benefit for the people will result from their conspiracy, but rather new increases of misery and disaster. For man is not empowered to establish new societies and unions which are opposed to the nature of mankind.[174]

The only further analysis as to why these theories are so "wicked" and "perverted" is in a sentence to the effect that they "falsely claim that . . . the property of others can be taken and divided or in some other way turned to the use of everyone."[175]

Lest the faithful conclude that he is insensitive to the sufferings of little children forced to work from pre-dawn to post-dusk in fetid factories, Pius IX points out that "pious institutions exist . . . for relieving the illness and want of the wretches."[176] And he does quote Matthew 25, from which he concludes that "the condition of the poor and wretched in Catholic nations is much less harsh than in any other nations."[177] Why, he does not say. As a final consolation he offers this:

> Let our poor recall the teaching of Christ himself that they should not be sad at their condition, since their very poverty makes lighter their journey to salvation, provided that they bear their need with patience and are poor, not alone in possessions, but in spirit too.[178]

The whole performance is painful and embarrassing for a loyal Catholic to contemplate. And the pain and embarrassment are not limited to *Nostis et nobiscum.* A check of all thirty-seven encyclicals of Pius IX and the nine of Gregory XVI, covering the years from 1831 to 1878, when "the odious abuses" of capitalism surpassed "anything similar in the centuries of barbarism" (Bishop Rendu's words) reveals not more than one hundred additional words devoted to the plight of the poor by either Gregory or Pius. The nearest thing to a rebuke to unjust employers appears in *Quanto conficiamur moerore* (August 10, 1863), where Pius denounces "that unbridled self-love and self-interest that drive many to seek their own advantage and profit with clearly no regard for their neighbor."[179] This could apply as much to a poor worker as to a wealthy and unscrupulous employer.

Yet these encyclicals return again and again to the duty of Catholics to obey "lawfully established authority." In a bald-faced appeal to *quid pro quo,* Pius IX, in one of his first encyclicals (*Qui pluribus,* November 9, 1846), urges the rulers of Europe to "defend the liberty and safety of the Church, so that 'the right hand of Christ may also defend their rule.' "[180]

In his defense it might be said (E. E. Y. Hales has said it in *Pio Nono*) that Pius IX was almost totally distracted and absorbed by his struggle against Mazzini, Garibaldi, Cavour, and King Victor Emmanuel to retain the Papal States, which were finally stripped from him in 1870.

Ironically, it was not the republican revolutionaries Mazzini and Garibaldi who did it, but the king of Sardinia, whose subjects the popes had reminded again and again of their duty to obey their sovereign. Of course, early in his reign, New Year's Day 1849, Pius IX had already threatened the Greater Excommunication, which attaches "*ipso facto* to any who shall dare to incur the guilt of any attack whatsoever upon the temporal sovereignty of the Chief Pontiff of Rome." Making such a sweeping threat of excommunication, it might also be said, "*ipso facto*" demonstrates how dangerous and debilitating the temporal sovereignty of the popes was to the spiritual health of the Catholic Church and what a blessing in disguise, what a *felix culpa,* it was for Victor Emmanuel to ignore it.

The turnaround began with the declaration of the doctrine of papal infallibility by the First Vatican Council on July 18, 1870. The vote was 533 to 2 in favor, about sixty bishops having left Rome on July 17 rather than vote against it.

The heralding of that doctrine as the beginning of a progressive renaissance may strike the reader as an absurd and contradictory statement in the light of the reactionary statements just quoted. In fact, it would have struck this aging son of the Church in the same way before he started reading the encyclicals of Gregory XVI and Pius IX. A paradox? Let me explain.

The doctrine of papal infallibility was a powerful, all-pervading reality in the Catholic Church long before July 18, 1870. It might be said to go back to Matthew 16:18–19 and other passages in the New Testament that give Peter primacy and, allegedly, his successors as well. In the nineteenth century, given the siege mentality that followed the attacks of Voltaire and his intellectual descendants, the doctrine became even more pervasive.

Consider Gregory XVI in *Singulari nos,* presuming to dismiss Lamennais's orthodox *Paroles d'un croyant* with these words: "By our apostolic power we condemn the book; furthermore we decree that it be perpetually condemned."[181] Consider Pius IX in *Qui pluribus* back in 1846, when his seat on the pontifical throne was barely warm, "This [papal] authority judges infallibly all disputes which concern matters of faith and morals."[182] Where is the limitation and the definition? There is none. It's "all disputes," take it or leave it. Consider what was even worse, the demand of Pius IX in *Quanta cura* (December 8, 1864) for total obedience by Catholics to the pope not just in "the dogmata of faith and morals" but also in "those judgments and decrees of the Apostolic See whose object is declared to concern the Church's general good and her rights and discipline."[183] Papal infallibility, by implication at least, has become a circus tent, or more accurately, a vast prison covering every conceivable question that the pope decides might "concern the Church's general good."

If the most conservative bishops had had their way at the First Vatican Council, the doctrine of papal infallibility might well have come out looking like these statements of Gregory and Pius. But those sixty bishops who left before the final vote made their presence felt. And there were many others who insisted that the doctrine be precisely defined and limited: infallibility therefore applies only (1) when the pope speaks *ex cathedra,* that is, in his official capacity as pastor and teacher, (2) when the pope speaks with the manifest intention of binding the entire church to acceptance, and (3) when the matter pertains to faith and morals.

The result? Looking back to 1870 from 1987 we see only one papal statement that qualifies under these limitations: the definition of the Assumption of the Virgin Mary by Pope Pius XII in 1950. In effect, the prison walls came tumbling down. But it was a long time before most of the prisoners realized they were free.

CONCLUSION

Jean-Baptiste Duroselle, perhaps the foremost authority on French social Catholicism of this period, concludes:

Before 1848 the influence of Buchez, of *L'Atelier,* of certain Fourierists, of Ledreuille had, in Paris and several other cities, reconciled the workers to the Church and one could ask oneself if socialism was not going to become Christian. The days of June [1848], the almost total disappearance of Christian democracy, the attitude of the hierarchy after December 2 [1851], the violent statements of *L'Univers* provoked a profound alienation of affections of the working classes in regard to the Church.[184]

As the reader might guess, my own list of influences and influencers leading socialism in the direction of Christianity would be longer than Duroselle's, but I cannot improve on his list of counter influences except to note again that the attitude of the hierarchy owed a great deal to the positions adopted by Gregory XVI and Pius IX.

With the publication of *Rerum novarum* by Leo XIII in 1891, antisocialist though it was, a beginning was made to the task of reconciling once again the workers of France and Catholic Europe to the church. As this process continued in the twentieth century through the pontificate of Pius XI and flowered in the pontificate of John XXIII, the whole question of reconciling socialism and Catholicism arose once again out of the dustbin of history to which it had been assigned, to the center of the stage.

The development is appropriate, for on the basis of the evidence in this chapter we can go even further than Duroselle and conclude, not simply that socialism might have become Christian, but that it was, in fact, largely, if not mainly, Christian in origin. And we mean that not simply as a body of ideals with roots in the Bible and Judeo-Christian tradition, but as a modern phenomenon growing out of certain intellectual, economic, and political conditions that coalesced in France in the first half of the nineteenth century. We mean it, finally, whether we consider the arguments used, those who used them, or the influence of those who used them on their contemporaries.

Meanwhile, however, in the second half of the nineteenth century Marx and Marxism were forging ahead, to be followed in due course by Lenin and Leninism in the twentieth century.

CHAPTER 8

England

JOHN LUDLOW AND OTHER EARLY SOCIALISTS IN ENGLAND

The young John Ludlow was living in Paris with his sisters and widowed mother. One day he heard a cry in the street outside, *"À bas les Ministres!"* (roughly translated, "Down with the Government!"). The maid, Marguerite, who remembered 1789, became very agitated, jumped on a chair and exclaimed, "Ah, Madame, it is like that that the Revolution began!"[1]

Why she jumped on a chair, as though a mouse were loose in the room, Ludlow does not tell us. In any case it was "the mouse that roared," the Revolution of 1830, and there seems little question that this revolution and his personal experience of the Revolution of 1848 had much to do with the fact that John Malcolm Ludlow (1821–1911) became the most intense and dedicated of the first self-styled Christian socialists of England. He was, in fact, the founder of the movement.

Born in India, his father a British colonel who died when John was still a baby, John lived in Paris until the age of sixteen, set a brilliant record at the elite Collège Bourbon, and determined to remain in France until the day his mother said to him, "I'm sure your father, had he been alive, would have wished you to be an Englishman."[2]

Reluctantly Ludlow moved to London with his mother and studied for the bar at Lincoln's Inn. He continued to visit Paris and came under the influence of the Evangelical Protestant Alexandre Vinet, the man who first used the word *socialisme*, and of Louis Meyer, a saintly Lutheran pastor who founded an organization called the Society of Friends of the Poor. In effect, Meyer said to Ludlow, "What are you doing for the poor in London?"

Moved by this challenge, Ludlow returned to Lincoln's Inn and tried to interest its chaplain, Frederick Dennison Maurice (1805–1872), in a visiting service he had started for the poor in the neighborhood. Maurice was not interested. Sixteen years older than Ludlow, he had already established a reputation as an unorthodox but popular preacher and professor of moral philosophy at King's College, London, but he was not yet excited about the condition of the poor. Ludlow had become aware of that condition, and also of

139

the feeble effects of the kind of personal charity that commended itself to religious Englishmen and women. Later he summarized his conclusion, "No serious effort was made to help a person out of his or her misery, but only to help him or her *in* it."[3]

When the Revolution of 1848 broke out Ludlow hurried to Paris and was delighted to see that "after the gagging of the Louis Philippe regime, the whole city seemed to be bubbling into speech."[4] A large part of that speech, he noted, was devoted to various kinds of socialism. Ludlow conceived the idea of "Christianizing socialism." If Christianity failed to meet this challenge, he believed, "it would be shaken to its foundations, precisely because Socialism appealed to the higher and not to the lower instincts of the working class."[5]

Strangely enough, neither then nor later was Ludlow much influenced by Buchez and his followers, even though his own brand of socialism was far more like that of Buchez than that of the French with whom he was more familiar: Fourier, Proudhon, and Blanc.

When Ludlow returned to London he gave a full report to Maurice, who was enthusiastic, partly because the Chartist movement, taking its cue from the revolutionary happenings on the continent and propelled by widespread suffering and depression, was threatening once again to challenge the supremacy of the landed and commercial aristocracy, which was supported in the main by the established Church of England. The Chartist movement was a mass movement, led in part by Owenite socialists, but concerned more with political than economic action. The goal of the Chartists was a new electoral law to include universal manhood suffrage, a secret ballot, salaries and no property qualification for members of Parliament, thereby making it possible for the workers to be represented in the House of Commons for the first time.

At this point English socialism was in a state of hibernation. Let us review its history briefly. Since the time of Thomas More an undercurrent of socialistic or communistic thought had moved beneath the surface of English society. Even Shakespeare reflects it. In *King Henry VI* he gives half-comic, half-sympathetic treatment to the real-life rebel Jack Cade (d. 1450) and has him say, "All the realm shall be in common . . . and when I am king . . . there shall be no money; all shall eat and drink on my score; and I will apparel them all in one livery, that they may agree like brothers, and worship me their lord."[6]

What had been an undercurrent surfaced in the time of Cromwell when a band of Diggers, led by Gerrard Winstanley and William Everard, dug up uncultivated common land in Cobham, Surrey, and pitched tents there for dwellings in 1649. In his *New Law of Righteousness* Winstanley claimed a direct revelation from God as the justification for this action:

Work together; eat bread together; declare this all abroad, "Israel shall never take hire, nor give hire. Whosoever labours the earth for any person or persons, that are lifted up to rule over others, and doth not look upon themselves as equal to others in the creation: the hand of the Lord shall be upon that labourer. I the Lord have spoken it and will do it."[7]

Unfortunately, Cromwell's troops did not recognize either the hand or the voice of the Lord. The Diggers were dispersed, Winstanley and Everard arrested, tried, and heavily fined. The movement died.

The first use of the word "socialism" in English, or more exactly "socialists," appeared in the November 1827 issue of *The Cooperative Magazine* to designate the view of Robert Owen (1771–1858) that industrial wealth should be owned in common, on a cooperative basis. Those who held this view were called "Communionists" or "Socialists." Owen was a fabulously successful operator of a large textile mill at New Lanark, Scotland, into which he introduced a number of enlightened labor policies. He went on to less successful experiments in establishing "home colonies," which were a combination of industrial and agricultural cooperatives with a touch of Fourierist *phalanstère* thrown in. The most famous failure was at New Harmony, Indiana. Owen also had a brief fling as a labor leader, heading up the first sizable union organization in Great Britain, if not in the world, the Grand National Consolidated Trade Unions.

By 1835 all these ventures had failed, not always because of their intrinsic weaknesses. The union effort foundered on a reef of intense and violent opposition by both employers and government. Part of the failure syndrome was due to the aggressive campaign of antireligious propaganda that Owen initiated. He preached a "doctrine of circumstances" that denied the reality of free will and insisted that the proper manipulation of environment could produce a "New Moral World" (the title of the Owenite newspaper) as well as new moral men and women without any reliance on religion or churches.

In this respect English socialism, in its origins, was most unlike French socialism. Its quiescent condition during the 1840s did, however, present an excellent opportunity for Christian socialism to rise to prominence.

The key date was April 10, 1848, when the Chartist-organized mass demonstration took place on Kennington Common in London. The Chartist proclamation was obviously written by a committee that included left- and right-wing representatives. The left must have been responsible for the sentence that read, "There is no telling what glorious Revolution a single hour may bring forth," the right wing for the reference to *"peaceful* revolution" and the instruction that demonstrators should *"peaceably* disperse" after they had marched to Parliament and presented their petitions for a more democratic electoral law.[8] In any case the government did not wait to see how this ambiguity would be resolved. It massed an overwhelming force of troops and volunteers at Kennington Common and dispersed the Chartists before they could even begin their march. This encouraged Parliament to ignore the petitions and discouraged the workers from any further confidence or hope in Chartist leadership. This all but did away with the English left.

On April 10 Maurice was in bed with a cold. Ludlow went to his law office, convinced that there would be no revolution that day. Into the office burst an excited young minister of the Church of England, Charles Kingsley (1819–75), who had come up to London from his rural parish out of sympathy for the Chartists, but also out of concern that he must do something to prevent violence and bloodshed. He actually thought he might be able to quell revolutionary fever with a leaflet. Kingsley persuaded Ludlow to go with him to Kennington Common, but before they could reach it they met the dispersed demonstrators going home. Disappointed, they went to see Maurice, who had sent Kingsley to Ludlow, and for the first time the three who were to create Christian socialism in England met together. At this point, however, they were not thinking of anything so radical. Maurice, in fact, was a conservative Anglican. His peculiar brand of theology emphasized the existence of "a Divine Order" of harmony and cooperation in existing society that would resolve all problems and conflicts if human beings would only recognize it and give it a chance. One of his critics, Aubrey de Vere, responded to this idea: "Listening to Maurice is like eating pea soup with a fork."[9]

Maurice did have a compelling effect on those who were not turned off by his intellectual fuzziness. With pride of intellect he combined an extraordinary humility and personal goodness. His warmth and intensity of feeling moved his listeners. Like Saint-Simon and Considérant, his accent was on the moral rather than the doctrinal content of Christianity. He even denied the existence of hell and eternal punishment, and this ultimately brought about his dismissal from the faculty of King's College. Meanwhile, however, he was a charismatic figure of established reputation in the social, academic, and ecclesiastical world of England, which still, unlike France, enjoyed undisputed dominance, particularly after the collapse of the Chartist movement. His effect on younger men like Ludlow and Kingsley, who called him "Master" and "Prophet," was alternately inspirational and negative, like a vehicle with a powerful motor and an even more powerful brake.

On this occasion, moved by the Chartist threat and recognition of the coexistence of great suffering and injustice alongside an even greater apathy and indifference on the part of the upper classes, the three men agreed that something must be done. First they decided to put up posters bearing a proclamation to "the Workmen of England," a leaflet that Kingsley composed, full of condescending advice to the lower classes, assuring them that they had more friends than they realized:

> friends who expect nothing from you but who love you, because you are their brothers, and who fear God and therefore dare not neglect you, His children, men who are drudging and sacrificing themselves to get you your rights, men who know what your rights are better than you know yourselves, who are trying to get you something nobler than charters and dozens of Acts of Parliament. . . . [The workers must] turn back from the precipice of riot, which ends in the gulf of universal distrust, stagnation, starvation. . . . [For] there will be no true freedom without virtue, no true science without religion, no true industry without the fear of God, and love to your fellow-citizens.[10]

The proclamation was signed "Working Parson." No record exists of a Chartist response to this unhappy overture. The wonder is that a movement so clumsily launched was able to stay afloat and eventually make an impressive showing in the regatta of British social reform. It says something for the learning abilities of its founders. Even Maurice learned something, though not as much as the others, who were still young enough to let go of inbred biases.

Kingsley was elated after that first meeting. He wrote his wife: "A glorious future is opening. Both Maurice and Ludlow seem to have driven away all my doubts and sorrows, and I see the blue sky again and my Father's face."[11]

The second thing the three agreed on was to start a weekly newspaper. *Politics for the People* was addressed to the workers. In it Maurice expounded his peculiar version of Liberty, Equality, and Fraternity. For example, equality could not be identified with "equality of property" or "equality of rank" nor equality of education:

> But you may have an education which is not merely one for works and of gifts—an education which will call forth the Man who is to do the work, who is to receive the gifts. Such an education will discover the real secret of equality. It will find that which lies beneath all distinctions of rank and property; that which alone prevents them or the absence of them from being a curse; that which no institutions created, and which alone can preserve institutions or reform them.[12]

Reading Maurice could also be like eating pea soup with a fork. He extolled liberty and fraternity, but that did not mean political enfranchisement, according to Chartist demands. If we only felt our fraternity with the rich strongly enough, and they their fraternity with us, then all would be well. He did not put it quite that baldly, but this was the general intent. The lower classes were not ready for the vote. Organizations, political parties, trade unions, strikes— these implied a denial of "the Divine Order." It was all rather pathetic. The message, in effect, was: "Politics are not for the people—at least not yet."

Eventually, even Ludlow, Maurice's disciple, had to take exception to this gospel according to Maurice. A letter to "the Master" in 1852 states the following:

> I have endeavored to study you very closely for the last year, both in yourself and through your books (I would especially refer to the *Moral and Metaphysical Philosophy*) and it does seem to me that you are liable to be carried away by Platonistic dreams about an Order, and a King- dom, and a Beauty, self-realized in their own eternity, and which so put to shame all earthly counterparts that it beomes labour lost to attempt anything like an earthly realization of them, and all one has to do is to show them, were it only in glimpses, to others by tearing away the cobwebs of human systems that conceal them. I do not think this is Christianity.[13]

Kingsley was better. He shared some of Maurice's aristocratic bias, but he felt more keenly the terrible injustice and oppression of the poor, and he was a better writer and did not shrink from the use of an occasional revolutionary phrase, even if he did not mean it literally. He was also honest enough to confess the sins of the Anglican clergy:

> I entreat you, I adjure you, to trust the Bible . . . the true *Radical Reformer's Guide. . . .* If you have followed a very different *Reformer's Guide* from mine, it is mainly the fault of us parsons. . . . We have used the Bible as if it were a special constable's handbook—an opium-dose for keeping beasts of burden patient while they were being overloaded—a mere book to keep the poor in order. . . . We have told you that the Bible preached the rights of property and the duties of labor, when God knows, for once that it does that, it preaches ten times over the *duties of property* and the *rights of labour.* We have found plenty of texts to rebuke the sins of the poor, and very few to rebuke the sins of the rich.[14]

Note the use of the opium metaphor, reminiscent of Marx's dismissal of religion as "the opium of the people," published in a German newspaper four years before, but not likely to have been known to Kingsley.[15]

Ludlow was even better. With his French background and French education, he leaned more decisively in the direction of democracy and he expressed his leanings in clearer and more logical language than either of the others. He supported most of the Chartist demands, including the elimination of property qualifications, but held that the vote should be limited first to those who paid taxes and had a minimal education. He tended to emphasize duties to the virtual exclusion of rights, but his emphasis on the duties of employers, and of the rich and powerful generally, was as sharp and bitter as that of any Owenite or Marxist.

> How comes it that the bulk of the working classes live their death-in-life upon wages permanently insufficient, and which fail wholly for months in every year? How comes it that the most filthy wretchedness should be seen side-by-side with the most gorgeous luxury. How comes it . . . that man's direct wickedness, or scarcely less wicked neglect, should create through town and country whole masses of suffering and mortality—or rather, wholesale murder? How comes it that thousands live and die unschooled, uncared for, godless, learning, to use Coleridge's awful words, their "only prayers from curses"?[16]

Politics for the People lasted only from May 6, 1848, to the end of July, a total of seventeen issues, perhaps the first attempt by any part of the English Church to break through the wall that separated it from the workers. The attempt was not really successful, but the Chartist newspaper unfairly showed its scorn for Kingsley and Ludlow, though not so much Maurice, when it accused them of telling the workers of England that "it is sinful to resist injustice and oppression."[17]

In the last issue Ludlow finally got around to the subject of socialism. Echoing Vinet and Leroux, he wrote that socialism was a reaction to the individualism that had caused a "splitting up of society under a thousand influences of sceptical and vicious selfishness," whereas the truth was that "we are all partners" and socialism was "the means of carrying out that partnership into new fields . . . better husbanding the common stock, more simply and successfully carrying on the common business, of assigning more judiciously to every partner such duties as he is best able to fulfill."[18] To everyone's surprise, Maurice, in the same issue, acknowledged the need to study the various forms of socialism "to see what great human sympathies are bound up with them, what there is in them which makes them inconsistent and unreasonable, what there is in them which has a divine root and must live."[19]

The movement grew, meanwhile, and more idealistic young men from the middle and upper classes were drawn to what Ludlow called "the band of brothers." One of these was Tom Hughes, (1822–1896), a cricket star at Oxford, who became a lawyer, member of Parliament, and author of *Tom Brown's School Days* and other popular books. Hughes was a great asset, unfailingly cheerful, friendly, loyal, and a good complement to the more shy and introspective Ludlow. Together they started a workers' night school in a London slum. Ludlow suggested weekly meetings at Maurice's house in Queen's Square to read and discuss the Bible, and so began in December 1848 a tradition that was to blossom again in the twentieth century: the use of Bible discussion as a rallying point and motive force for social action. Maurice, the dominant figure in these meetings, was highly effective, and his influence on the younger men grew, for good and ill.

The group was, however, still isolated in its middle-class ghetto. As Ludlow put it later, "The victims themselves of those fearful class-estrangements which they had come together to break down, they knew not a single working-man, of the thinking and reading class." This changed when a friend of Ludlow's introduced him to Walter Cooper in February 1849. Cooper was a journeyman tailor and a top Chartist leader. Ludlow brought him to hear Maurice preach at Lincoln's Inn, and Cooper, though not a believing Christian, liked Maurice. Meetings were arranged, Cooper brought other workmen, and larger meetings were held on a regular basis at Cranbourne Coffee Tavern. That a prominent Anglican minister wanted to meet with workers was a drawing card. Maurice was as effective with these men in the larger meetings as he was with his social equals in the smaller Bible-study groups. After one of them Kingsley wrote his wife:

Last night will never be forgotten by many, many men. Maurice was —I cannot describe it. Chartists told me this morning that many were affected even to tears. The man was inspired—gigantic. No one commented on what he said. He stunned us![20]

Despite the fuzziness of his appeal to "one great brotherhood," some quality of sincerity, some fire of passion made men believe and hope, if only for a time, that here was the secret, the key that would unlock the iron door that barred them from the good life.

Kingsley too made his contribution. Maurice, in one of his negative moods, had suppressed the publication of Kingsley's first novel, *The Nun's Pool*, in *Politics for the People*. Even though it was set in the reign of Henry VIII, Maurice thought it was too critical of the monarchy and the aristocracy for confiscating the church's property without assuming the church's role as an advocate of the poor. (The novel later appeared in *The Christian Socialist* under Ludlow's editorship.)

In his later novels, *Yeast* and *Alton Locke*, Kingsley zeroed in on the industrial evils of his own time. *Alton Locke* was a full-length, fictionalized version of an earlier pamphlet, *Cheap Clothes and Nasty*, that Kingsley had written, at Ludlow's urging, to expose the horrors of the "slop-system" of tailoring. Ludlow revealed his own passion in an article in *Fraser's Magazine* around the same time:

> If it be necessary in English society that from 13,000 to 14,000 females should in London be engaged in slop-work, earning on an average two-pence-half-penny a day, of whom one-fourth, being those who have no husband or parent to support them, have no choice but between starvation and prostitution—if this be necessary, I say, in English society, then English society is the devil's own work, and to hell with it as soon as possible![21]

This was language the workers could understand, language that persuaded the most skeptical that these middle-class reformers, these pious Christians, were the real thing.

Kingsley's novels were "crude"—as Carlyle described *Alton Locke*, even as he recommended it to a publisher—but people read them and were moved by them. Kingsley's church assignments kept him out of London most of the time and he was never a leader in the sense that Ludlow, Maurice, and Hughes were, but in the eyes of the British public he was probably the shining star of the Christian socialist movement.

THE ASSOCIATIONS

The "socialist" part of that movement, however, had not really surfaced. Again Ludlow led the way. A visit to his beloved Paris in the summer of 1849 gave him a chance to study the workers' cooperatives at leisure. "It was the golden age of the *associations ouvrières*," he later described it. "Never before or since have I seen anything to equal the zeal, the self-devotion, the truly brotherly spirit which pervaded those workshops."[22] Some of the workshops Ludlow visited may have been Buchezian, but they might just as well have been staffed by followers of Proudhon, Blanc, or Fourier. *Association* was the key concept of French socialism in that period.

Back in London, Ludlow told the band of brothers, "We must have an association like the French workingmen's associations."[23] Maurice tried to stop him, but Ludlow went ahead and called a meeting without him, and Maurice went along. Walter Cooper, the Chartist tailor, gathered a group of fellow tailors to form the first association. There followed two more tailors associations, three of shoemakers, two of builders, one of pianomakers, one of printers, one of bakers, one of smiths, and one of needlewomen. The "band of brothers" formed themselves into a Society for the Promotion of Workingmen's Associations to provide financial, legal and technical assistance. One member, Vansittart Neale, contributed his entire fortune of 60,000 pounds to help start associations and to make up operating deficits. Mistakes and deficits aplenty marked the effort. Enthusiasm was too often regarded as adequate counterpoise to incompetent management, careless screening of worker associates, inadequate planning and financing. At one point the Society had to insist that managers, who were elected by the working associates, must at least be able to read, write and do simple arithmetic.

Always Maurice was applying the brake, occasionally with good reason, but just as often with bad. The Society, composed of friends and supporters who all had other jobs, could not serve as a coordinating agency that would make sure the associations cooperated with each other to their mutual advantage. Ludlow therefore proposed a Central Board to represent them which would have power to insure a minimum of coordination. Maurice opposed it, and his reasons for doing so illustrate perfectly how he managed to conceal, from himself at least, a natural antipathy to organization and an inbred conservatism behind a veil of foggy theology. This is how he explained his opposition:

> Christian socialism is the assertion of God's order. Every attempt to bring it forth I honour and desire to assist. Every attempt to hide it under a great machinery, call it Organization of Labour [Louis Blanc's favorite phrase], Central Board, or what you like, I must protest against as hindering the gradual development of what I regard as a divine purpose, as an attempt to create a new constitution of society, when what we want is that the old constitution should exhibit its true function and energies.[24]

Ludlow, despite his reverence for Maurice, was smart enough to see through the fog. He wrote Kingsley: "This refusal is a serious affair, and if our Master has not the nerve to carry the thing out, some one must have it and soon."[25] Ludlow had it, and the Central Board was set up, but Maurice, going along reluctantly again, applied enough opposition to prevent it from having the kind of power that Ludlow and the other realists regarded as necessary.

Of course, Maurice was under pressure from conservative relatives and friends as well as the trustees of King's College. He and his Christian socialist brothers had made enough radical statements to send the right-wing press into paroxysms of abuse. A series of *Tracts of Christian Socialism* by the founders called forth reactions such as this:

> Tracts full of disreputable rant . . . mouthpieces of class selfishness, popular prejudice and ignorant passion . . . ravings of blasphemy . . . mischievous provocations clothed in oily phrases of peace and charity.[26]

We must, in the midst of our facile, post-mortem criticisms, give Maurice credit for risking as much as he did.

But his contributions to the sad story of what-might-have-been cannot be overlooked. The climax came in the case of the Amalgamated Society of Engineers, Machinists, Smiths, Millwrights and Patternmakers, usually known and hereafter referred to as the ASE. Thanks to the leadership of Robert Owen, the ideas of producer cooperation, socialism, and trade unionism had been linked from the beginning. The Christian socialists, at first, had discouraged this linkage. Even Ludlow had been infected with an antiunion bias, Maurice even more so, since he saw unions as class-war organizations sundering "the Universal Brotherhood" that should unite workers and employers. In a letter dated March 28, 1850, Maurice wrote:

> Every successful strike tends to give the workmen a very undue and dangerous sense of their own power, and a very alarming contempt for their employer, and . . . every unsuccessful strike drives them to desperate and wild courses.[27]

Walter Cooper and another effective Chartist leader, Lloyd Jones, joined the Christian socialists and were able to break down this isolation of the movement from the trade unions. Their greatest success was with the ASE, which in 1851 emerged as the largest and most powerful union in Great Britain. Cooper and Lloyd were able to interest the ASE's two competent leaders, William Newton and William Allen, in worker cooperatives as a practical way to reduce unemployment among their members and as a potential threat to be used in negotiations with the employers. Unfortunately, before they could set up any cooperatives of their own, the ASE leaders became embroiled in a battle to eliminate piecework and overtime. The union threatened a strike and the employers retaliated by locking out thirteen thousand workers in London and Lancashire. The ASE proposed binding arbitration by an impartial third party, but the employers responded with wild denunciations of "this conspiracy . . . an experiment of the dreams of Louis Blanc, embracing the visions of Owen and the extravagance of Fourier."[28]

Lord Goderich, one of the more attractive and progressive aristocrats among the Christian socialists, was moved to denounce this statement publicly in these words: "A more remarkable mixture of cold, hard greed and false, hypocritical sentimentality, has not for some time been sent forth by Mammon's worshippers."[29]

Faced with the lockout of its members, the ASE grew even more interested in worker cooperatives. Its paper, *The Operative* (January 1852) declared,

> The only remedy . . . is that the labourer should become a capitalist . . . making capital what it ought to be, the agent and instrument of labour, instead of what it is, the master, and too often the tyrant."[30]

Ludlow was ecstatic. This strong commitment to cooperation inspired him to scale the heights of Old Testament rhetoric in the pages of the *Journal of Association*:

> On, then, men of the Iron Trades, on! . . . Workmen of England, stand by the Associated Iron-Men! Their cause is your own! They are fighting your battle, and if I mistake not, they are fit to lead it. . . . [And] then shall be seen rising up in the midst of our country that city of the Future, of which only the practiced eye can discern a gateway here, and there a bit of wall, and here a watchtower for the seer, and there the frail huts of the builders, building as they of Jerusalem of old, with one hand only and a weapon in the other, building the temple of Brotherhood on the foundations of Righteousness, and yet accused of rebellion and sneered at for impotency by the Arabian and Ammonite without.[31]

The Christian socialists were unanimously in support of the ASE in its struggle against the lockout, with one fatal exception—Maurice. The employers had rejected arbitration and had even gone so far as to refuse to rehire any worker who would not sign a "yellow-dog contract," a declaration that he did not and would not belong to a trade union. Neale and his cousin, in close cooperation with the ASE, set up two cooperative workshops: the foundry in Cambridge Road, Mile End, and the Atlas Works, Southwark.

But the ASE needed even more help. Newton and Allen decided to call a meeting in London of representatives of all the unions, proposing to form one organization for joint action against the employers and also for "the realization of associated labour." They invited Maurice to preside. As a respected and eloquent representative of the Anglican establishment, as a confessed "Christian socialist," he was the natural choice.

Consider the opportunity that the ASE had here presented to Maurice and the Christian socialists. Consider the possible scenario if Maurice had gone to that meeting, convinced in heart and mind that justice lay, as it so clearly did, with the workers. Imagine him giving a speech only half as effective as the speech at Cranbourne Coffee Tavern that stunned the Chartist workers and reduced them to tears. It was all there. The undisputed leadership of the British workingclass was there for Maurice to pick up and hand over to Christian socialism. And what was his response to this invitation? In a letter dated February 21, 1852, to Kingsley he wrote:

> I am very anxious about the next step of the engineers. They purpose to call a meeting of all the trade societies [unions] to ask for their help and sympathy. They asked me, through Hughes, to preside. I said that if I had a case to go with, I would at once call on the Bishop of London and ask him what he would like me to do, but that I did not think that I had a case, that it seemed to me too much like throwing away the scabbard, and proclaiming that the war with capitalists was begun.[32]

"I did not think that I had a case." Incredible statement. The fact was that the *employers* had thrown away the scabbard and declared war on the organization of their employees, not in response to a strike, but simply in response to the threat of a justified strike against an iniquitous system of piecework and enforced overtime. Even if he had thought that he had a case, the idea of going to the bishop of London for permission to do something about it gives an indication of the state of Maurice's backbone at that moment. If only the heart, mind, and backbone of Ludlow had inhabited Maurice's body in the month of February 1852! What a difference it might have made for the history of Christian socialism, the English labor movement and the English church!

As it was, the meeting was held, was "densely crowded," and Vansittart Neale, the rich aristocrat who had spent his fortune for the worker cooperatives, presided. Unfortunately, he had been slightly infected by Maurice's caution, and he did not have the rhetorical ability to move anyone to tears. Nevertheless, the meeting voted to

> take such measures for the effectual organization of the trades as will ensure sufficient funds to conduct the present contest, and enable the workmen to establish themselves permanently in associative workshops.[33]

Other, larger meetings were held, the first steps of a united labor movement taken, the commitment to producer, worker cooperatives continued and was strengthened. But the immediate battle was lost. The ASE agreed to surrender on piecework and overtime if the employers would give up their insistence on the yellow-dog contracts, but even this was rejected. The workers crawled back and signed the contracts, which few had any intention of respecting.

The ASE, of course, recovered from the defeat and went on to become and remain one of the strongest and most influential unions in Great Britain. Nelson and Allen remained loyal to the cooperative movement, Neale and Hughes became leaders of the movement as it veered more and more toward the Rochdale emphasis on consumer as opposed to producer cooperatives.

THE DECLINE OF CHRISTIAN SOCIALISM

Christian socialism, however, having fumbled its great opportunity to weld the links of brotherhood and mutual support into an unbreakable chain binding it to the British labor movement, was on the way out. Maurice had made it clear that his idea of socialism was not one that could be reconciled with any realistic view of the class struggle and the realities of industrial life in England. Having killed *The Christian Socialist*, he went on to use his still powerful influence to disband "the band of brothers" and to kill the movement itself. The Society for the Promotion of Workingmen's Associations changed its name and then died, its last meeting taking place January 24, 1855.

By this time Maurice had been dismissed from the faculty of King's College because of his "heretical" notions about hell and heaven. He succeeded in switching the energies of most of the Christian socialists into the creation and maintenance of a Workingmen's College in London, which opened with one hundred twenty students on October 30, 1854, and has remained a successful educational institution to this day. This work was clearly more to Maurice's liking and abilities, and in his role as principal he made a valuable contribution, attracting such luminaries to the faculty as John Ruskin and Dante Gabriel Rossetti. They taught art.

Ludlow wrestled with the challenge of assuming leadership of the Christian socialist movement and keeping it alive. He finally decided it was too much for him. He was a small, shy man who never felt entirely at home, either with the workers or with the upper middle-class types who had been so important to its partial success, and he felt obligations to his wife and mother. He lost all his anti-union bias and served for a time as legal counsel of the ASE, but eventually became chief registrar of the Friendly Societies Office of the national government, in which capacity he was of significant value in promoting the legal interests of cooperatives, unions, and other benevolent organizations.

He swallowed his disappointment in Maurice and assisted him loyally in staffing and promoting the Workingmen's College, but the bitterness lingered like a bad taste. "So Mr. Maurice had his way," he wrote many years later in his unpublished *Autobiography*, "and the comparatively broad stream of Christian Socialism was turned into the narrow channel of a Workingmen's College."[34] And again:

Mr. Maurice himself at the time evidently did not feel . . . the crushing nature of the blow he was giving me. For to me the very bond of our friendship lay in the work to christianize Socialism. . . . But I saw that I was myself at fault; that I had wilfully blinded myself; that the Maurice I had devoted myself to was a Maurice of my own imagination, not the real Maurice. He was not to blame; I was.[35]

Ludlow did not entirely give up on Christian socialism, however. He maintained important contacts with kindred spirits in Germany and Denmark and in 1869 an article he wrote on German socialism attracted the attention of Karl Marx who, recognizing the rare combination of an Englishman who was sympathetic to the workers and fluent in German, sent him the first volume of *Das Kapital*, still untranslated, hoping for a review. Ludlow tried to read it, but he could not finish it and declared, somewhat hastily, that no Englishman would ever be able to read it, so heavy it was. Later he did review Marx's *The Eighteenth Brumaire of Louis Napoleon* and this was his shrewd analysis of the work and its author:

> Marx is an able, laborious, sharp-witted man . . . too really learned to be merely cynical, too cynically minded to make a favourable use of his learning; altogether a characteristic, clear-cut specimen of the German Reds, in whom righteous disbelief of the world's idols is not yet completed by belief in aught higher. . . . Marx's book is real history, full of thoughts, with all the facts ably and clearly marshalled, while the absence of favourable prejudice, whether as respects parties or individuals, gives it a position of acid impartiality.[36]

Ludlow lived to be ninety-one, long enough to become active again in the Christian socialist revival of the late Victorian period, and he served on the executive committee of the London branch of the Christian Social Union (CSU) from 1891 to 1903. One of the CSU founders, Scott Holland, recorded this memory of him:

> At the monthly meetings you would often see there a bent figure sitting with the face of one who had come out of other more heroic days. There was a nobility in the prophetic head which made the rest of us look very cheap. And now again when some pink, youthful, cheerful pessimist . . . had plunged us all into the abyss of despair, the old man would rise and shake with the passion of old days that forever haunted him with their wickedness and woe, and bid us cheer up. . . . The fire still gleamed in his eyes so that they shone with the passionate light which is only to be seen in men who have known Maurice. He quivered with an underground, volcanic vehemence which no years or gray hairs could tame; he was devoured by a great zeal for justice. We felt we were listening to the man Maurice found so hard to hold. . . . A deep, strong, noble soul, he retained to the last his democratic faith in the people, his passionate pity for the poor and downtrodden, his fiery cry for righteousness.[37]

I would suggest only one amendment to that account. That fire in Ludlow's eye was more likely not so much from knowing Maurice as from being restrained by Maurice from making that contribution to the poor and down-trodden that Ludlow was qualified to make.

Torben Christensen, the scholarly Dane, has written the best account of England's first Christian socialists, but his conclusion is too negative:

> Thus Maurice's final step to dissolve Christian Socialism as an organized force meant a personal tragedy for Ludlow. The man who above anyone else should be credited with the existence of Christian Socialism had become a broken man whose courage had deserted him when it came to striving for what he had regarded as his proper mission in life: to conquer the new industrial world for the Kingdom of Christ.[38]

I prefer the upbeat accent in the conclusion of an earlier historian, Gilbert Binyon:

> Largely through Ludlow's influence, there has been in England a comparative absence of that complete alienation between organized religion and the socialist movement which is all too common in the rest of the world.[39]

There is truth in both statements. After all, when you might have had a shot at the "Kingdom of Christ," who wants to settle for "a comparative absence of . . . complete alienation?"

THE GREAT REVIVAL

The ambiguities and paradoxes surrounding socialism and Christianity in England may be inferred from the following facts and quotations:

1. During the period between 1854 and 1877 virtually no organized socialist activity took place in Great Britain at all, and during this time Marx was resident in London. The period began with the demise of Christian activity and ended with the renewal of Christian activity in Stewart Headlam's Guild of St. Matthew.

2. At the height of the ensuing revival of British socialism, a leading Marxist, Ernest Bax, announced happily that Christianity had been a total failure. About the same time George Bernard Shaw (1856–1950), no martyr for the faith, wrote of that period, "Religion was alive again, coming back upon men, even upon clergymen, with such power that not the Church of England itself could keep it out."[40]

3. And yet, following the Lambeth Pan-Anglican Conference of 1888, three years before Leo XIII's *Rerum Novarum*, an encyclical letter from Lambeth signed by 145 bishops of that same Church of England deplored "excessive inequality in the distribution of this world's goods, vast accumulation and desperate poverty side by side" and insisted that "the Christian Church is bound, following the teaching of the Master, to aid every wise endeavor which

has for its object the material and moral welfare of the poor." In striking contrast to *Rerum Novarum,* the bishops added that the clergy should, in their preaching, show "how much of what is good and true in socialism is to be found in the precepts of Christ."[41]

4. And yet, in the poor sections of London only one in fifteen attended church regularly by the end of the century. Keir Hardie (1856–1915), leader of the Independent Labour Party, wrote in his paper, *The Labour Leader,*

> The Archbishop of Canterbury . . . said he had to devote seventeen hours a day to his work and had no time left in which to form opinions on how to solve the unemployment question. The religion which demands seventeen hours a day for organization and leaves no time for a single thought about starving and despairing men, women and children has no message for this age.[42]

5. And yet, after Hardie's death in 1915 a friend wrote of him, "Toward the end of his life he said that were he to live it again he would devote it to the advocacy of the Gospel of Christ."[43] Methodism alone produced over eighty full-time union leaders who owed their careers to Methodist experience and training.

6. And yet, Ben Tillett, leader of the great dock strike of 1889, had nothing but contempt for Frederick Temple, bishop of London at that time and later archbishop of Canterbury, who had sent Tillett a "brutal letter" about the struggling dockers.

7. And yet, Tillett, a Congregationalist, expressed great admiration for Cardinal Manning's "more humane and subtle" diplomacy in the same strike.[44] And Manning, despite Leo XIII's condemnation of socialism, publicly expressed admiration for a pro-socialist book by the Italian scholar and statesman Francesco Nitti (*Catholic Socialism*). William Temple, son of Frederick, also became archbishop of Canterbury and one of the great Christian socialists of the twentieth century.

During the period from 1877 to 1914 there were in England *over one dozen national and local Christian socialist organizations*. Two of these existed simultaneously in the Anglican Church; a third Anglican organization, the largest of them all, though not explicitly socialist, counted many militant socialists among its leaders.

THE GUILD OF ST. MATTHEW (1877–1914)

The man who founded and dominated the Guild of St. Matthew, a socialist organization of the Anglican Church, was the Rev. Stewart Headlam (1847–1924). One of those who tried unsuccessfully to challenge his domination was the Rev. Henry Shuttleworth (1850–1900). The Rev. Scott Holland (1847–1918), a fellow Anglican, who founded the larger but vaguer Christian Social Union, called those two "Headlong and Shuttlecock."

The two were a sort of composite model for Shaw's clergyman in *Candida*.

Peter Jones summarizes Shaw's portrayal, especially as it related to Shuttle-worth. I quote at length, partly because it presents an interesting portrait of a typical Christian socialist of that period and partly because it reveals Shaw's awareness of Christian socialism. This awareness was itself a significant factor in the intellectual life of the period and was expressed sympathetically in the preface to *Androcles and the Lion*. Though Shaw dismisses Jesus' claim to be God as "psychopathic delusion," he still concludes, "Decidedly, whether you think Jesus was God or not, you must admit that he was a first-rate political economist."[45] Herewith Jones's summary of *Candida's* stage directions:

> Reverend James Mavor Morell is also terribly charming and popular, a little too good to be true (or too good for his own good), artistic and vain ("a great baby") . . . and Shaw pits against him (as a possible rival for his wife's affections) the self-seeking poet Marchbanks, in Shaw's own words "a dramatic antagonist for the clear, bold, sure, sensible, benevolent, salutarily short-sighted Christian Socialist idealism" of Morell. In one of his brilliant and characteristically detailed stage directions Shaw sets the Headlam-Shuttleworth scene: "An adept eye can measure the parson's casuistry and divinity by Maurice's *Theological Essays* and a complete set of Browning's poems, and the reformer's politics by a yellow-backed *Progress and Poverty, Fabian Essays, A Dream of John Ball,* Marx's *Capital. . . .*" On stage Morell "glances through Mr. Stewart Headlam's leader and the Guild of St. Matthew news in the *Church Reformer* between planning talks to anarchists and countless other self-imposed social duties.[46]

Shaw's stage directions are virtually an outline of Christian socialism in England. Headlam was a student of Maurice at Cambridge and from him he gratefully derived the conviction that a Christian need not believe in hell. *Progress and Poverty* by the American Single Taxer Henry George was very popular in England following its publication there in 1880 and greatly influenced most of the English socialists, both secular and religious, including Headlam—especially Headlam. George was a popular lecturer in England. At a farewell banquet for him in 1884 Headlam went so far as to declare that private property in land was in oppostion both to the Ten Commandments and to the teaching and life of Jesus Christ. How he did this is not clear, since "Thou shalt not steal" has traditionally been a conservative's first and last refuge.

The Fabian Society was probably the most influential socialist organization in England, especially among the intellectuals, and many Christian socialists belonged to it. Seven of them, including Headlam, served on its executive committee at one time or another, and several contributed to *Fabian Essays. A Dream of John Ball* was writtten by William Morris, author of the popular utopian phantasy *News from Nowhere*. Ball (d. 1381) was one of John Wycliffe's Poor Preachers who made famous the text: "When Adam dalf [delved] and Eve span,/ Who was thanne a gentilman?" Ball supported Wat

Tyler and the Peasant Rebellion of 1381 and for his support lost his head in the presence of Richard II.

The Church Reformer was the newspaper of the Guild of St. Matthew, called elsewhere by Shaw "one of the best socialist journals." "Leader" is the British word for leading editorial. The paper died in 1895, though the Guild kept going to 1909. Shaw's characterization of his parson as "a great baby" could not have been meant to apply to Headlam. He was a complex character, but basically tough. He worked for years in the slums of London. He loved the theater and organized a Church and Stage guild for chorus girls. Keir Hardie described him as "a dapper little gentleman puffing contentedly on a big cigar" and added, "As a Scotsman and a Non-Conformist I well remember the shock it gave me that the leading member of the Guild [of St. Matthew] divided his attention fairly evenly between socialism and the ballet."[47]

Though small like Ludlow, Headlam did not share his introspective shyness. Percy Dearmer, another socialist Anglican parson, wrote of Headlam to a friend, "I wish I had his lovely manners."[48] Headlam had courage to match his manners. Already in trouble with Bishop Temple for his unorthodox views about hell, Headlam did not hesitate to rebuke the bishop for failing to support the London Matchgirls Strike of 1888 and referred to him in print as "the rich, hard, narrow Bishop." . . . [49]

Perhaps his greatest act of courage was his decision to stand bail for Oscar Wilde (1854–1900) when Wilde was tried for sodomy in 1895, although he hardly knew him at the time. Headlam's own wife was a lesbian, and this was a factor in leading him to brave the fury and hostility displayed by Victorian London toward Wilde and himself.

In areas other than hell Headlam was theologically conservative, believed in the Real Presence of Christ in the Eucharist and liked to speak of his movement as "sacramental socialism." In the following typical passage, the reader may detect a preview of Harvey Cox's *The Secular City*:

> In the worship of Jesus really present in the Sacrament of the Altar before you, all human hearts can join, and especially secularists, for when you worship Him you are worshipping the Saviour, the social and political Emancipator, the greatest of all secular workers, the founder of the great socialistic society for the promotion of righteousness, the preacher of a revolution, the denouncer of kings, the gentle, tender sympathizer with the rough and the outcast who could utter scathing, burning words against the rich, the respectable, the religious.[50]

An uncompromising egalitarian in most of his work and words, who hated all class distinctions and the "aristocracy of intellect" as well as of land or family, Headlam still insisted on limiting the Guild to members of the Anglican Church and narrowed his appeal even further by opposing Hardie's Independent Labour Party (ILP). He shared a Maurician, elitist distrust of any party that relied mainly on the workers for its constituency. And yet he believed strongly in political action and tended to disparage as utopian the efforts of those who, following Buchez and Ludlow, preached the virtues of producer cooperation, as in the following:

> While showing all respect for cooperative shirtmakers and cooperative decorators, and for the many little communistic societies of monks and nuns and for all other little private experiments, we at the same time call upon churchmen to take a wider view, and advocate and support such legislation as will help to remedy private evils.[51]

That second "little" gives away the show of "all respect."

THE CHRISTIAN SOCIAL UNION (1889–1919)

Headlam's stand against the ILP, his militant opposition to church schools and support for an exclusively secular system of public education (which gave rise to Shuttleworth's rebellion), his brave gesture in aid of Oscar Wilde, and his authoritarian style of leadership all worked against the growth of his Guild. The membership never exceeded four hundred nationally, of which, in its peak year of 1895, more than 25 percent were clergymen.

Jones, in a military metaphor that seems slightly exaggerated, concludes that "Stewart Headlam and his disciples were the shock troops of sacramental socialism. The Christian Social Union was the army of occupation."[52] Anyone who has tried to interest Christians in social reform has to be impressed, however, with the CSU's success. At one point it had six thousand members and, of the fifty-three men appointed Anglican bishops between 1889 and 1913, sixteen were members of CSU, appointed by Liberal prime ministers like Gladstone and Asquith as well as Conservatives like Cecil and Balfour.

The two most influential leaders were Holland and Charles Gore (1853–1932), a lean, aristocratic, saintly High Churchman who became successively bishop of Worcester, Birmingham, and Oxford. G. K. Chesterton (1874–1936) wrote a delightful poem about a CSU meeting in Nottingham as seen by a local tradesman. Chesterton was one of the speakers and included himself in the lampoon, but this was his summary of Gore and Holland:

> Then Bishop Gore of Birmingham
> He stood upon one leg
> And said he would be happier
> If beggars didn't beg,
> And that if they pinched his palace
> It would take him down a peg.
>
> He said that unemployment
> Was a horror and a blight,
> He said that charities produced
> Servility and spite,
> And stood upon the other leg
> And said it wasn't right . . . .

Then Canon Holland fired ahead
Like fifty cannons firing,
We tried to find out what he meant
With infinite enquiring,
But the way he made the windows jump
We couldn't help admiring . . . .

He said the human soul should be
Ashamed of every sham,
He said a man should constantly
Ejaculate, "I am."
When he had done, I went outside
And got into a tram.[53]

The same poem includes these lines about Holland, "He said he was a Socialist himself,/ And so was God." Although Chesterton was later to become an important antisocialist, he retained great admiration for Holland and in his *Autobiography*, immediately after the above, adds,

He was a man of great clearness and fairness of mind, and what he said always meant something and was a result of the unpopular sport of thinking. . . . He was also a man with a natural surge of laughter within him.[54]

As time went on, militant members, such as Conrad Noel (1869–1942), grew impatient with the vagueness of the Union's program and moved away in different directions. Noel described the union as "forever learning but never coming to a knowledge of the truth."[55] Even Holland lamented that in CSU debates

no subject may be introduced which "sets class against class." . . . The city branch may safely discuss rural housing; the rural branches will do well to discuss town planning. . . . This policy is the main cause of our weakness.[56]

Despite that weakness the Christian Social Union attracted many of the best and most intelligent Christians of England, and there is no doubt that it was the major vehicle by which the Social Gospel arrived in that country. As such it remains a key factor in the development of Christian socialism in the English-speaking world.

THE CHURCH SOCIALIST LEAGUE (1906–1924)

Unlike Paris, London at that time was not a capital that was also the industrial center of the country. England's industrial centers were—and are—

mostly in the north—in Manchester, Liverpool, Newcastle-on-Tyne. It was in cities like these that the Christian Social Union's aristocratic parsons from Oxford and Cambridge seemed most irrelevant, and some of those same parsons, like Noel and W. E. Moll (?1857–1932), realized their irrelevance and took steps to change things. Moll left London to take a poor working-class parish in Newcastle, where Noel later joined him, and both became active in socialist politics, Moll sitting on the national committee of Hardie's ILP and Noel on the executive committee of the British Socialist Party, an amalgam of left-wingers from the ILP and from H. L. Hyndman's Marxist Social Democratic Party (SDP). While serving as a curate at Moll's church on the Tyne, Noel preached openly against the Boer War (1899–1902) to munitions workers, who then threatened to blow up Moll's church.

Moll, a hard-shell anti-imperialist himself, reassured Noel, "My dear Noel, by all means let it go on, as it is the truth; and if we lose our church, which is the ugliest structure in Newcastle, we can build a new one with the insurance money."[57]

Noel, a grandson of Lady Gainsborough, was one of the great Christian socialist characters of all time. "No priest in the country," said fellow socialist Rev. P. E. T. Widdrington,

> could claim so wide a knowledge of the Labour movement. His name was familiar in every industrial area . . . . In ILP branches and Labour Churches [the Labour Church was a peculiar form of non-Christan religion] his lectures and debates created a deep impression and a friendliness which did much to remove the suspicion in Labour circles that the Church was hostile.[58]

In hot water with the bishops, Noel shuffled from one assignment to another, but finally, in 1910, received a church at Thaxted from the hand of the aristocratic socialist who controlled it, the Countess of Warwick. There he remained for thirty years, until his death in 1942. He made of Thaxted a lively center of High Church radicalism, displaying the Red Flag and the green banner of the Sinn Fein, attracting Gustav Holst to train his choir and a Marxist from Hyndman's SDP, George Chambers, to be his first curate.

Noel lashed out in all directions. Time was, he wrote in *The Church Socialist* in February 1912, that the worst social hindrances were "the Bishops, the Brewers and the Brothels, [but] . . . our deadliest foes now are the Daily Press, the Liberal Government, the Party System and the Religious Newspapers."[59] Journals like the *Church Times* "call evil good and good evil, and champion a materialism more deadly than that of Marx under the specious cloak of next-worldliness."[60]

Despite his radical eccentricity Noel had a sound and clear idea of the dividing line that must separate politics and religion when a minister of God enters the pulpit. He expressed it in a letter to the parishioners before he took over at Thaxted:

By my ordination I am bound to preach that God's kingdom and will shall come and be done on earth. I am bound to point out all things that offend against that kingdom, and to urge upon you the sole duty of hastening the coming of that divine kingdom by public spiritedness and personal reformation. If this be called preaching politics from the pulpit, then I am a political preacher. But if by politics people mean party politics, then I want at once to assure you that I do not intend to advocate the solution of our evils, which is called socialism, from the pulpit of Thaxted Church. . . . Why? Because, although the preacher must from time to time deal with public as well as private evils, I do not think he has any right to urge upon his people either the Liberal, or the Conservative, or the Socialist method of dealing with those evils. . . . It is the business . . . of the clergyman to stir up people's hearts and consciences, to help inflame them with a passion for personal and social righteousness, to implore them to consider their commerce, their home, their politics in the light of their religion. But it is for themselves, each one of them, to apply the principles laid down in church to the problems of life. . . . [The clergyman] has no right, as preacher, to force upon his people his particular solution of our public difficulties. *Besides it would be unfair of him to do so in a pulpit where no man can discuss with him or answer him.* If a clergyman feels strongly one way or the other about politics, when he has made friends with his people, why should he not talk these matters over with them in a friendly way, just as one of themselves? In this way, as well as by meetings and conferences, we may study questions of public interest, and learn how to serve our country wisely and effectively [emphasis added].[61]

Noel wrote the first comprehensive history of Christian socialism, at least as far as he (and I) were (and are) aware. The book, *Socialism in Church History*, published in England in 1910 and in America the following year, is a fairly competent job, but flawed by several assumptions that are false or at least dubious. One is the assumption that the taking of *any* interest on financial loans is a serious sin. The frequent reiteration of this opinion gives the book an air of unreality. Another assumption is even more serious. On the first page of the first chapter Noel writes,

All socialists, however much they may differ on other points, are in absolute agreement on one point, and that point is their socialism.

He quotes as a universal norm the definition of the Church Socialist League, which he helped to found:

Socialism is the principle according to which the community shall own the land and industrial capital collectively and use them cooperatively for the good of all.[62]

This definition covered the belief of *most* English socialists, both secular and Christian, in 1910, but certainly not all, and it was totally inaccurate as a description of the socialism of Ludlow, Buchez, and virtually all the pre-Marxist socialists of both England and France. Even Louis Blanc's collectivism did not go this far. Robert Owen would not have accepted it. In 1906, four years before Noel published his book, a prominent Christian socialist architect, A. J. Penty (1875–1937), published a book, *The Restoration of the Gild* [sic] *System*, which set off a revival of that notion of worker ownership and control that had characterized the first socialists. Unfortunately, the Fabian Society, dominated by Shaw and the Webbs, had done an effective job of selling the Marxist notion of public ownership, even though they rejected other Marxist notions of revolution and economic determinism.

Noel is clearly familiar with the *theology* of Maurice and Kingsley, and knows they did not agree with his idea of socialism, but he mentions neither Ludlow nor Buchez nor the workers' cooperatives organized by those pioneers. The emphasis on "state socialism," which characterized the Victorian revival, and the idea that socialism necessarily involves a public takeover of farms and every kind of productive enterprise, was then and is today an important factor in alienating the Christian population of the Western world. Historically, I cannot repeat too often, this statist approach was a later idea of socialism that was largely but not totally successful in replacing an earlier and sounder idea. The later idea eventually became flesh in Russia and China, which have now forced thinking socialists to re-examine the earlier idea.

Noel and Moll had both been members of Headlam's Guild of St. Matthew, Noel of the CSU as well, and in 1906 they joined with other dissatisfied members of both organizations to form a new, more radical, more political, more pro-labor, more socialist, but still Anglican organization that they called the Church Socialist League.

Among the other founders were a group of militant monks from the Community of the Resurrection, a religious foundation started by Bishop Gore at Oxford but later settled at Mirfield in the northern county of York. The leaders were Fathers Paul Bull and J. N. Figgis.

The CSL counted about twelve hundred members in its peak year of 1912. It had important strength in the industrial centers of northern England but also boasted seventeen branches in London alone. Its motto, "Christianity is the religion of which socialism is the practice,"[63] was contributed by the Rev. Frederick Donaldson, who led a spectacular march of the unemployed from Leicester to London in 1905, starting off to the strains of *Lead Kindly Light* and the cheers of a crowd of a hundred thousand, who lined the streets of the depressed city. Arriving in London a week later, they discovered that "everybody whom they had come to find was out of town, except the Archbishop, and he alas would not see them."[64]

CSL's first president, Rev. G. Algernon West, wanted to affiliate the League with the Socialist International abroad and the Labour Party at home, a party that was slowly evolving from the chaotic divisions of the English left. At the

Leicester conference of 1909, West's proposal was voted down and West resigned.

Opposition, meanwhile, began to develop within the CSL to the collectivist tendency of the leaders. This opposition eventually coalesced into a movement known as Guild Socialism, a many-sided-and-splendored thing, which, in the words of one of its CSL spokesmen, Maurice Reckitt, combined

the craftsman's challenge and the blazing democracy of William Morris; the warning of Mr. Belloc against the huge shadow of the servile state, and perhaps, something also of his claim of the individual's control over property; the insistence of Mr. Penty on the evils of industrialism and its large-scale organization; . . . something of French syndicalism, with its championship of the producer, something of American industrial unionism, with its clear vision of the need of industrial organization; and something of Marxian socialism, with its unsparing analysis of the wage-system by which capitalism exalts itself and enslaves the mass of men.[65]

Reckitt joined the Church Socialist League in 1908 and for several years served as editor of its newspaper, *The Church Socialist*. He wrote several books about Guild Socialism, but in his autobiography, published in 1941, by which time he had long since ceased to be a socialist, he makes this incredible statement,

None of the ideas [of Guild Socialism] . . . were present, or at any rate conspicuous, in the Socialist philosophy before the Guild propaganda arose to challenge it.[66]

The only explanation for such a statement is that Reckitt thinks of socialism, by his own confession, "as popularized in England by Keir Hardie and [Ramsay] MacDonald, or Shaw and the Webbs." Reading on, one is therefore not surprised to find no mention of Ludlow, Buchez, or the workingmen's associations. This is also true of the book Reckitt published in 1918 with C. E. Bechhofer, *The Meaning of National Guilds*. (It is also true of books on Guild socialism by S. G. Hobson and G. D. H. Cole.)[67] This ignorance of, and/or indifference to, the rich tradition of French and English socialism, both secular and Christian, on the part of leading Christian socialists of that period is one of the more baffling features of the period. Ignorance of, or indifference to, French socialism is perhaps understandable; ignorance of, or indifference to, the English socialism of the Owenites is less so; ignorance of, or indifference to, the Christian socialism of Ludlow and the Society for the Promotion of Workingmen's Associations is incomprehensible.

Reckitt joined with Hobson and Cole, the socialist historian, to form the

National Guilds League in 1915, and this organization attracted many Christian socialists who were turned off by the collectivist, state-oriented tendency of Fabian and Marxist brands of socialism. Cole, its most brilliant advocate, unfortunately blunted the attraction by introducing the idea that parliamentary representation should be abolished and replaced by functional representation through the Guild system. As finally developed, the aims of the Guild League were listed as "the abolition of the Wage System and the establishment of self-government in industry through a system of National Guilds working in conjunction with the state."[68] They also promoted a strong emphasis on the trade unions as providing the nucleus for the Guilds. This amalgam of sensible and not-so-sensible ingredients highlights a recurring difficulty with the socialist movement. In exaggerated form the difficulty was expressed by the anti-socialist-historian-of-socialism Alexander Gray when he wrote of William Godwin, the anarchist father-in-law of the poet Shelley,

> Never was there anyone who was more the embodiment of intellect and reason. . . . It follows from this peculiarly intellectual bias that he was utterly destitute of common sense.[69]

This weakness is so common in the history of both socialism and Christianity that by way of shorthand I will refer to it hereinafter as "Godwin's disease."

Socialism has been for the most part the creation of intellectuals, and Christian socialism in England the creation, mainly, of intellectual clergymen. Buchez was a doctor and Ludlow a lawyer. Both had more knowledge of ordinary life than clergymen, and both realized early on that they must test their theories in the crucible of everyday working-class experience. I think it follows from these circumstances that there is a better ratio of common sense to idealism in their proposals than in that of many other of their socialist comrades.

Bernard Shaw is a good example of those comrades. He gives the nod to common sense when he writes, "Most theories will work if you put your back into making them work, provided they have some point of contact with human nature."[70] How much one can expect people to put their backs into making a theory work if it has only a *slight* contact with human nature is, of course, another question. A serious question arises with Shaw. A few pages before the sentence quoted above he had written, "It was believed that you could not make men good by act of Parliament. We now know that you cannot make them good in any other way."[71] As you might expect from that sentiment, which was shared in a less absolute way by the Webbs, all three eventually became, as Anne Fremantle puts it, "senile dupes of Soviet Communism, because they loved good blueprints, and Soviet blueprints are admirable; they only suffer from being untranslatable into comparable action."[72]

Guild socialism was upstaged by World War I and then by the Russian Revolution and then by all the intellectual confusions that flowed from those events and the further development of capitalism. It could stand another look today as we grope for more attractive alternatives to the dominant systems of the Soviet Union and the United States.

THE CHESTERBELLOC VS. THE SHAWELLS

Let us return to 1907 and what may well have been the turning point that marks the beginning of the post-World War I decline of Christian socialism in England. In its issue of December 7 of that year, the socialist weekly *The New Age* printed an article by Hilaire Belloc (1870–1953) that touched off a brilliant, funny debate between Belloc and G. K. Chesterton on the one side and Shaw and H. G. Wells (1866–1946) on the other.

These were probably the four most popular and widely read writers of the time in England, and among the most popular in the English-speaking world. Belloc and Chesterton were certainly the most articulate champions of Christianity in England at that time, though Belloc's view of Christianity was badly distorted by anti-Semitism. Chesterton, then thirty-three years old, had been a socialist, a member both of the Guild of St. Matthew and of the Christian Social Union. He was still a devout Anglican, not becoming a Roman Catholic until 1922, largely under the influence of his dear friend Belloc. Belloc, in addition to being a witty versifier and an all-purpose writer of history and fiction, was at this time a Liberal member of Parliament and a few years later was to write an influential book, *The Servile State*. Maurice Reckitt said of it, "I cannot overestimate the impact of this book upon my mind, and in this I was but symptomatic of thousands of others."[73] Without question Belloc deserves major credit for turning both Reckitt and Chesterton away from the socialist camp, and with them, thousands of other Christians who were either in it or thinking seriously of joining it. In his initial article Belloc identifies socialism with collectivism and then adds,

> The criticism I offer to collectivism is offered by the whole weight and mass of Catholic opinion . . . by all that is healthy and permanent in the intellectual life of Europe. . . . The sentiment of property is normal to and necessary to a citizen. . . . The divorce of personality from production is inhuman, and of itself just as inhuman when it is effected by collectivism with a charitable object as when it is effected by the present industrial system with an immoral and selfish object.

Chesterton comes to Belloc's support with a front-page piece on January 4, 1908, under the title "Why I Am Not a Socialist." He seconds Belloc's "expression of ordinary human disgust at the industrial system" and adds, "No one but Satan or Beelzebub could like the present state of wealth and poverty." To the socialist writers he says, "You have left certain human needs out of your books; you may leave them out of your republic." Speaking of the common people and their "instinctive aversion to socialism," he notes,

Individualism was imposed on them by a handful of merchants; socialism will be imposed on them by a handful of decorative artists and
Oxford dons and journalists and countesses on the spree.

He dislikes the socialists' "talk about the inevitable, the love of statistics, the
materialist theory of history, the trivialities of sociology, the uproarious folly of
eugenics." He concludes, "I am not a socialist, just as I am not a Tory, because I
have not lost faith in democracy."

A week later Wells enters the discussion in defense of socialism, but emphasizing his agreements with Belloc and Chesterton: "We all three want . . . the
fullest and freest development of individual life . . . . We all three want people
to have property of a real and personal sort." Presumably he meant such things
as house, garden, and consumer goods.

Our real difference is only about a little more or a little less owning. . . . State or Plutocrat, there is really no other practical alternative
before the world at the present time. . . . The organized Christian state
of [Belloc and Chesterton] is nearer the organized state I want than our
present plutocracy. Our ideals will fight some day . . . but to fight now
is to let the enemy in.

Wells pleads for "a working political combination between the socialist
members in Parliament and just that noncapitalist section of the Liberal Party
for which Chesterton and Belloc speak." He concludes,

Chesterton isn't a Socialist—agreed. But which side is he on? I want [a
Utopia] from Chesterton. . . . It isn't fair for him to go about sitting on
other people's Utopias. . . . It isn't an adequate reply to say that nobody
stood treat, and that the simple, generous people like to beat their wives
and children on occasion in a loving and intimate manner, and that they
won't endure the spirit of Sidney Webb.

On January 25, 1908, Chesterton responded to this with a somewhat slight
contribution entitled "On Wells and a Glass of Beer." His major point:

Liberalism must come before Socialism. Brown must be a citizen and
have a certain spirit, and all these things shall be added unto
him. . . . What influences will give him this spirit? There are many
reasonable answers; but one of our answers is—property.

Belloc chipped in with a further elaboration of this point two weeks later:

What constitutes our modern economic trouble . . . is the disproportion
in control of the means of production; for with the means of production
in few hands, no one is secure except those few who own.

He might have added "or control," and he would have scored a clean hit both on the plutocrats and the centralized state collectivists.

The following week Shaw, a regular contributor of money and articles to *The New Age*, finally joined the fray with a piece entitled "The Chesterbelloc":

> The Chesterbelloc is European democracy, is the Catholic Church, is the Life Force, is the very voice of the clay of which Adam was made, and on which the Catholic peasant labors. . . . Wells' challenge to Chesterton is irresistible: he must plank down his Utopia against ours. . . . Now Chesterton and Belloc have their failings like other men. They share one failing . . . addiction to the pleasures of the table. As to Wells, his Utopia is dismally starved. There is not even a mound of buttered toast in it. . . . What this must mean to Chesterton no words of mine can express. Belloc would rather die than face it.

(Both Chesterton and Belloc were stout-bellied men.)

A lesser man might have wilted before the Shavian wit, but Chesterton was equal to the task. In the issue of February 29, 1908, he disarms his adversaries with flattery—"the two most brilliant writers alive"—and continues with some effective thrusts at the chinks in their armor:

> Shaw and Wells are two men of genius. Chesterton and Belloc is mankind. The two best jokes against us, as uttered by the best jester of the age, are also jokes against mankind. . . . We believe in the naturalness of drinking fermented liquor and in the possibility of miracles. . . . The proposed abolition of personal property (Socialism) has its only practical parallel in teetotalism, the abolition of normal drink. . . . We do not "plank down" a Utopia, because Utopia is a thing uninteresting to a thinking man; it assumes that all evils come from outside the citizen and none from inside him. But we do "plank down" these much more practical statements: (1) that a man will not be humanly happy unless he owns something in the sense that he can play the fool with it; (2) that this can only be achieved by setting steadily to work to distribute property, not to concentrate it; (3) that history proves that property can be so distributed and remain so distributed, while history has no record of successful collectivism outside monasteries.

Comment: "Play the fool" can be a costly condition, especially with greedy fools.

On March 21 Belloc joined the counterattack with this:

> I want someone to tell me why a social system in which the legal control of modern means of production was widely distributed among the citizens would not endure? It is irrelevant to say that redistribution in a

congested state is much harder to effect than further centralization. If I show a man a way to get slowly out of debt and he says, "It wouldn't work, so I'll cut my throat," and then adds, "It would be quicker to cut my throat," his replies betray muddleheadedness.

Wells responded in the next issue:

Belloc's question would be answered in the affirmative did he omit the word "modern". . . . Belloc's proposal as an alternative to socialism is simply the suggestion of the least efficient as against the most efficient way of managing wholesale production, and all to meet an alleged passion in the individual to "own."

Belloc had the last word on May 2, but it was not really an effective response to Wells's objection that the Chesterbelloc's plea for a return to handicrafts, small shops, and family farms would not meet the demands of modern production. In 1926, eighteen years later, Belloc and Chesterton, and Reckitt, organized the Distributist League and publicized it in their books and in *G. K.'s Weekly*. Though it had some initial success and exerted influence in such far-flung corners as *The Catholic Worker* movements in the United States and Australia, the Antigonish movement in Canada, and the *Free America* movement of Herbert Agar, Ralph Borsodi, and Monsignor Luigi Ligutti, it never improved very much on Belloc's inadequate response of 1908, or Chesterton's appeal to a history of small-scale production that could no longer meet the challenges of modern technology and large-scale industrial organization.

"History has no record of successful collectivism outside monasteries." This was Chesterton's challenge to socialism as Shaw, Wells and the Webbs (and Marx) defined it. And assuming a belief that Russia and China, despite their success as formidable survivors, have not achieved success as societies that meet minimum requirements in the areas of freedom and human fulfillment, or efficiency, one would have to concede that Shavian socialism has not met Chesterton's challenge any more effectively than the Chesterbelloc met that of Shaw and Wells.

I have dwelt on this debate at length, not simply because it is a fascinating episode in the history of socialism, but because it is, I firmly believe, a key episode in the history of *Christian* socialism. At one point Shaw, who despite all this remained a good friend of Chesterton, complains about the influence on the latter of an even better friend: "For Belloc's sake Chesterton says he believes in the Bible story of the Resurrection. For Belloc's sake he says he is not a socialist.[74] One wonders how much Belloc's hostility to socialism derived from Leo XIII's simplistic treatment of socialism in *Rerum Novarum*. The key role played by the question of the *alleged* incompatibility of Catholic notions of private property and socialism in both *Rerum Novarum* and *The New Age* debate would seem to answer, "considerably, if not more so."

The central questions posed by the debate—and especially the questions revolving around the great P's, property, power, and personality, and their relation to those other P's, poverty and politics—remained, and still remain, the questions that have plagued socialism, both secular and Christian, almost as much as they have plagued capitalism. The passage of time has supplied some answers that seem more satisfying than those of the Chesterbelloc or the Shawells, but these will have to wait for a later chapter. Meanwhile, we resume our history.

OTHER ORGANIZATIONS

Peter Jones, in his excellent account of English Christian socialism between 1877 and 1914, describes two more Anglican organizations—Conrad Noel's Catholic Crusade and the League of the Kingdom of God, organized by Reckitt and other Anglicans attracted to Guild Socialism. He also names seven "non-conformist" organizations (Methodist, Baptist, etc.): the Christian Socialist Society (Rev. C. I. Marson and W. H. P. Campbell), the Christian Socialist League (Rev. John Clifford, a popular Baptist preacher); its direct successor, the Christian Social Brotherhood, the Christian Socialist Fellowship (an English branch of an American group), the New Church Socialist Society (Swedenborgian) the Socialist Quaker Society, and the Free Church Socialist League.

The most famous member of the last-named was Philip Snowden (1864–1937), a Methodist weaver's son who became a member of several Labour Party cabinets in the 1920's and 1930's. He was a kind of freewheeling Christian, but coined one aphorism that might rank with the best as a summary of the gospel: "Personal Salvation and Social Salvation are like two palm trees which bear no fruit unless they grow side by side."[75] In his *Autobiography* Snowden tells a story about himself that speaks volumes about English socialism:

> A working-class socialist from the town of Wibsey, chairman of a labor meeting in the 1890's, instructed his speaker: "Now look here, Fred. Tha' knows they're an ignorant lot at Wibsey, so don't be trying any of that scientific socialism. We want no Karl Marx and surplus value and that sort of stuff. Make it plain and simple. Tha' can put in a long word now and then so as to make them think tha' knows a lot, but keep it simple, and then when tha'rt coming to finishing up, tha' mun put a bit of Come-to-Jesus' in, *like Philip does.*"[76]

Despite the Vatican's hostility to socialism a few Catholic Socialist Leagues did exist, notably in Leeds. One was also founded in Glasgow in 1906 among Irish immigrant workers. The Catholic Social Guild was a kind of Catholic equivalent of the Christian Social Union.

Jones believes that all of these organizations, plus the Progressive League (1907–1910), a vehicle for the spellbinding Congregationalist, Rev. R. J. Campbell and his socialist New Theology, did not all together equal the membership or the influence of the three major Anglican organizations, the Guild of St. Matthew, the Christian Social Union, and the Church Socialist League.

His conclusion about this revival, which had pretty much petered out by the 1920's, is both positive and negative. These Christian socialists, though more labor-oriented and involved than the Mauricians, "failed in the end to break through the class barrier and to make sustained and successful communication with the urban masses."[77] Still, echoing Binyon's judgment about Ludlow, their successful effort to make Great Britain conscious of the Social Gospel did help "to prevent the total and final alienation of Church and people, although it could not prevent the continuing erosion of the Christian faith."[78]

A SOCIALIST ARCHBISHOP

William Temple (1881–1944) managed both to violate and to observe the minister's-son-reacts-against-father syndrome. He violated it by following, career-wise, in his father's footsteps to an almost carbon-copy degree: Oxford don, school headmaster, minister, canon, bishop, to the top of the British hierarchy as archbishop of Canterbury. He observed it by reacting against his father's more conservative and cautious stance on social and economic questions. He joined the Labour Party in 1918, but resigned from it three years later upon appointment as Bishop of Manchester, for which Tawney chided him. He apparently felt that as a bishop he should not identify himself publicly with a political party, which leads one to wonder if an Anglican Bishop ever resigned from the Conservative Party for that reason. (An English wit once called the Anglican Church "the Conservative Party at prayer.")

In his youth, 1908, he had gone so far as to write: "The alternative stands before us—socialism or heresy . . . *Socialism* is the economic realization of the Christian Gospel."[79] He drew back from this hard line in later years. In his major work, *Christianity and Social Order*, he put the choice differently: "The question now is not—shall we be socialists or shall we be individualists? But how socialist and how individualist shall we be?"[80] But this book, published in 1942, two years before his death, makes it clear that, even as the highest ranking prelate in the Anglican Church, he remained in heart and mind a Christian socialist.

Temple also reacted against his father by supporting a strike of national importance—the great Coal Strike of 1926, which followed and was directly related to the disastrous General Strike of that year. He may have remembered Ben Tillett, leader of the Dock Strike of 1889, chastising the elder Bishop Temple for the "brutal letter" he had written about the strikers.

William Temple took pains to write no brutal letters to the coal strikers. He was out of the country when the strike broke, but, unlike his father, who left the country during the dock strike, he hurried back to join a group of fellow bishops who were urging the government and the mine owners to try a little harder to settle the strike.

Stanley Baldwin, the Conservative prime minister, asked publicly how the bishops would like it if he referred to the Iron and Steel Federation a revision of the Athanasian Creed. Joseph Fletcher notes in his biography that in his response "Temple heatedly repudiated any pietistic divorce of Christian duty and social concerns."[81]

Temple, one of the most intelligent and articulate men to head the Church of England, also displayed intelligence in his career as a socialist. In his youth, as at the Pan-Anglican Congress in London in 1908, the year of the Chesterbelloc-Shawells debate, he reflected the socialist bias of the time when he declared, "The Christian is called to assent to great steps in the direction of collectivism."[82] The Congress, incidentally, which represented Anglican and Episcopalian churches from all over the world, concluded that " 'capitalism' was both immoral and unmoral."

By the time of the Malvern Conference of 1941, which Fletcher calls "the most dramatic episode in Temple's history," his knowledge of life, his observations of Soviet aberrations and his familiarity with Christian tradition had brought him to a more balanced, nuanced vision of socialism.

Fletcher wrote:

> He agreed with St. Ambrose "—a great officer of State as well as a Bishop"—that common use is natural and that usurpation and avarice caused private property. For this reason almsgiving is an act of justice rather than of mercy. But he held with Ambrose and Augustine that the law of private property, when properly qualified, is a constructive form of realism about human selfishness. Frequently he followed a usage of the English Distributists (e.g., G. K. Chesterton), i.e., the observation that every argument for private property is an argument for its widest possible distribution.[83]

The Malvern Conference, called in the early days of World War II to discuss "the ordering of a new society," was not an official Anglican conference. It included 23 of the 98 bishops, 140 priests of every rank, and about 250 lay men and women, including such distinguished personalities as T. S. Eliot, Dorothy Sayers, Middleton Murry, Alec Vidler, and Maurice Reckitt. Sir Richard Acland led a strong collectivist faction that wanted a statement that "common ownership of the means of production is a fundamental Christian principle." After three days of debate, Temple, then archbishop of York, the second-ranking position in the Anglican Church, drafted a compromise resolution saying that "the ultimate ownership of the principal resources of the community" in the hands of private owners "is" a stumbling block to a just society. This was too strong for the majority, who voted to replace "is" with "may be," and the resolution passed without a dissenting vote, but with many abstentions. T. S. Eliot and Vidler, two of the "aye" votes, later made a public announcement of their change of heart to "no" votes.[84]

Almost immediately the Church League for Industrial Democracy in the

U. S. A. followed up with a similar conference, held in New Haven, which brought together 350 Christians, clergy and laity, who voted unanimously for Acland's original proposal. Temple sent his greetings to the American conference.

Shortly after the Malvern Conference the arch-conservative Winston Churchill named Temple archbishop of Canterbury. He did so reluctantly, much as Baldwin had named him archbishop of York. Churchill had little respect for the clergy in general and Temple's socialism appalled him, but he had to acknowledge (years later) that Temple was "the half-crown article in a penny bazaar." Back in the thirties Temple's good friend R. H. Tawney had felt compelled to warn the American Fletcher, "You speak as though Temple is representative of the churches. Unfortunately, he is not."[85] Nevertheless, if Temple had not died in 1944, only two years after his enthronement at Canterbuy, it might have made a difference to the fortunes of Christian socialism in the postwar era.

Temple had an appreciation for Catholic tradition that is unusual in a Protestant bishop. He admired the work of Jacques Maritain and he studied Thomas Aquinas, and took from both fundamental ideas about property, natural law and just price theory. He tended to agree with the analysis, outlined in chapter 1 above, to the effect that the Protestant Reformation gave a significant push to the progress of capitalism. For example:

> In its whole social teaching the [medieval] Church stood on a firm Biblical foundation. The Reformers repudiated large parts of the tradition in the desire to return from ecclesiastical to Biblical authority; but in fact their position was in this respect [property theory] less fully Biblical than that of the medieval Church.[86]

Temple's contention was that the Reformers relied too much on the Eighth Commandment ("Thou shall not steal") for their property theory and neglected Biblical, Patristic and Thomistic emphasis on the obligation to share superfluous wealth, as well as the notion of "common use" of a world created by God for the benefit and enjoyment of all his children. The effect was to shift sharing from the realm of justice to that of charity.

Gary Dorrien has pointed out, "He frequently cited as his own feeling the banner carried in parades of the unemployed: 'Damn your charity—we want justice.' "[87]

"I am convinced that St. Thomas offers exactly what the modern world needs," Temple wrote, "in his conception of property and in the principles which underlie the doctrine of the Just Price . . ."[88]

He summarized the latter as follows: "There is a price which it is reasonable and right to charge, and to take more, however willing purchasers may be to pay, is avarice."[89]

This was his condensation of Thomas's natural law theory and its application to economics:

Thus it is a Natural, not a Supernatural, Order with which we are concerned; but as God is the Creator, this Natural Order is His order and its law is His law. Thus, in the economic field, the reason why goods are produced is that people may satisfy their needs by consuming those goods. Production by its own natural law exists for consumption. If then a system comes into being in which production is regulated more by the profit obtainable for the producer than by the needs of the consumer, that system is defying the Natural Law or Natural Order.[90]

Here again we catch the echo of the socialist slogan, "Production for use and not for profit."

A large part of Temple's influence stemmed from his personal charm. Tawney liked to tell the story of Temple receiving an aristocratic visitor in his office:

TEMPLE: Take a chair, Mr. Jones.
VISITOR: Mr. *Montague*-Jones, if you please.
TEMPLE: Indeed? Take two chairs.[91]

Temple's loud, high-pitched laugh was one of his most prominent and, to some, most endearing characteristics. The sufferings of the poor did not amuse him, but it was his consolation that he could laugh at the arrogance and pretensions of the rich and powerful.

TOO GOOD TO BE TRUE

R. H. Tawney (1880–1962) was almost too good to be true. Consider the following opinions:

On the occasion of his eightieth birthday the *London Times* noted, "No man alive has put more people into his spiritual and intellectual debt than has Richard Henry Tawney."[92]

Talcott Parsons, the American sociologist, wrote, "His name will long be remembered among the founders of twentieth century social thought."[93]

Right, left, and center of the British Labour Party revered him. Hugh Gaitskell on the right: "I always think of him as *the* democratic socialist *par excellence*."[94] Richard Crossman on the left: "Tawney's *The Acquisitive Society* is my socialist Bible."[95] Farther left, even the editors of *The Tribune* saluted him. Ross Terrill, perhaps his best biographer, concludes,

Commanding an audience in church as well as labor circles, Tawney was able to exercise on Christians an influence unmatched by any other socialist of the twentieth century.[96]

Though he disagreed with them frequently, Sidney (1859–1947) and Beatrice (1858–1943) Webb were among his most enthusiastic admirers. After he and

Sidney served as labor representatives on the Coal Commission in 1919, Beatrice wrote in her diary,

Sidney has come out of the Commission with a great admiration for Tawney, for his personal charm, his quiet wisdom, and his rapier-like intellect. Tawney has in fact been the great success of the Commission.[97]

In chapter 1, I considered Tawney's contribution to Max Weber's thesis that Protestantism had, in large part, miraculously turned wine into water, made Christian virtues vices, Christian vices virtues, and thereby sanctified the greedy motivations that powered the engine of capitalism and drove it roughshod over the bodies and souls of the poor. I quoted mainly from Weber because he was the pioneer and the more prestigious figure, but it was Tawney who wrote the better book. It was Tawney who, because he was a loyal Christian, unlike Weber, and a Protestant, had the greater influence on Christians in Great Britain and made it the more difficult for them to escape the profound implications of the conclusion of the book *Religion and the Rise of Capitalism*:

Compromise is as impossible between the Church of Christ and the idolatry of wealth, which is the practical religion of capitalist societies, as it was between the Church and the state idolatry of the Roman Empire.[98]

The book developed from a series of lectures sponsored in 1922 by friends of Scott Holland in his memory, to celebrate "the religion of the Incarnation in its bearing on the social and economic life of man."[99] Rejected by one publisher as too dull, it was published by another in 1926 and quickly won sales in six figures and eight languages.

The book is a masterly combination of research and clear, incisive interpretation. Here are some representative quotations from it.

About human nature:

While men are born with many of the characteristics of wolves, man is a wolf domesticated, who both transmits the arts by which he has been partially tamed and improves upon them.[100]

About Calvinist notions of predestination:

The demonstration that distress is a proof of demerit, though a singular commentary on the lives of Christian saints and sages, has always been popular with the prosperous.[101]

About Weber's *The Protestant Ethic and the Spirit of Capitalism*:

Both the "capitalist spirit" and "Protestant ethics" were a good deal more complex than Weber seems to imply. What is true and valuable is his insistence that the commercial classes in seventeenth century England were the standard-bearers of a particular conception of social expediency, which was markedly different from that of the more conservative elements in society—the peasants, the craftsmen and many landed gentry—and that that conception found expression in religion, in politics, and not least, in social and economic conduct and policy.[102]

Like still another great Christian socialist, John Ludlow, R. H. ("Harry") Tawney was born in India. He was the son, not of a soldier, but of a college principal in Calcutta.

Tawney met Billy Temple at the railroad station as both of them were entering Rugby School, on their way to Balliol College at Oxford and a full helping of *noblesse oblige* and what has been called "the effortless superiority" of England's upper middle class. Considering his background and education, one is impressed with Tawney's disdain for that "servile respect for wealth and social position" that he said "remains even today [1935] the most characteristic and contemptible vice of large numbers of our fellow countrymen."[103]

At Oxford Harry Tawney came under the influence of Bishop Gore and joined the Christian Social Union. Some years later Gore visited Tawney as he lay in bed recovering from wounds suffered at the Battle of the Somme in World War I. Tawney, rejecting an officer's commission, had enlisted as a private and, as sergeant, led an attack by a battalion that was reduced from 820 to 54 men in two days of fighting. Tawney was part of the reduction.

The army hospital to which Tawney had been sent was one assigned to lower ranks. As Gore was leaving after his visit he said to the head nurse, "Remember you have in your care one of the most valuable lives in England." The nurse hustled to Tawney's bed and reproached him, "Why ever didn't you *tell* us you were a *gentleman*?"[104]

A gentleman was what Tawney was, but not in the sense meant by the nurse. On the day before the *Times* described him as one of the most influential men alive, Tawney told a friend in reference to a dinner arranged at the House of Commons to honor him, "It is very kind of them, but I don't know why they are doing it. I have had no influence."[105] On another occasion, being told Simone Weil was not an orthodox Christian, he replied, "The Christian religion is for bad people like me, not good people like her."[106]

This stubborn humility was wedded to a sweetness of temper which, despite an ability to lacerate the hides of fools with wit and irony, seems to have captivated almost all who came in contact with him. One of his working-class students in the Workers Educational League said of him, "Tawney was not a teacher; he was a man with a soul. He was one of us."[107] Harold Laski, a man with whom Tawney often disagreed, described him as "the friend who has meant more to me than any man I have ever met."[108]

He was not pious in the usual sense and not even very regular in church-going until his later years. He told Beatrice Webb that he "disliked theology" and though he read widely in the field early in life, exposure to Adolf von Harnack "convinced me that the most acceptable offering to the Almighty would be a holocaust of theologians."[109]

After several years in social work Tawney settled down to a career in workers' education, the writing and teaching of economic history at the London School of Economics, and the role of a valued expert and consultant to the Labour Party. He was, in fact, the principal author of the Labour Party's platforms in 1928 and 1934.

Tawney had, unlike Shaw and the Webbs, his fellow Fabians, no admiration for the "police collectivism" of the Soviet Union. Nor was he tolerant of radical chic, as indicated by this sample of his sometimes caustic style at its most caustic:

> After the collapse of 1931 an epidemic of the "infantile disease of leftism" was obviously overdue. It raged for some years like measles in Polynesia and set thousands gibbering. . . . The great game of over-trumping the Left of today for fear of not being in the swim of tomorrow went merrily forward among the intelligentsia. . . . [They] discovered the recondite truth of the existence of a class struggle and announced their conversion to it with blood-curdling bleats.[110]

"Blood-curdling bleats." A great phrase.

Few socialists have expressed so clearly the necessity for an indissoluble marriage between socialism and democracy:

> The question is not merely whether the state owns and controls the means of production. It is also who owns and controls the state. It is not certain, though it is probable, that Socialism can in England be achieved by the methods proper to democracy. It is certain that it cannot be achieved by any other; nor, even if it could, should the supreme goods of civil and political liberty, in whose absence no Socialism worthy of the name can breathe, be part of the price.[111]

This same passage gives a hint of Tawney's weakness as a Christian socialist thinker. He was a little too partial to nationalization, probably in part the result of his experience on the Coal Commission and also, probably, because the Webbs did influence him to favor consumers against the selfish tendencies of producers.

And yet he once wrote,

> The past has shown no more excellent social order than that in which the mass of the people were the masters of the holdings which they ploughed and of the tools with which they worked.[112]

Certainly that sentiment should have prejudiced Tawney in favor of the producer-cooperative approach of Ludlow and Buchez. For a time he was drawn toward guild socialism as a counterpoise to the dangers of collectivism, but G. D. H. Cole's aberration in the direction of vocational representation in Parliament instead of geographical representation seems to have cooled him off.

The Coal Commission was a formative experience that highlighted some of the absurdities of private ownership of the means of production in England around 1919 (and even in present-day America). One exchange between Tawney and a management representative went as follows:

> TAWNEY: What is the mine owner paid for?
> ANSWER: He is paid for his property.
> TAWNEY: That is to say, the royalty is simply payment for a private right quite irrespective of any function which is performed or any work that is done. Is that a fair statement?
> ANSWER: I think that is fair.[113]

Terrill's conclusion emphasizes the eclectic quality of Tawney's socialism, which was both its strength and its weakness:

> If Tawney differed from each major strand of British socialism, he fertilized them all. He is the one twentieth century British socialist thinker who can be saluted from every quarter: Bevanite left, Gaitskellite right, guild socialist, Marxist, Fabian, Christian socialist—the philosopher who has most nearly provided an overall framework for socialism in British conditions and according to the British temper.[114]

In the history of Christian socialism in England, Tawney occupies, if possible, an even more central position than Terrill assigns him. During the 1920s the flame of Christian socialism flickered and nearly died. It flared again in the depressed 1930s with the organization in 1931 of the Socialist Christian League. Tawney later became president. In 1937 John Macmurray and Hewlett Johnson, the "Red Dean of Canterbury," led a Christian flirtation with the Soviet Union. As a result in 1942 the Council of Clergy and Ministers for Common Ownership was created.

After World War II the electoral triumph of the Labour Party stimulated another burst of interest in Christian socialism and in 1945 over a hundred Labour MP's (members of Parliament) formed their own Parliamentary Socialist Christian Group.

During the 1940s and 1950s tension continued between the SCL and the CCMCO over the question of the Soviet Union and relations with the Communist Party of Great Britain. The question became largely academic when CP membership collapsed in 1956 with the Soviet invasion of Hungary. In 1960 Tawney presided over the merger of the SCL and the CCMCO. They became the present Christian Socialist Movement, which then adopted a policy of "critical friendship" with the Soviet Union.

The CSM has over a thousand members in seven or eight branches, the great majority being Anglicans, followed by Methodists and a small number of Roman Catholics, Quakers, and other denominations. Only 10 percent are manual workers, a recognized weakness. Among recent leaders have been Lord Donald Soper, Canon Edward Charles, Peter Dawe, Paul Derrick and David Ormrod. In one form or another Christian socialism has maintained continuity in England since 1877, the current world's record.

The CSM has had as many as a score of its members sitting in Parliament on the Labour benches. The spring 1986 issue of its lively, well-edited quarterly *The Christian Socialist* features CSM's submission to a Labour Party study of "common ownership." Making it evident that the producer cooperative is CSM's favorite form of socialism and common ownership, the submission includes the following:

> We in the CSM are proud to be in the tradition of the Christian socialists who pioneered cooperative production societies in the 1850s. . . . We are now asking the party to devote more consideration to encouraging [workers' cooperatives]. . . . In particular, the party should consider means to convert large as well as small companies to a common ownership basis.

The Christian Socialist Movement of England has not forgotten John Ludlow and the Society for the Promotion of Workingmen's Associations. Praise God.

CHAPTER 9

German-Speaking Europe

What shall we make of the Germans? The German-speaking population of Europe numbers about 90 million. Of this number nearly 80 million live in East and West Germany; the rest are in Austria, Switzerland, and neighboring countries. As a language group, German speakers are second in number in Europe only to Russian-speakers, who make up about half of the Soviet Union's 260 million people.

Sitting astride the center of Western Europe, the Germans have been in a position that would naturally tempt them to dominate it. They have qualities of passion, energy, creative thought, and imagination, which, linked to a strong sense of discipline and organization, have produced great musicians, poets, philosophers, reformers, revolutionaries, and formidable armies.

Twice in this century America has sent its young men across the sea to help stop German armies, to discourage the Kaiser and Adolf Hitler from fastening their particular brands of capitalist imperialism and Nazi racism on the continent of Europe. Millions have died on the battlefields, in the bombed cities, in the concentration camps.

Germany, like the United States, contains a more equal mix of Catholics and Protestants, and a more equal mix of Catholic and Protestant influences than was the case in either France or England. But there the similarities stop. Christian socialism, or at least Christian social theory, has been a factor in Germany, thanks to men like Emmanuel von Ketteler, the Catholic archbishop of Mainz in the nineteenth century, and Protestants like the two Blumhardts, Ragaz, Barth, and Tillich.

But Christian socialism in Germany pales before Marxist socialism. Cole has written:

> Marx created that distinctively German socialism which was soon to assume an ideological dominance over most of the continent, driving the older forms of socialism before it as chaff before the wind. Not that Marxism ever succeeded in expelling the earlier doctrines. What it did was to drive them for the most part out of the socialist movement to seek habitations elsewhere—in cooperation, in the various forms of anar-

178

chism . . . and in so-called "Christian socialism" within the bosom of the Catholic Church. . . . But Marxism drove them out of the center of both argument and organization.[1]

In producing Marx and Marxism it might be said that Germany has, over the last century, influenced the history of the world as much as France had influenced it over the previous eleven centuries.

This is not the place to analyze Marxism and its various components— French Enlightenment and German philosophy, Fichte, Feuerbach, Hegel Upside Down—or its practical results in world history. For this there are far better authorities, notably G. D. H. Cole and his five-volume *History of Socialist Thought* (even more history than thought) and Leszek Kolakowski, the exiled former-Marxist professor of philosophy at Warsaw University, and his three-volume classic *Main Currents of Marxism* (more thought than history).

MARX VS. WEITLING

Let us begin the history of Christian socialism in Germany with a description of Marx's confrontation with it in the person of Wilhelm Weitling (1808–1871). The date was March 30, 1846; the place, Brussels. The occasion was one of a series of small, clandestine meetings of German exiles—socialists and communists—who conspired together during the 1830s and 1840s under such names as the League of Outlaws, League of the Just, German Educational Association (*Deutscher Bildungsverein*) in such places as Paris, London, and Brussels. These meetings culminated in the formation of the Communist League in 1847, which entrusted Marx (1818–1883) and his good friend and collaborator Friedrich Engels (1820–1895) to draw up *The Communist Manifesto*.

At the time of the 1846 meeting Marx was twenty-seven years old, had briefly served as editor of the *Rheinische Zeitung* (Rhineland News), a radical newspaper in Cologne, had written a good deal but published little outside of left-wing journals. By comparison with Weitling he was a relative unknown. Weitling, then thirty-seven, was the top German radical in Europe and had already published three books, one of which (*Guarantees of Harmony and Freedom*) Marx himself had praised in a Paris paper as "the tremendous and brilliant debut of the German working class."[2] Weitling, however, was no match intellectually for Marx. He was a self-educated tailor, the illegitimate son of a German servant and a French officer who was on his way to death in Napoleon's invasion of Russia. Unlike Marx, he was an authentic member of the working class, had known bitter poverty (Marx came to know it later), and had written a book, *The Poor Sinner's Gospel,* which portrayed Jesus Christ as a revolutionary communist. The book was widely read by European radicals and had won Weitling ten months in a Zurich prison in 1843. He had been driven out of Paris in 1839 because he had taken part in an abortive uprising led by Auguste Blanqui.

A report of the Brussels meeting has come down to us in the recollections of a young Russian intellectual, Pavel Annenkov, who seems to have been an impartial observer. I quote at length because Annenkov gives us, as few others have, a sense of the atmosphere of those meetings of exiled German communists at which Marx presided and how and why Marxian socialism "drove the older forms of socialism before it as chaff before the wind."

Marx was a type of man all compact of energy, force of character and unshakable conviction—a type who was highly remarkable in his outward appearance as well. With a thick black mane of hair, his hands all covered with hair and his coat buttoned up askew, he gave one the impression of a man who had the right and the power to command respect, even though his aspect and his behavior might seem to be rather odd. His movements were awkward but bold and self-assured; his manners violated all the social conventions. They were proud and slightly contemptuous, and the metallic timbre of his voice was remarkably well adapted to the radical verdicts which he delivered on men and things. He never spoke at all except in judgments that brooked no denial and that were rendered even sharper, and rather disagreeable, by the harsh tone of everything he said. This tone expressed his firm conviction of his mission to impress himself on men's minds, to dominate their wills, and to compel them to follow in his train.

The tailor-agitator Weitling was a good-looking blond young man in rather a foppishly cut frock-coat and with a beard rather foppishly trimmed, and resembled a commercial traveler rather than the stern and embittered worker whom I had imagined . . . .

We sat down at a little green table, at the head of which Marx took his place, pencil in hand and with his leonine head bent over a sheet of paper, while his inseparable friend and companion in propaganda, the tall erect Engels, with his English distinction and gravity, opened the meeting with a speech. He talked about the necessity for labor reformers arriving at some sort of clarity out of the confusion of their opposing views and formulating some common doctrine which should serve as a banner to rally around for all those who had neither the time nor the ability to occupy themselves with questions of theory. But before Engels had finished his speech, Marx suddenly raised his head and hurled at Weitling the following question: "Tell us, Weitling, you who have made so much stir in Germany with your communist propaganda and won over so many workers so that they have thereby lost their work and their bread, with what arguments do you defend your social-revolutionary activity and on what basis do you propose to ground them?" . . .

A painful discussion began, which, however, as I shall show, did not last very long.

Weitling seemed to want to keep the discussion on the plane of the commonplaces of liberal rhetoric. With a serious and troubled face, he began to explain that it was not his task to develop new economic theories, but to make use of those which, as was to be seen in France, were best adapted to open the eyes of the workers to their terrible situation, to all the wrongs committed against them . . . .

He spoke at length, but to my surprise and in contrast to the speech of Engels, unclearly and even with confused delivery, frequently repeating and correcting himself; and he had difficulty in reaching the conclusions that sometimes followed, sometimes preceded his premises . . . .

He would no doubt have spoken longer had not Marx broken in upon him with angrily glowering brows. He said that it was simple fraud to arouse the people without any sound and considered basis for their activity. The awakening of fantastic hopes . . . would never lead to the salvation of those who suffered, but on the contrary to their undoing. "To go to the workers in Germany," he said, "without strictly scientific ideas and concrete doctrine would mean an empty and unscrupulous playing with propaganda, which would inevitably involve, on the one hand, the setting-up of an inspired apostle and, on the other hand, simple asses who would listen to him with open mouth." Weitling's role, he added, with a gesture toward me, might be all very well in Russia, but in a civilized country like Germany one could do nothing without solid doctrine.

The pale cheeks of Weitling colored, and his speech became animated and direct. In a voice that quivered with excitement he began to insist that an individual who had brought together hundreds of men in the name of the ideas of Justice, Solidarity and Brotherly Love, could hardly be characterized as a lazy and empty fellow; that he, Weitling, was able to console himself against the present attack by recalling the hundreds of grateful letters, declarations and demonstrations that had come to him from all the ends of the fatherland; and that it might be that his modest efforts for the common good were more important than closet analysis and criticism carried out far from the suffering world and the oppression of the people.

This thrust might well have silenced a less formidable, humbler man than Marx, for it struck at a major weakness in his arrogant assumption of command. But that kind of man he most decidedly was not. Annenkov continues:

These last words made Marx lose his temper; enraged, he struck his fist on the table with such violence that he shook the lamp, and leaping up, he shouted, "Ignorance has never helped anybody yet!"
    We followed his example and stood up too. The conference was at an end.[3]

So began the descent of Wilhelm Weitling from top German radical in Europe to a minor player in the history of German communism. He must have realized that he was up against superior competition. A few months later he departed for New York and except for one year, when he returned to Germany to participate in the (failed) revolution of 1848, the rest of his career was spent in the United States, mostly in New York City. For five years he edited a German-language newspaper *Die Republik der Arbeiter* (The Worker's Republic), which was the organ of a national movement of German-American radicals that Weitling organized and dominated in dictatorial fashion. This *Arbeiterbund* (Workers' Association) was sizable enough to accumulate a substantial treasury, which Weitling proceeded to sink in one more utopia called Communia on the plains of eastern Iowa near Dubuque. The *Arbeiterbund* and its *Republik* followed Communia into bankruptcy in 1855.

Truth to tell, Weitling was a pathetic representative of Christian socialism or, more accurately, Christian communism. The first seventy pages of his most Christian book, *The Poor Sinner's Gospel*, are devoted to an effort to prove that the Bible is full of errors and contradictions and that Jesus Christ was merely another sinner like the rest of us. Weitling confesses, "It is a long time since I went to church or prayed and I am not likely to start praying again in the near future."[4] The rest of the book, paradoxically, is devoted to proving that "we will only get out of this mess when the poor have become less ignorant and the rich more sensitive through the teaching of Christ."[5]

Here are some of Weitling's conclusions.

• "Poverty must be overcome, not by almsgiving but the abolition of private property."[6]

• "Our modern property laws were drawn up originally by Roman jurists, the greatest rogues and babblers under the sun, and they are as great a shock to the law of Moses as a clenched fist in your eye."[7]

• Weitling's interpretation of the Parable of the Ten Virgins and the Wedding Feast (Mt. 25:1–13): "The lamps are propaganda, the oil is the material means necessary for the propaganda. . . . Foolish propagandists are those who are not ready for a revolution when it comes suddenly; they let their opportunity slip by them and the power falls to those who are better prepared, as for example happened in the 1830 revolution in France."[8]

Weitling had a good knowledge of French and he had translated Lamennais and Considérant for German publication. He was familiar with the writings of Saint-Simon; indeed *The Poor Sinner's Gospel* was a kind of poor person's *New Christianity*. He shared with Saint-Simon a low opinion of German philosophy ("an artfully constructed metaphysical hocus-pocus")[9] and of democracy ("humbug" and "political frippery").[10] He also shared with the Frenchman the delusion that you can sell Christianity as a handy manual of social and economic axioms without the religious dogma or any faith at all in Jesus Christ as Lord, Savior, and the risen, triumphant Son of God.

A few weeks after the stormy session with Weitling, Marx and Engels convened a board of inquiry to condemn and, in effect, excommunicate a friend and disciple of Weitling, a man named Hermann Kriege, who had emigrated to America and was publishing the *Volks-Tribun* and pretending to speak for German communism and the League of the Just. Weitling, in fact, was a member of the board, the only one of eight members who voted against the condemnation, realizing as he must, that the condemnation was actually aimed at himself. (At that time the League of the Just had only eighteen members in all, so one must not think that this proceeding was highly important at the time. It became important only in retrospect.)

The *Manifesto* or *Circular Against Kriege*, which reveals the tell-tale bite of Marx's sarcastic wit, shows Kriege to have been an even more sentimental advocate of Christian communism than Weitling. One issue of his paper, the *Circular* notes with distaste, included thirty-five separate references to "love." Kriege's feminist leanings were another object of scorn. "Woman was destined to give birth to the Son of Man," wrote Kriege, and after extolling the feminine preference for love over hate, he continues, "That is why your voice is important also in politics."[11]

Although the *Circular* accuses Kriege of having, while in Europe, "always passed himself off as an atheist," or perhaps because of that fact, the trial board was especially incensed that Kriege invoked "the holy spirit" of love and community, "the spirit that commanded the tempest and the storm, the spirit that cured the blind and the lepers." This "old religious dream," the board concluded, "is in direct contradiction with communism." It charged further that "the *faith*, and more precisely the faith in 'the holy spirit of community,' is indeed the last thing necessary to the realization of communism."[12] This notion of a community that unites men and women of all classes remains anathema to certain Marxists down to the present day, as we shall see when we consider the views of Louis Althusser and Gustavo Gutiérrez.

Perhaps even more significant than the *Circular's* condemnation of any messing around with religious versions of communism was its horror at Kriege's proposal that the United States divide up its public land into 160-acre lots and give them to all comers, as was later done by the "homestead laws" of 1862 *et seq*. This idea, "of transforming all men into private landowners," the board protested, "is as realisable and communistic as transforming all men into emperors, kings and popes."[13] God forbid that any man, safe and secure on his own land, should feel like an emperor or a king, and least of all, a pope.

Finally, with an ironic lack of self-scrutiny, the board condemns Kriege to outer darkness because he is intolerant of those who disagree with him. This, mind you, is a product of the *young* Marx, the one who is supposed to have been so much warmer, idealistic, and humanistic than the old Marx.

Henri Desroche has made the excellent point that this excommunication of Kriege and, in effect, Weitling, who quit the League shortly thereafter, was "a kind of counterpart to the condemnation of Lamennais" by Gregory XVI. "The *Circular Against Kriege*," Desroche points out, "is one of those scissor-cuts that henceforth serve to separate the two histories (*dossiers*)." The final irony: one of the slaps at Kriege was that he regarded Lamennais as "his father."[14] Lamennais, condemned both by the far right and the far left, must then have been pretty close to the truth.

At any rate, when Marx knocked over the particular brand of Christian socialism, or communism, represented by Kriege and Weitling, it is safe to conclude that he was knocking over the flimsiest of straw men, an unrecognizable caricature of the real thing, even though Kriege's version did include some valid ideas, such as the support for family farms and "the holy spirit of community."

Marx was equally contemptuous of other, more authentic forms of Christian socialism. The whole idea he dismissed as "the holy water with which the priest consecrates the heart-burnings of the aristocrat."[15] Therefore it might be interesting to examine the Christian socialism—the same "so-called Christian socialism" that Cole says Marx drove out of the socialist movement into "the bosom of the Catholic Church"—of one who was both a priest *and* an aristocrat, Wilhelm Emmanuel von Ketteler.

KETTELER'S PRECURSOR

Before exploring the career of Wilhelm Emmanuel von Ketteler, archbishop of Mainz, we should acknowledge the contribution of his John the Baptist, the layman Franz von Baader, who was ennobled in 1820 for his work as a mining engineer in the Bavarian government.

Franz von Baader (1765–1841) has been described by one historian as "the first to create the concept of 'Christian socialism' [and] the true initiator of Catholic sociology and social doctrine in Germany."[16] Born in Munich the son of a Bavarian court physician, Baader suffered a precocious period of depression between the ages of seven and ten, from which he was suddenly freed while looking at some geometrical figures. He became a doctor, but the sight of his patients' sufferings was too painful for him and he took up the study of mining. In this field he spent several years in Scotland and England, where he was deeply moved by the suffering of the industrial proletariat. In fact, he was one of the first, if not the first, to focus attention on the proletariat, the "property-less wage earners," as he called them in his 1835 study *On the Present Faulty Relationship Between the Property-less, or Proletarians, and the Propertied Classes of Society.*

Baader read widely—Locke, Hume, Hobbes, Kant, Augustine, Aquinas, Meister Eckhart, Fichte, Hegel. He was a personal friend and admirer of Lamennais, particularly in the latter's middle period, after the conservative phase and before Gregory XVI drove him into apostasy. He was fascinated by the seventeenth century mystic Jakob Böhme, though he was at first so outraged by the theosophical obscurities he was reading that he flung the book against the wall. Finally he taught at the University of Munich under the all-purpose title Professor of the Philosophy of Nature, Civil, and Religious Society.

This dazzling variety of social, economic, scientific, philosophical, and religious study and experience Baader condensed, or expanded, into sixteen volumes of diverse writings that lay buried and unknown for many years, surfacing briefly in the 1860s when Ketteler was doing his serious work on the social question, returning to obscurity, and then surfacing again after World

War I when they were rediscovered by Kierkegaard, the Great Dane, who singled Baader out as his own precursor and wrote that he "should be known as a matter of course to all those who wish to ponder these matters," that is, the existential problems of evil and liberty.[17]

Consider a few samples of Baader's thought, which combine an understanding of patristic and scholastic notions of property with a somewhat romantic evocation of medieval institutions and modern and progressive calls for a new application of those notions and institutions in the total separation of church and state, popular sovereignty, and worker associations.

On property:

Christianity has also fundamentally reformed all doctrines and notions of acquisition, possession and consumption of property by doing away with the pagan concept of absolute property without, however, barring individual acquisition and possession. But every use and consumption of property that is not social is anti-social. [Current echo: If you're not part of the solution, you're part of the problem.] For he who does not live for society lives against it, and every separatist is a fool in theory and a criminal in practice. No Christian may declare: this property, this right, this office are mine, to handle as I please; for in reality these are God's gifts and tasks (*Gaben und Aufgaben*). . . .[18]

On church and state:

While many regarded it as an evil that in our day the secular power became separated from religion and the Church, *Avenir* [the paper of Lamennais, Lacordaire, and Montalembert] has taught us to recognize that God has given this an unanticipated turn; for we can already see that the separation has caused the emancipation of religion and its resurrection from the dust.[19]

On popular sovereignty:

It is surely God's will and imposition that there shall be Government, but it is up to men to decide who shall govern and how. Accordingly Paul says: *Omnis potestas est a Deo* [All power (authority) is from God]. Note that "*potestas*" here signifies the government or office of power, not the holder of power, and if this maxim is taken to imply that God has instituted this or that person, this or that constitution, it is *wrongly* interpreted.[20]

Note the revolutionary implications in that last sentence, which are of course only a restatement of the notions of popular sovereignty in Aquinas, the sixteenth-century Italian Robert Bellarmine, and his Spanish Jesuit contemporary Francisco Suárez. These same notions are linked to the "social contract" of Rousseau and whatever was decent and legitimate in the French Revolution.

Baader on worker associations:

> When recently the extinction of Christian sentiment and the new sanctioning of pagan jurisprudence gave renewed support to egotism and separatism in the dealings of the powerful and propertied with the poor and powerless, this was bound to debase the state of the proletariat more and more and finally . . . to render it quite unbearable when total irreligiosity had prevailed. Is it therefore surprising that these proletarians, after having frequently enough been thrown together, *ex officio*, into a rabble, finally get the idea to foregather in their own interest or, as they call it, to form associations?[21]

Baader was the first German to use the phrase "Christian social principle," which was to become popular among Christian socialists. This is how he defined it:

> Religion in its supreme commandment says: Love God above all, and thy neighbor as thyself. This is the principle of every truly free community of life and of every commonwealth, of all true liberty and equality. This is the Christian social principle![22]

Saint-Simon, Cabet, Weitling, and others then and now have emphasized the love of neighbor alone in Christ's teaching as a basis for Christian socialism. Baader believed that, for the ordinary mortal, love of neighbor goes nowhere without the love of God.

KETTELER, BISMARCK, LASSALLE, MARX

The life of Archbishop Ketteler (1811–1877), by a happy stroke of providence, fell within that period of German history when the man could most effectively impact and influence in a lasting way his country and his church.

In the early nineteenth century, Germany—unlike France and England—was not really a country. It was little more than a bewildering multiplicity of kingdoms, princedoms, states, estates, municipalities, and archbishoprics with temporal power (as in Cologne, Trier, Mainz, and Salzburg). At the time of the French Revolution (1789), Germany was made up of 1,789 autonomous political authorities. Among these, two major powers, Protestant Prussia and Catholic Austria, struggled for dominance. The Austrians had the initial advantage, thanks to the political genius of Metternich, but the Prussians had the superior organization and, during the crucial years, the political genius of Otto von Bismarck (1815–1898). Also, they did not suffer from Austria's distraction of having to preside over an empire of 10 million Germans and 40 million Hungarians, Czechs, Poles, Ruthenians, Slovenes, Slovaks, Serbs, Rumanians, and Italians.

Bismarck and his excellent Prussian army eliminated Austria from contention in the Seven Weeks War of 1866. The defeat of France in 1870 took only six weeks, although Paris held out for a few months longer until starvation and defeat drove it into the chaos that gave rise to the Paris Commune and, finally, the Third Republic. Bismarck and Germany were the undisputed masters of Europe, and Bismarck's king, Wilhelm I, reluctantly accepted the title of Emperor of Germany in the great Hall of Mirrors in Louis XIV's palace at Versailles. He preferred the title King of Prussia.

But Bismarck did not feel entirely secure. The Catholics and the socialists worried him. The Catholics, already suspect as potential supporters of a potential resurgence by Austria, became even more menacing when Vatican Council I declared the pope infallible on July 18, 1870. This moved Bismarck to initiate the persecution of the church known as the *Kulturkampf* (1871–1882), during which bishops and priests were imprisoned, thousands of pastorates in Prussia were vacated and the Jesuit, Redemptorist and Lazarist orders were suppressed. Bismarck abandoned the *Kulturkampf* when he saw that it had welded the Catholics into a formidable political bloc, which, behind the banner of the Center Party, continued to elect between ninety and one hundred delegates to the Reichstag until it died a somewhat ignoble death under Hitler's evil spell in 1933. Bismarck also knew that he would need Catholic support in his struggles with the National Liberals and the Social Democrats.

Unlike in France and England, the bourgeoisie in Germany was never able to win clear, undisputed control of the government. The Prussian Junkers—landed aristocrats—stood in the way, behind the supreme Junker, Prince Otto von Bismarck, and his Junker king, Wilhelm I. From the hostility of the Junkers toward the bourgeois upstarts there came, in fact, unlikely advantages for the poor and the peasants—universal suffrage for men and some of the first social insurance and regulation of industrial abuses in Europe. Although he did not live to see most of this, Ketteler was a major factor in bringing it about.

Wilhelm von Ketteler was born in 1811, seven years before Marx, the son of Baron Maximilian von Ketteler, on the baronial estate in Westphalia near the Rhine. He grew to be a husky extrovert who angered his father by getting the tip of his nose sliced off at the University of Göttingen when he challenged a fellow student to a duel for stepping on his foot. This led to transfers to the University of Berlin and then to the University of Munich, where he finally earned a law degree. He went on to service with the Prussian government in Münster.

Concluding that this line of work "involved too much paper and too little heart,"[23] Ketteler was further alienated when the Prussians imprisoned a friend of his family, Archbishop Clement August of Cologne, because the archbishop would not accept a Prussian decree that the children of mixed marriages must take the faith of the father. So Ketteler quit. He drifted for a few years, coming briefly under the influence of the eccentric Joseph Görres, who had journeyed intellectually from a radical devotion to Rousseau to Catholic romanticism. A visit to the Marian shrine at Altötting in Bavaria seems to have moved Ketteler to study for the priesthood and he was ordained in 1844.

His first assignments were in country parishes, but he quickly made an impression that was strong enough to persuade the people of Teklenburg to elect him, against his will, as a delegate to the first national assembly at Frankfurt, a product of the Revolution of 1848. He never addressed this short-lived assembly, but when two aristocratic delegates—Prince Lichnowsky and General von Auerswald—were assassinated, Ketteler, the aristocratic priest-delegate, was chosen to give the funeral oration. It was the impact of this oration before the leaders of Germany that led, within eighteen months, to his appointment as archbishop of Mainz in March 1850.

Ketteler must have been a powerful speaker—powerful in a way that cannot be appreciated by reading his sermons and orations. The style is typical of nineteenth-century oratory, leaning toward the florid and sentimental, but marked by flashes of effective imagery and metaphor. The funeral oration struck a note of concern for the poor that was characteristic of Ketteler. One particular sentence expressed an idea that was as radical as anything he said or wrote for the rest of his life. Some excerpts:

> I hear cries for help from among our poor, suffering brethren. . . . Who that is not heartless is not in full sympathy with this cry for help? I see greed and miserliness on the increase. I see the pursuit of pleasure taking over. . . . He [Christ] is the Way, the Truth and the Life. Without him there is only folly, dishonesty and death. . . . With him . . . we can turn the earth into a paradise. . . . Yes, it is my deepest conviction that *we could even bring about common ownership of the goods of this world* as well as eternal peace along with maximum freedom in our social and political institutions. . . . That is the truth that cries out to us from these graves [emphasis added].[24]

That the ghostly shades of Prince Lichnowsky and General von Auerswald, leaders of the right wing of the Assembly, would be crying out for "common ownership of the goods of this world" or "maximum freedom" seems unlikely, but there must have been something about the delivery and the aspect of this young aristocrat that impressed that august assembly. Overnight Ketteler became a national figure. He was invited to be one of the two principal speakers at the first national Catholic Congress in Mainz later that same year, 1848. The other speaker was the Congress president, Joseph von Buss (1803–1878), a layman who as early as 1837 had proposed a Factory Bill in the *Landtag* of Baden, thereby becoming "the first German to propose a bill of social reforms in any parliament."[25] The bill would have put an end to Sunday work, provided technical training, state contributions for health insurance, and a system of savings accounts that would have made it possible for workers to buy their own factories.

Ketteler's contributions to the Congress were not overly impressive, but at least he reminded the delegates of the major problems. "The most difficult question in political life," he said,

> is the social question. . . . The Catholic Church has the final solution. . . . Let the state legislate as it may, it has not the strength for this task. . . . The starving laboring masses, whose ranks are swelling daily, are raising their voices in protest and demand. May the Catholic societies show the world that the true spirit of Jesus Christ is not dead upon the earth.[26]

At the Congress banquet Ketteler toasted the poor and took up a collection for them which netted the equivalent of about $150. Hostile critics asked if this was the capital with which the Catholic Church proposed to solve the problem of poverty.

The pastor of the Mainz cathedral invited Ketteler to give six Advent sermons a few weeks later. His subject was "The Great Social Issues of the Present." In his first sermon Ketteler took pains to straighten out anyone who may have misunderstood his reference to "common ownership" in the funeral oration at Frankfurt. He also developed a theme that was to be the centerpiece, literally, of Catholic social teaching right up to the present day, to wit:

> Today the haves and the have-nots confront each other with animosity, and the poverty of the masses grows daily. . . . On the one side we witness a stubborn, narrow interpretation of the property right, and on the other a determination to abolish that right completely. We look desperately for moderation between these two extremes.[27]

Like so many before and since, Ketteler went to Thomas Aquinas for the happy medium:

> One cannot speak of a full and absolute right—that belongs only to God—but only a right to use. . . . [and to use only] as the Creator has ordained that use . . . to serve the needs of all mankind. . . . The Catholic Church's concept of property has nothing in common with the prevalent view, which regards man as the absolute lord of that which he owns. . . . According to [Aquinas] man should never regard the fruits of his own stewardship of property as his exclusive possession, but rather as the common property of all.[28]

As one Father of the Church put it, stealing means not only to take what belongs to others, but also to hold back what rightfully ought to belong to others. The notorious saying, "Private property is theft" [Proudhon] is not purely and simply false. Aside from enormous falsehood it contains a grain of uncomfortable truth. . . . So long as there is a spark of truth in it, it is capable of setting the world on fire.[29]

But, "experience teaches how easily common ownership leads to quarrels and disputes."[30] And, *on the other hand,* "the wealthy indulge themselves in a lavish and wasteful satisfaction of every sensate whim [and] are indifferent to the plight of their less fortunate fellows, who must often do without the bare necessities of life."[31] *But,* "if this matter were determined somehow by government regulations, then the finest wellspring of human nobility [charity] would be stifled."[32]

Ketteler, at this point in his life, was clearly opposed to the use of state intervention to right the wrongs of capitalism. His second sermon enlarges on this theme and on "The Obligation of Christian Charity." He quotes St. Matthew on love, the Good Samaritan, the Works of Mercy: "My Christian brethren, if we would all obey these teachings for one single day, all of our social problems would disappear as if by magic."[33]

But even as the preacher gave expression to this excessive faith in the magic of personal charity, he dropped a hint that more than that was necessary, a hint that he himself would come to realize it and become an eloquent champion of state intervention:

> It is not enough to provide more food and clothing for a few poor people or to send a few florin more to our favorite charity. . . . We must seek out the poorest of the poor in their hovels, *study the causes and conditions of their poverty*, share their sufferings and their tears . . . [emphasis added].[34]

Over the next sixteen years Ketteler did not have much time to "study the causes and conditions of poverty," given the demands of his office as archbishop of Mainz, but what time he had he used. Surprisingly, he used a large part of that time studying the ideas and actions of Ferdinand Lassalle (1825–1864), one of the most fascinating characters in the whole history of socialism. Fascinating for two reasons: (1) his life and death at the age of thirty-nine read like an unlikely Hollywood movie, and (2) the question "What would have happened to the socialist movement if he had lived another twenty or thirty years?" is surely one of the biggest If's in the history of that movement.

As a young man Lassalle had taken part in the Revolution of 1848 and served a brief term in prison. As a lawyer he had taken up the cause of an older woman, the wealthy Countess Sophie von Hatzfeldt, who was involved in a sensational divorce case that dragged on for ten years and made household names of both lawyer and client. Lassalle wrote books on philosophy (*Heraclitus the Obscure*), history (*The Italian War and Prussia's Mission*), and economics (*The System of Acquired Right*). He was probably the most eloquent speaker in Germany, one of the first to exploit the mass meeting, and he organized the first substantial socialist party in the world, the General German

Workers Association (1863). At the height of his popularity and influence (even Bismarck met with him and took him seriously) he fell in love with a young woman, whose father was so upset at the idea of his daughter marrying a socialist Jew that he arranged for a former lover, a Wallachian prince, to challenge Lassalle to a duel. Lassalle accepted the challenge and stood motionless, his pistol unraised, while the prince shot and killed him.

For several years he had been a friend and admirer of Marx, but Marx grew jealous of his popularity with the German workers and turned against him. When Lassalle was killed, Marx expressed regret about their falling out and praised and lamented Lassalle with genuine sincerity. But they were bound to fall out, for there were basic differences between them.

Despite his flamboyant ways and revolutionary youth, Lassalle was at heart a reformer and not a revolutionary. The first plank in his party's platform was universal suffrage. He believed that once the workers could all vote they would inevitably take control of the state and should then vote into law a system of state-financed producer cooperatives so that the workers could at last enjoy their fair share of the profits of industry. Marx, however, had little faith in the vote or in producer co-ops, believing that only violent revolution could wrest control of either the state or the means of production. Although vague about what should follow the revolution, Marx and his followers tended to prefer state ownership and control over worker ownership and control, with the state initially run by a "dictatorship of the proletariat."

Lassalle, though by no means religious himself, disagreed with Marx on toleration of the religious viewpoint. He was, in fact, more of a Hegelian idealist than a materialist and while he was head of the socialist movement in Germany there was none of the violent and bitter hostility toward Christianity that later marked that movement as it came more and more under the influence of the Marxists. The Marxists, led by Wilhelm Liebknecht (1826–1900) and August Bebel (1840–1913), organized their own rival party in 1869, the Social Democratic Workers Party, and in 1875 the two parties merged at Gotha to form the ancestor of today's Social Democratic Party, then called the Socialist Workers Party.

Archbishop von Ketteler never met Lassalle but, with reservations because of his lack of religious faith, he praised him and his ideas frequently in books, speeches, and letters. He accepted in toto Lassalle's faith in "the iron law of wages," Lassalle's incisive denunciations of economic liberalism and the capitalist structures built upon it, and, in particular, Lassalle's enthusiasm for the producer cooperative, or productive association, as it was usually called.

Countess Sophie von Hatzfeldt, Lassalle's friend, wrote him a letter in which she told of meeting with Ketteler and of his telling her that

> I have taken a deep interest in Lassalle. I have learned much from him. I favor his social plans entirely. . . . Up to now Lassalle has carried on his mission of defeating error and lies with the greatest of success and he must be allowed to continue his work.[35]

Making allowances for some exaggeration, this was not too far from the truth, as revealed in other documents.

In 1864, however, when Ketteler wrote his book *The Labor Question and Christianity*, he still disagreed with Lassalle on the key issue of state support for producer cooperatives. This was also the point on which Buchez had parted company with Louis Blanc in France. Ketteler did, however, propose that the state should spend in behalf of the poor the money realized from the sale of church properties confiscated by the edicts of 1782–1785.

Ketteler wrote an anonymous letter to Lassalle in 1864:

> I could place 50,000 gulden [about $50,000] for the purpose of subsidiz-ing [producer] associations . . . one for cigar workers, one for women craft workers, one for industrial workers, and two for other popular industries. . . . Do you consider this plan practical? Would you be willing to outline a plan of organization, or name a person who would? The position I have in life makes it impossible to give my name. I ask you therefore to send your reply to MZ35, Frankfurt, collect. The founding of productive associations for the workers, membership in which will, besides their salary, give them a share in the profits, seems to me a wise thing to do.[36]

Lassalle responded almost immediately, but the only advice he had to offer Ketteler was to read two of his books. The fact was that Lassalle knew very little about how to operate a successful cooperative. Little came of Ketteler's plans to organize producer co-ops. Although he started with high hopes for raising money from loyal Catholics—after all, hadn't German Catholics col-lected 23,000,000 thalers for the pope in the last five years?—he soon realized that there wasn't the same kind of interest in doing something for the workers. In 1865 he was already telling the Journeymen's Union in Mainz: "Religion and morality alone cannot solve the labor question. The state must help, the community must help, the Church must help, all must put their hand to the task."[37]

Being a practical man, he soon realized that productive associations alone would not solve the problem either, not in the current state of affairs. He therefore began to promote the idea of trade unions: "The idea behind this movement is completely meritorious and it requires serious attention. We extend to it our cordial support."[38] A few years later, in an address to ten thousand workers gathered in the open air before a shrine of the Blessed Virgin near Offenbach on July 25, 1869, he went even further:

> Given these principles [of economic liberalism] the need for workers to organize has become an inevitable, natural consequence. Religion can do no less than bless the endeavor . . . and offer support . . . if the working-class is not to be completely vanquished by the power of centralized

capital. . . . The demand [for wages that reflect the true value of a man's labor] is fully justified.[39]

Having given full recognition to the reality and justice of class conflict and class struggle, Ketteler did not shrink from giving his approval to labor's principal weapon in that struggle:

> Many have maintained that the strike, because of the disruptions which it causes in the business and the loss of wages that workers suffer during the course of the strike, does more harm to the workers' cause than it is worth. This is not true, overall. Strikes have resulted in significant wage gains, as the English writer Thornton proved decisively. Since the trade unions began their activities, wages have risen by as much as 50 percent in certain industries, in others by 25–30 percent and in all other industries generally, by at least 15 percent. Thornton also demonstrated that even as a result of strikes that workers appeared to have lost, wage increases were granted soon afterward.[40]

Ketteler, incidentally, does not seem to have realized how much these facts compromised his faith in the iron law of wages.

To the argument that unions were too often led by atheistic radicals Ketteler responded with a passage that reminds one of John XXIII in *Pacem in Terris:*

> The air remains God's air even when the atheist breathes it, and the bread we eat remains nourishment provided by God even when the baker who prepares it is godless. That is precisely how things stand with the principle of association. It is rooted in the divine plan and is basically Christian, even though the men who nurture the idea fail to recognize God's will in it.[41]

While the archbishop was doing the job of a union organizer, his classmate of seminary days, Father Adolf Kolping (1813–1865) was building an organization of eighty thousand workers in four hundred *Gesellenvereine* (Journeymen's Associations). This organization provided hostels, clubs, educational and spiritual services; it spread to America and endures to this day.

Small wonder that a few months after Ketteler's address to the mass meeting at the shrine near Offenbach, Marx wrote to his friend Engels:

> My trip up the Rhine has convinced me that the priests, especially in the Catholic districts, must be energetically attacked. I shall work along these lines through the International. The dogs (for example, Bishop Ketteler in Mainz and the parsons in the Düsseldorf Congress) flirt with the labor question where they find it suits their purpose.[42]

If Ketteler's interest in the labor question could be described as a flirtation, it would be interesting to see how Marx might have defined true love. The books, sermons, and speeches of the archbishop, as well as the record of his life, are so full of that concern that it might almost rival his interest in the religious question. Better, one might say that it became a major focus of his effort to apply the teachings of his religion to the life of the temporal world.

The fact that Ketteler was unwilling to sign his name to that letter to Lassalle indicates that the atmosphere in Germany at the time was not ripe for a marriage between the Catholic Church and secular socialism. But when three Catholic members of Lassalle's party asked Ketteler in 1866 if they could in good conscience belong to the socialist party, he told them that the goals of the General German Workers Association (GGWA) were "compatible with the spirit of Christianity" and praised Lassalle, despite his lack of faith, for having "a deep respect for the doctrine of Christianity."[43] His only note of warning was that since Lassalle's death the organization may have come under anti-Christian leadership. In fact, *The Social Democrat*, published by followers of Lassalle in Berlin, was soon calling Ketteler "an accomplished hypocrite"[44] and dismissing his ideas as "ultramontane medieval propositions" whose consideration was "entirely a waste of time."[45]

By contrast, in his last public speech before the fatal duel, Lassalle spoke with pride of Ketteler's support and referred to him as

> a servant and prince of the Church . . . a man who in the Rhineland is considered almost a saint, a man who for many years has interested himself in the labor question.[46]

In that same speech Lassalle said that he did not believe in the divine character of private property, but had no intention of abolishing it, and added that the workers knew they must accomplish their goals peacefully.[47]

As long as Lassalle lived, as long as socialism in Germany stood for religious toleration and producer cooperatives, that half-way house between common and private property, just so long was it well within the realm of possibility that socialism and Christianity might make their peace. But the Marxists would not permit that to happen. As late as 1875, when Lassalle's GGWA merged with the Marxists' Social Democratic Workers Party, enough Lassalle influence remained to dictate the inclusion of a plank in the Gotha program for religious toleration, as well as a proposal that the state should fund producer cooperatives. In a savage attack on that program Marx denounced both ideas and in regard to religious toleration said this:

> But the workers' party ought at any rate in this connection to have expressed its awareness of the fact that bourgeois "freedom of conscience" is nothing but the toleration of all possible kinds of *religious freedom of conscience* [emphasis in the original], and that for its part it endeavors *rather to liberate the conscience from the witchery of religion* [emphasis added].[48]

In short, if words have any meaning, Marx's view was that a socialist state should actively seek to discourage the practice of religion, not to tolerate it. This kind of aggressive hostility did, in fact, increasingly mark the policies of the Social Democratic Party (SDP) and its leaders, as well as the worldwide socialist movement, until well into the twentieth century and, in some quarters, right up to the present moment.

The extent and intensity of that hostility is hard for a modern reader to appreciate, it has now been so long since most socialist leaders and writers moderated their views of religion, at least for public consumption. Following are some examples.

Wilhelm Liebknecht in his book *The Materialist Basis of History* wrote: "It is our duty as socialists to root out the faith in God with all our zeal, nor is anyone worthy of the name who does not consecrate himself to the spread of atheism."[49]

Liebknecht again: "Socialism must conquer the stupidity of the masses in so far as this stupidity reveals itself in religious forms and dogmas."[50]

August Bebel in *Vorwaerts*, a Berlin socialist daily of which he was editor: "Christianity is the enemy of liberty and civilization. It has kept mankind in slavery and oppression. The Church and State have always fraternally united to exploit the people. Christianity and socialism are like fire and water."[51]

In the Reichstag session of December 31, 1881, Bebel declared: "In politics we profess republicanism, in economics socialism, in religion atheism."[52]

Liebknecht and/or Bebel dominated the SDP virtually until Bebel's death in 1913, by which time the party had long since become the largest, best-organized, most successful socialist party in the world and had acquired a dominant position in the Socialist International. Together with militant atheism the socialists threw their weight with equal effectiveness in the direction of total abolition of private ownership of the land and of other means of production, although they did make an exception for producer cooperatives (but not state-supported) and these were not, in fact, dropped from the SDP program until 1921. Karl Kautsky (1854–1938), who as editor of *Die Neue Zeit* (The New Time) became the leading intellectual and Marxist theoretician of German socialism, continued both emphases and was a leader in the successful movement to condemn the "revisionism" of Eduard Bernstein (1850–1932).

This controversy, which flared up in the late 1890s, was actually an attempt by Bernstein and pro-peasant socialists like the Bavarian Georg von Vollmar, the Hessian Eduard David, and the trade unionist Adolf von Elm to move the party away from rigid Marxism back toward the reformist, pluralist kind of socialism represented by Lassalle. Its defeat at the German party congress of 1899 and the international congress at Amsterdam in 1904 (at one point there was a tie vote of 21–21) was not entirely avenged until 1951, when the new Socialist International declared itself at Frankfurt an even more revisionist movement than Bernstein himself might have approved. And yet, such has been the dominance of Marxism in the intellectual wing of the socialist movement that even today "revisionism" remains a term of reproach.

But back to Archbishop Ketteler. The return need not be abrupt because there are several logical connections between Ketteler and Bernstein's defeat. Ketteler represented the high-water mark of a possible rapprochement between socialism and the Catholic Church, and Bernstein represented the high-water mark, prior to 1851, of the tendency within secular socialism to move toward a rapprochement with a complex of economic, political, and intellectual values that were clearly more congenial to Christians in general and Catholics in particular. Both failed, and the Catholic Church went on to become the most militant and effective opponent, worldwide, of secular socialism until the revisionism of 1851 began to meet with an affirmative response from the church in the sixties, seventies, and eighties.

There was another, more immediate connection. In the early 1870s Ketteler was one of the founders of the Center Party, working largely through his clerical disciples Canon Christoph Moufang (1817–1890) and Father Franz Hitze (1851–1921), both of whom, as members of the Reichstag, vigorously promoted Lassalle's idea of state support for producer cooperatives as well as most of the other items in the Gotha program of the Social Democratic Party. Part of Bernstein's lifelong effort was to encourage socialist coalitions with the more progressive elements on the right. Of these, the Center Party, with its solid ninety to a hundred votes in the Reichstag, was the most substantial as well as the most progressive, despite its own splits between left and right factions. The Liebknecht-Bebel-Kautsky leadership of the SDP, however, consistently opposed any thought of coalition governments as a betrayal of "revolutionary Marxism."

This doctrinaire stand endured until 1920. By then the split between socialists and Catholics was so definite that any attempt at a coalition between the two parties could not withstand the combined pressures of the punitive Versailles Treaty, the worldwide depression, the rise of the Communist Party on the left and the Nazis on the right. Russia had already been overwhelmed, Italy was soon to be overwhelmed, and a decade later Germany would be overwhelmed. So came to pass the words William Butler Yeats wrote in 1921:

Turning and turning in the widening gyre
The falcon cannot hear the falconer;
Things fall apart; the center cannot hold;
Mere anarchy is loosed upon the world,
The blood-dimmed tide is loosed, and everywhere
The ceremony of innocence is drowned;
The best lack all conviction, while the worst
Are full of passionate intensity.[53]

Archbishop Wilhelm Emmanuel von Ketteler journeyed to Rome in 1869 to take part in Vatican Council I, where, with most of the German bishops, he was one of a sizable group of "inopportunists" who opposed the declaration of papal infallibility, not on doctrinal grounds, but on the ground that it was inopportune to declare it at that time. It was indeed inopportune for the Germans, since it was a factor leading to Bismarck's declaration of war on the Catholic Church with the *Kulturkampf*.

Ketteler returned to Rome in 1877 for the jubilee of Pope Pius IX, who stood for so many things that Ketteler did not. On his way home he fell ill, probably of pneumonia, and died in the Franciscan monastery of Burghausen. A copy of *Das Kapital* was found in his traveling bag, which leads one to speculate on the odds against a book of Ketteler's ever being found in the traveling bag of Karl Marx.

Pius IX died the next year and was succeeded by a pope very different from him, Leo XIII, who was wont to refer to Ketteler as "my great predecessor"[54] and once told Ketteler's former secretary that the archbishop was "the first openly to declare that employers *and* government had a responsibility and a duty to the workers of our time."[55]

Actually, Ketteler was not the first, but he was the first archbishop to do so with so much power and eloquence that the world had to sit up and take notice. Leo certainly did take notice, but of that more in another chapter. To that same chapter we will leave the further study of German "so-called Christian socialism" in the Catholic Church. It was to be a significant factor in shaping the thought of Leo XIII as well as of subsequent popes.

ON THE PROTESTANT SIDE

In the early days of the Christian social movement in Germany, there was too much hostility to make possible any significant collaboration between Catholics and Protestants, though later the Christian unions, encouraged by Ketteler, were able to organize both groups under the same roof.

One exception was Victor Aimé Huber (1800–1869), who had some influence on Ketteler's circle. Like Baader before him he visited England, in 1844 and 1854, and became friendly with Ludlow and the Christian socialists. He brought back an enthusiasm for producer cooperatives and spread it through his books, the periodical *Janus*, which he edited from 1838 to 1848, and an organization he founded, the Association of Christian Order and Liberty. He also promoted the idea of utopian colonies, according to the gospel of Fourier, Cabet, and Owen. In 1851 he left his teaching position in Berlin to live among the workers in a small mountain town.

Another pioneer was the Lutheran pastor Joseph Hinrich Wichern (1808–1891), who worked among the poor in Hamburg and Berlin and organized schools for vagrant boys, youth hostels, orphanages, and something called "the Inner Mission," intended to revive the flagging faith of the German people and to persuade them to apply the teachings of Christ to every aspect of social and industrial life. Another instrument of this mission was his *Kirchentag* (Church Day), an annual conference that met in a different city each year between 1848 and 1871 to discuss Wichern's social teachings.

Like the early Ketteler, Wichern distrusted the state and preferred individual action and charity to relieve poverty. Also like Ketteler, his disciples came to realize the inadequacy of this approach and looked more and more to the state. Most prominent among these were the pastors, Adolf Stöcker (1835–1909) and Rudolf Todt (1839–1887). Todt took as the text for his social gospel Ephesians 4:25: "We are members of one another." With Stöcker he organized a Central Association for Social Reform in 1878. Stöcker went even further and in the same year founded the Christian Socialist Workers Party, which he saw as a rival to the Social Democratic Party, organized three years before at Gotha from the merger of Lassalle's GGWA and the Marxist SDWP. When Stöcker's CSWP failed to elect any candidates, Stöcker struck out the words "Socialist" and "Workers" and renamed it the Christian Social Party, adding a heavy dose of anti-Semitism. He flirted briefly with the Junkers' Conservative Party, but his socialism was too much for them and they expelled him in 1896. He reconstituted the CSP, which then elected him to the Reichstag along with two other delegates. He served there until 1908. He had been an army chaplain during the Franco-Prussian War and this experience led him to preach patriotic sermons in the spirit of his political creed, which he summed up in the words, "Christianity, monarchy, the Fatherland, and social reform."[56] Such sermons led to his appointment as court preacher, but his anti-Semitism was too much even for Bismarck and Kaiser Wilhelm, who forced him out in 1890.

Stöcker is significant mainly as a kind of precursor of those Christians who supported Nazism, whose full name was, after all, National Socialism. He was also responsible for the conversion of Friedrich Naumann (1860–1919) to a kind of Christian socialism. Naumann wandered off to the left and then came back to the right, combining anti-Semitism with a virulent form of militaristic nationalism. For both Stöcker and Naumann, Christianity and socialism became less and less central as they yielded to the pressures created by the rise of Germany as a world power. Naumann justified German power with such statements as, "The struggle for existence has taught the nations to be armour-plated beasts."[57]

Naumann, however, played a role by reason of his influence in reverse on a major figure in the history of Christian socialism in German-speaking Europe, Karl Barth (1886–1968). One day in 1915, Barth, then a socialist pastor in the Swiss town of Safenwil, met with Naumann. They had an angry argument over German responsibility for World War I and the relation of Christians to that war. Barth was entirely in sympathy with Rosa Luxemburg, who in a bitter comment on the collapse of socialist resistance on both sides of that conflict remarked that the Marxist *Manifesto's* "Workers of the world, unite" had been changed on the battlefield to "Workers of the world, slit each other's throats."[58]

On that same day Barth went from his visit with Naumann to a visit with Christoph Blumhardt (1842–1919), who commented somewhat cryptically on Barth's argument with Naumann, "The world is the world, but God is God."[59] This was not the first exposure of Barth to the Christian socialism of the younger Blumhardt, but it was clearly the most influential, and the cryptic ambiguity of Blumhardt's statement about God and the world was to mark

Barth's own contribution to modern theology and the history of Christian socialism. The contrast with Naumann added to the impact of that meeting.

THE BLUMHARDT MIRACLE

Christoph was the son of Johann Christoph Blumhardt (1805–1880), a Lutheran preacher with a gift of healing. This gift climaxed at Christmas 1843, the year after Christoph's birth, when his father drove what he believed to be a demon out of the soul of a young woman named Gottlieben Dittus. This "miracle," one of the most famous and significant in the history of modern Protestantism, was later reported by the elder Blumhardt to church authorities. The report is available in English under the title *Blumhardt's Battle*. I quote from a summary of that report by James Luther Adams, the much-loved dean of Christian socialists in America:

> Blumhardt's report narrates such fantastic phenomena of mental hallucination and bodily distortion that it is scarcely credible. So puzzled was he by these phenomena that he repeatedly called for assistance at the hands of physicians. Here is his description of the climactic episode in an eighteen-month struggle against the dark powers that possessed Fraulein Dittus:
>
> > "Foam flowed again from her mouth. It had become clear to me that something demonic played a role here after what had happened so far, and it hurt me to think that there should be no means of help in such a horrible affair. While in these thoughts, a sort of wrath gripped me. I jumped forward, took her stiff hands, pulled her fingers together with force as for prayer, loudly spoke her name into her ear in her unconscious state and said, 'Fold your hands and pray: Lord Jesus, help me. We have seen long enough what the devil is doing, now we want to see what Jesus can do.' After a few moments she awakened, prayed these words after me, and all convulsions ceased, to the great surprise of those present."[60]

One of those present was Gottlieben's sister Katherina, who at that moment cried out, "Jesus is victor!" in a voice "almost inconceivable in a human throat," which the elder Blumhardt took to be the cry of the devil himself.[61]

This healing made the father famous and left an indelible impression on his son Christoph and on Karl Barth as well. In some mysterious way it confirmed their faith not only that Jesus was Son of God and Lord of heaven and earth, but also that he desired more than the salvation of individual souls, that he desired the temporal salvation of the world, the kingdom of God on earth. Barth later quoted the elder Blumhardt:

> Yes, dear Christians, make sure that you die saved. But the Lord Jesus wants more. He wants not only my redemption and yours, but the

redemption of all the world. He wants to finish off the evil that dominates the world and to make the whole world free from its preoccupation
with godlessness.[62]

Barth added this comment on the confrontation between Johann Blumhardt
and the demonic possession in the soul of Gottlieben Dittus: "The contrast was
not between Jesus and the unconverted heart of man, but between Jesus and
the real power of darkness."[63] The son Christoph wrote, "Jesus is victor over
every devil, over hell and over death! And today he is likewise victor over all
flesh, over the whole world, over all mankind in its earthly concerns."[64]

As these quotes indicate, there was more than a touch of utopian optimism
in the Blumhardts. The upshot, however, was that Christoph was moved
finally to join the Social Democratic Party in 1899 despite what others
described as its "godlessness." He responded,

> The heart of a man who denies God with his reason more often contains
> God in spirit and in truth than does that of one who confesses with the
> mouth. . . . If then today socialism has its eye on the goal that specifies
> an equal right to bread for everyone, which necessitates that property
> relationships assume such a form that the life of man, rather than money
> and possessions, has the highest value—why is that an objectionable
> desire? I am certain that it is based on the spirit of Christ . . . and that
> there will be uprisings until it is reached.[65]

Blumhardt was the first Lutheran pastor in Germany to join the SDP, and in
that same year, 1899, he committed the unforgivable sin of expressing public
support for picketing strikers in Würtemberg, in the face of a new law that
imposed severe penalties on picketing. Three years before this, Kaiser Wilhelm
II, head of the Evangelical Church, had written even about the conservative
Stöcker: "Pastors should concern themselves with the souls of their parishioners, should promote charity, and keep out of politics."[66] Clearly Blumhardt's
more radical activity could not be tolerated and the church authorities forced
him to resign from the ministry.

But Blumhardt held firm. For six years he represented the Social Democratic
Party as principal spokesperson for the five opposition deputies in the Stuttgart *Landtag*. Repudiated by his church, he left instructions that at his death
there should be for him, as for Lamennais in France, no funeral service, only
the reading of Psalm 46:

> God is our refuge and strength, a very present help in trouble. Therefore
> we will not fear though the earth should change, though the mountains
> shake in the heart of the sea. . . . Come, behold the works of the
> Lord. . . . He makes wars cease to the ends of the earth; he breaks the
> bow, and shatters the spear, he burns the chariots with fire! "Be still, and
> know that I am God. I am exalted among the nations, I am exalted in the
> earth!" The Lord of hosts is with us; the God of Jacob is our refuge.

Martin Rumscheidt credits the Blumhardts with beginning "the movement in Lutheranism away from inwardness and concentration on the soul to the new comprehension of Christ's political and social commission to the Church." He further credits Christoph, with later and more substantial help from Dietrich Bonhoeffer, with the discrediting of Luther's "doctrine of the Two Kingdoms, which asserts that the measures of the state, achieved through power, are compatible with the demands made in the gospel of the community of love, the church."[67]

The year of Blumhardt's death, 1919, was a critical year in the history both of socialism and of Christian socialism in Germany. Defeat in the war had driven the Kaiser from his throne and from his position as head of the Evangelical Church. In the chaotic aftermath of that defeat the SDP emerged as the majority party with 163 delegates in the Reichstag and 22 delegates elected by its left-wing splinter, the Independent Socialist Party. The Catholic Center was the second largest with 88 delegates, the Democrats had 75 (Max Weber and other intellectual liberals were members of this party) and 47 delegates belonged to several right-wing parties. The Spartacists, a Communist party, attempted a coup on the Russian model even before the election, and their leaders, Rosa Luxemburg and Karl Liebknecht, son of Wilhelm, were assassinated by cavalry officers while under arrest. All this in January 1919.

Communist uprisings in Berlin and Munich during the months of February and March were suppressed by the government, now controlled by the SDP, with over a thousand casualties. In April the Communists were successful in setting up a Soviet republic in Bavaria, the heart of Catholic Germany, but this was liquidated in May, leaving a kind of permanent "Red scare" in Munich, the Bavarian capital, which not only gave Hitler his start but fortified Catholic conservatism in southern Germany, where it remains strong up to the present day.

RAGAZ, FOUNDER OF "RELIGIOUS SOCIALISM"

This then was the backdrop against which a group of religious-socialists known as the Schlüctern Circle, centered around their publication, *The Christian Democrat*, organized a conference in the town of Tambach, in November 1919. About a hundred kindred souls attended. Leonhard Ragaz (1868–1945) had orginally been invited to be the principal speaker, but he was sick, so Barth was invited in his place. Barth, another Swiss socialist, was apparently believed to agree fundamentally with his older countryman, Ragaz, on the need for a Christian socialist movement.

This was a big mistake. But before we get to that, we must consider the life and work of the man Barth replaced, Leonhard Ragaz, who had been since 1908 professor of theology at the University of Zurich and the most prominent Christian socialist in Europe. A disciple of the Blumhardts, Ragaz made a powerful impact on the intellectual and religious life of Zurich. Emil Brunner, a founder of "dialectical theology," one of his students, looking back on that time, wrote,

That was a great time, when Ragaz came to Zurich. Then theology was interesting, not as a science, but as a proclamation in our time, as encounter with historical reality, with the labor question, with the war issue.[68]

Ragaz had begun his ministry as a Reformed village pastor in 1890 with a leaning toward "undogmatic Christianity" and a kind of liberal theology seasoned with Hegelian abstractions. He became concerned with the poverty of his parishioners and, through the influence of Kierkegaard, disillusioned both with the institutional church and with liberal theology. He gave up the ministry for a few years, but returned to it and accepted in 1902 a call to the cathedral in Basel. The following year a great bricklayers' strike led to violence and the calling in of troops. From the pulpit of the cathedral Ragaz preached what came to be known as the "Bricklayers' Strike Sermon." As Christoph Blumhardt had done four years before with the strike in Wurttemberg, so did Ragaz stir up and upset the religious and political establishment of Switzerland. He declared that Christ was on the side of the oppressed, that the socialist movement was pursuing "the humanization of humans" and was thereby a sign of the kingdom of God, and that Christians should at least join in this general endeavor. The sermon was printed and widely distributed, with both plus and minus reactions.

About the same time a Zurich pastor named Hermann Kutter (1863–1931) wrote a book, *Sie Müssen* (They Must), which said substantially the same thing that Ragaz was saying and which became very popular. Together in 1906 Kutter and Ragaz founded a movement that they first called "religious-social" and later "religious-socialist." Although they had much in common they also had differences. These differences happened to correspond to conflicting tendencies in Karl Barth's own life and theology, and it is appropriate that in 1915 Barth, in a letter to his friend Eduard Thurneysen, set down the differences between Ragaz and Kutter in outline form. Some examples:

RAGAZ: Experience of social needs and problems. Belief in development. Optimistic evaluation of Social Democracy. Opposition to the church. Religious-socialist party with conferences and "new ways." Emphasis upon sympathy with workers and other laymen. Martyrdom hoped for and sought. Protest against war.

KUTTER: Experience of God. Insight into the enslaved condition of man without God. The Social Democrats can never understand us! Religious responsibility *in* the church in continuity with the pietistic tradition. Circles of friends for *spiritual* deepening and for work. Concentration primarily on the pastors.[69]

Ragaz, in short, was more activist, political, union-oriented, Kutter more spiritual, religious, church-oriented. The Two Kingdoms again. Strangely enough, however, when the war broke out it was Ragaz who opposed it and

Kutter who supported the German side. This led to a final break between them. Ragaz became more and more concerned wiith pacifism and nonviolence, more and more hostile to the spirit of German nationalism and militarism. He was an admirer of Woodrow Wilson and his proposal of a League of Nations. When Wilson came to Paris for the peace conference, Ragaz wrote him a prophetic open letter warning that unless the punitive provisions of the Treaty of Versailles were changed, there would be literally hell to pay.

> Militarism in Germany, strengthened by the treaty, is raising its head again. The proletarian revolution opposes it in a violent way. It is likely that this revolution will turn into a world revolution unless some saving force intervenes. If it does not, there will be a catastrophe in comparison with which the biblical flood was child's play. Hunger, despair, violence and murder will make a real hell out of the earth, and death will reap unheard-of harvests. Nor will America be spared from it.[70]

Although Ragaz was not an absolute pacifist, believing that there were occasions when nations must defend themselves, his Christian bias in favor of nonviolence turned him strongly against the Bolshevik, Leninist brand of revolution. He had joined the Social Democratic Party of Switzerland in 1913 and was active in it. In 1919 this party was faced with the decision whether to join the Third (Communist) International. Ragaz had begun editing *Neue Wege* (New Ways) in 1906 (it is still being published today). Through the pages of this periodical and through pamphlets, speeches, and sermons, he and his fellow religious socialists exercised a significant degree of influence within the SDP. They have often been given credit for tipping the scales against affiliation with the Third International. Some key quotes in Ragaz's battle against Leninism:

> The World War is over, but now the danger of an international civil war hangs over mankind like a heavy cloud. And on that cloud is written in large letters the name "Lenin." . . . Often people battle Bolshevism for pocket-book reasons, though they are actually practicing minority rule themselves. Our opposition is different. We fight as socialists against a perversion of socialism . . . .
> Socialism lives and breathes respect for the freedom of people. It takes seriously the fact that a person is an end in himself and not just a means for other purposes. . . . Socialism is not just an economic or political system as such. . . . Socialism is a moral ideal, and the political or economic system is simply the means by which it gets realized . . . .Without this ideal it would lose its worth. . . . Socialism is a form of community that is based on the principle of solidarity rather than on the principle of mutual combat. This solidarity does not rest simply on egotism but on the feeling of mutual responsibility, mutual respect for the worth and sacredness of each person. Strike this factor and replace it, if

you can, with pure materialism and egotism, with a mere calculation of what is useful to everybody, and you will have robbed socialism of its soul. You will have taken from it all that is great, holy and exciting in it. This is the idealism without which all socialism collapses . . . .

One hears repeatedly the charge that socialism is a new Catholic Church. There is something true in this statement insofar as it stresses the right and necessity of a community and of solidarity as opposed to an exaggerated individualism. . . . But when one thinks that present-day socialism is dominated by Marxism, and that Marx comes from Hegel, the greatest advocate of state absolutism, a man who declared the individual conscience to be "the radical evil," then one realizes that something of this spirit of absolutism has infused socialism as a whole . . . .

Socialism has to combine in itself the truth of Catholicism and the truth of Protestantism and thus help free the world from the one-sidedness of a confused individualism on the one hand and an authoritarian despotism on the other. Since for socialism the emphasis on community is a matter of course, special care must be taken not to betray freedom, but to make the community that it is building into a fortress of freedom.[71]

Ragaz was an interesting mix of radical and conservative ideas, radical and conservative interpretations of the gospel. One of his more conservative traits was his emphasis on sexual morality, which led him to be critical of some of his Marxist comrades. He lamented the fact that Marxist socialism

sometimes believes that it must exalt adultery for the greater honor of socialism. If it sets out to work with enthusiasm for birth control and abortion—an enthusiasm that deserves to be spent on a better cause—then, in addition to its libertinism, there can also be seen at work that kind of rationalism and intellectualism that militate against a deeper sense of values. . . .[72]

Ragaz preached a brand of socialism that one might expect Swiss Christians to find attractive. Some did. Many did not. Ragaz had grown up in a mountain village of farmers, the son of a farmer, and the cooperative forms of economic life practiced by those farmers impressed him and helped to shape his own ideas about a decentralized form of socialism. But he did not sufficiently develop those ideas in practical economic terms nor did he draw out the relationships between that "fortress of freedom" he wrote of and the necessary distribution of power over the means of production.

Another problem with Ragaz was the violent animosity toward organized religion that began to mark his writing and preaching after World War I. Barth once remarked that he and Ragaz were like two express trains passing each other in opposite directions, he going into the church and Ragaz out of it.

Much of Ragaz's criticism was eminently fair and necessary. The trouble was that he often gave the impression that *all* religion, *all* churches, were reactionary, perverted forms of Christianity and basically alien to the spirit of Christ. For example:

> The Kingdom of God is no religion, but rather the abolition of all religion. . . . Not only does [Jesus] not bring a new religion, he does not bring any religion at all. . . . He does not want a religion, but rather a Kingdom, a new creation, a new world. He wants God, the people, the brother, a new justice, the liberation of the world from fear and sensuality, from Mammonism, from despair, from death—and from religion. . . . What Jesus wants is a world order based on God, not a religion. . . . No religious dogma. . . . The world is truly his temple; therefore the special temple falls by the wayside. All people automatically become priests; therefore a special priesthood is not needed. All days become holy: therefore special holy days are not needed. Every deed becomes an act of worship; therefore worship services are no longer needed.[73]

Quite apart from the holes one might find in the logic of this statement, one can understand how it would turn off church-going Christians, even those who might otherwise have been disposed to accept Ragaz's socialist gospel.

One of the more admirable contributions of Ragaz was his promotion of Christian-Jewish dialogue, mainly through his friendship with Martin Buber (1878–1965), who was editor of *Der Jude* from 1916 to 1924, professor of religion at Frankfurt University from 1923 to 1938, professor of social philosophy at the Hebrew University in Jerusalem from 1938 to 1951, and author of many important books on Judaism and philosophy. He became and remains one of the outstanding voices of German Jewry, Zionism, and authentic religious faith.

At his first meeting with Paul Tillich in 1928, at a conference in his home village of Heppenheim, Buber objected when Tillich suggested that a new word be found to replace "God" in order to unite in the cause of socialism those who could use this name and those who could not. Tillich later reported that after he had made this suggestion, a short man with a black beard and fiery black eyes rose in the back and protested, "Aber Gott ist ein Urwort!" (But God is an *Urwort*). *Urwort* is not easily translated into English. "Primordial word" is perhaps closest. It was Buber's view that even for the sake of unity one could not dispense with a primordial word like "God." Tillich later admitted, "And he was right."[74]

In that same year, 1928, Buber wrote a short essay, "Three Theses of a Religious Socialism," which opens with a quotation from Ragaz: "Any socialism whose limits are narrower than God and humanity is too narrow for us." In the essay Buber defines religious socialism:

Religious socialism can only mean that religion and socialism are essentially directed to each other, that each of them needs the covenant with the other for the fulfillment of its own essence. . . . Religion without socialism is disembodied spirit, therefore not genuine spirit; socialism without religion is body emptied of spirit, hence also not genuine body. But—socialism without religion does not hear the divine address, it does not aim at a response, still it happens that it responds; religion without socialism hears the call but does not respond.[75]

In 1922 Ragaz had written, "But before all else I remind you of men like Gustave Landauer and Martin Buber, who proclaim a state-free and nonviolent socialism in the sense of a genuine community of people built upon love."[76] Landauer, a German Jew, had been kicked to death by soldiers in 1919.

Buber wrote to Ragaz in 1932 of his intention to organize a "union of Jewish religious socialists" that could send representatives to conferences of religious socialists, but the advancing horrors of Nazism prevented this idea from coming to fruition.

Perhaps the long-range significance of Leonhard Ragaz is best expressed in those of his writings that drew the attention of German Christians away from Paul and Luther and Barth's emphasis on faith (to the possible neglect of works) and back to the simple, stubborn insistence of James (2:24,26) that "faith apart from works is *dead.*"

Ragaz, protesting the emphasis of Barth and other dialectical theologians, wrote:

The Gospel is different. It knows no such slogan as "first faith, then works" or "There is no doing, there is only grace." Everything is more organic, dialectical in a deeper sense. Action has its direct meaning and decisive importance, *but the importance of grace is not thereby diminished* [emphasis added]; its value is debased when the other member, the works, loses its meaning. Not faith *or* works, grace *or* action, but the Kingdom *and* its pursuit [emphasis in the original]. One of the main points of the New Reformation must be the restoration of the importance of works.[77]

Unfortunately, Ragaz alienated himself increasingly from the institutional church, which he saw as a tool of reaction, and in 1921 he gave up his position on the theological faculty and moved from an upper-class to a working-class section of Zurich, where he set up an educational center for workers, led Bible discussions, and edited his *Neue Wege.* He was not the theologian that Barth was, and the ascendance of Barthian theology among left-wing Protestants meant the decline of the more active, explicit "religious socialism" that Ragaz clung to until his death in 1945.

Religious socialism, in turn, must pay tribute to the German-speaking Swiss.

Barth, Ragaz and Kutter all made major contributions to the movement, one of which was the pacifist tendency—for good or ill—that has characterized Christian socialism in Germany ever since. The passionate urgency that marked the work of Ragaz and Kutter is eloquently expressed by Mattmüller and Buess in their recent book:

Instead of the Church as a quiet, healing element, they demand the Kingdom of God. For them the condition of the world is not an un-changeable order. . . *God is still at work, and we have to work with him, so that the world becomes filled with his splendor* [emphasis added].[78]

BARTH THE AMBIGUOUS

When members of the Schlüctern Circle invited Karl Barth (1886–1968) to replace the ailing Ragaz as their keynote speaker at the Tambach conference in 1919, they thought they were inviting a younger edition of the Zurich theolo-gian. Apparently they had not yet read the book that propelled Barth into the center of German Protestantism, his *Epistle to the Romans*, which had just been published.

They certainly knew that Barth had established a reputation as "the Red Pastor" of Safenwil in Switzerland, that he had followed Ragaz in joining the Swiss Social Democratic Party in 1915, and that he had been saying and writing things like the following:

Jesus *is* the movement for social justice, and the movement for social justice *is* Jesus in the present. . . . *Real* socialism is real Christianity in our time. . . . Jesus rejected the concept of private property; of that . . . there can be no doubt.[79] [Ah, but there was, and is.]

A real Christian must become a socialist if he is to be in earnest about the reformation of Christianity. A real socialist must be a Christian if he is in earnest about the reformation of socialism.[80]

They also knew, undoubtedly, that here was a new and arresting voice, a man who spoke as one having authority, who proclaimed the divinity and power and wisdom of Jesus Christ, Son of Man and Son of God, as no one had pro-claimed him in Germany for years and years, who made them forget the corrosive skepticisms of theologians like Friedrich Strauss and Rudolf Bult-mann. Here was a man whose erudition, subtlety, and style, almost in and by themselves, *seemed* to give the lie to such pontifical certainties as Bultmann's later statement that "no one can use the electric light and the radio or the discoveries of modern medicine and at the same time believe in the New Testament world of spirit and miracle."[81] Here at last was a man who, appar-ently, did believe in precisely that world and who could express his faith with such intellectual force that others felt compelled to believe as well. Here was a man who could belittle human arrogance with just as sharp a pen as human arrogance had ever employed to belittle God.

> He [man] thinks he sits on a high throne, but in reality he sits only on a child's stool, blowing his little trumpet, cracking his little whip, pointing with frightful seriousness his little finger, while all the time nothing happens that really matters.[82]

So they settled back in their seats, those "religious-social" Christians at Tambach, expecting a word to rouse and spur them on, and before they had been listening for ten minutes, this is what they heard from the Red Pastor of Safenwil:

> Immediately to hand we have all those combinations—Christian-social, evangelical-social, religious-social and the like—but it is highly question-able that the hyphens we draw with such intellectual courage do not really make dangerous short circuits. Clever enough is the paradox that the service of God is or must become the service of man; but that is not the same as saying that our precipitate service of man, even when it is undertaken in the name of the purest love, becomes by that happy fact the service of God.[83]

And much more to that ambiguous, plausible but nonetheless discouraging effect.

If they had read Barth's *Epistle to the Romans*, they might have been forewarned. There Barth, disillusioned by the socialists' decision to "slit each other's throats" in World War I and by Bolshevik extremism in the Russian Revolution, had come to view negatively politics, the state, and all human endeavor as over against God, "the wholly other." Politics was *grundschmut-zig*, "dirty to the roots."

> The revolutionary must, however, own that in adopting his plan he allows himself to be *overcome of evil*. He forgets that he is not the One . . . that for all the strange brightness of his eyes, he is not the Christ who stands before the Grand Inquisitor, but is, contrariwise, the Grand Inquisitor encountered by Christ. . . . He too usurps a position which is not due him, a legality that is fundamentally illegal, an authority which— as we have grimly experienced in Bolshevism, but also in the behavior of far more delicate-minded innovators—soon displays its essential tyr-anny.[84]

A salutary warning, but in Barth it became more than a warning. It was the way things must inevitably be.

In another place the ultimate ambiguous put-down:

Let there be strike, general strike, and street fighting if need be, but no religious justification or glorification of it . . . ; military service as soldier or officer, but on *no* condition as military chaplain . . . ; social democratic but not religious socialist.[85]

The Christian could be, *should* be, socialist, but not *religious* socialist: the old distinction without a difference, the characteristic mark of Gray's intellectual, so totally the embodiment of intellect and reason that he becomes destitute of common sense. Godwin's Disease. For if the Christian socialist is not a religious socialist, words have no meaning. At the very least Christian socialists are religious socialists in the sense that they are both religious and socialist, even if they see no necessary connection between the two. But if their socialism flows naturally from their religion, and their religion naturally supports and corrects their socialism, then they are twice, thrice, four times religious socialists. No wonder that, as Markus Mattmüller, Ragaz's biographer, put it, "Barth's speech left the Tambach Congress with a feeling of hopelessness."[86] And the religious socialist movement, at least as far as formal organization went, in that fateful year of 1919, when it might have made a difference, died aborning. As Mattmüller put it,

The Tambach Congress of 1919 was a crossroads in the history of religious socialism. Many German sympathizers from then on got to know the Blumhardt message in Barthian clothing and were fascinated by it, as an earlier generation of religious socialists had been fascinated by the original: The sovereign God, God the wholly other, the Kingdom of God, were totally revealed by Barth within Blumhardt's meaning of those words. But the Kingdom of God, as Ragaz once said, now put on an academic gown and read from a prayer-book, and from being a movement for the world became a movement for the church.[87]

And yet he was a great theologian. The American Will Herberg called Barth "beyond all doubt the master theologian of our age."[88] He could write so profoundly, with such dialectical, paradoxical subtlety, that few dared to question absurdities like the following from his *Epistle to the Romans*:

Human action neither assists the victory of God nor hinders it. It must follow then, from His freedom and sole dominion, that men are not responsible, and, from His overcoming of sin by grace, that men are free to do both good and evil.[89]

Unfortunately, it was not human freedom, the latter part, that came through most strongly, but the former contradiction, human irresponsibility and inability either to assist or hinder the victory of God. This Gospel of Helplessness moved one wit to rewrite the old hymn "Rise Up, O Men of God," as "Sit Down, O Men of God, Ye nothing can do." Reinhold Niebuhr called it "sanctified futilitarianism."[90]

Shortly after his appearance at Tambach, Barth, on the strength of his popular *Epistle,* was offered a professorship at the University of Göttingen and the rest of his life was spent in Academe, either in Germany or Switzerland, where he was isolated for a time from the world of work and politics, which he had once known as a pastor in Geneva and Safenwil.

His socialism, though muted, did not die in Academe. The Nazis saw to that, or rather the Nazis supplied the challenge that Barth's valid Christian faith could only answer with the words of Peter, "We must obey God rather than men." For Barth, obeying God came down to reaffirming his socialist faith by publicly joining the Social Democratic Party in 1932 and giving vigorous public support to Günther Dehn, one of the first targets of Nazi persecution in Academe, a man who, ironically, had first been led to left-wing Christianity through the influence of the anti-Semitic Stöcker.

Even though the SDP, as Hitler assumed power, urged its members in the universities to resign in order to keep their jobs, Barth refused to do so and the Nazis drove him back to Switzerland and the University of Basel in 1934.

In later years, after the war, Barth revised somewhat his theology and his view of religious socialism. He stressed a little more "the humanization of God" in Jesus Christ and grew more tolerant toward political action and the need for Christians to play an active role. In a private meeting with Mattmüller he even admitted that the reading of a new volume of Ragaz's letters "showed him to me in a new light" and that "this man was a passionate theologian who wrestled with the Gospel."[91]

In 1948 a battle broke out between Barth and Reinhold Niebuhr, who at the moment were probably the two most influential theologians in Christendom. The debate highlights both theological and sociological, or socialist, differences between them, differences that have troubled and divided Christians since Paul and James wrote their separate epistles, emphasizing respectively justification by faith and justification by works.

Although Barth did not seem to realize it at the time, the first shot was fired by Niebuhr at the founding congress of the World Council of Churches at Amsterdam in 1948. Barth had given the opening address and, in a real sense, returned to the discouraging ambiguities of his Tambach speech. He criticized the four volumes of preparatory studies because they embodied the view that

. . . as Christians and church people we ought to achieve what God alone can accomplish and what he will accomplish completely by himself. . . . We shall not be the ones who change this wicked world into a good one. God has not abdicated his lordship over us. . . All that is required of us is that in the midst of the political and social disorder of the world we should be his witnesses. . . .

We may be his witnesses, but he has not called us to be his lawyers, engineers, managers, statisticians and administrative directors. We are therefore not burdened with the cares that go with such activity in his service.[92]

It was a very biblical, Christ-centered speech. He called twice for faith in the resurrection and second coming of Christ, faith in the Trinity, faith in "the real Gospel of Jesus Christ."

[The question of Barth's orthodoxy has also been an ambiguous one because Barth, in Pierre Benoit's analysis, "can accept the results of modern *historical* criticism without excitement. . . . If you call into question the historical value of his biblical documents, you are merely removing a support upon which he has never relied. God speaks to him equally as well through the 'faith of the community' as through the actual miracles or the explicit declarations of Jesus."][93]

Whether or not Niebuhr, in his address to the same congress, was responding explicitly to Barth's address, the latter, if he was listening, must have recognized himself. Niebuhr starts with a clear, brilliant call for "a plague on both your houses" to both capitalism and Marxism, but with this tribute to a Marxian insight:

> In a sense the word of Marx is true, "The beginning of all criticism is the criticism of religion." For it is on this ultimate level that the pretensions of men reach their most absurd form. The final sin is always committed in the name of religion.[94]

He makes his own claim to orthodoxy with an expression of "faith in the One who died and rose again," (see chapter 10 below for more on this question) and then acknowledges both his agreement and disagreement with Barth in these two sharp sentences:

> The final victory over man's disorder is God's and not ours, but *we do have responsibility for proximate victories.* Christian life without a high sense of responsibility for the health of our communities, our nations and our cultures *degenerates into an intolerable other-worldliness*[emphasis added].[95]

After he returned home Niebuhr wrote a more explicit response in *The Christian Century.* (This appeared Oct. 27, 1948, but Barth's address did not actually appear in the magazine until December 8.)

Niebuhr pays tribute to Barth's heroic stand against Hitler and to

> a very powerful witness to Christ in the hour of crisis. But perhaps this theology is constructed too much for the great crises of history. It can fight the devil if he shows both horns and both cloven feet. But it refuses to make discriminating judgements about good and evil if the devil shows only one horn or the half of a cloven foot [p. 1139].

The following February 16, 1949, Barth replied to Neibuhr in the same magazine. He expressed his "utter surprise" that Niebuhr, whom he regarded as an ally, should be so critical of his address. He can only explain it on the ground that Niebuhr has completely misunderstood him. He excuses his inexcusable remarks to the effect that God "has not called us to be his lawyers, etc." and that "we are therefore not burdened with the cares that go with such activity in his service" with a plea that this was "a touch of irony." Irony? There's no irony visible within a hundred miles. The truth is that Barth had, one more time, failed to resist the temptation to play the prophet and confound the Philistines with a few more overstated expressions of his conviction that "the world is the world and God is God." Faced with a man who would not let him get away with it, Barth retreated to a porous defense based on a line of Biblical-vs-non-Biblical, he being Biblical and Niebuhr non-Biblical. This didn't work too well either.

Niebuhr responded in the next issue (February 23, 1949) where he maintained that Barth's method leads to

> two errors . . . one is the introduction of irrelevant detailed standards of the good, when the Christian life requires a great deal of freedom from every kind of law and tradition, including the kind which is woven together from proof-texts. The other is that it fails to provide sufficient criteria of judgment and impulses to decisive action in moments of life when a historic evil, not yet full-blown and not yet requiring some heroic witness, sneaks into the world upon the back of some unobtrusive error which, when fully conceived, may produce a monstrous evil (p. 236).

Despite the cheap shot about "proof-texts" (fascinating how easily quarreling theologians can dismiss appeals to biblical authority with that little phrase) Niebuhr proved again that he could think more clearly and logically than Karl Barth.

From there things went from bad to worse in the relationship between the world's most influential theologians. A few years later Barth was heaping scorn on Niebuhr's somewhat feverish anti-communism with such statements as "anti-communism [is] an even greater evil than communism itself."[96] In this case, however, Barth himself exposed the fallacy of the statement a few years later still:

> Anti means *against*. God is not against, but *for* men. The communists are men too. God is also for the communists. So a Christian cannot be against the communists but only for them. To be for the communists does not mean to be for communism. I am not for communism. But one can only say what has to be said *against* communism if one is *for* the communists [emphasis in the original].[97]

The conclusion seems to be that anti-communism is all right if you are Karl Barth, but not all right if you are Reinhold Niebuhr. He wrote a public letter to an East German pastor who had asked his advice on how the Lutheran Church should deal with the communist government of East Germany and whether the church should not defend its right to "proclaim the gospel publicly." In answer Barth advised submission and made the incredible statement that "I do not believe that [the church] can claim to be legally entitled to freedom of speech." He also suggested that any prayers for a change of government "might be awfully answered, so that some morning you would wake up among those 'Egyptian flesh-pots' as one obligated to the 'American way of life.' "[98]

This response, reprinted in America, angered Niebuhr, who commented in *The Christian Century,* contrasting Barth's counsel of submission to communist tyranny with his brave defiance of the Nazis:

> Barth is a man of talent to the point of genius. But even a genius cannot escape the dilemma that the price of absolute purity is irrelevance and that the price of relevance is the possible betrayal of capricious loves and hates even in the heart of a man of God.[99]

Years later, after Barth's death in 1968, Niebuhr partially retracted this harsh judgment on Barth's anti-Americanism and anti-anti-communism and, with reference to the Vietnam disaster, concluded,

> While I do not share his sneer at the "flesh-pots of Germany and America," I must admit that our wealth makes our religious anti-communism particularly odious. Perhaps there is not so much to choose between communist and anti-communist fanaticism, particularly when the latter, combined with our wealth, has caused us to stumble into the most pointless, costly and bloody war in our history.[100]

The Christian socialist, finally, should not leave Karl Barth without reminding him or herself of this salutary warning:

> All reformers are Pharisees. They have no sense of humor. Deprive a total abstainer, a really religious socialist, a churchman, or a pacifist, of the pathos of moral indignation, and you have broken his backbone.[101]

TILLICH AND THE *KAIROS*

If a vote were taken, the odds are that students at the main-line Protestant seminaries in America would name Barth, Tillich, and Niebuhr as the three top theologians of the twentieth century. All three were Christian socialists, of a sort.

The major event in the religious life of Paul Tillich (1886–1965) was the Battle of Champagne in World War I. Tillich was twenty-nine years old and a Lutheran military chaplain in the German army. He had grown up in the family of a Prussian pastor, whose orthodox devotion to Christ and the Kaiser he entirely shared. He became president of a Christian fraternity at the University of Halle and in that role was a delegate to a national congress of that fraternity in 1907.

Tillich's father was also a delegate. After the congress Paul wrote a letter to his father on the occasion of his fiftieth birthday. Although much has been made of Tillich's rebellion against his father, one would never guess it from this affectionate letter, which includes the following sentence about the Wingolf Society congress: "You cannot know what a joy it was for me that it was possible for both of us standing shoulder to shoulder to fight for the same goal."[102]

What was that goal? It was an effort to retain faith in the Apostles' Creed as a requirement for membership. They were outvoted and the requirement became merely a statement of loyalty to "the Christian faith" without definition of what that meant.

The evidence indicates that this was Tillich's frame of mind when, as a newly married assistant pastor in a workers' section of Berlin, he volunteered for duty as chaplain on the Western Front. Filled with patriotic optimism, he believed the war would be over in a few months. The Battle of Champagne in 1915 destroyed whatever was left of that optimism. This is how he described it forty-four years later:

> A night attack came and all that horrible, long night I moved among the wounded and the dying as they were brought in—many of them my close friends. . . . What I saw absolutely transformed me.[103]

He suffered two nervous breakdowns over the four long years of horror, but he survived them both and returned to active duty and performed with such bravery that he was awarded the Iron Cross. Mind and body survived, but his faith did not. "When the German soldiers went into the First World War," he later wrote,

> most of them shared the popular belief in a nice God who would make everything work out for the best. Actually, everything worked out for the worst, for the nation and almost everyone in it.[104]

In this mood of despair Tillich turned for consolation to a most unlikely source, Friedrich Nietzsche (1844–1900).

> I well remember sitting in the woods in France reading Nietzsche's *Thus Spake Zarathustra* in a continuous state of exaltation. This was the final liberation from heteronomy. European nihilism carried Nietzsche's prophetic word that "God is dead." Well, the traditional concept of God was dead.[105]

"Heteronomy" became one of Tillich's favorite polysyllabics, and he had many. It means "rule by another," in this case God or Christ.

Tillich returned to Berlin shortly before the end of the war. For him God was indeed dead, and the Kaiser was exiled. The revolution prevailed and the socialists controlled the government. During the war, one of his best friends had seduced his wife, and this led to divorce and a second marriage, to Hannah Werner, "a handsome young woman with magnificent large eyes and a deep melodious voice," who also happened to be entirely irreligious. Tillich had stopped going to church and was living the life of what he described later as that of "a wild man."[106] The two remained together until death, but it was a stormy union, starting from the wedding night, when Tillich left his bride at home while he went off with the man who had seduced his first wife and enjoyed a fling in the company of other lady friends. Hannah never forgave him for that indignity and matched his frequent infidelities with infidelities of her own, all of which she detailed after his death in a steamy memoir.

Before the war Tillich had earned degrees that entitled him to teach both theology and philosophy. One would think that he would have abandoned theology and stuck to philosophy, but he eventually taught in a half dozen universities in Germany and America a kind of philosophical sociology of religion and, finally, a theology of his own invention.

This included a doctrine of sin without sinning, faith without believing, God without God, and Christ without either a virgin birth or a resurrection. Wilhelm and Marion Pauck, his dear friends and biographers, describe his teaching as follows: "Sin became separation, grace reunion, God the Ground and aim of Being, and faith ultimate concern."[107] Once in the fifties I asked Tillich if "this God as the Ground of our Being has anything in common with the personal, self-conscious God of the Gospels." I don't recall his precise answer, but I recall very vividly how stupid he made me feel for supposing that it might.

In his later *Systematic Theology* Tillich defended his "demythologizing" of Christ by protesting that to deny him a human father would be to "deprive him of full participation in the human predicament."[108] One could not help thinking that rejection by the highest religious and political authorities of his country, scourging and humiliation, abandonment by his friends, and death on a cross might qualify as an adequate portion of the human predicament on the part of one who could not, by definition, share it fully because the essence of the human predicament is that human beings are not God, do not rise physically from the grave, and will not come at the end of time to judge the living and the dead.

But Tillich was brilliant, and in many ways an exemplary character—brave and generous and good. Among his virtues his defense of the Jews stands out, especially in the early thirties as the tide of Nazi anti-Semitism was rising. One night in a bar some tipsy customers asked him, "Professor, can you tell us whether there are any Christians in the world any more?" Tillich responded, "No, not a single one. The only Christians in the world today are Jews."[109]

And he was a loyal socialist. His experience in the war had acquainted him for the first time with the common person, with the proletariat, and made him think about the exploitation of the lower classes by the upper classes, by the rich Junkers and the demonic powers of capitalism. "Demonic," another one of Tillich's special words, had nothing to do with faith in demons. It was Tillich's version of original sin, a combination of creative and destructive forces that inhabited the souls of human beings and was especially active, he believed, in "capitalism, nationalism and Bolshevism." And he was honest enough to acknowledge its power in himself. His faith in it saved him from buying all the utopian illusions of Marxism, which otherwise fascinated and fastened itself upon his mind. He was especially skeptical about the chances of a classless society or "a New Man" once the revolutionaries had expropriated the capitalists. He knew that they would quickly fall to arguing among themselves about the division of power and pelf.

Back home in Berlin in 1919, amid the turmoil of the country's defeat and the revolutionary situation, Tillich conceived the idea that this moment was "the *Kairos,*" the Greek term used by St. Paul in 2 Corinthians 6: "Behold, now is the acceptable time; behold, now is the day of salvation" (v.2).

For strangely enough, beneath his uncontrolled obsession with sex, beneath and behind his Nietzschean denial of the Christian God, Tillich still thought in religious categories, and some lingering faith that Christ at least was a New Man, or as he later called him, a New Being, still captivated him. He founded a discussion group, which he called the Kairos Circle, and it soon began to publish a *Journal of Religious Socialism.* Carl Mennicke, the journal's editor, Tillich's fellow minister, who was described by other members as "the heart" of the group as Tillich was "the head," jokingly described the founders of the Circle as "three Jews and three pagans." One of the Jews, Eduard Heimann, an economist, described the members as "naive, optimistic, esoteric, eccentric academicians."[110]

Their political sympathies lay with the Independent Social Democrats, a splinter party of defectors from the more stodgy SDP who were democratic enough to resist the lure of the Spartacists, who reincarnated as the Communist Party. Tillich spoke at a meeting of the independent socialists, although it appears that he never actually joined the party. He later wrote, in fact, "in domestic politics commitment to a political party is out of the question."[111]

Nevertheless, for this action he was called on the carpet by the Lutheran Consistory of Brandenburg, of which his father was a member. Paul defended himself, for he was still combining part-time work as a minister with a modest position as lecturer at the University of Berlin on "Christianity and the Social Problems of the Present." In his response to the Consistory, Tillich took a leaf from Christoph Blumhardt's defense against those who drove him from the Lutheran ministry for his affiliation with the SDP in 1899. At that time Blumhardt recalled that the heart of an atheistic socialist "more often contains God in spirit and in truth than does that of one who confesses with the mouth."[112] Tillich reminded the Consistory that "it is a higher goal to destroy the bases of economic misery than to rescue the sufferers through the works of Christian charity."[113]

Superintendent Bartels, spokesperson for the Consistory, made a negative response that Tillich described as "soft as a plum," and warned him not to do it again. He took no action and Tillich did not do it again, but in 1929, forgetting his nonpartisan prejudice, he joined the SDP as a gesture of protest and resistance to the growing menace of Nazism. The following year he extended his influence beyond the little band of Kairos Circlers by helping to found and edit a *New Journal of Socialism,* striking the "Religious" but retaining a reference to "spiritual and political formation" in the subtitle. The journal appeared monthly until 1933, when it was suppressed by Hitler. Meanwhile Tillich had long since left Berlin and was teaching at the University of Frankfurt, where he was a member of the neo-Marxist group that included Marcuse, Fromm, Adorno, and Horkheimer. In that same year Tillich published *The Socialist Decision,* the book he told James Luther Adams he was most proud of, which in turn led to its confiscation and public burning, his dismissal from the faculty, along with a number of Jewish professors, and subsequent departure for America, at the invitation of Reinhold Niebuhr, to teach at Union Theological Seminary in New York City.

Heimann's word "esoteric" was the right one to describe the Kairos Circle, its publications and, especially, Tillich's writing and speaking style. His performance was brilliant, particularly on the lecture platform. He was featured in 1959 on the front cover of *Time* magazine, which called him "the foremost Protestant thinker" in America. Too often the meaning of what he wrote or said was hidden or hopelessly obscured behind the kaleidoscopic dazzle of his encyclopedic mind. Economics, however, was not one of his strong points, and in this area the confusion was not necessarily in the eye of the beholder or the ear of the listener. Consider the following from the *Journal of Religious Socialism,* an article entitled "Basic Principles of Religious Socialism" written in 1923:

Where social relations are determined by the intrinsic power and erotic energy of the individual and of communities that posit justice, there appears, in spite of the full recognition of the personality formally equal before the law, the idea of the fief, that is, the idea of a possession or disposition (*Verfügung*) of goods according to the intrinsic power and significance of the individual and of the particular community for the life import of the whole.[114]

From the context it is clear that Tillich is trying to say something about public and private ownership of the means of production, but what precisely it is only God and he would know. Like Ragaz and the young Barth, Tillich wanted to make the Christian churches more appreciative of the religious elements in socialism and the socialist movement more appreciative of the socialist elements in Christianity. These were his major considerations in writing *The Socialist Decision.* Several things therefore strike one as extraordinary about the book.

Although he mentions Christianity a number of times as a significant sociological phenomenon, in 179 pages of text he neither quotes nor mentions Jesus Christ once. References to Marx and Marxism are frequent, but it becomes evident that Tillich neither understands the implications and assumptions of classical Marxism nor appreciates what it is in Marxism and the program of the Social Democratic Party that is making it impossible for the SDP to attract the German peasants and the middle class, and thereby counteract the appeal of Hitler and the Nazis.

For example, Tillich has an important insight about the failure of socialism to relate itself to what he calls "the myths of origin . . . soil, blood, group and community,"[115] at least insofar as these have their roots in real values and are not grossly magnified into a monstrous kind of "political romanticism," as Hitler so magnified them. (Incidentally, this complaint about the bloodless rationality of socialism is one that has continued within the movement up to the present, at least in the United States.) What Tillich does not seem to have understood is that a major reason for this failure goes back to Marx and Marx's ideas about private property and the employer-employee wage relationship.

These ideas are laid out most explicitly in *The Economic and Philosophical Manuscripts of 1844,* which had just been published in a full German edition for the first time when Tillich was working on *The Socialist Decision.* These manuscripts, which clearly influenced Tillich's thinking, are filled with statements such as this:

> Wages and private property are identical . . . the wage is but a necessary consequence of labor's estrangement, for after all, in the wage of labor, labor does not appear as an end in itself but as the servant of the wage. . . . Estranged labor is the direct cause of private property. The downfall of the one aspect must therefore mean the downfall of the other. . . . Communism, as the annulment of private property, is the justification of real human life.[116]

This theme, which Marx and Engels continued in *The Holy Family* and *The German Ideology,* brought them logically to their theory of class struggle, not, mind you, as an observation about historical reality, but as a demand for the total elimination of private property and private owners by means of a violent revolution, which would, simultaneously, transform the human nature of the revolutionaries and make them fit to organize and run a society without wages, division of labor, or private ownership of the means of production.

> Both for the production on a mass scale of this communist consciousness, and for the success of the cause itself, the alteration of men on a mass scale is necessary, an alteration which can only take place in a practical movement, a *revolution*; this revolution is necessary, therefore, not only because the *ruling* class cannot be overthrown in any other way,

but also because the class *overthrowing* it can only in a revolution succeed in ridding itself of all the muck of ages and become fitted to found society anew [emphasis in the original].[117]

Why and how Marx imagined that once people started working for the state they would automatically be freed from the "alienation" of wages and the division of labor is hard to understand. But he did:

> In communist society, where nobody has one exclusive sphere of activity but each can become accomplished in any branch he wishes, society regulates the general production and makes it possible for me to do one thing today and another tomorrow, to hunt in the morning, fish in the afternoon, rear cattle in the evening, criticize after dinner, just as I have a mind, without ever becoming hunter, fisherman, shepherd or critic.[118]

This is Godwin's Disease with a vengeance. At any rate, the Social Democratic Party of Germany, to which Tillich belonged, had in practice become a revisionist party closer to Bernstein than to Marx. In theory, however, it was still a revolutionary party wedded to the whole dreamy complex of Marxian notions about the replacement of private property with total collectivism. When Georg von Vollmar, the "peasants' socialist," was defeated at the SDP congress of 1899, the last hope vanished of any clear, unambiguous statement by the party that the peasants were safe in their unshakable determination to hold on to their own land. Lenin had fooled the Russian peasants, but the German peasants were not so gullible.

Judging from *The Socialist Decision,* Tillich seems to have missed all this, and all his talk about socialism getting in touch with "the myths of origin" was about as productive as shouting down a rain barrel. Ironically, in the last chapter, Tillich, advised by Adolf Löwe, another Jewish member of the Kairos Circle, proposes a revisionist program that would limit state ownership to "the landed estates, heavy industry, major manufacturing concerns, banking, and foreign trade."[119] If he and the SDP, using words of one or two syllables, had made it clear a few years earlier that this was the limit to their dreams of Marxist collectivism, both might have been more successful in stopping Hitler and the Nazis.

Tillich's socialism, after he emigrated to America, endured for some years. He was active with Niebuhr in the Fellowship of Socialist Christians. After the war, in the "flesh-pots" of American prosperity, Tillich concluded that "the *kairos*" had passed and his socialism became more muted. His Christianity, if one can call it that, was a much more salable product and Tillich went from strength to strength, from Union to Harvard to the University of Chicago to the Waldorf-Astoria Hotel, where in 1963 he was the principal speaker at Henry Luce's gala party in celebration of the fortieth anniversary of *Time* magazine. Before a distinguished audience of *Time* "cover" personalities Tillich spoke on "The Ambiguity of Perfection." This was the oblique reference, and the only one, that he made to whatever was left of his socialist convictions:

> The awareness of ambiguity . . . is alive in those who realize that the immense success of our economic system, though justified by this success, is not an unambiguous criterion for all other systems.[120]

THE "PRACTICAL-POLITICAL" ONES

In a 1930 essay Tillich distinguished the *Kairos* brand of religious socialism, "which seeks to resolve the static opposition of the concepts of religion and socialism by demonstrating their dialectical relationship," from the more "practical-political type [which] attempts to unite the present socialist movement with the actual forms of religion."[121]

The "practical-political" types had taken a whack from the great Karl Barth at the Tambach Conference in 1919, and this served to discourage them for a few years. The great Paul Tillich never invited them to his *Kairos* meetings and they probably could not have understood him if he had. Even Günther Dehn, a theologian himself, confessed that "sometimes the discussions were over my head."[122]

Fortunately, the practical-political types were not easily discouraged. In 1926 they regrouped and founded the Association of Religious Socialists. They answered Barth with an excellent formula of Ragaz: "The Kingdom of God is not *of* this world but *for* this world." Their first president was the Lutheran pastor Erwin Eckert. They fought for the right of Lutheran ministers to join socialist parties, with some success. Unfortunately, Eckert gravitated so far to the left that he was expelled from the SDP in 1931 and joined the Communist Party, which did result in the loss of his church position. In 1933, after establishing a solid record as a foe of militarism, nationalism, and Nazism, the Association was disbanded by the Nazis and its paper, *The Sunday Paper of Working People,* died with it. Within the Association a group of Catholic socialists had organized under the leadership of Heinrich Martens, Ernst Michel, Otto Bauer, and the militant priest Wilhelm Hohoff, but this group of course died too. Many of the members were imprisoned or lost their jobs during the Nazi regime, but many continued their activity within the anti-Nazi Confessing Church.

After the war, groups of religious socialists came together again in West Germany, but a real breakthrough did not occur until 1972 with the republication of Ragaz's book *From Christ to Marx, From Marx to Christ.* The Association reformed, with chapters in Bochum, Bielefeld, Darmstadt, Duisberg, Kassel, Marburg and Tübingen. It publishes an excellent magazine, *Christ und Sozialist* (Christian and Socialist), although Ragaz might have preferred the title *Religiös und Sozialist.*

Günter Ewald, a professor at the University of Bochum and president of the Association, summarized its purpose as follows:

We are working for a new order of society, where people will no longer be treated as objects, a society different from both Western capitalism and Eastern communism. Methods and goals of production should be built on democratic structures of economic life and on a concept of the person not simply as the consumer of a maximum quantity of material goods but as a total human person. For this reason we favor the cooperative form of production.[123]

The Association is still relatively small, largely academic in membership, active mainly in the left wing of the Social Democratic Part,', with antinuclear, pacifist, and environmental interests, and it favors coalition with the Greens. As Ewald's statement indicates, it may also be said that the Assocation reflects the best traditions of Christian socialism in Germany.

In German-speaking Switzerland, as noted above, Ragaz and Kutter inaugurated the Christian socialist movement in 1906 and Ragaz began editing *Neue Wege* . In 1930, Ragaz presided over the founding of a religious socialist organization, *sozialistische Kirchgenossen*. After his death in 1945 the group split over the question "To be anti-communist or anti-anti-communist?" In 1980, during the fiftieth anniversary year of the organization the two factions came back together and formed the present *Ökumenische Konferenz der Religiösen Sozialisten*. The dominant personality is Markus Mattmüller, Ragaz's biographer, who has played a leading role in the International League of Religious Socialists.

In Catholic Austria, because of the long-standing hostility of the church toward socialism and the close relations of the Austrian clergy with the conservative People's Party (before World War II even with the pseudo-Fascist movements of Dollfuss and Schuschnigg), there was little action until after the war. An amorphous "Movement of Religious Socialists" did exist before World War II, but only in 1951 did Alfred Strobl take the lead in organizing a Working Group of Church and Socialism, then in 1958 the Working Group of Socialist Catholics, and finally in 1966 the present ACUS (*Arbeitsgemeinschaft für Chrisentum und Sozialismus*), which since 1977 has been an affiliate of the Austrian Socialist Party.

Gerhard Steger, a Catholic official in the Socialist government, has served as chairperson. He is the author of *Marx Kontra Christus* and of *Der Brückenschlag,* a book about the Catholic Church and Social Democracy in Austria. Franz Gundacher, another active member, has made important contributions as vice-chairman of the International League of Religious Socialists, of which ACUS is the only predominantly Catholic affiliate.

CHAPTER 10

The United States

During most of the nineteenth century the role of the United States in relation to the history of socialism was mainly that of a graveyard for utopian colonies founded by socialists and communists from England, France, and Germany. Previous chapters have dealt with the typically unhappy ventures of Owen, Weitling, Cabet, and Considérant. The Hutterites were and are, of course, the major exception, indicating that an insistence on religious orthodoxy and discipline is necessary to any long-term vitality for such communes outside of celibate monasteries and convents.

In 1872 Marx and Engels used their majority at the Hague congress of the First International to move the headquarters to New York City, largely as a stratagem in their battle for control with Mikhail Bakunin (1814–1876) and the anarchist faction. The International died four yours later, although it once boasted about thirty branches in the United States, consisting mostly of German immigrants.

To fill the vacuum created by the death of the International, Marxists in America organized the Socialist Labor Party in 1877. Daniel DeLeon (1852–1914) took over its leadership in 1890. His insistence on organizing socialist unions in competition with the American Federation of Labor and his extreme, doctrinaire Marxism led to defections and to the eventual creation in 1901 of the Socialist Party of America by followers of Eugene Debs (1855–1926), Morris Hillquit (1869–1933), Victor Berger (1860–1929) and George Herron (1862–1925), a Congregational minister and Christian socialist who rivaled Debs himself in florid eloquence.

The story of George Herron is a fascinating one and serves admirably to demonstrate the significance and tragedy of the Christian element in the socialist movement during its peak years in the first two decades of the twentieth century. The height of that period, though modest by European standards, was impressive by current American standards when we consider that if a 1984 candidate for president had received the 6 percent vote that Debs received in 1912 (900,000) it would have amounted to 5,580,000 votes. In addition the Socialist Party that year had 120,000 dues-paying members and 1,200 elected officials. Well over 300 socialist periodicals (including 13 dailies) were being published with a combined circulation of about 2 million. One of these was a weekly, *The Christian Socialist,* which at one point had 20,000 subscribers. This was a substanial movement, and Herron was a substantial leader while he lasted, but first, some background.

Although William James, Sr., insisted as early as 1848 that the goals of socialism and Christianity were identical, there was little follow-up on this sentiment either before or immediately after the Civil War. The abolition movement absorbed and drained most of the reformist energies of the Northern churches. The issues, and the conflict, were then nicely highlighted by statements of two of the seven clergymen-sons of the Presbyterian theologian Lyman Beecher. Son Edward said, "Now that God has smitten slavery unto death, he has opened the way for the redemption and sanctification of our whole social system."[1] His more famous brother, Henry Ward Beecher (1813– 1887) was more typical of the clergy of that period. Although he had been active in the abolitionist movement (his sister was Harriet Beecher Stowe, author of *Uncle Tom's Cabin*), this was Henry's view of poverty in 1877:

> God has intended the great to be great and the little to be little. . . . The trade union, originated under the European tradition, destroys liberty. . . . I do not say that a dollar a day is enough to support a working man. . . . But it is enough to support a man. Not enough to support a man and five children if a man insist on smoking and drinking beer. . . . But the man who cannot live on bread and water is not fit to live.[2]

Henry was a fabulously popular preacher (one wonders why) and his income from salary and lectures was $40,000 a year (the equivalent of $440,000 in 1987 dollars), more than enough to cover smoking and drinking beer. Whether it was enough to cover adultery was the subject of a suit brought by a former friend, Theodore Tilton, whose wife was the lady in question. Beecher was acquitted, but his influence, fortunately, was thereafter somewhat diminished.

Mark Twain was wont to refer to that period as "The Great Barbecue," during which time the common folk were kept quiet with the gift of free land out West, at the Indians' expense, and the "Iron Buccaneers" of finance and industry carved themselves generous helpings of coal, iron, oil, railroads, or all of the above. The common folk grew less quiet as the Buccaneers carved and carved, but the latter were not visibly moved. "The public be damned,"[3] said Cornelius Vanderbilt (ships and railroads). "I can always hire half the working class to kill the other half,"[4] said Jay Gould (railroads), and this was the general policy in the bitter railroad strikes of 1877 (over 30 killed) and 1885–86, in which the Knights of Labor rose and fell. In 1886 there were 1,600 strikes involving 600,000 workers, and the first May Day demonstration ended in the Haymarket Riot in Chicago, during which some unknown person threw a bomb that killed seven policemen and led to the hanging of four probably innocent anarchists and the imprisonment of four others. These were troubled and violent times.

Most of the strikes were lost, and to the victors fell the spoils. A reputable newspaper reported as follows in January 1880 (to translate into today's dollars, multiply by eleven):

The profits of the Wall Street kings the past year were enormous. It is estimated that Vanderbilt made $30,000,000, Jay Gould $15,000,000, Russell Sage $10,000,000, Sidney Dillon $10,000,000, James R. Keene $8,000,000, and several others from $1,000,000 to $2,000,000 each."[5]

By contrast the standard daily wage in manufacturing was about $2.50 for a 10-hour day (or longer), so if a man worked a full 6-day week 52 weeks a year (no paid vacations), he would have an annual income of $780 and consider himself lucky. The average income of workers was far less, more like Beecher's $1 a day. Well into the twentieth century weekly wages of $4 and $5 were not uncommon. *The Dawn*, a Christian socialist paper, reported that in 1890 children were working for 6 cents a day in Cincinnati.[6]

Many of the Iron Buccaneers were faithful churchgoers. James J. Hill (railroads, mining, stocks, banking) once gave half a million dollars to a Catholic seminary, although he was a Protestant, because he was concerned about his Catholic immigrant workers. Out loud he worried, "What will be their social view, their political action, their moral status, if that single control-ling force should be removed?"[7] Obviously Mr. Hill was all compassion. Jay Cooke (banking and mines), whose zeal in self-aggrandizement brought on the panic and depression of 1873, gave bells, steeples, organs, Sunday-school books, rectories and cold cash, and exhorted his fellow countrymen, "We must all get down at the feet of Jesus and be taught by no one but Himself."[8]

Clearly there was confusion as to what Himself was teaching. Luther's "justification by faith," Wesley's "gain all you can, save all you can" (without the "give all you can") and the Calvinistic tendency to recognize the elect by their success in this world—these were the most popular interpretations of the teachings of Christ.[9] But fortunately, there were other interpreters—a minority—who began to talk about that phrase in the Lord's Prayer, "Thy kingdom come, thy will be done, on *earth* as it is in heaven." True, there was a great deal of vagueness as to what that might mean in specific terms. True, there were curious mixtures of Rousseau, Darwin, and Spencer in among the gospel quotes. True, there was a tendency to believe that humanity was just naturally so rational and enamored of the True, the Good, and the Beautiful that, once a few minor adjustments had been made and the educational system improved, God's Kingdom *would* come on earth as inevitably as spring follows winter and summer spring.

THE CHRISTIAN LABOR UNION (1872–1878)

Boston was the center of much of the early action in Christian socialism and social Christianity. After the distractions of the Civil War, the first organized movement was the Christian Labor Union (CLU), founded in Boston in 1872 by a brilliant, quixotic minister of the Congregational Church, the Rev. Jesse Jones.

The financial angel of the movement was another quixotic character, Judge T. Wharton Collens, a Roman Catholic from New Orleans, who in 1868 had written that communism is "the outward evolution of the teachings of Moses and Jesus."[10] Another substantial supporter was George McNeill, a leader in the Eight-Hour-Day movement, sometimes described as "the father of the American Federation of Labor."[11]

With Collens's money and Jones as editor the group published the first Christian socialist publication in the United States, *Equity*, a monthly that lasted from April 1874 to December 1875, and also the second, *The Labor-Balance*, which survived from October 1877 to February 1879. Collens died in 1878 and the loss of his financial support killed both CLU and its publication.

But they left their mark. Jones had no illusions about the difficulty of solving the labor question, which he called "the most gigantic and complex problem which has ever challenged human society."[12] The CLU's answer was three-fold: (1) mutual benefit societies in the churches to care for the sick and those in financial distress; (2) support by the churches for "all forms of industrial cooperation" and trade unions [that sounds like two folds in one]; and (3) an economic order based on a labor theory of value, enforced by patronizing only those merchants and manufacturers "who adopt the cost system."[13]

There is no evidence that any of the CLU leaders had read Marx. What they meant by "labor theory of value" and "cost system" seems to have been closer to the medieval notion of the just price, which in turn represents a combination of just wage and just profit, which in turn are related to the Thomistic notion of "appropriate style of life." There was also in the CLU literature a somewhat contradictory, more Marxian idea that the wage relationship was basically bad because it inevitably created conflict, hostility, and exploitation, and this was part of the motivation for promoting producer cooperatives.

The CLU and *Equity* backed the Erie Railroad Strike of 1875 with revolutionary rhetoric:

> Our fathers began the Revolution for less cause. . . . The Erie Railroad is the George III of the workingman's movement . . . and this event is the first gun of the new revolution. . . . It is the beginning of the war between the corporations and the people.[14]

In the same year CLU officers sent a letter of protest to the YMCA of New York City for supplying scabs and strikebreakers in a strike of longshoremen and they supported the great strikes of 1877, quoting Jesus, "I came not to bring peace but a sword."

Sometimes, however, they came down on the nonviolent side of the Christian gospel. Although they were apparently not familiar with Marx, they were familiar with the First International and the Paris Commune of 1871, and Editor Jones took pains to distinguish the CLU from such movements. Christian communism, he declared, favored more pacific methods than the "petroleum communism" of the Paris Commune. (This was probably a reference to the alleged arsonist tendencies of the Communards.) Speaking of the CLU members, he wrote,

> Every one of the chief principles of the International they hold, and can show chapter and verse for in the Bible; but in place of the spirit and method of the International they put the spirit and method of Jesus.[15]

The editors of *The Labor-Balance* endorsed the program of the Socialist Labor Party, which had been organized in 1877, and printed the entire text in the paper in April 1878. That text included this radical passage:

> We demand that the resources of life—the means of production, public transportation and communication, land, machinery, railroads, telegraph lines, canals, etc., become as fast as possible the common property of the whole people through the government; to abolish the wages system, and substitute in its stead cooperative production with a just distribution of its rewards.[16]

Exactly how cooperative production and the abolition of the wage system were to be reconciled with total state ownership and control was about as clear as the syntax of that paragraph. But this was typical of early socialists, whether Christian or secular, Marxist or non-Marxist. Jones, Collens, and the CLU were no exception.

GLADDEN AND THE SOCIAL GOSPEL

One of the better preachers of what came to be known as the Social Gospel was the Rev. Washington Gladden (1836–1918), who capped a long and useful career when, as moderator of the National Council of Congregational Churches in 1905, he vigorously opposed the acceptance of $100,000 from John D. Rockefeller, Sr. The Rockefellers have become so respectable and even progressive—we now have a Democratic Senator in Washington following a liberal Republican Vice-President—that we tend to forget that the man who amassed the family fortune used tactics in the amassing that he certainly did not learn at the feet of Jesus, by any interpretation.

In describing these tactics and the Rockefellers, Gladden used such terms as "the iniquity of conscienceless and predatory wealth . . . no better moral title than the booty of the highwayman . . . oppressors and despoilers of the people."[17] By the time he entered his protest, however, the money had been accepted and partially spent, and it developed that it had also been solicited.

Gladden, backed by a number of other prominent Congregationalists, including President William Tucker of Dartmouth, made enough of a fuss so that the solicitation of funds from the more prominent Buccaneers was not soon repeated.

Gladden opposed the Marxist, collectivist socialism of his day, but by my measuring rod, he was a socialist in the best pre-Marxist and post-Frankfurt tradition. He published thirty-six books, most of which were collections of sermons or lectures. In one of the first, *The Working People and Their Employers* (1876), he came out strongly for producer cooperatives:

> The subjugation of labor by capital is the first stage in the progress of industry; the second stage is the warfare between capital and labor; the third is the identification of labor and capital by some application of the principle of cooperation.[18]

He concluded:

> The gains which have come to workmen through the introduction of machinery have . . . not kept pace with the increase of wealth. Nor will they until the machines are owned, as well as operated, by the workmen.[19]

Gladden was a shrewd, practical man who worked as a farmhand, newspaper reporter, and editor before he settled down to the life of a popular preacher and lecturer in Columbus, Ohio. He served a term on the Columbus City Council and it was this experience that fortified his conviction that "the people must own all the monopolies. . . . If democracy is to endure, it must assert and maintain this prerogative."[20]

In the paragraph that precedes this statement, however, Gladden strongly opposes the "attempt to put all our industries upon the basis of collectivism,"[21] a goal that marked the writings of Edward Bellamy, Herron and W. D. P. Bliss (see below) as well as the Marxists and Fabians who had come to dominate the socialist movement in both Europe and America. His knowledge of life and human nature told him that once the state took over the land, the farms and all productive property, it would enjoy a concentration of power that could not be reconciled with freedom and democracy.

Gladden was a "liberal" Christian in the sense that he did not insist, or apparently believe, in the Virgin Birth or the unique divinity of Christ. Christ was "more, but not *other*"[22] than the rest of us. Gladden was not one of those Social Gospelers whom Reinhold Niebuhr accused, sometimes unfairly, of not believing in sin. In *Working People* he says flat out, "Men are not just; the great majority of them are governed in their conduct, not by the principles of equity, but by their selfish interests and passions."[23]

At the same time Gladden had a most naive faith in progress and in the perfectibility of unjust humanity, another characteristic of Social Gospelers that Niebuhr held in scorn. Consider the following from a sermon preached in

1909, when Gladden was seventy-three years old—old enough to know better: "We have come to a day in which it does not seem quixotic to believe that the principles of Christianity are soon to prevail; that all social relations are to be Christianized."[24] Gladden then quoted "a journalist": "The seed was sown two thousand years ago and *the plant is now preparing to burst into bloom,* and the next thousand years may see some real fruit of the spirit of brotherhood" (emphasis in the original).[25]

Five years later what burst into bloom was not the spirit of brotherhood, but the spirit of fratricide, as Germany, Austria, France, and England, four of the most "civilized" nations on earth, followed by Russia, Italy and the United States, began driving their young men to slaughter. The journalist was more cautious than Gladden. Gladden was ready to pick the fruit "soon." The journalist was willing to wait a thousand years, a much more realistic hope.

Gladden remains, however, a stand-up, stand-out representative of the Social Gospel and Christian socialism. He was at his best, and most valuable, in his cool, rational analysis of the class war that raged in the America of his day and in his eloquent plea for industrial peace and justice. The most famous expression of this was his lecture "Is It Peace or War?" (1886), which he gave once to a large audience of workers and employers in Columbus and twice to audiences in Boston, one consisting of employers and the other of workers. Such was the force of his logic, fairness, and rhetoric that both workers and employers were constrained to applaud him, the workers with better reason than the employers.

Gladden's answer to his own question was that it *was* war, primarily of the employers' making, and that it *ought* to be peace, but "if war is the order of the day, we must grant to labor belligerent rights."[26] By which he meant the right to organize and strike. "War is always a terrible evil, but it is sometimes the lesser of two evils,"[27] and in his view the subjugation and pauperization of the working class was a worse evil than class war.

Gladden, as evidenced in this same address, was not a socialist in the sense then understood by that word, in the sense still understood, or misunderstood, by many today, but he was a socialist in the best sense: in recognition that the answer was not simply exchanging a private employer for a public employer, although some of this was necessary, in recognition that there was a better way than both of these, a way that could not come overnight or by violent revolution, but must be fought for, worked for, prayed for over the long and patient years. Toward the end of "Is It Peace or War?" he reiterates his faith in that better way:

> Some of [the workers] are hoping for cooperation, for an organization of industry in which the men who do the work shall own the capital, and receive both profits and wages. To every such enterprise, Godspeed! It takes a high degree of intelligence and self-control to cooperate in production; workingmen are gaining these qualifications steadily; they will be ready for it before long.[28]

There's that Social Gospel optimism again. We can laugh, or weep, but then we don't have to conclude that the time may be never, or even in a thousand years. There is enough evidence today that the time is ripe, and has been for some years.

BELLAMY'S BIG BOOK

Not too long ago three eminent critics—Charles Beard, the historian; John Dewey, the philosopher; and Edward Weeks, editor of the *Atlantic Monthly*—independently making lists of the most influential books published since 1885, all listed *Looking Backward* by Edward Bellamy (1850–1898) as second only to Marx's *Capital*. Published in 1888, by 1900 it was surpassed in popularity only by *Uncle Tom's Cabin* and *Ben-Hur*, sold millions of copies in over twenty languages, and stimulated utopian thinking to the point that forty-six utopian novels were published in the United States within twelve years after its first printing.

How bad those novels were is hard to imagine, for *Looking Backward*, from a literary standpoint, must be one of the worst best-sellers ever written. The characters are all cut out of cardboard, converse in the most stilted clichés when they are not delivering lectures at each other, and with the exception of the hero, who does confess to some imperfections, remain painfully perfect and virtuous throughout. The male reader's eyes may light up when Bellamy, describing his heroine, drools briefly over "the faultless luxuriance of her figure," but they will dim again quickly as worse writing follows bad.

The hero, Julian West, admits to some imperfection only because he is the only contemporary character, a young man who went to sleep in a sort of underground bomb shelter in 1887 and woke up 113 years later in the year 2000. The place is Boston, but one is tempted to conclude that he went to sleep in Boston and woke up in Moscow. The utopia that Bellamy's characters proceed to describe bears an uncanny resemblance to the regimentation of the Soviet Union, except that in Bellamy's society everything and everyone have become perfect in utility, virtue, and happiness. Behaviorism has gone wild. Also gone wild is the notion of Progress that Gladden and other Social Gospelers shared in modified form and that Reinhold Niebuhr took such mordant pleasure in skewering.

In Bellamy's utopia the state—more precisely, the nation—owns and runs everything. The term "industrial army"[29] is frequently used to describe the set-up. In his words,

The nation [was] organized as the one great business corporation in which all other corporations were absorbed; it became the one capitalist in the place of all other capitalists, the sole employer, the final monopoly in which all previous and lesser monopolies were swallowed up, a monopoly in the profits and economies of which all citizens shared.[30]

Whether Bellamy ever read Lord Acton (1834–1902) is uncertain, but if so, somebody should have made him stand in a corner and repeat a hundred times, "Power tends to corrupt and absolute power corrupts absolutely."[31] The only explanation for the popularity of this book must be the intensity of the revulsion created by the misery of the poor in Bellamy's day as contrasted with the ravenous greed of the Vanderbilts, Goulds et al., that plus the pervasive fascination with the idea of Progress.

Within a few years of its publication, 162 Nationalist Clubs were organized throughout the United States, whose purpose was to discuss and promote the "nationalization" advocated in *Looking Backward*. Most of them folded within a few years. The same fate befell the two publications, *The Nationalist* and *The New Nation*, which Bellamy himself financed out of the income from his book.

Bellamy was not a Christian in the orthodox sense, but religious references are common in his writings and many ministers applauded his book and joined his Nationalist Clubs. Professor Graham Taylor, then at Hartford Theological Seminary, went so far as to say, "I suppose that in the broad meaning of the terms, Nationalism and Christianity are synonymous."[32]

A term, or tent, big enough to cover Bellamy's Nationalism and Christianity may be imagined from a few quotes from *Equality*, a sequel to *Looking Backward* that Bellamy published in 1897. One of the characters in the book, a sort of lay minister named Barton, explains to Julian West the status of religion in utopian America as contrasted with Bellamy's day when the churches were "the champions and apologists of power, privilege and vested rights against every movement for freedom and equality":[33]

> At the time of the great Revolution [early in the twentieth century] sectarian demarcations and doctrinal differences . . . were completely swept away and forgotten in the passionate impulse of brotherly love which . . . destroyed the soil of ignorance and superstition that had supported ecclesiastical influence.[34]

Barton goes on to explain that there are no churches and no clergy, only the opportunity for anyone to broadcast his or her passionate impulses on the "free telephone," a sort of precursor of the radio, or on the "electroscope," a precursor of television.

"God is love" (1 John 4:16) is the tent-like quote from the Bible that serves to cover all doctrinal difficulties, in Bellamy-Barton's view, and of course one must admit that it does cover a lot of ground.

James Dombrowski, a historian of Christian socialism in the United States, has written, "Because of its literary excellence *Looking Backward* deserves to rank with the great classics of Utopian romance from Plato to Moore [*sic*] and Morris."[35] Even prestigious readers like John Dewey, William Allen White, Eugene Debs, Norman Thomas, Thorstein Veblen and Erich Fromm have been attracted and deeply influenced by it.

One can respectfully dissent from the view that *Looking Backward* is any kind of a classic and still agree with Dombrowski's conclusion that Bellamy's book and movement "quickened the social conscience of multitudes within and without the Church."[36]

As Protestant ministers and theologians gave serious thought to the implications of the book for religion, politics, and economics, most of them cooled in their estimates of its value. Perhaps a more important question is this: To what extent were *Looking Backward* and *Equality* responsible for fixing in the mind of the American people the idea that socialism is synonymous, not with Christianity, but with nationalization, totalitarianism, and a corrosive contempt for formal religion?

The asking of this question detracts nothing from Edward Bellamy, who was in many respects an admirable individual who sacrificed wealth and health to promote his idea of the revolutionary triad: liberty, equality, and fraternity.

ELY, THE CHRISTIAN ECONOMIST

Dombrowski's judgment on Richard T. Ely (1854–1943) is more credible than his opinion of *Looking Backward*. "Previous to 1890," he wrote,

> probably no other man did more to turn the attention of organized religion in the United States to the ethical implications of the industrial revolution and to the religious obligations in the field of economics than Richard T. Ely.[37]

Ely repeatedly called attention to the neglect that the second commandment, "Thou shalt love thy neighbor as thyself," was suffering at the hands of Christians. He insisted that seminaries, instead of spending all their time on theology, the study of the first commandment, should give equal time to the social sciences, which incorporate the study of the second commandment and its implications. As a result of his books and lectures seminaries did begin to include sociology, economics, and other social sciences in their curricula.

One might conclude from this emphasis that Ely was one of those Saint-Simonian Christians whose interest in Christ is limited to the social implications of his teaching. Far from it. Born the son of a Presbyterian farmer-engineer, Ely could not accept the doctrine of predestination and went over to the Episcopal Church, "which I thought offered a fuller and richer life."[38] Ely's writing is more crowded with quotes from, and references to, Jesus than almost any other advocate of social Christianity, lay or cleric. The religious emphasis was all the more newsworthy in a professor at secular universities like Johns Hopkins and the University of Wisconsin.

For almost the first time since the Fathers of the Church, Matthew 25 received a major emphasis. In his most influential book, *Social Aspects of Christianity*, Ely quotes verses 31–46 in their entirety, lists all the things Jesus might have mentioned as requirements for salvation, and concludes,

> These are all doubtless important; but these are not the distinctive things by which Christ separates the good from the bad. The performance or

non-performance of social duties separates the doomed from the blessed. . . . I say this is something new in religious systems.[39]

Ely had something else in common with the Fathers of the Church: he derived a strict code of duty toward the poor from such gospel passages as Matthew 25. For example:

If I love my neighbor as myself, my necessities are as important as his. True, but my comforts are not as important as his necessities, nor are my luxuries and superfluities as important as my neighbor's comforts. Luxury can never be indulged in by a Christian so long as he can minister to the real well-being of others, and supply them with material goods helpful for their development; and this forever renders luxury an impossibility for a Christian.[40]

Ely's influence sprang from his role as the leading economist of his time. His *Outlines of Economics* went into six major editions and sold over a million copies. He was a founder of the American Economic Association in 1885 and described its purpose as "to study seriously the second of the great commandments on which hang all the law and the prophets, in all its ramifications."[41]

The platform of the Association, as orginally worded, read, "We hold that the doctrine of *laissez-faire* is unsafe in politics and unsound in morals."[42] The original membership list included the names of twenty-three ministers, among them Gladden. This Christian and anti-Manchesterian bias, of course, did not last.

Ely believed strongly in public ownership of monopolies. He dismissed the alternative of public regulation and control of monopolies with this wise observation: "Expert knowledge must for the most part be on the side of those over whom it is designed to exercise this control. . . . Can ignorance control knowledge, inexperience experience?"[43]

Like Gladden, Ely was not a socialist in the meaning of that term as accepted by his contemporaries—namely, total collectivisim—but, like Gladden, he was a socialist in the sense of favoring a pluralist society that combined private ownership in agriculture and competitive industry with cooperative enterprise and public ownership of monopolies. His support of cooperatives, however, was not as strong as Gladden's.

His significance for Christian socialism and the Social Gospel lay mainly in his giving these movements a solid foundation of economic facts and intellectual competence, a much-needed antidote to the outbreaks of Godwin's Disease among the socialistic divines and utopians like Bellamy. These were useful, however, to the latter mainly in their critique of contemporary capitalism, not in their advocacy of collectivism, for *Outlines of Economics* is about as cogently critical of collectivism as one could be, and it was Ely's reputation as a progressive economist that probably prevented a large number of Christian Americans from joining the socialist movement.

BLISS AT *THE DAWN*

William Dwight Porter Bliss (1856–1926), more commonly known as W. D. P. Bliss, was, next to Herron and Frances Willard (see below), the best-known Christian socialist in the United States in the nineteenth century and, far more than Herron, the most dedicated and productive. Consider this thumbnail sketch of his life and activity.

First a Congregational, then an Episcopal minister, he joined the Knights of Labor, moved partly by the reading of Henry George, went as a delegate to the Knights convention in Cincinnati in 1887, was a founder of the Church Association for the Advancement of the Interests of Labor (CAAIL), to which forty-two Episcopal bishops belonged, helped found the first of Bellamy's Nationalist Clubs in 1888 and the Society of Christian Socialists (SCS) in 1889, edited the latter's publication, *The Dawn*, from 1889 until its death in 1896, was a leader of the Christian Social Union, modeled on the English organization of the same name, founded and pastored the Episcopal Church of the Carpenter in Boston (1890–1896), helped edit *The American Fabian*, wrote and/or edited six books on social questions, topped by the monumental *Encyclopedia of Social Reform* in 1897 (revised edition 1908), organized in 1898 the Union Reform League as an American edition of the Fabian Society, served as an officer of the Christian Socialist Fellowship, and all over the country lectured and preached the Social Gospel, which to him meant Christian socialism, as expressed in this quotation from the SCS publication, *The Dawn*:

> *The Dawn* stands for Christian Socialism. By this we mean the spirit of the socialism of the New Testament and of the New Testament church. In man's relations to God, Jesus Christ preached an *individual* gospel; accordingly, in their relations to God, Christ's disciples must be individualists. In man's relations to man, Jesus Christ preached a *social* gospel; accordingly, in these relations, his disciples must be socialists.[44]

Bliss was an interesting, almost unique, kind of Christian. Early in his ministerial career he converted to the Episcopal Church because he thought the Congregational Church too restrictive, but also for a very different reason, namely, that he believed the Episcopal Church to be best situated for the reunification of all Christians. He once wrote:

> Roman Catholicism is monarchy. Protestantism is anarchy. We needed to experience both, and may thank God for them, but now we need to press on to Catholicism, or democracy organized in Christ.[45]

Seldom has one man said so much in so few words or raised so many difficult questions. *The Dawn* often said nice things about Catholics, such as "the noble Bishop Ketteler, the truest Christian socialist bishop of the world."[46]

This tilt toward Catholicism might lead one to think Bliss was partial to orthodox theology. Not so. "Questions of theology," he wrote in the first issue of *The Dawn*, "we do not attempt to raise. . . . Orthopraxy is for us the road to Orthodoxy."[47] The idea was that if Christians would work together, they would inevitably come to worship and believe together. The following year, 1890, he wrote:

We believe that [the church's] theology needs simplifying. Various theologies, various systems, orthodox or unorthodox, have overgrown the simple religion of Jesus Christ. Christianity . . . has come to have little in common with the faith, and love, and life inculcated by The Master. Christianity is a life, not a creed, a way, not a philosophy, "a battle, not a dream."[48]

In passages like this, one hears echoes, or premonitions, of that other religious activist, Leonhard Ragaz. But unlike Ragaz, Bliss remained a faithful churchman. True, in Boston, he had a sympathetic bishop, the great Phillips Brooks, who gave his approval to Bliss's socialist Church of the Carpenter. Even so, he was an organization man, both in politics and religion.

Although Bellamy was one of the original associate editors of *The Dawn* and Bliss was one of the founders of the Nationalist movement, both Bellamy and Nationalism were too antichurch for Bliss's taste. He was always laudatory toward Bellamy, but Bliss had other difficulties with Nationalism, and Bellamy did not remain long on the masthead of *The Dawn*.

Already in 1890 Bliss was writing in *The Dawn*:

Socialism is the extension of democratic government. . . . The greatest fault of *Looking Backward* [is] that it uses a somewhat military phraseology and a somewhat regimented conception of society.[49]

A few months later he devoted a two-page editorial to "Why We Prefer Socialism to Nationalism." Some excerpts (emphasis in the original):

Nationalism, insofar as it differs from Socialism, emphasizes first . . . the thought of *nation*ality. . . . The *nation* is its unit. Here, then, we first take issue. . . . The unit of Socialism is not the nation so much as *society*, the collectivity of people in *any* organic form. It may be as a nation, but also as a world, as a church, as a trade union, as a township, as a municipality, as a cooperative factory—wherever people enter into organic relations, there is a social unit. State socialism is only one part of Socialism, and Nationalism seems to us only one part of State Socialism. . . .

While we, with Karl Marx and most German and American Socialists, do believe in the State, we believe that the State should be very decentralized. We believe that great emphasis should be put upon local government. . . . On that great line which has continuously, and we believe healthfully, divided every American political movement, we take position on the side of the democracy, the side of the common people. Paternalism in every form we fear; fraternalism we believe to be the salvation of the future. The danger we see before Nationalism is that it may become popular among the rich. The tendency today is beyond all question to combination and centralization. The rich men of this land are not wanting in shrewdness and cunning. They may see that Nationalism may prove a popular war cry, and under the cover of that war cry they may nationalize the railroads and municipalize the gas; and then quietly see to it that they are the government, so that the last state of this nation may be worse than the first. . . .

Nationalists say, "Turn everything gradually over to the State and all will be well." Socialists say, "Turn everything over into the hands of the producers, and then there will be justice."[50]

Fascinating confusions and distinctions. Bliss marshalls a number of excellent arguments against Bellamy's Nationalism. The irony is that he appealed for support to Marx and to "most German and American Socialists," and these were heading in the same direction as Nationalism. In fact, in the second issue of *The Dawn* Bliss himself printed this definition of socialism by Lawrence Gronlund, the foremost Marxist in America at that time (whom Eugene Debs used to read in prison):

> Socialism consists in converting all private capital, i.e., land, raw material and instruments of labor into collective capital, to be controlled and employed by society for the public benefit. That would include the abolition of all forms of profit, interest and rent, and negative all private business. . . . The wage-system will be abolished . . . no employers and employees; but all will be public functionaries, all dependent on the impersonal collectivity.[51]

Bellamy himself could not have put it better. True, Gronlund did include with his awesome "collectivity" a dash of Guild Socialism, with organizations of "tailors, bakers, teachers, physicians" who would

> settle their hours of work . . . and divide the payments among themselves. . . . Only the value of the goods they produce are determined by the central authority, which has the limited functions of general manager, statistician and arbitrator."

Those functions don't sound very limited.

But, "turn everything over into the hands of the producers, and then there will be justice." Not the whole answer perhaps—producers can also be unjust—but the beginning of wisdom, as it was the beginning of socialism, once, B.M., Before Marx.

Bliss seemed to be a sort of one-man Christian socialist movement, but he was not entirely alone. The first meeting of the Society of Christian Socialists (SCS) was held in the Baptist Tremont Temple in Boston (still standing) on February 18, 1889, on the call of Bliss and the Rev. Francis Bellamy, a cousin of Edward. Nineteen persons attended, of whom nine were clergymen representing most of the major Protestant denominations. Two women were elected as officers: Mrs. Mary Livermore and Mrs. L. L. Norris. Two other outstanding women, Frances Willard and Vida Scudder, a Wellesley professor, were frequent contributors to *The Dawn*.

Other chapters of the SCS were organized in New York City and in the states of Ohio, Illinois, and Kansas. None of them developed into anything like a mass movement, and by 1896, when the *Dawn* faded, all of them had faded as well. Although Bliss once expressed the opinion that "a large majority of the [Episcopal] clergy are secretly favorable to a churchly Christian socialism,"[52] and conservative publications sometimes complained that the churches were all going socialist, it wasn't really true. The Society's goal, "to awaken members of Christian churches to the fact that the teachings of Jesus Christ lead directly to some specific form or forms of socialism,"[53] was far from realization. Perhaps if Bliss had not bounced around so much, he might have kept the movement going longer, but follow-through was not his strong suit. That he kept *The Dawn* alive, almost single-handedly, for seven years, is significant.

Bliss died in 1926 and his funeral service was held at the Cathedral of St. John the Divine in New York City. Since I was a young member of the cathedral choir at that time, it is probable that I sang at the funeral. A comforting thought. There is continuity, there are connections, in this seemingly disconnected world.

HERRON, THE MARBLE JEREMIAH

William Allen White, "the sage of Emporia," once described George Davis Herron (1862–1925) as "one of God's pedestal dwellers, always moving about in bronze or marble . . . yet a kindly and some way sweet and gentle soul withal."[54] White knew Herron well, since the two worked together in Europe in what was for Herron an incongruous role, special emissary of Woodrow Wilson for the critical negotiations immediately following World War I.

"Sweet and gentle soul" also seems incongruous as a description of the man who simultaneously inspired and infuriated thousands of Americans, alternately blasted the capitalist moguls and *all* Christian churches, helped found the Socialist Party, and served as one of its most popular spokespersons—and all in the self-confessed role of one "bought by the blood of Christ, cleansed by the sufferings of God."[55] There was a bit of Jekyll-and-Hyde in this man.

W. D. P. Bliss was an effective preacher of the Social Gospel, but he was nothing compared to Herron. Just reading Herron's rhetoric makes you feel that you are in the presence of a kind of verbal wind machine. You feel like reaching out for something solid for fear of being blown away. At his best, he sounds like an authentic voice of Christian prophecy, a latter-day Jeremiah:

The jubilees which the church holds in honor of so-called benefactions of stock-gamblers and railroad wreckers, of trust monopolists and oppressors of the poor, are but a ridiculous and ill-disguised religious hoodwinkery. Christ did not send his church into the world to get the money of mammon, but to defend the oppressed, denounce wickedness, establish justice, and work righteousness.[56]

Or this:

God is pressing for a deeper incarnation of himself in the race. He calls for souls who shall make themselves of no reputation, seek not their own, be not anxious for the morrow's food and property . . . [to] go out into this great, starving, striving, staggering, doubting humanity, to be beaten with its stripes, bleed with its wounds, stricken, mangled, poor and lonely with its sins, taking no thought of reward, popular churches, or church year-books, in order to become divine righteousness in its life, and Christ-builders of its character; in order to become the strength of God to the weak, the joy of God to the wretched, the wealth of God to the poor.[57]

At its worst, Herron's rhetoric was a mishmash of half-baked Christian theology *cum* sociology *cum* unintelligible pantheism. The following, for example, is from "The Scientific Ground of a Christian Sociology," one of a series of lectures to students at Union Theological Seminary, at Princeton and at Michigan, Lawrence, and Indiana State Universities in the year 1894. The lectures were published as *The Christian Society* along with the 1890 lecture that lifted Herron to national prominence, "The Message of Jesus to Men of Wealth":

Society must be unity with all that is, with God and man, with the moral and the physical, with the known and the unknown, or it cannot be society in fact. The realization of society will be the realization of the universal unity in human relations. The just society, the society that perfectly apprehends the resources and directs the forces of nature, will be the unity of the life of the people with the life of God. For, if there be any sense in the universe, if there be a universe, the nature of man, the nature of nature, and the nature of God are one. And, according to Jesus the one, the all, the universe is Christian.[58]

Herron did not have much formal education, scientific or otherwise. He attended Ripon College in Wisconsin for a few years, but poor health and poverty forced him to leave. He found employment in a print shop, where he began to identify with the world of work and workers. In 1883, at twenty-one years of age, he entered the Congregational ministry in Zanesville, Ohio, apparently without further training, went on to preach in pulpits in Wisconsin and Minnesota, and finally, by the mysterious providence of God, in December

1891, received the position of associate pastor in the Congregational Church of Burlington, Iowa.

There his mellifluous sermons bewitched a rich widow, Mrs. Elizabeth Rand and her daughter Carrie. The relationship that developed among these three henceforth molded and in the end destroyed the career and effectiveness of George Davis Herron as a spokesperson and champion of Christian socialism.

First Mrs. Rand endowed in 1893 a special "chair of applied Christianity" at Iowa College (later Grinnell College) which, by agreement with President George Gates, was reserved for her protégé. Herron accepted the honor with his typical sense of humorless mission. "I have no choice in the matter," he told his Burlington congregation, "I go to suffer for the truth and the name of Christ."[59] *Suffer*? Mrs. Rand and Carrie followed him to Grinnell and took up residence.

But he did fill the chair. His classes became so large that they had to be held in the college chapel. He was in great demand as a preacher and lecturer. A reporter in Montreal wrote that his talk there shook up the town as if "a dynamite bomb had exploded in the square of the city."[60]

The *New York Post*, in fact, charged Herron, along with Richard T. Ely, a more surprising target, with being comparable to the anarchists who allegedly motivated the Haymarket bomb-throwers of 1886:

> Their offence differs little in its essence from that of Parsons, the Chicago anarchist, who was convicted and hanged for inciting others to murder. . . . It is the Elys, the Herrons . . . who are responsible for such men as Debs and his host of ignorant followers.[61]

Controversy followed him from coast to coast. After he had declared the United States a failure during a commencement sermon at the University of Nebraska, Governor Crowse followed him to the podium and called him "an anarchist." *The Kingdom*, a weekly edited by Herron disciples, reported that of the ministers on the platform at that time, "two doctors divine made haste to shake hands with the governor; four slipped away quickly; and three came to Dr. Herron with hearts greatly stirred and grasped his hand."[62] Probably a fair representation of the reaction of Protestant clergy throughout the land. The Catholic reaction was more uniformly negative.

In San Francisco Herron filled one of the largest halls and spoke for two hours between bursts of applause, declaring that

> competition is not the law of life, but a contradiction of every principle of Christianity. . . . Our economic system is organized social wrong. . . . The wage system is economic slavery, a profane traffic in human flesh and blood.[63]

He insisted, however, that the necessary changes would be effected gradually, not by violent destruction. At the end of his address a local Congregational minister, C. O. Brown, rose to attack him, once again as an "anarchist." Ever since the Haymarket bombing "anarchist" had been the all-purpose epithet for left-leaning activists, much as "Communist" and "Marxist-Leninist" are today.

Throughout most of the 1890s Herron did not publicly play a political role, although he later confessed that he had been voting for candidates of the Socialist Labor Party. Over those years his economic, political, and religious views solidified and leaned further leftward, until he was preaching a hard-line brand of economic determinism worthy of Marx himself, as, for example:

> Socialism begins with this—that the history of the world has been economic. The world's sentiments and religions, its laws and morals, its art and literature, are all rooted in the struggle between classes for control of the food supply. Moses and Jesus, Wycliffe and Mazzini, Marx and Millet are products of the stress and injustice of intensified economic conditions.[64]

In 1901 Herron played a leading role in the convention that united various rival factions in the Socialist Party, which then became the vehicle for the presidential candidacies of Eugene Debs and Norman Thomas and still today maintains a precarious national existence. A socialist paper, *The Worker*, reported:

> The selection of Herron as temporary chairman was unanimous and satisfactory to all parties. . . . He steered the convention through some threatening breakers during the opening and most trying hours of the convention.[65]

Subsequently Herron received the top vote in a referendum of the Party for delegate to the Socialist International. David Goldstein and Martha Moore Avery, two former Socialists, who became Catholic converts and whose book *Socialism: The Nation of Fatherless Children* is virulently antisocialist and anti-Herron, expressed the opinion that "the socialist movement of the United States, from 1902 to 1908, probably owes more of its progress to [Herron] than to any other person."[66] This seems doubtful in the case of Herron vs. Debs, although Debs had not at this time reached the degree of popularity that would mark his career. Herron was probably more influential than the other two leaders, Morris Hillquit, an immigrant labor lawyer out of the Jewish garment trades of New York City, and Victor Berger, a German immigrant best known in his home state of Wisconsin.

By 1908, however, Herron was well on the road to obscurity and was, in fact, living in a comfortable villa near Fiesole, Italy, with his new wife Carrie Rand. Mrs. Rand had died in 1905, having become the most generous contributor to the Socialist Party. She endowed its most prestigious institution of higher learning, the Rand School of Social Science.

In order to marry Carrie, Herron, with the help of Mrs. Rand's money, persuaded his first wife, Mary, mother of his five children, whom he had once called his "living conscience," to grant him a divorce. This action moved a council of the Congregational Church of Grinnell, Iowa, on June 4, 1901, to denounce "the criminal desertion of a worthy wife and devoted mother by a man who has deliberately falsified his marriage vows" and declare him "deposed from the Christian ministry."[67] Herron responded, accepting the decision, "I do not believe that the present marriage system is sacred or good. . . . Love must be set free and liberty must be trusted."[68]

Although he shortly thereafter made his permanent residence in the Italian villa, where he entertained lavishly, Herron continued to speak frequently in the United States and was chosen to nominate Eugene Debs at the 1904 convention of the Socialist Party. He was not, however, welcome in many churches. Teddy Roosevelt attacked him and Debs defended him, rebuking Roosevelt and saying of Herron, "those who know him know that Christ himself was not more cruelly maligned by the pharisees of his day, and that a purer soul never walked this earth."[69]

To the abuse Herron himself did not exactly turn the other cheek. Making a distinction between Christ and Christianity, he cut whatever umbilical cord remained:

Christianity today stands for what is lowest and basest in human life. . . . [The church] is the most degrading of all our institutions. . . . For socialism to use it, to make terms with it . . . is for socialism to take Judas to its bosom. There is not an instance, in sixteen centuries, in which the church has not betrayed every movement for human emancipation it has touched.[70]

So departed from the Christian socialist movement one who might have made a major contribution to it. One inevitably wonders what would have happened if Herron had never encountered the Rands. Probably something equally discouraging. When one considers the aphrodisiacal effects of successful oratory on both the speaker and the listener, it is perhaps a wonder that more popular preachers, teachers, and politicians don't weary of the bonds of matrimony.

SEX, CARR, *THE CHRISTIAN SOCIALIST,* AND THE FELLOWSHIP

Even today a Protestant minister who divorces his wife is not usually encouraged to remain in the church in which he has been serving. In other matters sexual there can scarcely be any comparison between our day and the early years of this century.

The Rev. Edward Ellis Carr, editor of *The Christian Socialist* from 1905 to 1922, wrote the following in a piece on "Socialism and Sex":

SEDUCTION IS WORSE THAN MURDER AND SHOULD BE
PUNISHED ACCORDINGLY. . . . Any man willing to destroy trusting
affection and murder a long life's joy for a brief personal gratification is a
demon unfit for human society [emphasis in the original].[71]

Carr's indignation was probably typical of the more self-righteous Christians of that era, though he does not seem to have remembered Jesus' treatment
of a case of similiar indignation (John 8:1-11).

"Free love" was a major issue both in and out of the Socialist Party and it
surfaced prominently in the pages of *The Christian Socialist* in 1911 as well as
in a major work of antisocialist propaganda published the same year and
bearing the imprimatur of William Cardinal O'Connell, archbishop of Boston.
The book was by Goldstein and Avery. They relied heavily on Carr and *The
Christian Socialist* for much of their ammunition.

Carr was an extraordinary character in the history of Christian socialism.
An early picture, frequently printed in his paper, reveals a large, handsome
young man who looked like a college football player. Circumstantial evidence,
but little known biographical material, indicates he was born somewhere in the
Midwest about 1877. He was influenced early in his life by reading Bellamy's
Looking Backward and he was converted to "a Marxian, class-conscious
socialism"[72] in 1899 by *Capital* itself. He joined Debs's Social Democratic
Party in 1900 and organized the first Socialist Party branch in Danville,
Illinois, where, until his radical activities became too much for his congregation, he was a practicing Methodist minister. In December 1903, a layman
named Oscar Donaldson began publishing *The Christian Socialist* as a monthly
in Webster City, Iowa. He and Carr joined forces in 1904 and Carr took over
the following year, moving the paper to Danville and then in 1906 to Chicago,
by which time it was coming out twice a month and had built up a circulation of
five thousand subscribers plus ten or twenty thousand who bought "special
editions." These included a Temperance Edition and one for every major
denomination, including the Roman Catholic, and some minor denominations, including the Swedenborgian. The Baptist edition featured Walter Rauschenbusch, the Episcopal one, Bishop F. S. Spalding of Utah.

Although he was expelled twice from the Socialist Party, Carr remained loyal
to it and was for several years sponsored by the Party on lecture tours. He
served as a delegate to the Stuttgart congress of the Socialist International and
his wife Ella was elected a member of the national executive committee of the
Party's women's auxiliary. The success of the paper led to the creation of a
Christian Socialist Fellowship in 1906, which lasted until about 1917 and
numbered over fifteen hundred members, including hundreds of Protestant
ministers and twenty-seven chapters across the country. A Christian socialist
manifesto signed by 160 clergymen appeared in the paper on April 15, 1908,
declaring that capitalism is based "upon the sin of covetousness" and makes
"the ethical life as inculcated by religion impracticable," whereas socialism
would create an environment favorable to the practice of religion.

At its peak, having become a weekly, *The Christian Socialist* boasted two thousand ministers among its twenty thousand readers. Its influence was considerable, both within and outside of the Socialist Party. Among two hundred delegates at the Party convention of 1908 Carr reported a dozen ministers and "scores" of Christian laypersons. This was the period in American history when socialism made its greatest gains. It is certain that it would have made even greater gains among the Christian population if it had not been for three factors: (1) the opposition of the Catholic Church, (2) the personality of Edward Ellis Carr, and (3) the heavily Marxist bias of the Socialist Party.

Carr had a florid, sentimental writing and speaking style, somewhat like his idol Eugene Debs, but without the aura of gaunt passion and suffering and occasional flashes of genius that made Debs a memorable figure. A devoted Marxist, Carr described himself as "an extreme liberal in theology" who "accepts Jesus as my Teacher, Leader and Master,"[73] but not, apparently, as Lord or God. "Christianity is not a dogma but a life,"[74] he wrote once in a phrase probably borrowed from W. D. P. Bliss, who served as secretary and treasurer of the Fellowship at one time or another.

The CSF convention in New York City in 1908 featured a rally attended by three thousand and addressed by Debs, Hillquit, Edwin Markham, and Rose Pastor Stokes. The next year in Toledo the New York chapter tried to take the Fellowship out from under the control of Carr's faction, but this effort failed and only served to weaken the organization.

In 1910 Carr joined Thomas J. Morgan, a prominent Chicago socialist and editor of *The Provoker*, and several other leading socialists, including Mother Jones, the miners' champion, in an effort to oust J. Mahlon Barnes, national secretary of the Socialist Party. Charges had been brought against Barnes simultaneously by Mother Jones, by James Brower, a Socialist candidate for governor of Illinois, and by a former SP office secretary, Marguerite Flaherty. The charges involved financial irregularity, incompetence, drunkenness, and sexual immorality, the latter depending mainly on the guesswork—probably accurate, as it turned out—of Marguerite Flaherty.

The National Executive Committee—a seven-member body that did not include Debs—dismissed the charges without trial and little more than a cursory investigation. Carr, too quick to assume the sex scandal was true, filled pages of *The Christian Socialist* with lurid detail supplied by Flaherty and threats of retaliatory action if Barnes and the women involved, one of whom sat on the NEC, were not brought to justice. "If free lovers are to receive official protection," he declared, "no power on earth can prevent our protest reaching from sea to sea."[75]

Shaken by this furor, the NEC appointed a trial committee that acquitted Barnes and made countercharges against Mother Jones, accusing her, in effect, of blackmailing Barnes. Carr and Morgan were then expelled from the Party, and a short time later Barnes was revealed to be living with two wives at once. The NEC, highly embarrassed, encouraged Barnes to resign, and Victor

Berger, by now a member of the U.S. Congress representing Milwaukee, speaking for the committee, explained this action:

> The party is careful on the moral conduct of its officials because of the fact that the Roman Catholic Church is basing, in large part, its war against socialism on the charge that socialism means, in its entirety, free love.[76]

Simultaneously, and somewhat inconsistently, Berger and the NEC bemoaned the "malicious campaign of gossip [that] has cost the Party a most efficient and conscientious national secretary."[77] *The Christian Socialist*, stricken from the list of recognized socialist publications, was now restored to that list and Carr himself readmitted to membership, but the readmission was immediately revoked by a referendum of the four thousand socialists in the city of Chicago.

This was a significant vote. Carr won the English-speaking locals 288 to 159 and lost the foreign-speaking locals 604 to 50. These included Scandinavians (strongly pro-Carr) and Germans, Slovaks, Bohemians, and Italians (all almost unanimously anti-Carr). The significance of the vote, apart from reflecting the difficulty of communicating with non-English-speaking socialists plus some genuine concern about Carr's common sense, reflected even more the hard-line, antireligious, Marxist prejudices of the European immigrants who made up the majority of the more active and devoted members of the Party, especially in urban centers like Chicago and New York.

Such men also made up the majority of the more prominent and articulate leaders, men like Berger, Hillquit, and Adolph Germer, who later served as national secretary. Debs took almost no part whatever in the decision-making bodies of the Party. His functions were public-speaking and running for president, which he did six times between 1896 and 1920. He was the 100-percent-American front who could even write tributes to Jesus, "the grandest and loftiest of human souls."[78] But behind the front the party was controlled by others who came out of continental European Marxism.

An example of their true feeling about the prejudices of American Christians occurred at the Socialist Party convention of 1912 that nominated Debs for president for the third time. In the confusion of the closing moments, Hillquit nominated the discredited Barnes to be Debs's campaign manager, and he was elected. This so infuriated the Carr followers that they appealed the election to a referendum of the entire membership, which then numbered about 120,000. Barnes, in the middle of Debs's own campaign, was only confirmed by a vote of 18,000 to 11,000.

Despite this disastrous distraction Debs polled the largest vote, percentage-wise, ever secured by a socialist candidate for president, as noted above. Such was the strength of the revulsion against the horrors of early American capitalism.

Ironically, Carr himself was an orthodox Marxist—with a difference. He quoted Karl Kautsky to the effect that "economic determinism, surplus value, class struggle, and collectivism are the four fundamental principles of scientific socialism." Then he added, and this is what made his orthodoxy different, "The atheism of Marx and Engels is to socialism no more than the yowling of a black cat is to the rings of Saturn."[79]

Carr loved an argument. One thing that kept his paper going was his willingness to print opposing views, from inside the Party and inside the Christian Socialist Fellowship. One view from the Party was that of Professor Ernest Untermann, a member of the NEC, who protested that "the philosophy of Jesus is no more reconcilable with that of Marx than is that of Plato, Aristotle, Berkeley, Kant or Hegel."[80]

One from inside the Fellowship came from an early supporter and member of its executive committee, M. Kathryn Spiers of Virginia, who wrote these well-chosen words:

> The materialist bias of our Socialist leaders has produced a doctrine of economic determinism which is only apparently and not really true. . . . That erroneous doctrine . . . has given rise to over-emphasis on another apparent truth—the class struggle—thus diverting their powers from the true line of attack. . . . Motive is beyond the foreseeable control of circumstance, and good and true motives cannot be produced by external environment alone. Neither can false and evil ones. . . .
>
> To foster class hatred and mouth inflammable periods about an ines-capable class war, is therefore against any common-sense psychology of human nature, and will eventually kill any party which adheres to it as a factor in the adoption of Socialism.[81]

So much for two of Kautsky's and Carr's four fundamental principles of "scientific socialism." Actually, Spiers might simply have mentioned the Christian doctrines of free will, grace, and love of neighbor and let it go at that.

The third principle, collectivism, as understood by both Carr and the socialist movement, was total: "Collective ownership of the means of producing and distributing wealth, such as land, mines, factories, railroads, mail, express, telephone, and telegraph services, light, water, heat, stores, etc."[82] If we accept the Judeo-Christian view of human nature, such a concentration of power in the hands of a few individuals (the executive branch of the state) clearly cannot be reconciled with the free practice of Christianity, not to mention democracy.

There remains the fourth principle: surplus value. In one of the early issues of *The Christian Socialist* a man named George Littlefield contributed a ten-paragraph summary of Marx's *Capital*. Paragraph 4 reads:

> The withholding of this surplus value from labor prevents the exploited workers from buying or consuming but a fraction of their full product—hence periodic over-production and consequent "hard times."[83]

This single sentence contains a large, if not dominant, portion of the wisdom of both Karl Marx and John Maynard Keynes. That wisdom, however, is not inextricably tied to the concept of "surplus value." Marx defined it differently in different sections of *Capital*, but the most common definition is that it represents the difference between the income of the entrepreneur and the *legitimate* costs of production plus the wage actually paid to labor. The argument then revolves around the word "legitimate." Marx, as explained in the section above on Tillich, did not recognize the legitimacy of any return to capital, investors, and owners, since all productive enterprise should be owned by the state. Therefore, the more clarifying concepts for a Christian are the ancient Judeo-Christian concepts of just wage, just price, and just profit and the further clarifications of Thomas Aquinas about "appropriate style of life." But in the first two decades of the twentieth century few Christians, and certainly not Edward Ellis Carr, ever thought about such things. So totally did men like Marx, Engels, and Kautsky dominate socialist discourse.

The Socialist Party and Carr's *Christian Socialist*, as well as the Christian Socialist Fellowship, did adhere to these principles and, as Kathryn Spiers predicted, they all either died or were reduced to a condition of advanced debility that greatly resembles death. In all fairness, of course, we should mention such contributing factors as the effects of World War I, the Bolshevik Revolution (which Carr called "the greatest hour the old earth ever knew"),[84] and the complex reactions of Americans to both, from within and without the socialist movement.

Walter Rauschenbusch, who was too smart to get too close to either Carr or the Christian Socialist Fellowship, did write for the paper on occasion. In the issue of March 15, 1914, he wrote, "The pluck of Mr. Carr in keeping the paper going has been worthy of all admiration." That tribute one can warmly second. At the time of its death in 1922 it was probably the second oldest English-language socialist paper in the United States. It was, and remains, the Christian socialist publication with the longest life—nineteen years—published in the United States. By the time of its death, however, it was a pathetic creature and Carr's name alone remained on the masthead. He was reduced to printing such material as the following, from "A Theology for Socialism" by the Rev. Elmo Robinson:

> Theologians have wasted a great deal of time in trying to decide who Jesus was. It does not particularly matter who he was. The important thing is to understand what Jesus himself was driving at.[85]

Who Jesus was seems to matter. If he was a mere man like the Reverend Robinson, then we know that we can take or leave what he was driving at as we would the opinions of any other human. If, on the other hand, he was the one-and-only Son of God, with no other father but the Holy Spirit, a coequal partner in the wisdom and power of God, who will raise us up to heaven or cast us down to hell if we do or do not feed the hungry, clothe the naked, or shelter the shelterless, that realization on our part might just matter as we decide how seriously we will consider what he was driving at.

That does not mean that those who conclude that he was a mere man cannot take what he was driving at more seriously than those of us who take the other view. Far from it. And so much the worse for us.

RAUSCHENBUSCH, PRIDE OF THE SOCIAL GOSPEL

Reinhold Niebuhr decribed Walter Rauschenbusch (1861–1918) as "not only the real founder of social Chrisitanity in this country, but also its most brilliant and generally satisfying exponent to this present day."[86]

"This present day" was 1935, and this statement was made during Niebuhr's most socialist period. Later, in 1957, Niebuhr was more critical and included Rauschenbusch in his complaint that the Social Gospel "did not understand justice because it did not measure adequately the power and persistence of man's self-concern, particularly in collective self-concern."[87]

Karl Barth was even more critical. According to Paul Merkley,

> Barth's view of the Gospel played havoc with all efforts at accommodation between the doctrine of progress and the concept of the Kingdom of God. The Social Gospel of Walter Rauschenbusch was thus a heresy. The Kingdom lay beyond human history and would emerge in judgment of man's failure, which would be just as evident at the end as at the beginning of the human story.[88]

Where and what is the truth? To each his own interpretation of Rauschenbusch, and Barth, and Niebuhr, but taken all in all, Rauschenbusch earned Niebuhr's first judgment. He was the best of the prophets of the Social Gospel. His faith in Progress with a capital P was a touch on the naive side, but he was not oblivious to the power of sin. Six chapters of *A Theology for the Social Gospel* are devoted to it. Niebuhr was just plain wrong when he wrote, "Proponents of the Social Gospel . . . did not believe in sin."[89]

As for Barth, we have seen how utterly "other" was his notion of the kingdom. Jesus himself was a hopeless optimist by the Barth criteria. By the same criteria Barth's own Christian socialism was a heresy because by definition it assumes that human beings can, with God's help, bring the world closer to the divine image and likeness.

Rauschenbusch had his faults. He shows signs of Aryan racism. His liberal theology suffers from the usual weaknesses of that school, the cloudy imprecisions and the hopeless effort to reconcile antidogmatism with some meaningful content to Christian faith. Even Vida Scudder, a Protestant socialist herself, felt constrained to rebuke him for his anti-Catholicism and his antisacramental, antiecclesiastical bias, which she found at odds with the gospels and with "all sound psychological development of the religious life through history."[90] In a friendly letter she wrote, "I know many people who can hardly receive your splendid teaching because your anti-Catholic animus so distresses them."[91] His statement that "scarcely any personality who bears the marks of the prophet can be found in church history between A.D. 100 and A.D. 1200" is simply absurd.[92]

Nevertheless, any student of Christianity in the United States would be hard pressed to argue with A.W. Beaven, a former president of the Federal Council of Churches, who wrote in 1937 that "the greatest single personal influence on the life and thought of the American Church in the last fifty years was exerted by Walter Rauschenbusch."[93]

One of Rauschenbusch's strongest points was his readability. The sentences tend to be short and the meaning clear, illustrated with vivid metaphor, simile, and anecdote. Later books suffer from the theologian's occupational weakness of playing endless variations on one or two favorite themes, but the book that catapulted him to national fame in 1907, *Christianity and the Social Crisis*, is outstanding. It sold fifty thousand copies, a sensational number for a religious book at that time, and was translated into eight languages, making its author an international celebrity.

The book concludes that the hope of the future lies with the labor movement and that "socialism is the ultimate and logical outcome of the labor movement."[94] The final appeal is to members of the professional class, moved by Christian faith, to "contribute scientific information and trained intelligence" and to "throw their influence on the side of the class which is now claiming its full rights."[95]

Unlike Niebuhr, Rauschenbusch lived and died a Christian socialist. He never joined the party, which was too antireligious for his tastes, but his second most important book, *Christianizing the Social Order*, like the first, concludes with a plug for socialism. And it contains a virtual appeal for Socialist votes: "The Socialist Party represents the point of view and the interests of the working class just as accurately as the old parties have represented Capitalism."[96]

Small wonder that Norman Thomas, a Presbyterian minister who ran for president on the Socialist ticket six times, could write: "Insofar as any one man, or any one book, or series of books, made me a Socialist, it was probably Walter Rauschenbusch and his writings."[97]

The question remains: How could a *socialist* exert "the greatest single personal influence on the life and thought of the American Church" in the fifty years between 1887 and 1937? Was the Federal Council of Churches' Beaven just being kind to Rauschenbusch's widow when he wrote this? The next few pages will certainly not answer that question definitively, but they may throw light in the direction of an answer.

What strikes one about the man's personality and his books are the following: intelligence, wide knowledge of the world and world literature, a strong faith in Christ (however imprecisely expressed), sweetness of temper mingled with a great capacity for indignation at the sight of injustice, and, for an intellectual and a theologian, a remarkably high level of common sense.

Walter Rauschenbusch, a strikingly handsome man, was born in Rochester, New York, in 1861. He died of cancer in 1918 at the relatively young age of fifty-six, his life not quite spanning the years between the beginning of one terrible war and the end of the next.

The Civil War he could justify on the ground that its bloody, fratricidal battles put an end to slavery. The World War could claim no such justification. A few months before his death, weakened by disease, he wrote, "Since 1914 the world is full of hate, and I cannot expect to be happy again in my lifetime." The sentence that precedes this one, however, reads, "I had long prayed God not to let me be stranded in a lonesome and useless old age, and if this is the meaning of my present illness, I shall take it as a loving mercy of God toward his servant."[98]

His anguish over World War I did not spring simply from the realization that his faith in human progress had been dealt a heavy blow. He was torn between love and loyalty to America and a strong attachment to Germany, from which his parents had emigrated and where he had received a large part of his education.

His father, August, had come to the United States in 1846 as a Lutheran missionary, the sixth in a line of ministers and writers. After becoming a German Baptist, August became a professor of church history at Rochester Theological Seminary, in which role his son, the seventh minister in the line, eventually succeeded him.

First, though, Walter received a splendid education in the United States and in Germany. He mastered Latin, Greek, French, German, and Hebrew. He traveled throughout Europe, and he would later contrast the beauty of its cities with the public ugliness and squalor of so many American cities.

Returning to the Rochester Seminary to complete his training for the Baptist ministry, Walter spent one summer as a substitute pastor in a little church in Louisville, Kentucky, where he discovered that

> it is now no longer my fond hope to be a learned theologian and write big books; I want to be a pastor, powerful with men, preaching to them Christ as the man in whom their affections and energies can find the satisfaction for which mankind is groaning.[99]

Driven by this new ambition, Rauschenbusch first volunteered for the foreign missions, but was turned down for holding too liberal a view of the Old Testament. He became pastor of a small German Baptist church on the West Side of Manhattan on the edge of a tough slum known as Hell's Kitchen.

Just as Niebuhr's thirteen years in a Detroit parish had done for him, Rauschenbusch's eleven years (1886–1897) in Hell's Kitchen made an indelible impression on his mind and soul, taught him unforgettable lessons about the real world, and eventually made a Christian socialist out of him. Since Rauschenbusch and Niebuhr are two of the most influential theologians of the twentieth century, perhaps an extended time in a poor parish should be a required condition before any theologian is permitted to put pen to paper. There, like Rauschenbusch, they "could hear human virtue cracking and crumbling all around."[100]

The year of his arrival in New York, 1886, was a fateful year. Pulling out of the depression of 1885, American workers were on the street in over 1,600 strikes, many of which were brutally and bloodily defeated. Then there was the Haymarket Riot in Chicago and Henry George's campaign for mayor in New York. George's religious fixation on the Single Tax on land values deeply moved Rauschenbusch, though he could never agree with George's exclusive concentration on that solution. He later wrote:

I owe my own first awakening to the world of social problems to the agitation of Henry George in 1886. . . . Dear friends, there is a social question. No one can doubt it, in whose ears are ringing the wails of the mangled and the crushed, who are borne along on the pent-up torrent of human life. Woe to the man who stands afar off and says, "Peace, peace" when there is no peace.[101]

Scandalized by the indifference of Christians to the sufferings of the poor and by their self-centered obsession with individual salvation, Rauschenbusch began searching his Bible for ammunition to explode these distorted interpretations of the gospel. He was also looking for an all-inclusive concept that would crystallize his own synthesis of both personal and social Christianity. He found it in that same George campaign of 1886:

I remember how Father McGlynn, speaking at Cooper Union in the first Single Tax campaign in New York in 1886, recited the words, "Thy kingdom come, thy will be done on earth," and as the great audience realized for the first time the social significance of the holy words, it lifted them off their seats with a shout of joy.[102]

This he wrote looking back from 1912, by which time the Social Gospel had won a measure of acceptance, and so he was moved to add to the above the following sentences:

In the first century "the Kingdom of God" meant a combination of the religious and the social hopes of the common people. Today the same elements are fusing once more under new conditions, and the same spirit has taken possession of the ancient word. One of the earliest services of social Christianity has been that it has revitalized the great idea and reintroduced the Church to her own earliest gospel.[103]

What did he mean by "the Kingdom/Reign of God/Heaven"? There is not simply the phrase in the Lord's Prayer. There is also Jesus' response to Pilate: "My kingship is not of this world" (John 18:36). Not exactly an encouraging quote for the Social Gospel. There are all the comparisons of the Reign of God to a wedding, a banquet, a farmer sowing seed, a fisherman separating good fish from bad, a woman mixing yeast and flour or searching the house for a lost coin, the innocence of children. The Kingdom of God is at hand, or has overtaken you, or is within you (not so good) or is among you (better).

Among Rauschenbusch's myriad definitions and statements about the Kingdom of God perhaps the following are the simplest and clearest:

> The Kingdom of God . . . demands an organized fellowship of mankind, based on justice and resulting in love, binding all men together in strong bonds of trust, helpfulness, purity and good will. . . . The Kingdom of God deals not only with the immortal souls of men, but with their bodies, their nourishment, their homes, their cleanliness, and it makes those who serve these fundamental needs veritable ministers of God.[104]

In relating this interpretation to the actual text of the Bible, Rauschenbusch was a little slipshod. For example:

> In the synoptic [Matthew, Mark, and Luke] teaching of Jesus all turns on the kingdom of God, and the life hereafter is rarely referred to; in the Gospel of John "eternal life" is the central word and the "kingdom of God" scarcely occurs.[105]

The point of this seems to be that John, under Greek influence, was largely responsible for turning the attention of the early Christians away from the Judaic emphasis on social salvation toward a preoccupation with personal salvation. Unfortunately for this exegesis, a careful reading of Matthew, for example, reveals a total of forty references by Jesus to "the life hereafter," about evenly divided between heaven and hell, which is two more references than he makes to the Kingdom, or Reign, of God and ten more than John's Gospel makes to "eternal life" or "the life hereafter."

What is really puzzling about Rauschenbusch, however, is that in his preoccupation with the Kingdom of God, he almost totally neglects Matthew 25 and Jesus' vision of the Last Judgment, a much more useful text for selling the Social Gospel. I could find no references to these at all in *Christianity and the Social Crisis*. In *Christianizing the Social Order* (pp. 61, 62), Matthew 25 gets its first real but brief emphasis, and in *A Theology for the Social Gospel* it receives three quick, glancing references. Two of these, oddly enough, are used by Rauschenbusch to argue against the traditional belief in hell, which has its most powerful and authoritative expression precisely in that passage. And here, no doubt, lies the clue to why Rauschenbusch, and so many theologians, priests, and preachers before and since, have been reluctant or unwilling to use Matthew 25 as an argument for the importance of social salvation as compared with personal salvation. They shrink from it, even though in it Jesus, in effect, makes our active pursuit of social salvation the absolute test of our eligibility for personal salvation. What indeed could be responsible for the failure of theologians to pick up this indispensable tool for the construction of the Kingdom of God on earth? Among the Social Gospelers it took a lay economist, Richard Ely, to give Matthew 25 its proper emphasis (see above).

Martin Marty, the Protestant theologian from Chicago, recently lectured at Harvard on the subject "Hell Disappeared and Nobody Noticed: An American Cultural Phenomenon." That says it all.

But he was also wrong. Rauschenbusch noticed. At the same time that he was helping to make it disappear he was also regretting its disappearance.

"The belief in hell has waned at a time we need it badly,"[106] he writes in 1912. He wrote in 1907:

> The fear of eternal punishment, the hope of eternal reward, held many a coarse nature from evil and to justice and mercy, who might not have done the right for the right's sake or through any higher motive.[107]

"Held many a *coarse* nature from evil." Niebuhr was right too about Rauschenbusch. He may have believed in sin, but he could not believe that ordinary human nature was so "coarse" that it needed the fear of punishment and the hope of reward to make it behave. As with many moderns, the dark side of Christianity both held and repelled him. In the same book he writes, "if any one has lost faith in the existence of the Devil, of the personal power of malicious evil, he can regain his faith by tackling Big Business hard enough to make it mad."[108] In another book he writes, with approval, "Satan and his angels are a fading religious entity"[109] and "popular superstitious beliefs in demonic agencies have largely been drained off by education."[110]

To which one is tempted to respond: What education? The education acquired at Auschwitz, Belsen, Buchenwald, and Dachau? Or the Gulag? But Rauschenbusch lived and wrote at a time when that kind of education was unavailable. He only had the Inquisition, the Roman Empire, and, of course, Big Business in the early twentieth century to instruct him.

If his grasp of Christian psychology was somewhat shaky, his grip on Christian social ethics was firm. He was one of the first theologians to make an intensive study of economics and sociology. His books are full of factual, balanced, but, where appropriate, hard-hitting analysis of economic and social realities. And he had the gift of expressing that analysis in clear, interesting detail and example.

And from that analysis he drew sharp conclusions:

> An unchristian social order can be known by the fact that it makes good men do bad things. . . . A Christian social order makes bad men do good things.[111]

> Political democracy without economic democracy is an uncashed promissory note, a pot without the roast, a form without substance.[112]

Jesus bids us strive first for the Reign of God and the justice of God, because on that spiritual basis all material wants too will be met; Capitalism urges us to strive first and last for our personal enrichment, and it formerly held out the hope [and still does] that the selfishness of all would create the universal good. . . . Christianity makes the love of money the root of all evil. . . . Capitalism cultivates the love of money for its own sake and gives its largest wealth to those who use monopoly for extortion. Thus two spirits are wrestling for the mastery in modern life, the spirit of Christ and the spirit of Mammon.[113]

THE PRACTICAL SOCIALIST

Living and working on the edge of Hell's Kitchen, where 1,321 families had three bathtubs among them and one could hear human virtue "cracking and crumbling," Rauschenbusch, Leighton Williams, another Baptist minister, and Elizabeth Post began in 1889 to publish a monthly called *For the Right*. They announced that they were doing it "in the interests of the working people of New York City . . . from the standpoint of Christian socialism."[114]

Rauschenbusch remained faithful to this standpoint all his life, though *For the Right* lasted only until March 1891. Before it died the paper printed a declaration of principles for the Christian Socialist Society of New York City, but it appears that the Society never actually functioned. Williams and Rauschenbusch decided that it would make sense to form a more general organization, based on the idea of the Kingdom of God. And so in 1892 they organized the Brotherhood of the Kingdom, restricted at first to Baptist ministers but later opened to all sorts and denominations. For twenty-three years it met annually at the summer home of the Williams family on the Hudson River. *The Christian Socialist* advertised and reported its conferences, but one notices that the words "socialism" and "socialist" are not often used.

In 1897 Rauschenbusch, who like Niebuhr made his reputation first as a writer for religious periodicals, was appointed to the faculty of the Rochester Theological Seminary. There he organized a chapter of the Brotherhood (Boston and Los Angeles also had chapters) and in 1901 he lectured to the union members of Rochester at the Labor Lyceum on the subject of socialism.

He had already distinguished himself with an article in the *American Journal of Sociology* in which he confessed that "I am myself a socialist," or at least enough so "to take natural monopolies out of private management."[115] He then became, with Jean Jaures, the insightful Frenchman, one of the few socialist spokespersons of that era to point out a major weakness of the prevailing socialist, Marxist bias in favor of total collectivization and public ownership. In this article he wrote:

When the entire nation is organized as a colossal machine, and every cog is dependent on its connection with the machine for its chance to work, will there be freedom enough to make life tolerable? If a man is harried by a tyrannous foreman or a spiteful fellow workman now, he can quit his job and try elsewhere. He may be out of a job for a while, but there are at least other employers to try. In the socialistic state there is to be only one employer, the state. If a man there quits his job, he cannot even employ himself.[116]

Although he never went as far in favor of private ownership as the Socialist International in 1951, this sensible reaction to total collectivism led to protest in *Christianity and the Social Crisis* that "a socialistic State could easily afford to allow individuals to continue some private production."[117]

In his talk to the union members of Rochester he opens with a similar confession of his own socialist sympathies and adds the rather surprising (to modern eyes) statement that "in the main this audience, like similar audiences in the cities everywhere, is composed of socialists."[118]

After identifying himself with the general socialist critique of capitalism, Rauschenbusch launched into a masterly analysis of "dogmatic and practical socialism" that compares favorably with anything done by Eduard Bernstein. He likens the dogmatic socialists to the Christian millenarians who

> believe that this is a bad world and getting worse all the time [and] stake all their hope on the return of Christ. . . . In the same way the revolutionary socialists regard the present order as hopelessly bad: they are pleased to see it getting worse; they expect their new Jerusalem to come suddenly, and they stake all on that hope; meanwhile they sit and wait. . . .[119]

He adds:

> All this is permissible tactics if the suffering is short anyway. If, however, the development before us is still a long one, it is both cruel and unwise. The starved and helpless poor, flabby of flesh, thin of blood, weak in energy and will, alternating between fits of rage and long despair, are not good material even for a violent revolution, and they will not do at all for a peaceful revolution, in which patience, staying power, intelligence and practical sagacity count.[120]

What is impressive and extraordinary about this speech is the telling, tightly argued critique of Marxism, which is almost unique in the history of socialist discourse before and since. Although he concedes that "posterity will, I think, ascribe a very high position to Marx," he proceeds to lower that position to a level considerably below that ascribed by most American socialists of both that time and this. He does this by demonstrating, with logic and statistics, that Marx greatly overworked his theory of surplus value, that he was wrong about the disappearance of the middle class, wrong about the ever-increasing impoverishment of the workers, and wrong about the imminent collapse of capitalism. This is perhaps the most telling thrust:

> Marx said that during the transition the proletariat would have to exercise dictatorial power. What does that mean? Unless there is a real social

organization of the people already in existence, it would mean that the club orators, the men who spout in places like this, would be entrusted with power, and the Lord have mercy upon us! Workingmen are still fascinated by the man who can do what they can't do—talk fluently. I am a talker myself, and consequently I prefer the silent man who does things to the man who is like a roof gutter in a rainstorm. It is no easy thing to run a satisfactory democracy. We have been testing methods in this country for a century and a quarter, and we haven't learned yet. Running an industrial democracy is harder than a political democracy. . . . The great cooperative societies in England have more money than they can profitably invest because they haven't got the men who can manage things successfully.[121]

In *Christianizing the Social Order* Rauschenbusch returns to the theme of cooperative socialism in the sense of direct, immediate ownership by the workers: "The running of cooperative stores and factories is a new art which has to be learned with losses and suffering."[122] He quotes John Stuart Mill, "that bold, clear mind":

The form of association which, if mankind continues to improve, must be expected in the end to predominate, is not that which can exist between a capitalist as chief, and workpeople without a voice in the management, but the association of the laborers themselves on terms of equality, collectively owning the capital with which they carry on their operations, and working under managers elected and removable by themselves.[123]

Rauschenbusch did not always distinguish clearly between socialism as direct worker ownership and socialism as public ownership in the form of some vague, amorphous "Cooperative Commonwealth," a favorite phrase among both Christian and secular American socialists. This confusion is even more striking in the recurring distinctions, or attempts at distinction, that both Christian and secular socialists were continually making between competition and cooperation. Rauschenbusch uses the famous quote from Maurice, "one of the finest minds of England in the Victorian Age: 'I do not see my way farther than this: Competition is put forth as the law of the universe; that is a lie.' " Rauschenbusch continues, "And his friend Charles Kingsley added, 'Competition means death; cooperation means life'." [124]

In socialist literature, and most particularly in Christian socialist literature, we continually run into this posing of competition and cooperation as opposites, competition being bad, unchristian, the essence of capitalism, and cooperation being good, the essence of Christianity and Christian economics.

Alec Nove, the British economist and socialist historian of the Soviet economy, startled a conference of American socialists recently with the suggestion that "the opposite of competition is not cooperation, but rather monopoly."[125] And, of course, monopoly is even more authentically capitalist than competition.

This insight was anticipated, quite unintentionally, by Frances Willard, the Christian socialist president of the Women's Christian Temperance Union, who was quoted in *The Christian Socialist* as follows: "The trusts, whose object is to abolish competition, have proven that we are better without than with it."[126]

Have they? Are we? The history of trusts and monopolies, the history of that great, bloated monopoly known as the Soviet Union, have demonstrated that the elimination of competition is not necessarily a good thing. Rauschenbusch was too intelligent not to see this. He distinguishes between "commercial competition" (bad) and "human competition"[127] (good) and he notes that "the only valid defense for the wastefulness and inefficiency of the competitive system is that it protects the consumer against the voracity of the monopolist."[128] He might have added his warning of 1897, "When the entire nation is organized as a colossal machine, will there be freedom enough to make life tolerable?"[129]

Unfortunately, by 1912 he seems to have forgotten this because he adds, in the next paragraph after his remark about "the voracity of the monopolist," "Christianity should end competition because it is immoral."[130] He was not quite intelligent enough, or perhaps rather he did not have the benefit of our hindsight experience, to realize that commerical competition can be made human, stimulating, and productive when properly regulated and, furthermore, can be reconciled with cooperative ownership of the means of production, can be reconciled, in fact, with the finest species of socialism.

Rauschenbusch was one of those people who said so many good things so well that one is tempted to go on quoting indefinitely. I close this summary with two of his best statements. Even today, they cry out for attention, and action.

> Wealth is to a nation what manure is to a farm. If the farmer spreads it evenly over the soil, it will enrich the whole. If he should leave it in heaps, the land would be impoverished and under the rich heaps the vegetation would be killed. . . .[131]

> The industrial worker needs some property right in the industrial system in which he works. If he cannot be sole owner of a small shop, he must be part owner of a large shop. . . .
> The simplest and most effective form which such property right could take would be the right of a man [or woman] to a job. . . . The right to employment is the next great human right that demands recognition in public opinion and human law. . . . If all other means fail, the worker should be able to fall back on the community itself for employment.[132]

In such statements speaks the authentic voice of Christian socialism, the voice of Buchez, of Ludlow, of Ketteler.

Finally, from Rauschenbusch's tribute to *The Christian Socialist*, printed in its issue of March 15, 1914:

> Thousands of Christian people have been aroused. . . . This great body of awakened religious people is at present the most important mission

field for socialism in America. . . . Non-religious socialism is raw and undeveloped socialism, which has angrily flung aside some of the most precious possessions of humanity. . . . Christian socialists. . . . must carry into the propaganda of socialism the moral appeal, the persuasiveness, and the balance of temper which they derive from their religious training. Christianity and socialism are the oldest and the youngest of the idealistic forces at work in our civilization. The future lies, not with those who choose either of the two and reject the other, but with those who can effect the most complete amalgamation of the two.

BLACK CHRISTIAN SOCIALISTS

When we consider the extreme poverty and injustice suffered by black people in the United States, it may be surprising that socialism has not been more popular among them. Reflecting its origins among the white workers and intellectuals of Western Europe, the socialist movement in the United States was, for most of its early history, a white phenomenon.

Significantly, most of the first black socialist champions were Christian ministers. At the 1904 and 1908 conventions of the Socialist Party, the only black delegate was the Rev. George Washington Woodbey (1854-?), a Baptist minister from San Diego, California, a contributor to *The Christian Socialist*, and a former slave, freed after the Civil War.

At the 1908 convention Woodbey rose in opposition to national leaders like Berger and Untermann, who had spoken against the admission to America of Chinese immigrants. Woodbey's protest drew applause: "I am in favor of throwing the entire world open to the inhabitants of the world," and again, when he quoted Thomas Paine to the effect that "the world is my country."[133] But the convention sloughed the question off to a committee for study. Although more progressive on race than most American institutions, including the church, the Socialist Party still mirrored the race prejudice of white America.

The Christian Socialist, as early as 1905, advertised and praised Woodbey's pamphlet *The Bible and Socialism*. As late as 1915, the last year in which there is any historical record of his existence, Woodbey's articles were being printed in Carr's paper. In one of them, Woodbey, in one sentence, shows that he was both an orthodox Christian and an orthodox socialist:

When you show the church member how the Bible, in every line of it, is with the poor as against their oppressors, and that it is only because we have not been following out its teaching that professed Christians have been found among the worst oppressors of the poor and that no man is entitled to be called a Christian who does not measure up to the teaching of the Bible, you have made the first step toward converting him to the idea that cannot be done in its entirety without the collective ownership and operation of the industries.[134]

The Christian Socialist charged only 20 cents for Woodbey's *The Bible and Socialism*, although it runs 114 pages (in Philip Foner's excellent collection of speeches and writings by black socialist ministers). The book/pamphlet reveals an excellent knowledge of relevant passages in the Bible, with the single exception, once again, of Jesus' vision of the Last Judgment in Matthew 25, which is not mentioned at all.

Woodbey moved from the Republican Party to the Prohibition Party to the Democratic Party and, finally, to the Socialist Party after reading Edward Bellamy's *Looking Backward* and listening to Eugene Debs speak in the presidential campaign of 1900. He resigned his pulpit in Nebraska and devoted himself to the socialist cause. In 1902 he moved to California, where he was a member of the Party's executive committee and became famous throughout the state as "The Great Negro Socialist Orator." His street meetings also gained him familiarity with the inside of several California jails. Although he was appointed pastor of Mt. Zion Baptist Church in San Diego, he eventually lost his position for mixing too much socialism with his Bible.

Despite his great devotion to the socialist movement, Woodbey did not hesitate to criticize socialist leaders and writers who identified socialism with an anti-Christian bias. In a *Christian Socialist* article, "Why the Socialists Must Reach the Churches with Their Message," he expressed the still valid opinion that "Socialists cannot win without reaching the millions of working people who belong to the various churches of the country." He added, "The only question is how best to reach them. I have found that there are a large number of our comrades who seem to think that the way to do it is to attack the Christian religion as such."[135] He might have included George Herron among those comrades.

One of Woodbey's converts was the Reverend George W. Slater, Jr. As pastor of the Zion Tabernacle in Chicago he had tried to organize a buying cooperative to help his poor parishioners survive the recession winter of 1907-08. He found that the wholesalers, by agreement with the retailers, would not sell supplies to such a cooperative. Thinking, rightly, that this was a violation of the Anti-Trust Act, Slater later wrote that he "began to inquire about President Roosevelt's 'trust-busters,' as they are called, but I soon found out that the trusts were busting the busters."[136] This experience made him receptive to Woodbey's street speaking.

During the years 1908 and 1909 Slater wrote a series of articles for *The Chicago Daily Socialist* and in 1912, having moved to the Bethel African Church in Clinton, Iowa, he was elected to the executive committee of the Christian Socialist Fellowship and named CSF Secretary for the Colored Race. In this capacity he carried the socialist gospel to black churches around the country and contributed a number of articles to *The Christian Socialist*. In the last of these he took issue with R. R. Wright, the editor of an influential black journal, *The Christian Recorder*, who had attacked socialism on the ground that it "would appeal to individual selfishness." Slater responded:

The Socialist appeal to individual selfishness is the same in kind as the Christian's. . . . They teach that the individual will find his largest good in the larger good of the whole. The Socialists teach that the present competitive industrial system is an exploitation of the real producers of the necessities of life—food, shelter and clothing. . . . They teach that if the producers will form a cooperative industrial government, democratically operating the means, and democratically producing and distributing the products, of production . . . [then] the individual will receive for his toil very much more of the good things of life. This is a commendable selfishness.[137]

Slater wrote a number of popular socialist pamphlets, notably *Blackmen, Strike for Liberty* and, in answer to an appeal from the Socialist local in New York City, *The Colored Man's Case as Socialism Sees It*. He also published a pro-socialist monthly, *The Western Evangel*, from his church in Clinton, where he served until 1919. No copies of this publication or of his pamphlets are known to exist. Nor is anything known of his birth or his life after 1919. Such has been the neglect or indifference of socialist historians (excepting Philip Foner) to the work of "black socialist preachers."

Two other predecessors of Woodbey and Slater should be mentioned. The first of these was the Reverend James T. Holly, a former shoemaker, who was so outraged by racial prejudice in the United States that he advocated the emigration of black Americans to Haiti, where he himself had gone to live. *The Church Review*, like *The Christian Recorder* a publication of the African Methodist Episcopal Church (but more open to socialism), published a long article of Holly's in its issue entitled "Socialism from the Biblical Point of View" (no. 9, 1892-93). It opens with the words, "Socialism is the subject now uppermost in all minds, almost to the exclusion of every other thought, in this closing decade of the nineteenth century."[138]

Holly was a bitter man, with some reason, and his article reads like a chapter out of Jeremiah or Revelation:

There is no Gospel morality in our organized modern industry, and therefore offerings from such ill-gotten riches are made as if God could be bribed by the mammon of iniquity. But such gifts, amassed by grinding the face of the poor and heartlessly wrung out of the blood and sweat of careworn toilers, are already smitten with the curse of Heaven in answer to the sighs and groans of the oppressed laborers that mount up thither, crying for vengeance on the avaricious oppressors; and thereby those offerings are an abomination in the sight of the Almighty, for He cannot and will not behold with pleasure iniquity, injustice and oppression. . . . And down will go the whole Babylonish fabric of Christendom, ecclesiastical, political and financial, in one general crash, as that great millstone cast by the angel into the sea, saying, "Thus with violence shall that great city, Babylon, be thrown down, and shall be found no more at all."[139]

A few years later a different voice was heard in the same *Church Review* (no. 13, 1896–97), that of the Reverend Reverdy Ransom, later Bishop Ransom. Even more eloquent than Holly, he was a good deal more positive and optimistic. A learned scholar, he quoted Ruskin and Bishop Westcott of Durham, the English Christian socialists, as well as the American Richard Ely, and came up with a workable definition of democratic socialism, which, he wrote,

is opposed to individualism and does not regard society as composed of an army of warring atoms, but believes that social system to be the best in which the interests of the individual are made subordinate to the interests of society, while allowing freedom for the highest development of his own personality.[140]

Ransom is at his best in his closing appeal to black workers to make common cause with white workers in the struggle for a more just society:

The battles of socialism are not to be fought by white men, for the benefit of white men. . . . This question cannot be settled without the Negro's aid. The cause of labor, of the industrial army, is one. . . . That the Negro will enthusiastically espouse the cause of socialism we cannot doubt. Social and industrial oppression have been his portion for centuries. . . . The day is not far distant, when with clearer eyes, through the smoke of battle, we shall see the steeples of a new civilization rising—a civilization which shall neither be Anglo-Saxon, Asiatic nor African, but one which, recognizing the unity of the race and the brotherhood of man, will accord to each individual the full reward which the free exercise of his powers has won, and the right to stand upon an equal plane and share all of the blessings of our common heritage.[141]

These words were written almost a hundred years ago. The steeples of that new civilization are not yet visible through the smoke of battle, but here and there a glimpse may be caught of their outline. U.S. Representative Ronald Dellums of California, a confessed socialist, in his foreword to Foner's *Black Socialist Preachers*, echoes Bishop Ransom and appeals to the "special responsibility of American Blacks to help all people understand together the changes that must be made together."[142]

Another sign of hope is the work of two contemporary black theologians, James H. Cone and Cornel West, both of whom are members of the Democratic Socialists of America. Cone has written:

If we define our struggle for freedom only within the alternatives posed by capitalism, then we have allowed our future humanity to be determined by what people have created and not by God. To believe in God is to know that our hope is grounded in Jesus Christ, the crucified Lord whose resurrected presence creates a new hope for a better world.

He asks, "Why are there no genuinely radical and independent voices coming from our leaders today? Why do they pose alternatives that exist only within capitalism, a system which offers no hope for the masses of blacks?"[143]

Cornel West, with a dazzling display of erudition in his book *Prophesy Deliverance!*, puts his finger even more firmly on the key question for American blacks, namely, would the total elimination of white racism solve the problem of Black oppression? And he answers it firmly, "Racial status contributes greatly to black oppression. . . . [But] class position contributes more than racial status to the basic form of powerlessness in America."[144]

CHRISTIAN SOCIALIST WOMEN

The history of the socialist movement has not only been predominantly a white phenomenon; it has also been mainly a male phenomenon. Rosa Luxemburg (1870–1919), a Polish woman, became a leader of the left wing of the German Social Democrats, and Golda Meir (1898–1978) was Israel's prime minister, but few other women have established international reputations in socialist circles.

Of the 128 delegates to the founding convention of the Socialist Party in 1901, only eight were women. One of these was Carrie Rand Herron. By the 1908 convention the number of women delegates had risen to twenty, but even more impressive were the two hundred vocal women in the spectators' gallery.

Germany and the United States had about the best records for female membership in socialist parties, both averaging between 15 and 20 percent. American socialism during the nineteenth century was largely a German by-product, but even among German-American socialists the men tended to adopt the view that women, like children, should be seen and not heard. The German-American women mostly accepted their inferior status.

The native-born women, led by Victoria Woodhull, challenged this state of affairs. Oddly enough, Karl Marx himself, at the 1872 convention of the International Workingmen's Association (IWA), the First International, recommended that the U.S. sections of the IWA that consisted of native-born Americans be expelled because they gave "precedence to the women's question over the question of labor."[145] The head of the American delegation responded, "The labor question is also a women's question, and the emancipation of women must precede that of the workers."[146]

Among the most active and vocal champions of women's rights were the Christian socialists, notably Bellamy, Bliss, and Herron among the men, and Mary Livermore, Frances Willard, and Vida Scudder among the women. Mari Jo Buhle, a firmly secular socialist, in her book *Women and American Socialism, 1870–1920*, neglects Scudder but gives major credit to Livermore and

Willard for laying the groundwork of socialist organization among American women during the late nineteenth and early twentieth centuries.

Mary Livermore (1820–1905) was the wife of a Universalist minister, a traditional Christian wife and mother until the Civil War. She then moved from New England to Chicago, and there, as a member of the Sanitary Commission of Illinois, she suddenly blossomed into a popular public speaker and a first-rate organizer. She promoted the organization of more than three thousand soldiers' aid societies. Learning, like many other women, from this wartime experience, she went on to call the first women's suffrage convention in Illinois and became a leader of the newly organized American Woman Suffrage Association. She lectured (averaging 150 appearances a year) and wrote for many years on many subjects, including socialism, literature, and women's history. Returning to New England she served as president of the Women's Christian Temperance Union of Massachusetts and vice-president of Bliss's Society of Christian Socialists. Encouraged by Frances Willard, she also joined the Boston chapter of Bellamy's Nationalist Clubs. By her own person and prestige she gave Christian socialism instant credibility and respectability.

In several of her lectures Mrs. Livermore repeated a warning to her male contemporaries to "awake to the consciousness that there were in women possibilities and potencies of which they had never dreamed."[147] Looking back from 1899 in her autobiography, her report on the progress of women struck a positive note and reflected, in large part, the effectiveness of her own life:

> Colleges, universities, and professional schools were opening their doors to women. Industries, trades and remunerative vocations which hitherto had ignored them now invited their cooperation, and women were becoming self-supporting members of the community. Hard and unjust laws which had grievously hindered them were repealed, and others affording larger protection and opportunity were enacted. Great organizations of women for missionary work were formed, and managed solely by themselves. Women by the hundred thousand wheeled into line for temperance work. Women's clubs sprang into being—clubs for social enjoyment and mutual instruction and help. Woman Suffrage Leagues multiplied. Everywhere there was a call for women to be up and doing, with voice and pen, with hand and head and heart.[148]

When Mary Livermore spoke of "women by the hundred thousand" wheeling into line for temperance work, she was speaking primarily of the Women's Christian Temperance Union and of the woman who stood at the head of the line and who, more than any other, was responsible for the wheeling of the women. That woman was Frances Willard (1839-1898), popularly known as "Saint Frances" and frequently referred to as "the Woman of the Century." These are accolades that Mari Jo Buhle seconds, for she refers to Willard as "the century's most influential and revered American woman."

Mary Livermore came from New England and her Midwest experience was mainly in the metropolis of Chicago. Frances Willard was born and raised on a

Wisconsin farm and her affinity with the Protestant heartland of America was deeper and stronger than Livermore's. She was a magnificent organizer. By the mid-1880s she had built the WCTU into a powerful movement of two hundred thousand dues-paying members. Like so many successful movements before and since, the organizational unit was the small cell meeting, in this case "the parlor meeting," where women could feel at home and express themselves freely.

Willard quickly broadened the interests and objectives of the WCTU beyond a concern with alcohol, first to women's suffrage and then to what she called, in an arresting phrase, "the reign of a religion of the body which for the first time in history shall correlate with Christ's wholesome, practical yet blessedly spiritual religion of the soul." She described the aim of the WCTU "to help forward the coming of Christ into all departments of life."[149]

As the years went by this came to mean socialism. Bellamy's *Looking Backward* was a major influence on her. She called it "a revelation" and "an Evangel." So sensitive did she find it to women's interests that she told her secretary it could not have been written by a man but by "a great-hearted, big-brained woman."[150] She used her position as national president of the WCTU to push Nationalism. At the 1889 convention she had the Nationalist program printed in the convention proceedings and urged the members to join Nationalist clubs. By 1893, though Bellamy himself shunned the words "socialism" and "socialist," Willard used her presidential address to tell the delegates that "in every Christian there exists a socialist, and in every socialist a Christian."[151] By 1897, not long before her death, the presidential address became such a strong plea for socialism that the Socialist Party circulated it as an organizing leaflet. *The Christian Socialist* featured it eight years later in its special Temperance Edition, of which Carr printed and distributed seventy-five thousand copies. In it Willard said:

> I would take, not by force, but by the slow process of lawful acquisition . . . and a wiser ballot . . . the entire plant that we call civilization . . . and make it the common property of the people. . . . I believe that competition is doomed. . . . This is the higher way . . . the very marrow of Christ's Gospel.[152]

As noted above, Willard's socialism, like Bellamy's, had an excessively centralized, monopolistic bias to it, a bias that would probably have been more pleasing to Marx than to Christ, but there is no question that Frances Willard did more than anyone else, male or female, to introduce the general idea of socialism to Middle America.

And it all began (and continued, right up to her premature death in 1898) with a Christian woman's crusade against the Demon Rum.

THE DELIGHTFUL VIDA

Walter Rauschenbusch may have been the most readable theologian, but the most readable Christian socialist was, by all odds, the delightful

Vida Dutton Scudder (1861–1954), for over forty years professor of English at Wellesley College.

Like John Ludlow and R. H. Tawney, Vida Scudder was born in India. Her father was an American Congregational missionary who drowned when a dam broke in a river across which he was swimming. Still a baby, she was brought home and brought up in her mother's home in Auburndale, a suburb of Boston. Like Rauschenbusch, she was born in 1861.

Like Rauschenbusch also, much of her youth was spent living and studying in Europe—in Italy, France, and England in her case—and this experience gave her a great love and appreciation of our European antecedents, of personalities and writers as diverse as St. Catherine of Siena, St. Francis of Assisi, Maurice, Marx, Bakunin, Ruskin, Lenin, Tolstoy, Berdyaev, Ibsen, Arnold, Browning, and Jaures. She was a woman full of love, love for people individually and in the mass. She was a fine writer—verbose at times, a little sentimental at times—but sharp, observant, insightful, and wise. Scarcely a trace of Godwin's Disease, though her socialism leaned toward a kind of contradictory, democratic Marxism that was sensible enough to see that "without intricate safeguards and guarantees, the control of resources by government might mean a worse menace to liberty than any riot of individualistic anarchy."[153]

The book that "clinched my socialism" was the first volume of *The Fabian Essays* (1889). In her autobiography, *On Journey*, published in 1937, Scudder writes movingly of her introduction to that book. The reference to "settlements" is to the settlement house movement that she, Jane Addams, and a number of other women pioneered:

How brilliant they were, and how persuasive, drawn from the stuff, not of dreams but of life. *The Historic Essay* by Sidney Webb gave me a reading of history which I have never repudiated. . . . Above all, I found something better than pyrotechnics, I found solid thinking as well as superb moral passion in the essays of George Bernard Shaw. . . . Poets and dreamers had fed my imagination, heart and conscience had profited, rather negatively, through compassion and inward rage, by all that settlements had brought me. But I was in a fog. Now my mind found the practical, constructive ideas for which it had been avid. I looked around the tangled web in which our feet were helplessly caught and behold, I held a clue! Oh, the relief!

Bureaucratic, limited, the conceptions of those Fabians? Never looking beyond the horizons of state socialism and a municipal milk supply? Well, perhaps. . . . But it may be remembered that Fabian theories were for me supplemented and in a way implemented by living contact with the labor movement. This saved me from ideology, made me a conscious and deliberate sharer in the class struggle, endowed me with humble, semi-mystical perception of the necessary initiative of the Workers. . . . Moreover, I was a Fabian with a difference. For the ultimate source of my socialist convictions was and is Christianity. Unless I were a socialist I could not honestly be a Christian, and although I was not sure I dared call myself by that name, I could use no other.[154]

Scudder's contact with the labor movement came through Denison House, the Boston settlement she helped found and run, which became involved in organizing drives and strikes, especially among women workers, and through an AFL Federal Labor Union to which she belonged and which sent her as its delegate to the Boston Central Labor Union. There "we sat, excited, suffocated by smoke, listening to interminable speeches, now wordy, now angry, now full of meat."[155]

About the same time, 1889, Scudder joined the Reverend W. D. P. Bliss in the newly organized Society of Christian Socialists and, having converted to the Episcopal Church—she preferred to call herself an Anglo-Catholic—worshipped with him and a small group of socialist faithful in "an Upper Chamber on Boylston Place" in the Church of the Carpenter. She wrote about it lovingly:

Not only did we worship together, singing with special zeal the Magnificat, but we had wonderful suppers, true agape, when the altar at the back of the little room was curtained off and we feasted on ham and pickles and hope of an imminent revolution. Mr. Bliss's socialist paper, *The Dawn*, for which I wrote now and then, was sunrise light to some of us.[156]

What is most striking about Vida Scudder is the rare, almost unique combination of appreciation both for the spiritual and the material, for "the poets and dreamers" as well as the pragmatic trade unionists *and* the tough-minded revolutionaries. Nowhere is this better expressed than in her excellent book *Socialism and Character* (pp. 132-34), which Rauschenbusch praised as "a rare book, with a feminine wealth of insight and spiritual experience."[157]

The passage opens with a solid insight:

Take the working girl, for example, and gather up in imagination the total effect of all the benevolent agencies which exist to help her: the girls' club, the settlement, the vacation house, the Associate Charities. . . . Measure the force of their reaction on her personality in comparison with that of two crude economic facts—the wage she receives and the duration of her working day.

She goes on to deliver this harsh judgment on some of her most beloved authors:

Tolstoy, Ruskin, Ibsen were all on the wrong tack. Close these authors; open your Engels, your Bebel, your Jaures; and, even though you may not agree with their doctrines, enjoy to full the relief afforded by their method and attitude. For here at last we meet minds free from sentimentality or personal obsessions, seeking eagerly to be at grips with the actual facts of human progress.

She concludes:

The determinist has perceived what the idealist has too often ignored, that the most effective type of spiritual power always arises as the natural product of a concrete situation.[158]

But most of all one loves her for her love of Christ and because she still loved Ibsen enough to quote, in the same book, the speech of Julian the Apostate in *Emperor and Galilean*:

I dreamed of Him lately. I dreamed that I ordained that the memory of the Galilean should be rooted out on earth. Then I soared aloft into infinite space till my feet rested on another world.

But behold, there came a procession by me, on the strange earth where I stood. And in the midst of the slow-moving array was the Galilean, alive, and bearing a cross on His back. Then I called to him and said, "Whither away, Galilean?" But He turned His head toward me, nodded slowly, and said, "To the Place of the Skull."

Where is he now? What if that at Golgotha, near Jerusalem, was but a wayside matter, a thing done as it were in passing, in a leisure hour? What if He goes on and on, and suffers, and dies, and conquers again and again, from world to world?

And, Vida Scudder adds, "From world to world, also from age to age."[159]

TWO CONTEMPORARY WOMEN

Rosemary Ruether is a feminist theologian and author of many books who teaches at Garrett Evangelical Seminary in Illinois. She is also vice-chair of the Democratic Socialists of America. In 1977 she gave the James Luther Adams Lecture at a general assembly of the Unitarian Universalists, from which the following is excerpted:

Christians concerned with social justice must also reopen the question of socialism. Socialism remains the key tradition for considering an alternative economic order to that of the capitalist class system. Socialism signifies both the will to seek new visions and new possibilities for a just ordering of the socio-economic order and the unwillingness to accept the present order as given and inevitable . . .

The [Democratic Socialists] see the issue of full employment as particularly crucial to this reform agenda, since the very logic of the question of full employment raises the issue of the bias of the present economic system. . . . [160]

All the people who are working on cooperative factories and farms, who are working on tenant self-management in housing, who are asserting neighborhood control of schools, organizing welfare recipients around their rights, creating health care or consumer cooperatives and in many other areas: these should be able to see democratic socialism as the umbrella under which they are all moving to a more just society.[161]

Dorothee Sölle, poet and theologian, divides her time between Hamburg in West Germany and a teaching post at Union Theological Seminary in New York. She has also been active in DSA. When asked to tell how and why she became a socialist, she gave this account in a pamphlet of DSA's Religion & Socialism Commission:

During the Vietnam War I met a small businessman who had been incarcerated as a socialist in Hitler's prison. One night coming home from an antiwar meeting he ached. When I asked him why, he told me that they had trampled on his ribs and broken some that never properly healed. I asked him for whom he had suffered this.

He was surprised that I as a Christian would ask such a question. "Don't you know why we are organizng the antiwar rally? For what is your faith good if it does not make a difference?" he said. Thus I became a socialist.[162]

Since the days of Livermore, Willard and Scudder women have become much more prominent in the socialist movement and this is also true among Christian socialists. Ruether and Sölle are only two of the most prominent.

RISE AND FALL WITH REINHOLD NIEBUHR

The effort to combine political radicalism with a more classical interpretation of religion will strike the modern mind as bizarre and capricious. It will satisfy neither the liberals in politics and religion, nor the political radicals nor the devotees of traditional Christianity.[163]

This is a quotation from *Reflections on the End of an Era*, the most Marxist book written by Reinhold Niebuhr (1892–1971), who is the most influential theologian yet produced by the United States and who for about twenty years was its most intelligent and articulate Christian socialist.

Ultimately the combination did not satisfy Niebuhr and he returned to the political liberalism from which he had begun. But before he returned he demonstrated an amazing ability to translate and communicate Judeo-Christian concepts in a way that caught and moved the minds and hearts of the secular liberals and intellectuals of his time.

Consider some of the tributes from men who, like Max Weber, might well have described themselves as "tone deaf" in matters of religion. Arthur Schlesinger, Jr.: "No man has had as much influence as a preacher in this generation; no preacher has had as much influence in the secular world."[164] Walter Lippmann placed Niebuhr in "the very highest ranks of thinkers in this country during this century."[165] This was a significant tribute because Niebuhr had once lacerated Lippmann for "suave and bland pretenses of disinterestedness."[166] Hans Morgenthau called him "the greatest living political philosopher of America."[167]

This homage is the more noteworthy because it is safe to say that before Niebuhr began to be much read and listened to, roughly around 1930, Christianity was a subject that was almost beneath contempt in the world of intellectual America.

In Europe as well Niebuhr was hailed as something special. John Baillie, head of New College in Edinburgh, had this reaction to Niebuhr's delivery of the prestigious Gifford Lectures at the University of Edinburgh in 1939: "Intellectually, Niebuhr is head and shoulders, he is legs and ankles, above any other American."[168]

Emil Brunner, Barth's partner in the development of "dialectical" or "crisis" theology, frankly acknowledging his own failure to catch the ear of his secular contemporaries, wrote, "With him theology broke into the world; theology was no longer quarantined, and men of letters, philosophers, sociologists, historians, even statesmen, began to listen."[169]

A word of personal testimony: In the early 1940s I heard Niebuhr speak at a luncheon meeting of New York liberals sponsored by the Union for Democratic Action, which Niebuhr organized to promote U.S. support of the Allies' struggling effort to stop Adolf Hitler. It was a sensational performance: funny, eloquent, luminously intelligent, vibrant with energy and passion, and capped by a characteristic touch of insight and courage when he warned us that "even more of a threat than Hitler is the Hitler in ourselves."

This "Hitler in ourselves," this emphasis on the ancient doctrine of original sin (Niebuhr liked to recall that the *London Times* once called it "the only empirically verifiable dogma of Christianity"), was perhaps the most distinctive note in Niebuhr's theology. How he came to find it and how it influenced his approach to both socialism and religious discourse is worth some exploration.

Karl Paul Reinhold Niebuhr was born in Missouri of a German Evangelical pastor who had departed Germany for America, not for economic reasons— *his* father was a prosperous landowner—but to escape the oppressive authority of his father and life in nineteeth-century Prussia. At about the age of ten, Reinhold decided that his father was the most interesting man in town—then Lincoln, Illinois—and had the most interesting job. He resolved to follow his father into the German Evangelical ministry. His familiarity with German, incidentally, turned out to be a great advantage, since it made it possible for him to read writers like Weber, Barth, and Tillich long before they were translated into English.

Niebuhr attended Eden Theological Seminary in Missouri, but was dissatisfied with the limited training he received there and spent two years at Yale Divinity School, picking up some Ivy League polish and a bit of the liberal theology that was typical of that time and place. His thesis, entitled "The Contribution of Christianity to the Doctrine of Immortality," attempted to reconcile belief in immortality with disbelief in the physical resurrection of Jesus. Since Niebuhr is usually classified as a "neo-orthodox" theologian and since he described his own faith as "classical," it is interesting to note that he retained this disbelief in later life. Still, he was far more biblical in faith than Tillich, somewhat less than Barth.

In the 1956 symposium on his thought, he thanks his friends for helping him "to come into a fuller knowledge of 'the unsearchable riches of Christ' "[170] and confesses his faith that "Christ is 'the light that shineth in darkness.' "[171] In that same symposium, however, he was pressed hard by the British theologian Alan Richardson, who challenged Niebuhr's disbelieving faith in "historical criticism." "The only Jesus known to contemporary historical and critical scholarship," Richardson insisted,

> is the Christ of the apostolic witness, the very Jesus who healed the sick, raised the dead, and was himself raised from the dead on the third day. There is no other *historical* Jesus [emphasis in the original].[172]

Responding to Richardson, Niebuhr questioned his confidence about contemporary scholarship, which Niebuhr believed, somewhat tentatively, "seemed to indicate that the story of the empty tomb was an afterthought and that the really attested historical fact was the experience of the risen Christ among his various disciples."[173] He did not address the question as to how the disciples could experience a resurrection that was not a fact but an afterthought.

Niebuhr's impact as an "orthodox" theologian, in short, was based mainly on his brilliant series of written and spoken variations on the theme of "original sin," which, from the 1930s sermons on, he composed in twenty-two books, hundreds of editorials and articles in over seventy periodicals, five of which he either edited or helped to edit, some simultaneously, and in untold numbers of meetings, conferences, classes, and sermons, which, finally, in 1952 drained his fantastic energy, broke his health, and diminished the influence of his last twenty years.

Finding precise definitions of original sin in Niebuhr is not easy, but the references, assumptions, implications, and inferences are everywhere. One of the most famous: "Man's capacity for justice makes democracy possible; but man's inclination to injustice makes democracy necessary."[174] Another: "In terms of social theory [the doctrine] implied the inevitability of tensions of interest and conflict in human affairs,"[175] an inevitability that Niebuhr frequently called to witness to the "naive utopianism" of Marx's faith in a world without conflict or alienation once the private ownership of productive property had been abolished.

Critics have pointed out that Niebuhr's view of original sin did not really need the Bible. As the *London Times* conceded, it was "empirically verifiable" by any honest, intelligent person's observation of reality both outside and inside his or her own body and mind. But Niebuhr maintained stubbornly that "the Bible . . . gives a truer view of both the nobility and the misery of man than all the wisdom of scientists and philosophers."[176]

Emil Brunner has testified that Niebuhr's fascination with original sin was sparked by a conversation Brunner had with Niebuhr shortly after Niebuhr joined the faculty of Union Theological Seminary in New York in 1928. But Niebuhr himself, in his "Intellectual Autobiography," lays more stress on the thirteen years that preceded that conversation, years that he spent as pastor of a small parish in Detroit, learning something about real life, and death, from the way his parishioners faced the one and the other, to the way Henry Ford exploited the auto workers and still managed to sell the American public the notion that he was an enlightened employer.

As a result of this experience and these observations, which he recorded in a delightfully wise little book, *Leaves from the Notebook of a Tamed Cynic*, Niebuhr "became a socialist in theory long before I enrolled in the Socialist Party and before I had read anything by Marx." In a somewhat self-deprecatory explanation in later life to June Bingham he said, "I became the prisoner of a very cute phrase: . . . 'when private property ceases to be private, it ought no longer to be private.' "[177] Clearly Henry Ford's plant at River Rouge did not seem very private.

As a result of his experience in Detroit, Niebuhr also turned sharply against the optimistic faith in progress and the feeble or nonexistent sense of sin that he identified with secular liberalism and also with the Social Gospel, more accurately in the case of Bellamy and Herron, less accurately, as we have seen, in the case of Gladden and Rauschenbusch. World War I, of course, added fuel to this smoky fire, which flared up when Niebuhr journeyed to Europe in 1923 and observed the baleful effects of the Treaty of Versailles in the Valley of the Ruhr, where the French forces of occupation were behaving like most forces of occupation and "you could see hatred with the naked eye." Niebuhr concluded, "This is as good a time as any to conclude that I am done with the war business."[178] So he became a pacifist. He wrote for *The World Tomorrow*, the lively publication of the Fellowship of Reconciliation, and eventually became one its editors, in the company of such other socialist pacifists as Norman Thomas, A. J. Muste, Paul Douglas (later U.S. Senator from Illinois), Sherwood Eddy, and John C. Bennett. The masthead read "A Journal Looking Toward a Social Order Based on the Religion of Jesus."

Niebuhr's German antecedents helped make him sympathetic to the residents of the Ruhr, but ironically he broke out of the obscurity of that Detroit parish with an article for *The Atlantic Monthly* in 1916 in which he chastised the German-Americans for "betraying the ideals of [their] own people."[179] The betrayal lay in their failure to correct the excessive individualism of America with the idealism and stronger sense of community that was characteristic of German theology and of that country's record of progressive social legislation.

Over the next seven years, despite the encouraging start with *The Atlantic*, Niebuhr's reputation as a preacher advanced faster than his literary career. In 1923 he caught on at the *The Christian Century* and a steady stream of articles not only built that magazine's circulation but landed him a position on the Union faculty in 1928. With characteristic honesty Niebuhr later confessed,

> I had no scholarly competence in my field [social ethics], not to speak of the total field of Christian theology. . . . It was a full decade before I could stand before a class . . . without the sense of being a fraud.[180]

That was a fateful decade. In 1929 came the Crash and the beginnings of the Great Depression. Niebuhr joined the Socialist Party and began to read Marx more seriously. Marx's brilliant, scathing laceration of the sins of capitalism and bourgeois liberalism struck a responsive chord in Niebuhr's developing sense of moral and social realism. He became a *critical* Christian Marxist, and in 1931 founded the Fellowship of Socialist Christians.

In explaining the reversal of the usual arrangement of adjective and noun, Niebuhr later explained that this was to emphasize "the primacy of its Christian, rather than socialist, convictions."[181] It is worth noting, however, that over the years, nine times out of ten, Niebuhr used the terms "Christian socialist" and "Christian socialism."

An editorial in *The World Tomorrow*, probably written by Niebuhr, hailed "with enthusiasm" the new organization and ended with this comment:

> If several thousand clergymen and laymen would identify themselves with the Fellowship of Socialist Christians [FSC], and if a similar Fellowship of Socialist Jews could be formed, such minority groups would be able to exert an exceedingly powerful influence in the endeavor to disentangle religion from capitalism.

Readers were encouraged to write to the chairman, Buell Gallagher in Passaic, New Jersey, or to "the editors of *The World Tomorrow*," which indicates how closely that publication was tied to the FSC. The editorial also printed a statement of purpose released by the FSC executive committee, which, besides Gallagher and Niebuhr, included Bennett, Roswell Barnes, Frank Wilson, and Francis Henson, secretary of the student division of the YMCA. The statement read:

> The Fellowship of Socialist Christians is a group who are agreed that a Christian ethic is most adequately expressed and effectively applied in our society in socialist terms. They believe that the Christian Church

should recognize the essential conflict between Christianity and the ethics of capitalistic individualism. They believe that the evolutionary optimism of current liberal Christianity is unrealistic and that social change fundamental enough to prevent destructive social upheaval will require a combination of social intelligence and ethical vigor not yet in sight. Remedies for specific abuses are no adequate substitute for the reconstruction of our economic order so that production may be primarily for the use of all and not for the profit of the privileged.[182]

Note the Niebuhrian dig at "the evolutionary optimism" of liberal Christianity. And there was cause for such skepticism. Unemployment was on its way to the figure of 15,071,000 in March of 1933, over 30 percent of the labor force. The gross national product had been cut in two. The Communist Party was enjoying a new lease on life, and such literary lights as Theodore Dreiser, John Dos Passos, Sherwood Anderson, Lincoln Steffens, Edmund Wilson, Sidney Hook, Malcolm Cowley, and Waldo Frank were either leaning toward or had already come down on the Communist side. Among the intelligentsia, and much of the unintelligentsia, the general consensus was that capitalism was done for, that it was indeed "the end of an era."

The seriousness of the crisis, plus his reading of Marx, plus his skepticism about the optimism of the Social Gospel and its heirs led Niebuhr to the conclusion that human history, in William James's phrase, "*feels* like a real fight."[183] This feeling, in turn, led to increasing tension, first within the staff of *The World Tomorrow* and the pacifist Fellowship of Reconciliation and then, later, within the Socialist Party, which FSC members usually joined, between the Niebuhr group and the pacifist majorities of those organizations. At first Niebuhr retained his pacifism as far as international war was concerned, but already in 1932 he had published a theory of just revolution in *Moral Man and Immoral Society* and expressed this favorable judgment of Marxism:

> It is a fact that Marxian socialism is a true enough interpretation of what the industrial worker feels about society and history, to have become the accepted social and political philosophy of all self-conscious and politically intelligent industrial workers.[184]

This was actually one of Niebuhr's typically confident exaggerations, but it is misleading if the conclusion is drawn that the judgment was *entirely* favorable. He quoted Trotsky with distaste, "As for us, we were never concerned with the Kantian priestly and vegetarian-Quaker prattle about the 'sacredness of human life'."[185] And he placed Marxist groups as well as capitalist groups firmly under the indictment that makes up the major theme of that book, to wit:

> It may be possible, though it is never easy, to establish just relations between individuals within a group purely by moral and rational suasion and accommodation. *In inter-group relations this is practically an impos-*

sibility. The relations between groups must therefore always be predominantly political rather than ethical, that is, they will be determined by the proportion of power which each group possesses at least as much as by any rational and moral appraisal of the comparative needs and claims of each group" [emphasis added].[186]

Note that Niebuhr fails to sustain the same degree of cynicism (so difficult to reconcile with a "classical" Christianity that taught that "wherever two or three are gathered together in my name, there am I in the midst of them") throughout the entire passage. Moral action between groups is "practically an impossibility," which should mean at least 90 percent of the time. In the first part of the final sentence it is "predominantly," which could mean 60 percent or less, and by the end of the sentence ("at least as much as") it has been reduced to a mere 50-percent factor.

Many years later Niebuhr conceded that a more accurate title for the book would have been "The Not So Moral Man in His Less Moral Communities." In one of his Gifford lectures he expressed the truth of his insight more accurately, "The group is more arrogant, hypocritical, self-centered and more ruthless in the pursuit of its ends than the individual."[187] Even there the insertion of a "usually" would have been more consistent with a classical faith whose teaching and history emphasize that *sometimes*, with the assistance of the Holy Spirit, the group can be more moral than the individual. This would have been more consistent with Niebuhr's insight that "man's capacity for justice makes democracy possible."

By the time he wrote *Reflections on the End of an Era* in 1934, Niebuhr was sounding even more like a Marxist revolutionary: "It is idle to hope that modern society will ever make the transition from capitalism to socialism by purely democratic processes."[188]

A year later, from the left wing of the Socialist Party, he was ridiculing the right wing:

> [The Old Guard] mouths the old platitudes about democracy. Its insistence that socialists must always remain within the bounds of legality is a perfect revelation of spiritual decay within socialism. No revolutionary group of whatsoever kind in history has ever made obedience to law an absolute obligation.[189]

The tensions created by this belligerent strain in Niebuhr's thought led to the demise of *The World Tomorrow* in 1934 and to the Niebuhr group's founding of *Radical Religion* in 1935 as the quarterly organ of the Fellowship of Socialist Christians, which by then was a flourishing organization, particularly among the more liberal Protestant clergy of the Northeast. In 1933, largely at Niebuhr's instigation, Paul Tillich, driven from Hitler's Germany, joined the faculty of Union Theological Seminary and added to the intellectual distinction of the FSC, to whose publications and meetings he contributed frequently, although, strangely enough, he never joined the editorial board or executive committee. He also insisted on using the term "religious socialist" rather than "Christian socialist" or "socialist Christian."

His standoffish attitude was in sharp contrast to that of Eduard Heimann, his fellow exile from the Kairos Circle in Berlin, who for most of the seventeen-year history of the FSC served on either the executive committee or the editorial board of its publication or both. Heimann taught economics at the New School of Social Research in New York.

Heimann was a competent economist and he encouraged Niebuhr in a healthy skepticism of Marxist and Soviet insistence on collectivizing the land. Even in his Marxist *Reflections* Niebuhr expressed doubts that "the agrarian problem demands the same degree of collectivization as the urban one."[190] He added, "No one can say how much communist intransigence against the peasant may have contributed to the stubborn resistance of European peasants to communism [and socialism] and their consequent identification with fascism."[191]

In its first statement of purpose the FSC singled out the Socialist Party as the favored medium of political action. Despite the failure of Norman Thomas (1884–1968) to convert the American workers to the socialist cause in the elections of 1932 and 1936, Niebuhr voted for him both times and also helped him capture control of the party from the more conservative faction of Morris Hillquit (1869–1933), the New York labor lawyer. Thomas had served an East Harlem parish as a Presbyterian minister from 1911 to 1918, but lost most of his Christian faith and resigned the ministry in order to devote his life entirely to the socialist movement.

Thomas was no Marxist. In 1951 he wrote, "For me the outstanding fact about [Marxism], despite its proven power, is its inadequacy for our time under any interpretation." He added,

> As the years have passed, my belief in the need for developing a more adequate socialist philosophy has increased. Marxism had its great insights, but today not one of its principal dogmas is maintained by Marxists of integrity without elaborate explanation and qualification.[192]

Unfortunately, Thomas had virtually relinquished the faith that might have provided him with such a philosophy. But he had not entirely relinquished it. One night in 1958, when he though he might be dying, he wrote his children a letter in which he noted that he did not "believe in most of the formal dogmas of the church," but

> the Christian tradition is so much a part of our life, or my life, and Christ is for me so commanding a figure, who so released all that I care most for, that I feel justified in asserting a Christian [funeral] service.[193]

When all else is gone, the personality of Jesus Christ still retains its power of attraction.

It was over World War II that Thomas and Niebuhr fell out. The Thomas faction that Niebuhr had helped to gain control of the Socialist Party maintained stoutly, in Thomas's words, that "the present struggle in Europe . . . is merely a clash between rival imperialisms."[194] In April 1940, the SP in convention voted 159 to 28 against the United States giving assistance to the Allies. Niebuhr, by contrast, had joined the Committee to Defend America by Aiding the Allies, and when Irving Barshop, executive secretary of the Party, wrote him a letter asking him to come in and explain, noting that "Party discipline demands conformance to Party policies,"[195] Niebuhr simply sent in his resignation without comment. For the SP it was an expensive insistence on protocol.

Niebuhr concluded, "Nothing is more obvious than that socialism must come in America through some other instrument than the Socialist Party."[196] He wrote this in the FSC quarterly, whose name had just been changed to *Christianity and Society*. It had been decided by the FSC membership that *Radical Religion* was too radical a name even for left-wing Christians. Although he retained the sole editorship of the FSC quarterly, Niebuhr started a new magazine, *Christianity & Crisis*, in February 1941, to promote his progressive line of interventionism among a wider spectrum of Christian readers. He cast his vote for Roosevelt in 1940 and proceeded to organize the Union for Democratic Action, which in 1947 became Americans for Democratic Action. In 1944 he helped found the Liberal Party so that he could vote for Roosevelt without voting Democratic.

As if all this were not enough to keep him busy, he continued to produce books (eight by 1940). In 1944 he published *The Children of Light and the Children of Darkness*. Of all his writings it is probably the most valuable to the Christian who is interested in a defense of both democracy and socialism and a critique of both Marxism and capitalism.

In the ten years since *Reflections*, Niebuhr had learned a few things from his observation of contemporary happenings. He was too intelligent not to revise his opinions accordingly. He had seen that "purely democratic processes" could make drastic changes in the raw capitalism that dominated America before Roosevelt and the New Dealers went to work on it. Even before the Nazi-Soviet Pact of 1939 had disillusioned most of the liberal community about the Russian brand of Marxism, the Moscow trials of 1937 had stripped Niebuhr of his illusions and forced him to rethink the whole question of whether or not Marx had, in fact, gone wrong in the matter of the Great P's: property, power, personality, and politics.

Arguments that were to reach full development in *The Children of Light* were already taking shape in 1938. For example, this editorial in *Radical Religion*:

Modern Christian socialists . . . believe that the socialization of property will eliminate the most basic form of inequality of power in modern society. But . . . a socialist society, without democracy, may merely combine economic and political power in the hands of a small oligarchy and thus make for new forms of injustice. After all, "ownership" of property is not the only form of power through property. The government official who hires and fires men in a socially owned factory may be unjust . . . even though he does not own the factory. It is for this reason Christian socialists are bound to be critical of Russia.[197]

By 1944 Niebuhr had come to realize not only that basic changes are possible through democratic process but that political democracy is not itself a sufficient guarantee of justice where productive property is concentrated in the hands of the state. For the first time since Rauschenbusch, an American socialist tackled head-on—as Buchez had done in France, Ludlow and Cole in England, Lassalle and Ketteler in Germany—the problem of reconciling the socialization of production with the preservation of freedom and justice.

The nub of the argument is in the third chapter of *The Children of Light* and the nub of the nub is in the following excerpt. I quote at length because here the problem is analyzed and resolved with rare clarity and insight:

The modern factory is a great collective process. . . . The "private" ownership of such a process is anachronistic and incongruous; and the individual control of such centralized power is an invitation to injustice. . . . Though Marxism is nearer to the truth than liberalism on the property issue, the socialization of property as proposed in Marxism is too simple a solution of the problem. . . . The Marxist illusion is partly derived from a romantic conception of human nature. It thinks that the inclination of men to take advantage of each other is a corruption which was introduced into history by the institution of property. It therefore assumes that the socialization of property will eliminate human egotism. Its failure to understand the perennial and persistent character of human egotism in any possible society prompts it to make completely erroneous estimates of human behavior on the other side of a revolution. A second source of Marxist illusions is its belief that the ownership of property is the sole and only source of economic power. . . . Since economic power, as every other form of social power, is a defensive force when possessed in moderation and a temptation to injustice when it is great enough to give the agent power over others, it would seem that its widest and most equitable distribution would make for the highest degree of justice. . . .

In communities such as America, where the Marxist dogma has never developed the power to challenge the bourgeois one, the primary requirement of justice is that the dominant dogma be discredited. The obvious facts about property which both liberal and Marxist theories have obscured are: that all property is power; that some forms of property are intrinsically more ordinate than others and therefore more defensive, but that no sharp line can be drawn between what is ordinate and what is inordinate; that property is not the only form of economic power and that the destruction of private property does not guarantee the equalization of economic power in a community; that inordinate power tempts its holders to abuse it, which means to use it for their own ends; that the economic as well as the political process requires the best possible distribution of power for the sake of justice and the best possible management of this equilibrium for the sake of order.

None of these propositions solves any specific issue of property in a given instance. But together they set the property issue within the framework of democratic procedure. For democracy is a method of finding proximate solutions for insoluble problems.[198]

In the entire chapter of thirty-three pages Niebuhr is guilty of only one serious error. It is this sentence: "Technical advance has made it impossible for the worker to own either his own tools or the place of his work."[199] This strange lacuna in Niebuhr's economic vision, which made him unresponsive to the history and the possibilities of pre-Marxian and non-Marxian socialism, appears all the stranger since a few pages later he writes again, "The tool has become too big for the worker to own" and then exposes the fallacy of the statement, noting on the same page:

"Mechanization tends toward large-scale agricultural production; and large-scale production tends to destroy the small owner *unless he learns to develop voluntary cooperation in the use of large-scale machinery* [emphasis added].[200]

In other words, if cooperative use is possible and advisable, then cooperative ownership is equally possible and even more advisable because it guarantees the right to cooperative use. There is no tool or factory too big for the worker to own.

The Children of Light, in my opinion, represents the high point of Niebuhr's career as a Christian theologian and political philosopher. Four years later, in May of 1948, by vote of the membership at a conference in Princeton, N. J., the name of the Fellowship of Socialist Christians was changed to Frontier Fellowship. In the next issue of *Christianity and Society* Niebuhr gave this explanation:

It has long been felt that the term "socialist" in this country is subject to too many misinterpretations. The official socialist party is pacifist, and we are not. On the other hand, orthodox Marxism is rooted in the belief, which we do not share, that the institution of property is the primary root of evil in human society and that the abolition of this institution will therefore usher in a kind of millennial age. The measure of that error is given by the nightmare of tyranny in Russia, into which the original dream of utopia was transmuted. On the other hand, we continue to be socialists in the sense that we believe that the capitalist order of society stands under divine judgment and that there is no justice in modern technical society without a completely pragmatic attitude toward the institution of property. It must be socialized whenever it is of such a character that it makes for injustice through inordinate centralization of power. There is, however, no redemption in the abolition of a social institution if too much is expected of it. Extravagant religious hopes become the basis of political errors. In the case of the socialization of property the most dangerous error is the centralization of both economic and political power in the hands of a communist oligarchy.

The idea of the "Frontier Fellowship" is that we want to be a group of Christians who seek to explore the frontier of Christian thought and life in the social, political and economic problems of our day.[201]

That's it. No more, no less. That was the epitaph of organized Christian socialism in the United States until it rose again from the dead in the 1970s, some thirty years later. And nothing has been said, really, that would make the Frontier Fellowship any less socialist than the Frankfurt Manifesto of the resurrected Socialist International a few year later in 1951, as we shall see in more detail in the next chapter. Note, incidentally, the assumption of identity between Marxism and socialism.

Ah, but the year Niebuhr wrote that was 1948. Marx's historical materialism—modes and relations of production determine ideology—might have told the student of intellectual history that a bright, decent man like Niebuhr would turn socialist under the impact of the Great Depression. But it was modes and relations of *politics* that turned him away from it, that and some personal history. It was the time of the Cold War, Henry Wallace, and the Stalinist-dominated Progressive Party, and Niebuhr, by now the undisputed champion of the anticommunist left, was appointed in 1947 to the position of advisor to George Kennan's Policy Planning Staff in the U.S. State Department. Niebuhr was now part of the Establishment. It was he who triggered the debate with Wallace over the question of U.S.-Soviet relations, the debate that forced Wallace out of Truman's cabinet. "Russian truculence," he wrote in perhaps his most widely read article, "cannot be mitigated by further concessions. Russia hopes to conquer the whole of Europe strategically and ideologically."[202]

Opinions differ radically as to the truth of those statements and the validity of such U.S. policies and actions as the Marshall Plan, the Truman Doctrine, and the Korean War, which Niebuhr also backed. I supported both the truth and the validity at the time and I am not going to fault Niebuhr now on either score. Niebuhr never wavered, in word or deed, in his abhorrence of the cheap, lying anticommunism of Senator Joe McCarthy and his imitators. Nevertheless, one can agree, in the wisdom of hindsight, with Paul Merkley, one of the best of the students of Niebuhr's life and thought, who suggests that the intensity of Niebuhr's anticommunism began to distort his judgment in the twilight of his life. Merkley writes,

He saw the Soviet hand everywhere. He saw phony revolutions where a realist might have expected to see real ones—as, for example, in South Vietnam, where he could see nothing more than Communist manipulation behind the Buddhist opponents of the Diem regime.[203]

As the 1960s wore on and the casualties and disaster of Vietnam mounted and deepened, Niebuhr's intelligence and decency, and his Christian faith, brought him around to a more balanced view of that unhappy conflict. This view I have cited in the previous chapter in his reflections in 1968 on the death of Barth and on America's "odious," fanatical anticommunism, which had "caused us to stumble into the most pointless, costly and bloody war in our history."[204]

Twilight is a time of both gathering dark and occasional flashes of returning light. The above view of Vietnam was one of the latter. One instance of the former was Niebuhr's acquiescence in the complacency and optimism, so untypical of his earlier life, brought on by the continuance of American prosperity through the 1950s and the 1960s. He was actually able to write in 1965 that "open societies of the West have eliminated the injustices of early industrialism" and that "American Negro citizens are the only genuine proletarians in a bourgeois paradise."[205] As early as 1952 he wrote, "American business in practice has accepted the power of labor. . . . It acknowledges the 'right of collective bargaining'."[206] Expressed in this unqualified way, a style too common in Niebuhr, it wasn't true then and it isn't true now. He should have known better.

A second darkening was in Niebuhr's loss of faith in democracy as a universal good. He had written in 1953 that "a democratic society [is] most compatible with the Christian faith,"[207] and his magnificent aphorism in *The Children of Light* had made the point that the nature of human personality has made democracy not only possible but *necessary*. But a growing elitism marked his writing after the war and he could say, "Few of the non-industrial nations have sufficiently high standards of honesty to make democratic government viable."[208] Or this:

A democratic society requires not only a spiritual and material basis which is lacking in the Orient, but a socio-economic foundation which primitive and traditional civilizations cannot quickly acquire. Many of the values of democratic society which are most highly prized in the West are, therefore, neither understood nor desired outside of the orbit of western society.[209]

Research more scholarly than Niebuhr found time for has established the fact that virtually all "non-industrial nations" have democratic traditions that go back, usually, to primitive times before the industrial nations fastened the arbitrary boundaries of colonialism upon them. Reconciling those traditions with and within those boundaries and building a modern democratic state upon them is not an easy chore. Democratic government has not been easy for some of the most advanced "industrial nations," notably France and Germany, but that doesn't make it any the less "possible" *and* "necessary." The major hope of the West lies in retaining faith in it and in practicing it, in the West, the East, the North, and the South. Niebuhr failed us there.

Despite the falling out between them over pacifism and over World War II, it seems reasonable to conclude that Niebuhr's devastating critique of Marxism was at least partly responsible for Norman Thomas's negative view of that school of thought, quoted above. Marxism was still dominant in the Socialist International when that body met at Frankfurt in 1951, and Thomas, together with British and Scandinavian delegates, representing countries in which Marxism had never been strong, was at least partly responsible for the decision of that body, quoted below, to begin the process of shaking that dominance and freeing the socialist movement for a more enthusiastic participation by Christians who share with Niebuhr what he called "a more classical interpretation of religion."

By that time, unfortunately, Niebuhr had already departed. But he left behind some important legacies. He also left behind a group of disciples and believers: people like John C. Bennett, Robert McAfee Brown, Georgia Harkness, Roger Shinn, James Luther Adams, Paul Abrecht, and also Jewish believers like Eduard Heimann, Adolf Löwe, and Will Herberg, people who may have followed Niebuhr away from a formal affiliation with religious socialism, but who never gave up their faith in the more general implications of the Judeo-Christian tradition.

Let us close this section with the great prayer that Niebuhr left us: "O God, give us serenity to accept what cannot be changed, courage to change what should be changed, and wisdom to distinguish one from the other."[210]

RESURRECTION IN THE 1970S

The Socialist Party continued to exist, though in a much weakened condition, and Christian members continued to meet, informally, at national congresses and conferences. In 1977, at the Chicago convention of the Democratic Socialist Organizing Committee (DSOC), which had split off from the SP in 1973, these meetings evolved into a formal committee of religious socialists within DSOC. This group eventually became the Religion and Socialism Commission of DSOC's successor, the Democratic Socialists of America (DSA), which functions as the socialist wing of the Democratic Party, under the leadership of co-chairs Barbara Ehrenreich and Michael Harrington, the latter a graduate of the Catholic Worker movement and author of many important books on socialism and poverty, notably *The Other America*.

Since 1977 the R&S Commission has published a quarterly, *Religious Socialism*, and includes among its members such distinguished writers and theologians as James Cone, Cornel West, James Luther Adams, Rosemary Ruether, Dorothee Sölle, Harvey Cox, Father Arthur McGovern, S.J., and Arthur

Waskow, a founder of the New Jewish Agenda movement. One of its members, Maxine Phillips, served for several years as national director of DSA and managing editor of its publication, *Democratic Left*.

PUTTING THEIR BODIES ON THE LINE

With all due repect to the theologians, the writers, and the Northern preachers declaiming safely from their pulpits, we must not close this chapter without some notice of those Christians who risked their lives fighting for socialism, trade unionism, and racial equality in some of the more murderous regions of the American South.

Most of them were influenced and inspired by Reinhold Niebuhr, some being students of his at Union Theological Seminary. One of these, James Dombrowski, director of the Highlander Folk School in Tennessee, organized a meeting at which Niebuhr spoke in 1934. This was the reaction of Howard Kester, one of the more admirable Southern Christian socialists:

> Dr. Niebuhr lost no time in unbuckling his flaming sword against . . . the denial of the basic teachings of Christianity. . . . [We] were thunderstruck by the depth of his knowledge about man's sinfulness and man's inability to cope with the evils of his own creation. . . . Scotty Cowan summed up our feelings by saying, "Reinie is Judgment Day in britches."[211]

Other disciples were Don West and Myles Horton, both of whom served as directors of the Highlander School, founded in 1932, which still stands today as a center of education in the techniques of political and economic democracy.

One of its students years later was a black woman named Rosa Parks. A friend of hers wrote Horton that when she returned to Alabama from Highlander

> she was so happy and felt so liberated, and then as time went on she said the discrimination got worse and worse to bear after having, for the first time in her life, been free at Highlander.[212]

On December 1, 1955, Rosa Parks refused to move to the back of the bus and that refusal sparked the Montgomery bus boycott and real progress toward desegregation in the South.

Kester, Horton, Dombrowski, West and the Rev. Claude Williams all put their bodies on the line and their Christian socialism in action as they went about the South organizing blacks and whites into unions of miners, textile workers, and tenant farmers. They suffered beatings and imprisonment, and narrowly escaped lynching from homicidal mobs of white bigots and landowners.

Among their more impressive accomplishments was the organization, with a more secular socialist, H. L. Mitchell, of the Southern Tenant Farmers Union (STFU), which at its peak in 1937 had over 30,000 members in seven states. In 1935 Kester wrote that of the fourteen members of the STFU executive council, six were preachers and of these, four were socialists. He said of them: "They believe in the tenets of Isaiah and of Jesus and Marx and they are by their deeds social revolutionaries with a religious drive that keeps them in the midst of battle."[213]

Kester was not totally accurate, or at least it must be noted that their faith in the tenets of Marx included this significant exception, expressed in a resolution of the STFU's 1937 convention which insisted that all "actual tillers of the soil be guaranteed possession of the land, either as working farm families or cooperative associations of such farm families, so long as they occupy and use the land."[214] If more socialists, and socialist parties, had always insisted on the wisdom of those words, the history of socialism—and the history of the world—might well have been radically different.

The little known history of these heroes, together with an admirably objective account of how some flirted with the Communist Party, may be found in Anthony Dunbar's *Against the Grain*. I recommend it.

CHAPTER 11

The Convergence of Socialism and Catholicism

"The Catholic Church is the chief bulwark against socialism." This sentence is from the preface to one of the more important books published in America in the twentieth century: *Socialism: Promise or Menace* (New York: Macmillan, 1914). The book is a reprint of a debate that appeared in seven issues of *Everybody's Magazine* in the years 1913 and 1914, a debate between Morris Hillquit, perhaps the most intelligent leader of the Socialist Party then, and Father John A. Ryan (1869–1945), who was clearly the best-informed exponent of Catholic social doctrine of the time.

Ryan's opposition to the Marxist socialism of Hillquit and to the Socialist Party of that era is understandable. Ironically, and significantly, in the very act of opposing the socialism of 1914, Ryan was contributing to the development of a body of theory that would, by 1951, leave no *essential* difference between Catholic social teaching and the Frankfurt Declaration of the Socialist International.

The Statutes of the Socialist International begin with these words: "The Socialist International is an association of parties which seek to establish democratic socialism as formulated in the Frankfurt Declaration of 1951." Although most current dictionaries still have not learned about it, the Socialist International, in effect, rewrote the definition of socialism at Frankfurt. In 1931, twenty years earlier, Pope Pius XI had rewritten the definition of Catholic social teaching, building on the ideas developed by Heinrich Pesch (1854–1926), a German Jesuit; his disciple, Oswald von Nell-Breuning, S. J., and John Ryan, whose ideas had been given official weight by reason of the fact that they showed up, almost in toto, under the title *The U.S. Bishops' Program of Social Reconstruction* in 1919.

A further irony is that Pius XI, in the encyclical that contained the church's own revisions, *Quadragesimo Anno,* stated very firmly, " 'Religious Socialism,' 'Christian Socialism' are expressions implying a contradiction in terms.

No one can be at the same time a sincere Catholic and a true Socialist."[1]

These paradoxes, these condemnations and oppositions that lead to their opposites, these love-hate relationships are perhaps best explained by a longish quotation from a piece by Thomas Molnar in *The New Oxford Review* (July/ August 1985):

> When a new political or social configuration emerged—the feudal system, Renaissance humanism, bourgeois power, royal absolutism, industrialization, science, republicanism, democracy, and now labor power or socialism—Rome waited until the new system or ideology eliminated its own sharp edges, then sought accommodation with the domesticated form. It entailed not doctrinal change on the Church's part, but political acceptance, and also the acceptance of a certain new style. By the time coexistence became possible, accommodation did not imply concessions; for the Church the relationship became rather a matter of emphasis.
>
> Today we are in a situation similar to past ages, something that the narrow mind cannot tolerate. Notwithstanding Reagan, Thatcher, or the (questionable) superiority of Giscardian policies over those of Mitterand, socialism is gaining ground, not just in the domain of economics, but also and more importantly in that of intellectual discourse and style, social choices, and vision of the world. Masses of the people in the capitalist world find in capitalism material satisfactions, but also find the human price paid for them too high. Masses of people in the Communist world find Marxism detestable and counter-productive, but if they were free to choose, would opt for a non-Marxist socialism, with more freedom of choice, with a more "human face."

This is an insightful statement, but not totally accurate. The church cannot be portrayed as a wise old mother waiting for the world to eliminate sharp edges before it becomes worthy of the maternal embrace. The wise old mother has at times been foolish and forgetful of the gospel principles on which, or from which, she was born. That was particularly true in the nineteenth century when, as Pius XI lamented to Canon Cardijn, "The scandal was that the Church lost the working class."[2] Also, the accommodations *have* involved concessions and changes in doctrine, if by doctrine we mean not simply dogmatic statements like the Nicene Creed, but also statements of social doctrine, statements of new applications of gospel principles and teaching. In that area there have been significant changes.

LEO XIII CHANGES COURSE

When last we left Catholic social doctrine in the nineteenth century it was beginning to take shape in the words and actions of the doughty Archbishop Ketteler. Ketteler died in 1877 and Pius IX the following year. Although the next pope, Leo XIII, was later to acknowledge his debt to Ketteler, one would scarcely guess it from the tone and content of his first encyclical on the social question, *Quod Apostolici* (1878).

He lumps together socialists, communists, and nihilists and anathematizes them all, "bound together in a wicked confederacy," who "have long been planning the overthrow of all civil society whatsoever."[3] He congratulates the church because it does "not neglect the poor or omit to provide for their necessities" and because it is constantly warning the rich that "unless they succor the needy they will be repaid with eternal torments." He concludes, "In fine, she does all she can to relieve and comfort the poor" and adds this final, embarrassing question: "But who does not see that this is the best method of arranging the old struggle between the rich and the poor?"[4]

We are, in short, back *before* Ketteler, before any awareness that personal charity is by no means the best method of "arranging" the class struggle. Already Ketteler, Buss, Moufang, Hitze in Germany, the Christian socialists of France, England, and the United States, even French Catholic aristocrats like La Tour du Pin and Albert de Mun, even Cardinals like Manning and Gibbons, had long since learned this lesson. As Father Hitze put it, "[The working class] claims *its rights* and not alms."[5]

Emmanuel Mounier, that master of the mordant critique, once wrote that there is no point in trying to derive from the papal encyclicals "a Christian social teaching that arrives panting, to the detriment of its prestige, fifty years behind the development of ideas and facts."[6]

This was a reference to *Rerum Novarum* (1891), Leo's landmark encyclical, which arrived forty-three years, not fifty, behind the *Communist Manifesto,* which itself certainly did not represent the full development of either the idea or the fact of European socialism. Nevertheless, Mounier's point is valid. It was fifty-nine years since Lamennais had gone to Rome with Lacordaire and Montalembert to plead with Gregory XVI to listen to the people. It was fifty-seven years since he had reminded Rome and the whole Western world of the right to rebel against tyranny and the duty to fight for the poor. It was fifty-seven years since Gregory XVI had, for his pains and his eloquence, driven Lamennais from the church. More importantly, it was 1860 years since Jesus Christ had reminded us all that our reactions to poverty will ultimately determine whether we are saved or damned.

Nevertheless, *Rerum Novarum* was an important turning point. Again, nevertheless, with due respect to Mounier, there is a point in deriving a Christian social teaching from the encyclicals as long as we keep in mind what Newman called "the development of doctrine."

Certainly there are conservative propositions and omissions in *Rerum Novarum,* some less excusable than others. Leo begins forcefully with a denunciation of current capitalism worthy of Marx himself:

The present age [has] handed over the workers, each alone and defenseless, to the inhumanity of employers and the unbridled greed of competitors. . . . In addition the whole process of production as well as trade in every kind of goods has been brought almost entirely under the power of a few, so that a very few rich and exceedingly rich men have laid a yoke almost of slavery itself on the unnumbered masses of non-owning workers.[7]

Immediately, however, Leo launches into another tirade directed at socialists and accuses them all, unjustly, of proposing that all private property, whether of productive or consumer goods, be held in common. To justify this, he devotes ten pages to an extended paean to private property during which, ironically, he reveals an ignorance, or misunderstanding, of the Thomist teaching on property. This is ironic, since Leo was mainly responsible for the revival of Thomist thought. The paean is not only inaccurate but internally contradictory, several times acknowledging, as Thomas, the prophets, and the Fathers held, that "the goods of nature . . . belong in common and without distinction to all humankind."[8] and, as Thomas held, that "the limits of private possessions [should] be fixed by the industry of men and the institutions of peoples."[9] These acknowledgments are nullified, one in an adjacent paragraph, when Leo insists that not human law but "nature confers on man the right to possess things privately as his own"[10] and that "no one *in any way* should be permitted to violate his right" (emphasis added).[11]

Other conservative positions or omissions:

1. Unlike Ketteler, Leo leaves the impression that the right to strike should be forbidden, or might well be forbidden.[12]

2. Although the antireligious nature of socialist unions created a genuine problem for Catholic workers, Leo nowhere acknowledges the existence of "neutral unions," as in the United States and England, which respected the religious beliefs of their members. He therefore urges all Catholics to join only Christian unions, or associations like the medieval guilds that would also include their employers. Leo was certainly influenced by German and Austrian Romantics and aristocrats like the Baron Karl von Vogelsang, his patron, Prince Johann von Liechtenstein, and his disciple, the French Romantic, the Marquis de la Tour du Pin. Curiously, some of these noblemen were even more critical of capitalism than fellow Catholics like Ketteler and Hitze, who tended to be realistic enough to favor legislative reform rather than total rejection of the industrial system.

This emphasis on Leo's part has led one commentator to ask, "What could seem more hilarious today than the portrait of the 'good worker,' sober, honest, and pious, getting together with his 'good employer' to form Catholic associations?"[13] More bewildering than hilarious, however, is Leo's misunderstanding of the purpose and function of labor unions apparent in his suggestion that "moral and religious perfection ought to be regarded as their principal goal."[14] A labor union is an *economic* organization that absolutely demands a maximum of unity and strength to confront the more powerful employer.

Before the encyclical appeared there was even talk to the effect that Leo might oppose the entire idea of separate organizations of workers. Further talk had it that Cardinal James Gibbons of Baltimore was largely responsible for persuading him to acknowledge their value and to defend the workers' right to organize them. Gibbons was even more certainly responsible for persuading the pope not to condemn the American Knights of Labor, which had already been condemned by the Canadian bishops as a subversive secret society.

On the other hand, there were good, progressive things in *Rerum Novarum*. Above all, the idea that charity alone would "arrange" the class struggle was not only abandoned, but in proclaiming the right and duty of the state to intervene, Leo insisted that in doing so "special consideration must be given to the weak and the poor."[15] In short, the "preferential option for the poor" was not totally absent from church pronouncements between the time of the Fathers of the fourth century and the time of the liberation theologians of the twentieth.

Further, Leo supports state intervention so strongly that one can legitimately conclude that he is endorsing legislation to provide minimum wages and maximum hours, particularly for the young and for women.[16] One can even, from the strength of the wording, anticipate statements that were to come later which would lay explicit claim to a right of government to take over the ownership and/or control of certain forms of productive property. For example:

> If, therefore, any injury has been done to or threatens either the common good or the interests of individual groups, which injury cannot in any other way be repaired or prevented, it is necessary for public authority to intervene.[17]

Another striking feature of the encyclical is this flat-out statement: "It is incontestable that the wealth of nations originates from no other source than from the labor of workers."[18] Marx himself might have hesitated to make such a claim.

Rerum Novarum, taken as a whole, is not a radical document. It defends private property and the wage contract and, though critical, sharply critical, of certain aspects of capitalism, does not really take an anticapitalist stance. Of the two classes Leo writes, "Each needs the other completely: neither capital can do without labor, nor labor without capital."[19]

The sainted Pius X, a more conservative, even reactionary, pontiff, who succeeded Leo in 1903, interpreted this sentence as asserting that, in John Coleman's words, "the authority of capital over labor was as essential to the social organism as that of the authority of the church, government or family." Father Coleman adds,

> "This was not simply . . . a creative footnote. It is a simple inversion of Leo's famous dictum. . . . However hierarchical Leo may have been in his general social theory, he did not extend this to his understanding of capital and labor."[20]

Pius X, incidentally, also distinguished himself in 1914 by instructing the Italian bishops to prohibit their priests from supporting "syndicalist associations" because "the situation is sliding toward open social conflict."[21] Whatever did he think syndicalist associations were organized for? Several years earlier Pius X had condemned the writings of Marc Sangnier, leader of the French movement *Le Sillon* (who had earlier been decorated by Leo XIII) for saying things about democracy that were scarcely more flattering than the Christmas Message of Pius XII in 1944. All of which goes to prove that sanctity and intelligence are not necessarily synonymous. On the positive side Pius X did give approval to Catholics who join neutral unions.

No, Leo XIII was no radical, but neither was he blind to the sufferings of the poor, the lessons of history, or the demands of the present and the future. He had sense enough to see that his earlier statement, *Quod Apostolici,* was hopelessly inadequate. He maintained an unfair position toward socialists, even given their strong Marxist bias in 1891. His German advisors should have been aware of the more moderate strains represented by Lassalle and Eduard Bernstein. Bernstein had been editing the *Sozialdemokrat,* organ of the German SDP, for ten years before *Rerum Novarum* was written.

Leo may have been forty-three years behind Marx and Engels, but in 1848 they did not have anything like the large and powerful constituency that Leo had. Nor did they in 1891. A sizable part, the most powerful part, of Leo's constituency, despite their professions of Catholic faith, had come to believe with Adam Smith that the best role of the state vis-à-vis the economy was, in Carlyle's phrase, "anarchy plus a constable." They reacted negatively to *Rerum Novarum.*

In 1961, on the seventieth anniversary of the encyclical, I sat in St. Peter's Basilica in Rome and listened to Cardinal Cento, an aged man himself, tell a vast congregation of Catholic workers from all over the world that as a young seminarian he had seen Leo XIII in that same basilica during the Holy Year of 1900, then an old man of ninety. "His face was emaciated, like parchment," the cardinal said, "but his eyes still shone with an effulgent brilliance." The cardinal also noted that five years before Leo wrote *Rerum Novarum* an industrialist had told the Belgian Labor Commission, "Industrial science consists in obtaining from a human being the greatest possible amount of work while paying him the lowest possible wage."

"Alas," Cardinal Cento added sadly, "the god of certain capitalists was none other than the golden calf." Many of these men were part of Leo's constituency and they took a dim view of Leo's statements that the requirement of a just wage is "greater and more ancient than the free consent of contracting parties" and that "if, compelled by necessity or moved by fear of a worse evil, a worker accepts a harder condition . . . he certainly submits to force, against which justice cries out in protest."[22] The concept of "institutionalized violence," like the "preferential option for the poor," was not invented out of thin air at Medellín in 1968. Conservative and patrician he may have been at heart, as Father Coleman and others have maintained, but those brilliant eyes of Leo

XIII saw a few things that were basic and powerful, powerful enough to move the world.

That same day in 1961 we listened to another great pope, John XXIII, give us a preview of another great labor encyclical, *Mater et Magistra.* He told us of "the misery and hunger in which millions upon millions of human beings are now struggling" and called for

> the recognition and respect of a moral order that is valid for all, which recognizes its foundation in God, the protector and defender, the distributor of goods, riches and mercy, and the terrible avenger of injustice and inequality from whom no one can flee."

Before we consider John XXIII and his relation to socialism, however, we must consider Pius XI, and before Pius XI we must deal with the men who were most influential in shaping his labor encyclical *Quadragesimo Anno.*

THE GERMAN JESUITS AND PIUS XI

Of the four German Jesuits who most dominated and influenced Catholic social theory in the forty years between *Rerum Novarum* and *Quadragesimo Anno,* the first in date of birth was Victor Cathrein (1845–1931), a Swiss German. His devotion to, one might even say obsession with, natural law was so pronounced that on one occasion he was moved to write, "Supernatural Christian revelation is not a proper source of ethics."[23] If you are a devotee of natural-law reasoning, this may make sense, but if you are just a run-of-the-mill Christian, it is monstrous nonsense.

Cathrein's major contribution to Catholic theory was his book *Socialism,* which by 1923 had gone into sixteen printings and been translated into eleven languages. The first German edition was published in 1890, in time to have an impact on the writing of *Rerum Novarum.* The first U.S. edition came out in 1904, expanded by an American Jesuit co-author, Victor Gettelman, who added a section on socialism in the United States. This was in time to have an impact on the opposition of most American churches, both Catholic and Protestant, to the rising tide of socialism in this country.

Even Karl Kautsky, who must have hated it, paid a tribute to the book: "Marx's theory has been rendered much better by Cathrein than by any of the liberalist 'socialist-killers'. The author has at least read the works which he discusses."[24]

Marxian socialism is, of course, the socialism that Cathrein is concerned with excoriating. He is a mite fairer to the more moderate strain than Leo XIII, but not much. In 1929 Cathrein wrote another study, *Sozialismus und Katholizismus,* which was not translated into English, perhaps because it evaluates more positively the moderate strain of socialism, which had grown more moderate in the interim as the less moderate hardened into Soviet communism.

Cathrein probably had an influence on a younger but much more important

Jesuit, Heinrich Pesch (1854–1926), father of "solidarism," which was designed to strike a balance between the excessive individualism of capitalism and the excessive collectivism of socialism. Solidarism is the theoretical core of *Quadragesimo Anno,* according to the man who actually wrote the encyclical, a third German Jesuit, Oswald von Nell-Breuning (b. 1890), a disciple of Pesch. He refers to Pesch, in fact, as "our highest authority"[25] in the book he wrote about *Quadragesimo Anno,* whose subtitle is "The Social Encyclical Developed and Explained."

Pesch was born in Cologne. After joining the Jesuits he spent four years of study in England, where he came to know the sorry lot of the Lancashire workers. This experience helped motivate him to devote his life to the cause of the working class. For this purpose he dedicated his religious career to economics and for the last twenty years of his life wrote and rewrote the monumental five-volume *Lehrbuch der Nationalökonomie* (Manual of National Economy). Pesch, in fact, is one of the very few economists writing from a Catholic position who is recognized by secular economists as having something important to say.

Part of this recognition is due to the fact that, like Cathrein, Pesch was a devotee of natural law and the notion that people could, with no other help than their natural reason, come to a code of conduct similar to, if not identical with, the Ten Commandments, with maybe even a little Love-of-Neighbor thrown in. Therefore, as Cathrein said about ethics, so Pesch said about economics: "Economics is a *natural* discipline. It has to do with a natural ordering of economic life, therefore with 'natural ethics'."[26]

Seen through these spectacles, economics was to Pesch a social science (as opposed to the natural sciences) whose "concern is ultimately about the knowledge of means and results in relation to a desired goal."[27] Here already Pesch differed from many, if not most, secular economists who, in the words of Lionel Robbins, insist that "there are no economic ends."[28]

What was the "desired goal" of Pesch's economics? Nothing less than "the sufficient provision of the people, especially at its broader, lower levels, with good, fair-priced food, clothing, shelter, with all the material goods which they require for the satisfaction of their wants."[29] A shorter answer: "the material welfare of the people,"[30] and from the longer answer we can reasonably assume that Pesch means *all* the people. Pesch concludes that "the economist should [not] theologize or moralize in the treatment of his subject matter or, what is worse, try to derive an economic system from Holy Scripture."[31]

An obvious difficulty arises in the mind of the untutored layperson upon reading Pesch—several difficulties, in fact. If "economics has to do with natural ethics," as Pesch tells us, how can the economist refrain, as Pesch says he must, from moralizing? If Holy Scripture is for the Christian the ultimate foundation and motivation for an effective ethics, how can Christian economists do anything but build their economic system on Holy Scripture, or at least acknowledge its relevance? After all, natural ethics does not tell us with any conviction that the goal of economics must be the material welfare of *all* the people. In fact, nice ethical economists keep telling us that a certain percentage of the people might have to do without, go unemployed, go hungry, maybe even die, so that the rest may enjoy material welfare. Also, motivation is acknowledged by all economists as an essential, rock-bottom economic factor, the very linchpin, in fact, of the whole greed-based, supply-side economics that runs from Adam Smith to Milton Friedman to Ronald Reagan. And where can we find more powerful, compelling motivation than in the Old and New Testaments?

The solidarity of the human race, the core of solidarism, the foundation on which rests the church's unyielding rejection of *Marxist* notions of class struggle, all this depends on a moral reading of human nature and human destiny, which in turns finds its most compelling statement in Holy Scripture. Of course, if you're writing economics for nonbelievers, as Pesch was, better to stick to natural law and natural ethics. But still, how could he refrain from moralizing? And, in fact, he did not.

Pesch also wrote a book about socialism, an even longer book than Cathrein's, but no less negative. However, and this is most extraordinary, in the revolutionary period immediately after World War I, Pesch wrote a pamphlet, which the Center Party, the Catholic party, published under the title *Nicht kommunistischer, sondern christlicher Sozialismus* (Not Communistic, but Christian Socialism).

Franz Mueller, a professor emeritus of economics at St. Thomas College in St. Paul, Minnesota, much later wrote an article entitled "I Knew Heinrich Pesch." In this article, published in April 1951 by the Jesuit magazine *Social Order,* Mueller tells how it felt for a young man in Germany in 1919 to come across that pamphlet with that extraordinary title. His account of it and his citations are so significant that I quote at length. He notes first that the pamphlet "made it quite clear that the solution could not possibly be Marxism, even with its anti-religious fangs removed." He goes on:

> Yet the author did not hesitate to point out in very forceful language that individualistic capitalism was hardly less opposed to Catholic social principles. It warmed my heart to read statements like these: Profit-seeking is not merely an occasional excess but "the normal thing in capitalist economic life." Under individualistic capitalism,
>
>> supplying the people with external goods has changed from being an end of the national economy to being merely a means for acquisition. . . . The business end of the capitalist enterprise now dominates the national economic process. . . . Everything is made subservient to the interest of capital, and, indeed, progressively to the interest of financial capital. . . . Capitalism has played itself out. It is irretrievably lost. A new epoch is beginning, in which the world will be ruled no longer by propertied men through the power of their possessions, but by honest men devoted to work, through

their proficiency and the value of their service. . . . We agree with Marxian socialism that the future no longer belongs to the economic license of individualistic capitalism. However, neither will it belong to the compulsory economic system of communism, but to a truly socialized national economy, i.e., regulated in accordance with its end. . . . which is the satisfaction of the entire national community in accordance with the prevailing level of civilization.

In another pamphlet, *Neubau der Gesellschaft* (Rebuilding Society), Freiburg i. B., 1919, also published in the days of the German civil war, after the collapse of the Hohenzollern monarchy, Pesch wrote that it is

the deep-seated suspicion towards Church and Christianity which bars our way to the soul of the people. They regard us as representatives of capitalist interests, as defenders of the capitalist economic system. This suspicion, which is entirely unfounded, must be combated forcefully, frankly and sincerely. In our programs we must also clearly define our position against capitalism. We must not merely accept the transition to a new economic order; we must demand it; we must accomplish it; we must seize the initiative; we must acknowledge that the present rise of the lower strata of the population is the fulfillment of our ardent wishes and the inspiring goal of our own political and social action. . . . We cannot be satisfied with merely patching up the hitherto prevailing capitalistic economic order, bringing about relief for the working class through protective labor legislation, social insurance and the like. Surface repair certainly has had its great merits: today more is involved, viz., work on a fundamental scale, the beginning of a new epoch. This complete break with the capitalist system is the *sine qua non* not only for overcoming the distrust of socialist workers but also for preventing a paralyzing doubt from rising in the minds of Christian workers [*Nicht kommunistischer*, pp. 7f.].

Mueller continued:

Needless to say, Father Pesch rejected the socialist identification of capitalism with the institution of private property and with free enterprise. But he also objected to the notion that the essence of capitalism consists merely in the extensive use of capital goods (produced means of production). "Capitalism," he said, "is control of the national economy through the unrestrained and uninhibited acquisitiveness of the owners of capital." Catholics cannot but agree that the idea of unrestricted liberty, typical of economic individualism, as well as the idea of profit as an end in itself (*finis ultimus*) cannot be reconciled with the natural moral law, much less with the supernatural ethics of Christianity.

Puzzled by these revolutionary statements of Pesch, and by the title of the first pamphlet, I called Professor Mueller and asked if Pesch considered himself a Christian socialist at that time. His answer was a trifle ambiguous. "Certainly not a Marxist socialist," he said. He then explained that the church, in that revolutionary period of German history, was deeply concerned about losing any more of the German workers, many of whom had remained faithful to the church despite the inroads of Marxian socialism. "The church was looking for a concept," he said, "that would be more—how do you say?—more . . . " I suggested, "Acceptable to the workers?" I gathered from his reply that that was the general idea.

Professor Mueller kindly loaned me one of the few remaining copies of the pamphlet *Not Communistic, but Christian Socialism.* I found such statements as the following:

> To the socialism of Marxist color there must be counterposed a workable system of Christian socialism. We, on the Catholic side, are in a particularly advantageous position in this respect, as such a system is already present in our scholarly literature. The leading idea on which Christian socialism would be based is the idea of cooperation that is grounded in German law as well as in Christianity. This idea is not to be considered in its narrow meaning as limited to economic and occupational associations, but in a broader meaning as applying to the totality of public life, to the citizens' relations to each other, to the state . . . as well as the relations between different nationalities within the community of God's family encompassing the whole human race. From this cooperative idea flows directly the demand for equal rights for all citizens as such, for occupations and members of different occupations and for different nationalities in their relations with each other.

A bit on the vague side, that. But further on I found this:

> The role of the state: to do what cannot be done without the state. . . . In case of extreme need everything becomes common property. . . . Public welfare is the direct purpose of the state. It consists in public arrangements making possible the attainment of individual well-being. [Very different emphasis from John Locke's "the great and chief end" of the state is "the preservation of property."]
>
> Christian socialism does not categorically reject every case of nationalization . . . but each case of nationalization requires its special justification. . . . Private monopolies aiming at the enforcement of high prices are inadmissible. There may be situations where a public monopoly should be substituted for such private monopoly.

This sounded more like authentic socialism. Curious, I quizzed Professor Mueller again. This is what he told me:

That pamphlet was written shortly after the end of World War I and during the 1918–19 revolution in Germany. I cannot help thinking that Pesch, when he saw the red flags all over Berlin, felt it necessary to make "solidarism" attractive to the masses by calling it Christian socialism. If I remember correctly, later he wasn't too sure that this was a prudent decision. I think he never again used that expression.

But note: The use of that expression was not simply Pesch's decision. The pamphlet was published by the Center Party. Today, red flags are flying all over the world, Berlin included. "Christian socialism" may not yet be an attractive expression to the masses in the United States. They don't even like the expression "the masses." Throughout most of the world, however, where the vast majority have long since given up on the peculiar American dream that it is only a question of time before we all strike it rich, there, I submit, Christians may find it a prudent decision indeed to revive, defend, and proclaim the ancient and honorable expression "Christian socialism." Even in the United States that day may come sooner than we think.

DIFFERENT EXPRESSIONS, SAME IDEA

To go from the two Pesch pamphlets of 1919 to Richard Mulcahy's *The Economics of Heinrich Pesch* is an even more puzzling experience than trying to explain Pesch's use of the expression "Christian socialism." Mulcahy nowhere mentions the pamphlets in his text, although he does include them in his bibliography. The quotations from Pesch's five-volume *Lehrbuch,* all from editions revised and published after 1919, repeat all the standard objections to socialism, which is identified with total Marxian collectivism and public ownership of the means of production, plus the further objection: "Proletarian dictatorship and socialism belong together."[32]

Mulcahy, another Jesuit, who has written the only work in English that gives book-length treatment to Pesch's thought, does provide us with clarification as to the different ways Pesch used the words "capitalism" and "capitalistic."

First, he refers to "capitalistic production," the technical fact of a rather intensive use of produced means of production. . . . Second, reference is made to the "capitalistic enterprise," . . . [which] assumes . . . private ownership of capital and the presence of a laboring force which cooperates in production under the guidance of a capitalistic entrepreneur" (IV, 561). . . . The third sense in which capitalism is used by Pesch is as "the embodiment of certain abuses which arose in the historical development of the capitalistic enterprise, specifically in the 'capitalistic epoch', but which are not essential to the capitalistic enterprise and are not found in every capitalistic enterprise" (IV, 561–62). Reference is primarily to the "spirit" of capitalism based fundamentally on an exaggerated individualism [The numerals refer to volume/page of the *Lehrbuch*].[33]

Pesch himself, however, does not seem to agree with Mulcahy's interpretation that he is referring simply to the "spirit" of *individualistic* capitalism, because we find this definition of capitalism in Vol. II, p. 230:

An economic *system* arising from the individualistic freedom of striving for gain, ruled by the principles of exchange and the practices of the liberal economic epoch, serving in the first line not the whole welfare of the people, but the owner of capital and his money interests [emphasis added].[34]

Pesch adds these further qualifications of the capitalistic system he is talking about: "The enterprise itself has become the goal and the end of the economic system" (III, 60). And further:

The providing for the needs of the people is less the task of the economy than a means for the enrichment of private enterprise. The subjective goal of private acquisitiveness is elevated above the objective task of the national economy. The private economy dominates the national (II, 277).[35]

We begin now to see the connection between the pamphlets of 1919 and the *Lehrbuch*. The language of the pamphlets, written in a revolutionary situation, is more impassioned and urgent, but the basic meaning is the same: Capitalism as Pesch knew it was a bad system. Note that this was Germany, the most welfare-oriented country of the industrial West. Bismarck's welfare system was frequently referred to as "state socialism." It even included some public ownership.

Franz Mueller, in his 1951 article, after quoting Pesch's anathemas of capitalism, adds this softening qualifier: "Yet there are many who will deny that the American economic system is 'capitalistic' in this sense."[36] To which we must add the hardening qualifier that there are many who affirm that the American economic system is capitalistic in precisely this sense.

To Marxian socialism and capitalism Pesch compares and contrasts his own system, solidarism, which he also refers to as "the social system of labor." Here is one of his thumbnail definitions:

The solidaristic principle . . . on the basis of the responsibility to the community (a norm binding on both citizens and public authorities) arising from the social end of the people united in a political community, determines measures, and limits the freedom, private property, and self-interest of the autonomous subjects and their associations, and likewise the authority of the state . . . (I, 451).[37]

PESCH TRANSLATED INTO *QUADRAGESIMO ANNO*

As must be evident already, I have delved into the thought of Pesch at some length and depth because his admiring disciple and fellow Jesuit, Oswald von Nell-Breuning, at the request of Pius XI, wrote the pope's encyclical *Quadragesimo Anno.* The encyclical's subtitle is "On Reconstructing the Social Order" and the reconstruction recommended is borrowed from Pesch's solidarism.

The first thing a reader may notice about *Quadragesimo Anno* is that, like the work of Cathrein and Pesch, the argumentation is based not on Scripture but on natural law. Nell-Breuning takes pains to point this out in his book "explaining" the encyclical:

> Only natural truths and logical reasoning will be used to derive and establish the Pope's teaching on human society and its members. Where the encyclical cites passages taken from Holy Scripture, careful examination shows that this is done not by way of proof, but rather to stress the conformity of his logical conclusions with the teachings of the Gospel, or in order to explain the meaning of certain words of the Scriptures that have been drawn into the controversy of opinions.[38]

Of course, natural truth and logical reasoning, as one critic has put it, "light no bonfires." This may have been one consideration leading to a change in the style and content of papal and other church statements on social questions in the years since 1931. *Quadragesimo Anno,* for example, has just five biblical citations in its first thirty-three pages (out of a total of forty-one). Nineteen more appear in the last eight pages, but this section is almost entirely exhortation. John XXIII's *Mater et Magistra* (1961), a longer encyclical of eighty-one pages, follows the same pattern with most of its twenty-three biblical citations falling in the hortatory pages at the end. By contrast John Paul II's *Laborem Exercens* (On Human Work), though shorter than John XXIII's encyclical, has one-hundred three biblical citations scattered throughout. The U.S. bishops' 1986 pastoral, *Economic Justice for All: Catholic Social Teaching and the U.S. Economy,* topped this record with 112 citations, almost all concentrated in an early section entitled "The Christian Vision of Economic Life."

The next thing one might notice about *Quadragesimo Anno* is that, as in Pesch's *Lehrbuch,* only more so, there is ambiguity as to whether the author is pro- or anti-capitalist. For example, insofar as capitalism is defined as "that economic regime in which [are] provided by different people the capital and labor jointly needed for production . . . the system itself is not to be condemned."[39] A few paragraphs later we read this:

> In our days not alone is wealth accumulated, but immense power and despotic economic domination is concentrated in the hands of a few. . . . *This accumulation of power is the characteristic note of the present*

economic order. . . . Free competition is dead; economic dictatorship has taken its place. . . . The whole economic life has become hard, cruel and relentless in a ghastly measure [emphasis added].[40]

Pius XI/Nell-Breuning defend the justice of the employer-employee relationship against the classical Marxists: "Those who hold that the wage contract is essentially unjust . . . are certainly in error." Then they add:

In the present state of human society, however, we deem it advisable that the wage contract should, when possible, be modified somewhat by a contract of partnership. . . . In this way wage-earners are made sharers in some sort in the ownership, or the management, or the profits.[41]

Thus, at the level of individual enterprise, a tentative step is taken toward socialization of the means of production. Another even more significant step is taken, a step that had already been taken years before by Heinrich Pesch and John A. Ryan, in these words of *Quadragesimo Anno*:

For it is rightly contended that certain forms of property must be reserved to the state, since they carry with them an opportunity of domination too great to be left to private individuals.[42]

Now we have public ownership where necessary—a very flexible formula—and we have worker participation in ownership, control, and profits. But that is not all. We also get a proposal for a major "reconstruction" of this "hard, cruel, relentless, ghastly, despotic economic order."

This reconstruction is lifted entirely from Pesch's solidarism. The encyclical proposes the organization of "vocational groups" that would combine representatives of labor, management, and the public in a system of self-government for each industry or profession. This would be parallel to the political structure, but presumably subordinate to it. Pesch at least makes that clear. The encyclical does not.

Almost as soon, however, as the proposal is made, it begins to run off the track. This seems to have been the doing of Pius XI independently of Nell-Breuning. In a 1971 article in the German publication *Stimmen der Zeit,* Nell-Breuning revealed, as Father Coleman reports in his *Origins* article, that "the only independent contributions of the pope to the text were sections of paragraphs 91ff., which said some ambiguously favorable things about Mussolini's fascist order."[43] The pope apparently wanted to throw a sop to Mussolini since he was about to issue a strongly antifascist encyclical *Non Abbiamo Bisogno.* Although *Quadragesimo Anno* immediately adds a criticism of Mussolini's scheme as being too authoritarian, state-controlled, "excessively bureaucratic and political," the fat was in the fire. Pesch's vocational group plan, which he and Nell-Breuning saw as a form of economic democracy, was tagged as "corporatism," which in turn was tagged with the label of "fascism" by all the church's enemies and even some of its friends.

Pius XI did not help matters when a few years later he said some nice things about the semifascist schemes of Engelbert Dollfus, the Catholic dictator of Austria. Dollfus, ironically, was the leader of the Christian Social Party, which in many histories is referred to as the Christian Socialist Party. Squeezed between the Nazis, by whom he was eventually assassinated, and the strong Socialist Party of Austria, he ordered government troops to shut down Socialist headquarters and, when resistance naturally followed, to shell the Karl Marx Hof, a socialist housing complex. This completed the alienation of the Austrian working class from the "Christian Socialists," and to a large extent, from the Catholic Church as well.

Unlike the German church, where the Christian unions had kept large numbers of workers loyal, the church in Austria was composed mainly of peasants and aristocrats.

Franco in Spain, Salazar in Portugal, Pétain in Vichy France all tried to hitch their fascist and semi-fascist tails to the papal kite. The negative reactions to them soon became attached to the vocational-group plan.

In the swirl of negative opinion several things have been overlooked. First, there are significant similarities between the plan and the Guild socialism that flourished in England from 1906 to 1923. Both had their origins in a nostalgic look backward to the Middle Ages, a nostalgia that united the more realistic Jesuits of North Germany with the Vogelsang Romantics of Austria, Bavaria, and France. Both were concerned to find worker-oriented alternatives to state socialism and class war, although most guild socialists were thinking to end class war by eliminating the employer class. Some of them eventually became the early leaders of the Communist Party of Great Britain.

Another curious oversight of encyclical critics is the failure to note that the more militant, radical wing of the American labor movement during the thirties, forties, and fifties, the CIO (Congress of Industrial Organizations), at every convention between 1941 and 1955, endorsed an "Industry Council Plan" that was based on *Quadragesimo Anno*. This was acknowledged by different parties who were in the best position to know. One was Philip Murray, a devout Catholic and one of America's most admirable labor leaders, who was president of the CIO from 1940 until his death in 1952. At a communion breakfast of the Association of Catholic Trade Unionists in New York City in 1942, Murray said that a critic "charged that I had taken the plan—body, boots and breeches—out of the encyclicals." Murray acknowledged that this charge was "almost completely true."[44]

The Association, or ACTU, as it was usually called, was founded in 1937 in New York City at the Catholic Worker, the radical movement led by the saintly Dorothy Day. Its founders, members of AFL and CIO unions, took their charter from that passage in *Quadragesimo Anno* wherein the pope agrees that Catholic workers may join "neutral unions," with this precaution:

Side by side with these trade unions there must always be associations which aim at giving their members a thorough religious and moral training, that these in turn may impart to the labor unions to which they belong the upright spirit which should direct their entire conduct.[45]

ACTU members helped organize Catholic workers into neutral unions, usually the CIO, marched on strike picket lines, ran labor schools, and fought racketeer and Stalinist control where these existed. ACTU publications strongly promoted the CIO's Industry Council Plan as an excellent application of *Quadragesimo Anno* to the American scene.

Another body that was even better qualified to make an authoritative judgment was the U.S. Conference of Catholic Bishops, which in 1948 took the position that the phrase "industry councils" was an accurate way "to designate the basic organs of a Christian and American type of economic democracy" derived from the encyclical *Quadragesimo Anno*.[46]

A significant footnote: In that same year of 1948, the Cold War having now begun, *The Daily Worker,* official newspaper of the Communist Party, labeled the plan "the ACTU Industry Council Plan," called it "fascism" and simply an American incarnation of "Mussolini's and Franco's 'corporate state.' "[47] The only problem with this verbal barrage was that all the Stalinist delegates to all the CIO conventions since 1941 had voted for it. William Z. Foster, chairman of the Communist Party, had himself in 1942 written a pamphlet entitled *Labor and the War* in which he said, "The Murray Plan of industry-labor-government councils in the various industries offers a practical means to accomplish the indispensable end of speeding up production by giving labor a real voice in war industry."[48] But by 1948 a "real voice for labor" had transmogrified into "fascism."

In Europe the fascist tag stuck, and so it was small wonder that in 1961 John XXIII simply dropped the plan from his encyclical *Mater et Magistra*. The principles behind the plan, however, the vision of an economic democracy that would replace the monarchies and oligarchies of capitalism, these Pope John supported and reaffirmed even more strongly than Pius XI.

PIUS XI AND SOCIALISM

Before discussing John XXIII let us return briefly to *Quadragesimo Anno* and the famous dictum that "no one can be at the same time a sincere Catholic and a true socialist."

In 1970 Father Nell-Breuning wrote an article for *Sacramentum Mundi,* an encyclopedia of Catholic theology, which contained the following:

It is certain that forms of socialism existed in 1931 which did not exhibit the features described in the encyclical (*Quadragesimo Anno*) and accordingly were not affected by the papal condemnation—the British Labor Party for one (which the Archbishop of Westminster hastened to reassure on this point) and probably Scandinavian socialism as well.[49]

Question: Why did not Father Nell-Breuning mention such facts when he wrote the encyclical? Why did he leave the impression that all socialist parties were forbidden territory for Catholics? In his 1970 article he concedes that "the libertarian, democratic socialism of the present day has clearly ceased to be" the kind of socialism condemned by Pius XI. But such socialism existed in 1931 and not simply in England and Scandinavia. Such socialism existed long before Karl Marx, during Marx's heyday, and after it. "True socialism," according to *Quadragesimo Anno,* is a socialism that insists that "man's higher goods, not excepting liberty, must, they claim, be subordinated and even sacrificed to the exigencies of efficient production."[50] Who claimed that? Did the Socialist International in 1931 make any such claim? If so, my reading has not revealed it.

A second question: If no one can be at the same time a sincere Catholic and a true socialist, why did not the encyclical also insist that no one can be at the same time a sincere Catholic and a true capitalist? Just as it concedes that the *structure* of a capitalist economy—capital and labor "provided by different people"—"is not to be condemned," so the encyclical concedes that the structure proposed by the more moderate branch of socialism—a combination of public and private ownership and social reforms—"often strikingly approaches the just demands of Christian social reformers."[51]

Not the structure, therefore, but the (alleged) spirit and philosophy of socialism is to be condemned. But the encyclical has also condemned the spirit and philosophy that would justify capital when it

> employs the working or wage-earning classes as to divert business and economic activity entirely to its own arbitrary will and advantage without any regard to the human dignity of the workers, the social character of economic life, social justice and the common good.[52]

The encyclical then tells us that this spirit has, in fact, prevailed so that the structure has been undermined, twisted out of shape and "the whole economic life has become hard, cruel and relentless in a ghastly measure." So capitalism is in worse shape than moderate socialism. Why then is it only socialists who cannot be sincere Catholics?

Ah, well, perhaps we should let bygones be bygones. The writer of the encyclical has conceded, in the 1970 article, that the situation has changed radically since 1931. Unfortunately, the condemnation had its effects, and some of them were tragic. Gregory Baum has detailed the harmful effects for the socialists of Canada.[53] Far more serious was the baleful influence of *Quadragesimo Anno* in Germany, where the Social Democratic Party, still given to Marxist rhetoric but practicing Bernsteinian moderation, might otherwise have been able to forge a coalition with the Center (Catholic) Party strong enough to hold off the Nazis. The consequences of that failure should not have to be spelled out.

Before leaving our discussion of Pius XI, we must strike a positive note by recalling his own "preferential option for the poor" in his advice to the priests of his church: "Go to the workingman, especially where he is poor; and in general, go to the poor."[54]

This admonition appears toward the end of another social encyclical, *Divini Redemptoris* (English title: On Atheistic Communism). It is significant that about one-quarter of this encyclical, published in 1937, is devoted to communism and three-quarters is devoted to "the lamentable ruin into which amoral liberalism has plunged us" and advice about how to scramble out of it.[55] The encyclical might better have been entitled "On Atheistic Capitalism."

In the years between Pius XI and John XXIII (1939 to 1958) a fourth German Jesuit, Gustav Gundlach (1892–1963), from his chair on the faculty of the Gregorian University in Rome, was to exert a major influence on a pope, Pius XII. Gundlach, another student of Pesch, made sure that Pius XII, in all his allocutions on social questions, kept Pesch's solidarism and vocational groups well in the foreground.

Christian socialism, meanwhile, was making headway in Catholic intellectual circles. German writers and scholars like Max Scheler, Father Wilhelm Hohoff, Theodor Brauer, August Pieper, Ernst Michel, Walter Dirks, Georg Beyer, Otto Bauer, and Heinrich Mertens were all either embracing socialism themselves or writing sympathetically about it from a Catholic viewpoint, many of them even before the publication of *Quadragesimo Anno*.

EMMANUEL MOUNIER

The figure among the intellectuals of Western Europe who most stimulated or provoked Catholics into taking a new look at socialism was undoubtedly Emmanuel Mounier, from 1932 until his early death in 1950 the editor of the French Magazine *Esprit*. English has no word that conveys the full meaning of *esprit*, which is a combination of spirit, soul, mind, and wit. All of these were characteristic of Mounier and of *Esprit*.

Mounier was not only a brilliant editor and writer. He was also the leading guru of a movement known as Personalism, which did not lack for gurus. Perhaps as good a definition of Personalism as any would be: Christianity translated for French intellectuals. An unfriendly critic, Paul Nizan, called it "a flotilla of abstractions, a fleet of capital letters."[56] Among the more prominent ones were "Person" and "Community." Note the blood relationship to Solidarism, which also tried to reconcile the individual and social aspects of the human personality.

Frankly, Mounier was such a mass of brilliant contradictions that I find it impossible to do him justice in the space left to me. The best I can do is refer the interested reader to John Hellman's excellent book *Emmanuel Mounier and the New Catholic Left 1930–50* (Toronto University, 1981). Hellman describes Mounier as "committed to revolution and indifferent to politics, an enthusiastic admirer of the Marxists and an anti-Marxist, a communist sympathizer and an anti-communist, a purist democrat and an authoritarian,"[57] who "tried to marry black France and red France, the priests with the Jacobins."[58]

Hellman might have added several more paradoxes: an elitist whose hero was Charles Péguy (1873–1914), the peasant and "mystic socialist" whose socialism was "simply the transposition of the proletarian and popular love of work well done"[59]—a socialism that Péguy had learned while caning chairs in Orléans. In his book on Péguy, Mounier included this lovely quote from his hero:

> A tradition, coming, welling up from the profoundest depths of the race . . . demanded that that chair leg be well made. Every part in the chair that one could not see was exactly as perfectly made as that which was visible. That is the very principle of the Cathedrals. It was a handsome continual sport, and yet more: they said while laughing, and to annoy the curés, that to work is to pray, and they did not realize how well they put it.[60]

This quotation recalls to me the Catholic Worker of the 1930s, when Peter Maurin, the French hobo-philosopher and Dorothy Day's guru, told us about Péguy and Mounier and also Eric Gill, the English artist-craftsman-writer, who wrote a sentence that has stuck with me ever since and still symbolizes my own favorite brand of socialism: "People work best when they own and control their own tools and materials."[61]

Still another Mounier paradox: he was contemptuous of the social encyclicals. Yet, when the socialists behind the Popular Front came to power in 1936, Mounier urged the Blum government to perform the necessary surgical operations, *"clearly prescribed in the papal encyclicals,"* such as

> dismantling of the financial fortress of capitalism, the abolition of the trusts and financial oligarchies . . . the nationalization of public services . . . the abolition of the proletarian condition . . . the collective organization of production, the substitution of a contract of association for the salary contract [emphasis added].[62]

But mostly Mounier was a kind of intellectual John the Baptist, the voice of one crying in a secular wilderness, a spiritual desert, warning his countrymen and his coreligionists to flee from the wrath to come:

> These crooked beings who go forward in life only sidelong with downcast eyes, these ungainly souls, these weighers-up of virtues, these dominical victims, these pious cowards, these lymphatic heroes, these colorless virgins, these vessels of ennui, these bags of syllogisms, these shadows of shadows, are they the vanguard of Daniel marching against the Beast?[63]

Or this:

> Whoever seeks the continuity of the Kingdom had better turn his attention away from the statistics of Massachusetts or the Ubangi, away from

the epaulets of Franco and the prestige of Cardinal Spellman in *The Reader's Digest*. He will find . . . in the workers' quarter of Montreuil . . . three priests living in community, in shabby clothes, and around them an obscure, stammering and shocking reality. . . . The church of the year 3000 will place these solitaries on pedestals when Franco . . . will not even leave a trace in the pitiless books of history. Before burying the Christian tradition, one had better direct a little attention to its avant-gardes.[64]

And finally some good advice for the socialists and the fellow travelers in the form of three lessons learned from the history of France after World War II (even though he had not always been wise enough to take them to himself):

Any attempt to reconstruct socialism on the plane of literary clubs, without the ballast and vigor of the proletariat, is headed for the morass. . . .

Any union of heretics and schismatics of the Left, without a forceful doctrine and a popular base, ends in impotence . . . .

All groups which through their ideological weakness, their mimicry of communist theses and absence of autonomy, only appear to be instruments of the Communist Party, are at present incapable of widening their activity.[65]

PIUS XII PICKS DEMOCRACY

The record of Pius XII's pontificate is not a clear blue sky. There have been questions about the strength and consistency of his stand against Hitler and the Nazis. Nevertheless, we do know that on Christmas Eve 1944 in a radio message to the world Pius XII put the papacy and the Catholic Church on record as a champion of democracy—note well—*Western-style*. It was an eloquent statement and worth quoting at length:

Moreover—this is perhaps the most important point—beneath the sinister lightning of the war that compasses them, in the blazing heat of the furnace that imprisons them, the peoples have awakened as it were from a heavy sleep. They have taken a new attitude toward the State and toward those who govern—they ask questions, they criticize, and they distrust.

Taught by bitter experience, they are more aggressive in opposing the concentration of power in dictatorships that cannot be censured or touched, and in calling for a system of government more in keeping with the dignity and liberty of the citizens. These uneasy multitudes, stirred by the war to their innermost depths, are today firmly convinced—at first perhaps in a vague and confused way but already unyieldingly—that had there been the possibility of censuring and correcting the actions of public authority, the world would not have been dragged into the vortex of a disastrous war, and that to avoid the repetition of such a catastrophe in the future we must vest efficient guarantees in the people themselves. . . .

It is hardly necessary to recall the teaching of the Church, that "it is not forbidden to prefer temperate, popular forms of government, without prejudice, however, to Catholic teaching on the origin and use of authority," and that "the Church does not disapprove of any of the various forms of government, provided they be by themselves capable of securing the good of the citizens" (Leo XIII, Encyclical *Libertas*, June 20, 1888).

This was Leo XIII solving the problem, among others, of Catholic support for the Third Republic in France. Now, however, the church is telling us that dictatorships are *dis*approved as being incapable of securing the good of the citizens and that democracy is preferred. Note:

Considering the extent and nature of the sacrifices demanded of all citizens, especially in our day when the activity of the State is so vast and decisive, the democratic form of government appears to many a postulate of nature imposed by reason itself.[66]

WHENCE ALL THOSE SOCIALIST VOTES?

French pollsters reported after their country's presidential election of 1979 that one-fourth of France's *practicing* Catholics had voted for François Mitterand, the Socialist candidate, thereby assuring his victory. This was a new high. French Catholics had traditionally voted for antisocialist candidates.

Where did all those swing votes come from? And why? Answers must be tentative, but one answer would go back to a young Belgian priest, Joseph Cardijn (1882–1967), who in 1912 began organizing young workers into small study groups. He used a technique which many years later was to be employed in Latin America by the *comunidades de base* (base communities). Many hailed this technique as a brilliant new invention. It was brilliant but not new.

Cardijn called the technique "See, Judge, Act." The idea was for young workers to observe the conditions of life that surrounded them, both at home and at work, then to judge those conditions in the light of the gospel, which they read and discussed at their meetings, and finally to act to bring those conditions closer into conformity with the gospel.

The technique was successful, sensationally successful. Father Cardijn, in addition, was a charismatic personality who, in small meetings, had the intelligence and the self-discipline to let the workers think and talk for themselves and, in large meetings, had the eloquence and the fire necessary to inspire and galvanize them into action.

The conditions in the factories where the young workers of Brussels were employed were no better than most other factories of that era. Inevitably as a result of Cardijn's activity, he and his Young Christian Workers (YCW) came under heavy attack from Catholic employers and politicians and from some of the more conservative clergy. They appealed to Cardinal Mercier, who had appointed Cardijn to the strategic position of social action director for the Brussels area.

Mercier bent to the pressure and was on the verge of stopping Cardijn, but Cardijn gave him an out by suggesting that he, Cardijn, go to Rome and put the question to the pope. This was 1924. The pope was Pius XI. The opposition was jubilant, confident that Cardijn would never get in to see the pope, much less swing him to his side.

Fortunately, this meeting was different from the meeting of Lamennais with Gregory XVI. Pius XI greeted Cardijn warmly. "At last," he said, "some one speaks to me of the working class."[67] This was the occasion on which he said, "The great scandal of the nineteenth century was that the church lost the working class."

For more than an hour the pope listened and then he told Cardijn, "Not only do we bless your movement—we make it our own." So armed, Cardijn and Mercier were able to sweep all opposition aside and Cardijn went on to worldwide success. The YCW spread to 109 countries, organized and activated millions of young workers who in turn became activists and militants in their unions. The working class was being won back. The YCW, in addition, gave birth to other, similar movements among students, farmers, intellectuals, and married couples.

In all accuracy, however, it must be added that all these movements have suffered losses since the sixties. This has been especially true of the Young Christian Students (JEC) in France, badly damaged by the forced resignation of most of its national staff in 1965 after the organization ran afoul of the rigidly conservative Cardinal Veuillot, archbishop of Paris. Over the next ten years the leadership drifted steadily toward Marxism. In 1970 the national secretary stated, "Our movement has analyzed society, not apart from the faith—that is impossible—but with secular, and especially Marxist tools."[68] In 1976 the JEC national council declared itself "sympathetic to the fight for a socialism of self-management" and warned the church that it must cease to be "an obstacle to the radical change in which the JEC participates." It also committed itself to assist in the creation of a national section of Christians for Socialism, the organization founded by Latin American Marxists in Chile in 1972 (see below).

This drift of the French Catholic left toward Marxism was abruptly checked about 1974 when Marxism suffered what students of intellectual life in France have described as "a deep crisis." This seems to have been a joint product of the publication in 1973 of Solzhenitsyn's *Gulag Archipelago* and the growing awareness of Soviet atrocities, together with a sharp decline in the popularity of the French Communist Party. The CP, which had been the strongest single party after World War II, had by 1981 slipped to only 44 seats in the National Assembly, to 269 held by the Socialists, out of a total of 491.

The drift both to and away from Marxism is even better illustrated by the history of La Vie Nouvelle (The New Life), an organization of left-wing Catholics that was founded in 1947 and owed much of its program and spirit to Mounier's *Esprit*. Originally anti-Marxist, it had by 1971 reached the point where its national council agreed that "Marxism is the only structured and coherent social theory." At the same time it rejected "dialectical materialism, or at least certain of its interpretations" as well as "certain Marxist governments." That year La Vie Nouvelle had about five thousand members, of whom perhaps six hundred were declared socialists. By 1976 membership had slipped to three thousand, but the number of socialist members had climbed significantly. Reservations about Marxism had also climbed, as is shown in this statement of the National Council: "La Vie Nouvelle does not declare itself Marxist; it recognizes that Marxism is an important factor in its internal dynamic." Further, it saw in Marxism

the absence of a credible theory of power, the Marx/Lenin theme of a revolutionary avant-garde that brings the theory from outside to the proletariat, the scientistic temptation of a pretension to absolute knowledge.[69]

By 1986 Christians for Socialism had virtually died in France and many aspects of liberation theology, its dominant ideology, were regarded by most left-wing Catholics as "naive Marxism." La Vie Nouvelle remained highly critical of the Soviet Union and predominantly supportive of the French Socialist Party. I asked a French friend, Danièle Hervieu-Léger, author of several important books on the sociology of religion, why La Vie Nouvelle was not affiliated with the International League of Religious Socialists. She did not know, but she hazarded the guess that it would be most reluctant to join any organization that could not bring itself to protest the suppression of Solidarity in Poland or the Soviet invasion of Afghanistan (see below). She also suggested that liberation theology was not popular among French Catholics because "it associates politics and religion too closely for the French. They are trying to *dis*associate them."

THE CHRISTIAN UNIONS BECOME DEMOCRATIC AND SOCIALIST

In 1961, at a meeting of the World Congress of Christian Workers in Rome, I met one of the graduates of the YCW. He was Eugene Descamps, newly elected general secretary of the French Confederation of Christian Workers (CFTC), which had become the largest labor federation after the Communist-dominated CGT. He expressed his desire to create a new federation that would not have the name "Christian" attached to it and would be able to appeal to the socialist workers. He told me,

> Thanks to the work of the Young Christian Workers, we have more young militants than the Communists have. And they are better militants than the Communists. If we can only give the French workers the choice between a Communist federation and one free, democratic federation, then I believe that the future belongs to us.

The CFTC did take the "Christian" out of its name and replaced it with "Democratic" in 1967. By 1985 it (now the CFDT) had increased its share of the organized labor movement from 25 percent to 34 percent and helped bring down the Communist share from 55 percent to 46 percent. It still had not persuaded the officially socialist *Force Ouvrière*, with 15 percent, to merge with it. The future did not yet belong to the CDFT, but the trend was auspicious.

The CFDT, though jealously guarding its independence from all political parties, has now become the largest and most dependable source of labor support for Mitterand's Socialist Party. Michael Harrington, co-chair of the Democratic Socialists of America, comments on this development:

> When [the CFDT] became a part of the new socialist movement led by François Mitterand in the seventies, they were the carriers of a distinctive idea of socialism: worker-managed, decentralized, communitarian. And that trend can now be found in almost all of the socialist parties of Europe.
>
> That French experience . . . did not involve the CFDT in a repudiation of its origins and an acceptance of the secular, anti-clerical socialism which Catholics had always fought in France. Rather it meant that both the traditional socialists and the new socialists changed themselves, that in the process of uniting they discovered (rediscovered) new (old) values. I am suggesting something like that as a political-spiritual project for all of Western society.[70]

Harrington, it seems, has even more grandiose dreams than Eugene Descamps. But who knows? He may be on to something. We can only applaud his intention and second his suggestion. Harrington, incidentally, is a graduate of the Catholic Worker in the 50s who lost his faith and now describes himself as "a Catholic atheist." His commitment to Christ's poor, however, would put most Catholics to shame.

THE RADICALIZATION OF CATHOLICISM

From John XXIII through John Paul II we can observe a steady radicalization of Catholic social teaching. In *Mater et Magistra* (1961) John insisted that the more profitable "large and medium-size productive enterprises . . . should grant to workers some share in the enterprise."[71] An echo and development of Pius XII on political democracy can be heard in John's statement that

> the greater amount of responsibility desired today by workers in productive enterprises not merely accords with the nature of human beings, but also is in conformity with historical developments in the economic, social and political fields.[72]

Not until a later encyclical, however—*Pacem in Terris* (1963)—did John give full expression to his ability to distinguish between what people say and what they do, to his wonderful openness to the good wherever it may be found, not excepting the movement of Marxian socialism. As in this passage:

> Neither can false philosophical teachings regarding the nature, origin and destiny of the universe and of humankind be identified with historical movements that have economic, social, cultural or political ends, not even when these movements have originated from these teachings and have drawn and still draw inspiration therefrom. . . . Besides, who can deny that those movements, insofar as they conform to the dictates of right reason and are interpreters of the lawful aspirations of the human person, contain elements that are positive and deserving of approval?[73]

In 1971, on the eightieth anniversary of *Rerum Novarum*, Paul VI developed this thought a little further and implied that if "careful judgment" were utilized, Catholics might well join socialist parties:

> Some Christians are today attracted by socialist currents and their various developments. They try to recognize therein a certain number of aspirations which they carry within themselves in the name of their faith. They feel that they are part of that historical current and wish to play a part within it. Now this historical current takes on, under the same name, different forms according to different continents and cultures, even if it drew its inspiration and still does in many cases, from ideologies incompatible with faith. Careful judgment is called for.[74]

Further cautions and qualifications follow, but, in effect, the bars were down.
Gaudium et Spes (The Church in the Modern World), a product of Vatican Council II, is perhaps the most authoritative statement of all, since it represents the thinking not only of Pope Paul VI but also of several thousand bishops from all over the world. Here is a sampling of that thinking:

> Active participation of everyone in the running of an enterprise should be promoted . . . workers themselves should have a share also in controlling these [economic] institutions [on a higher level], either in person or through freely elected delegates.[75]

The strike can still be a necessary, though ultimate, means for the defense of the workers' own rights and the fulfillment of their just demands.[76]

Insufficiently cultivated estates should be distributed to those who can make these lands fruitful.[77]

We have already noted that Paul VI finally acknowledged the continuing validity of Aquinas's theory of just revolution and tyrannicide (*Populorum Progressio*, 1967). In 1981 John Paul II set out to commemorate the ninetieth anniversary of *Rerum Novarum* with a new social encyclical, *Laborem Exercens*, but an almost fatal attempt on his life delayed it for a few months. This was perhaps the most radical statement of all. Explicitly describing what "should rightly be called 'capitalism,' " John Paul writes,

There is a confusion or even a reversal of the order laid down from the beginning by the words of the book of Genesis: *Man is treated as an instrument of production*, whereas he—he alone, independently of the work he does—ought to be treated as the effective subject of work and its true maker and creator [emphasis in the original].[78]

Further: "We must first of all recall a principle that has always been taught by the Church: *the principle of the priority of labor over capital*" [emphasis in the original].[79] Well, not quite "always taught."

In consideration of human labor and of common access to the goods meant for man, one cannot exclude the *socialization*, in suitable conditions, of certain means of production. . . . Merely taking these means of production (capital) out of the hands of their private owners is not enough to ensure their satisfactory socialization. . . . We can speak of socializing only when the subject character of society is ensured, that is to say, when on the basis of his work each person is fully entitled to consider himself a part-owner of the great workbench at which he is working with everyone else. A way towards that goal could be found by associating labor with the ownership of capital, as far as possible, and by producing a wide range of intermediate bodies with economic, social and cultural purposes [emphasis in original].[80]

The role of the agents included under the title of indirect employer is *to act against unemployment*, which in all cases is an evil [emphasis in the original].[81]

John Paul had previously described the "indirect employer" as "all the agents at the national and international level that are responsible for the whole orientation of labor policy."

There were interesting reactions to this encyclical. Father David Hollenbach, S.J., professor of social ethics at Weston School of Theology: "It really looks like the Pope's criticism of capitalism and collectivism argues for a form of democratic socialism."[82]

Nicholas von Hoffman, writing in the *New Republic*, characterized John Paul's position as "a form of soft, non-Marxist socialism."[83]

The trend toward the "socialization" of the Catholic Church did not occur only at the top. There was pressure from below, not only from Catholic workers, as with the French CFDT, but also from within the hierarchy. Back in the forties a French bishop, Pierre Théas, gave perhaps the strongest expression to it:

> Urged on by unrestrainable forces, today's world asks for a revolution. The revolution must succeed, but it can succeed only if the Church enters the fray, bringing the Gospel. After being liberated from Nazi dictatorship, we want to liberate the working class from capitalist slavery.[84]

Then in 1967 Dom Helder Camara, archbishop of Recife (Brazil), one of the most progressive members of the most progressive hierarchy, took the initiative in drawing up a "pastoral letter from the Third World" entitled *Gospel and Revolution*. It declared:

> Far from working against it, let us learn to embrace socialism with joy as a way of life better adapted to our time and more in accordance with the spirit of the Gospel. Thus we will avoid causing anybody to confuse God and religion with feudalism, capitalism and imperialism, the worldly oppressors of the poor and of the workers of the world. These inhuman systems have engendered others which, in their attempt to free peoples, have instead also become oppressors, falling into totalitarian collectivism and religious persecution.[85]

This last sentence was an obvious attempt to distinguish socialism from communist and/or Leninist regimes. The letter was signed by fifteen bishops and two apostolic vicars—from Brazil, Colombia, Algeria, China, Egypt, Indonesia, Laos, Lebanon, Oceania and Yugoslavia.

Dom Helder, an engagingly enthusiastic prelate, presided, until his recent retirement, over a cathedral whose walls are pockmarked by the machine-gun bullets of right-wing elements intent on scaring him into silence. He is clearly the most popular, best-known and most widely traveled of all the spokespersons of Christian socialism in Latin America. He has encouraged the effort to incorporate elements of Marxism into Christian thought, making the analogy of Thomas Aquinas's successful effort to incorporate Aristotelian philosophy. Therefore it is the more significant that he is also one of the more outspoken critics of Soviet or Cuban style "socialism." He has said,

I don't see any solution in capitalism. But neither do I see it in the socialist examples that are offered us today, because they're based on dictatorship and you don't arrive at socialism with dictatorship. My socialism is a special socialism, that respects the human person and goes back to the Gospels. My socialism is justice.[86]

One might fault this statement for its current identification of socialism with dictatorships, ignoring democratic socialism in the West European style. The repudiation of Leninist, Soviet, and Cuban-style claims to the name "socialism," however, is most welcome and somewhat rare among exponents of the notion that Marx, like Aristotle, might well be incorporated into Catholic thought. It is notably rare in Latin America. This is not to deny that there is much in Marx, or in some of his more democratic disciples, such as Michael Harrington, that we can profitably study. The best full-length examination of what in Marx can be reconciled with Christianity and what cannot is *Marxist Analysis and Christian Faith* (Orbis, 1985) by the French theologian Father René Coste. I commend it to all.

Just as Freud, with a similar gift for forceful exaggeration, stripped away our illusions and revealed the power of sexual drives, so did Marx tear away our illusions and reveal the power and pervasive influence of the economic factor on almost every element of society's superstructure, including religion and the academy, not to mention our own personal illusions of disinterested altruism.

Despite the staggering ignorance of life that moved Marx to write that once "society regulates the general production," this will "make it possible for me to do one thing today and another tomorrow," his vision of a world that was free from alienation and exploitation has made a difference over the years. Today auto manufacturers like Volvo and Saab are breaking up the assembly line and allowing groups of workers to function as a team responsible for producing cars, rotating jobs and using all their skills instead of just one or two. Marx deserves some credit for that.

Saying that, however, or saying any number of nice things about Marx's contributions to human progress, is not the same as saying that Marx can be incorporated into Catholic thought as easily as Aristotle or can be fundamentally reconciled with Christianity.

LIBERATION THEOLOGY

Reconciling Marx and Christianity is one of the concerns of liberation theology, and most, if not all, liberation theologians would identify themselves as Christian socialists. Although it dates only from 1968, liberation theology has produced a voluminous literature and it is not appropriate to add much to that here. (The term "liberation theology" here refers only to that body of thought originating in Latin America, concerned purely with "class injustice" and, usually, favoring a socialist solution. We will not deal with liberation theologies that are concerned primarily with injustices that involve a) women,

b) racist or ethnic groups, c) the environment, or d) the arms race. A Christian socialist would share those concerns, but the solution to them may or may not be a socialist one.)

This theology is now being studied with enthusiasm all over the world in both Catholic and Protestant seminaries. Its dean and most persuasive practitioner is Gustavo Gutiérrez, Peruvian author of *A Theology of Liberation* (Orbis, 1973), which is still the seminal book on the subject. Other important representatives are Hugo Assmann who has worked mainly in Brazil and Costa Rica; Leonardo Boff in Brazil; Enrique Dussel in Argentina and Mexico; José Míguez Bonino, in Argentina; José Miranda in Mexico; Juan Luis Segundo in Uruguay; and Jon Sobrino, a Spanish Jesuit who has studied in America and Germany and has taught in El Salvador.

These theologians encompass a variety of emphases. What they have in common is a passionate commitment to the plight of the poor and an insistence that Christ came not simply to save souls but to save bodies as well, not simply to preach the kingdom of God in heaven but also the kingdom of God on earth. Matthew 25 (unless you feed, clothe and shelter the poor, you don't get to heaven) is of course a basic text, but more common are references to the Exodus, the archetypal liberation from slavery and oppression.

The latter-day Pharaohs are, locally, the military juntas and dictators, behind them the native capitalists, and behind these the international capitalists—most especially, those of the United States. There is no lack of evidence to support the thesis that the First World's most profitable export, the multinational corporation, is knee-deep in the sweat and blood of the Latin American worker and peasant, and the history of the Reagan years in the White House will add to that evidence.

Most, if not all, liberation theologians are Christian Marxists, casting aside the atheism and materialism, but accepting the class analysis, the dominance of the economic factor, tending to accept the necessity of violent revolution, tending to accept the possibility, if not probability, of some form of the dictatorship of the proletariat as a sort of necessary evil. I have not yet read anything by any of them that could be construed as critical of Fidel Castro and Cuba, although my reading has not been exhaustive. It is understandable that Castro would be admired, or at least respected, as one who delivered his people from a reactionary dictator stood up successfully to the Colossus of the North, and gave his people significant improvements in health, education and security of employment.

In a popular new book, *Fidel and Religion*, Castro tells his interviewer, Frei Betto, a Dominican priest from Brazil, that "absolute respect for the religious beliefs of citizens is established and guaranteed in our constitution."[87]

Sixteen pages earlier Castro had conceded, in response to Betto's question, that "those who believe in God" are excluded from membership in the Communist Party of Cuba. Since very few good jobs are available to those who don't belong to the Party, Castro's subsequent claim to "absolute respect for the religious beliefs of citizens" is farcical at best.

THE RATZINGER INSTRUCTIONS

In August 1984, and again in April 1986, liberation theology could be found on the front pages of the world's newspapers. Cardinal Joseph Ratzinger, the controversial prefect of the Vatican Congregation for the Doctrine of the Faith, issued two Instructions that either explicitly or implicitly criticized liberation theologians.

The second was more positive than the first. Long, repetitive, and abstract, it made one yearn for the day when seminaries will insist that degrees in theology will be awarded only to those who have passed a Good Writing course. But in effect it justified the *New York Times* headline: "Vatican Backs Struggle by Poor to End Injustice." The negative part followed in the subhead: "But Document Also Sees New Forms of Slavery" (April 6, 1986).

Neither Instruction quoted any liberation theologians. Less understandable was the failure to quote Marx, especially when Ratzinger, in the first Instruction, made such sweeping generalizations as this: "Atheism and the denial of the human person, his liberty and his rights are at the core of Marxist theory." A case could be made for the statement, but it should be made.

Another weakness of the first Instruction was the false impression it gave that absolute pacifism is part of Catholic teaching, that violence in pursuit of justice is never justified. Fortunately, this was corrected in the second Instruction. Someone must have reminded Ratzinger that Paul VI, true to the teaching of Aquinas, had written in 1967 that "a revolutionary uprising" could be justified "where there is manifest, long-standing tyranny which would do great damage to fundamental personal rights and dangerous harm to the common good of the country."[88]

In fact, any number of Latin American countries have, at one time or another, qualified as such tyrannies. One has to ask oneself this question: "If I lived in such a country and I were young and healthy, shouldn't I be out there in the bush with the guerrillas fighting to free the people from tyranny, hunger, and oppression?" A second question: "If I didn't have the courage to join the guerrillas, would I have a right to complain because those who did have the courage also had some Marxist-Leninist ideas which they proceeded to implement once the tyrant had been overthrown?"

Dom Helder Camara once said, "I would a thousand times rather be killed than to kill." A very Christian sentiment, also dependent on whether one has the courage to mean it, as I know the archbishop has. Karl Popper, sitting safely somewhere in England, once gave this excellent advice to revolutionaries:

The use of violence is justified only under a tyranny which makes reforms without violence impossible, and it should have only one aim— to bring about a state of affairs which makes reforms without violence possible.[89]

But then Popper did not live in Latin America. He did not wait half a lifetime for a reasonably honest election, then see a man elected who had promised "reforms without violence" and watch him either (1) sell out to the rich and the military or (2) if he meant business, be replaced by the military in behalf of the rich, often with the overt or covert assistance of the United States of America, leaving hunger and oppression precisely where they were before.

Small wonder that "reformism" and "compromise" and "democracy" (usually with the prefix "bourgeois") and "the United States of America" have become dirty words in Latin America and appear so in the writings of certain liberation theologians.

All this being cheerfully, or sadly, admitted, one must also admit that there are grounds on which to criticize liberation theology. Let us take the best of its representatives, Gustavo Gutiérrez. More than any other person he has been responsible for attracting the attention of us comfortable, complacent Christians of the North and forcing us to focus on the misery of the South. He has made us consider the extent to which we are responsible for that misery. He has also done more than any other person to place the question of Christian socialism on the agenda of the Catholic Church and of the whole modern world.

Some of his contributions will become evident if we examine one of his recent books, *The Power of the Poor in History*, a collection of essays revised and printed in English in 1983 (Orbis Books), but first published in Spanish between 1969 and 1979.

If one can hold on for the first 110 pages, which suffer from an excess of theory and a repetition of the same ideas in too many different ways, then rewards and revelations await the reader. On page 111 begins a thrilling exposition of one of the great moments of current religious history and a fascinating exercise in theological thrust and counterthrust. Gutiérrez begins by taking apart the Preparatory Document of the Conference of Latin American Bishops (CELAM) held at Puebla (Mexico) in 1979. This document was drawn up by the conference secretariat, controlled by the more conservative bishops behind CELAM president, now Cardinal, López Trujillo of Colombia. Its obvious purpose was to reverse the radical trend begun at the previous conference at Medellín (Colombia) in 1968. Medellín marked the debut of the liberation theologians, led by Gutiérrez, who served as *periti* (expert consultants) to the more progressive bishops. At Medellín the Latin American church, urged by Paul VI during the opening session to cultivate "freedom of the spirit with regard to riches,"[90] cut its ties to the rich and powerful and placed itself solidly beneath a banner emblazoned with the words "Preferential Option for the Poor." The conference made a historical break with the past when it coined the phrase "institutionalized violence" to describe the social, economic, and political structures of Latin America that doom millions to suffering and premature extinction, even when no guns or physical violence are employed.

In 1978 the conservative bishops tried, through such devices as the Preparatory Document, to change all that. Gutiérrez, in an article first published in

Peru in 1978 and reprinted in *The Power of the Poor in History,* pulls apart the honeyed ambiguities of the Document and, in masterful fashion, demonstrates how it would constitute a repudiation of the letter and spirit of Medellín. He then details how the Puebla conference rejected the conservative line and remained faithful to the letter and spirit of Medellín. Whatever slight leaning to the right occurred might be symbolized by the preferred use of "institutionalized injustice" instead of "institutionalized violence," although the latter expression did appear again.

Some liberation theologians, Catholics, talk and write as though Pope John Paul II were leader of the opposition. This hostile strain was evident at a Conference of Christians in Popular Liberation Struggles held in Barcelona in January 1984, a conference that was made up mainly of devotees of liberation theology from thirty different countries. Not so Gutiérrez in *The Power of the Poor in History.* He makes John Paul look very good, very much on the progressive side, and emphasizes repeatedly the agreements between the pope and liberation theology.

Of course he does not quote the pope's warning, in his address to the opening session at Puebla, that there are some for whom "the Kingdom of God is emptied of its full content and is understood in a rather secularist sense," as if it were to be realized "by mere changing of structures and social and political involvement."[91] This was interpreted as referring to certain liberation theologians. Gutiérrez does, however, in a note, quote the Puebla bishops in this significant passage of the final document:

> Fear of Marxism keeps many from facing up to the oppressive reality of liberal capitalism. One could say that some people, faced with the danger of one clearly sinful system, forget to denounce and combat the established reality of another equally sinful system (cf. Pope John Paul II's Homily in Zapopan) [92].[92]

So Marxism, ultimately, did not fare much better than capitalism. Even so, the liberation theologians who had assembled "outside the walls" (unlike Medellín they were excluded from the conference itself) greeted the end of the conference with glad relief, and "well past midnight their songs echoed through the streets . . . sounding suspiciously like a victory celebration."[93]

Yet the question of Marxism remained, and still remains. In 1976 Dow Kirkpatrick, a Methodist missionary in Peru, interviewed Gustavo Gutiérrez for *The Christian Century*:

KIRKPATRICK: What are the main principles of Marxism which liberation theology finds useful?

GUTIERREZ: I would make the question more precise. I don't believe that liberation theology needs to decide which aspects are important in

Marxism. Liberation theology does not evaluate the Christian and non-Christian in Marxism. It [Marxism] provides an analysis of the surrounding reality for Christians and non-Christians alike in the struggle for freedom.[94]

Gutiérrez, in the last sentence of his response, shows that he has decided that Marxist analysis is an important and valuable aspect of Marxism. But let us ignore the evasion and extract a few Marxist notions from his writings and consider whether, in fact, they do provide "an analysis of the surrounding reality" that might prove useful to anyone in "the struggle for freedom."

Here it is only fair to point out that the reality that surrounds Gutiérrez in a poor barrio of Lima (Peru) is not exactly the same as the reality that surrounds me, although I sit in the middle of a black ghetto that does, in fact, reveal some very similar kinds of poverty and oppression. Nevertheless, Gutiérrez frequently makes statements that apply not only to the Latin American reality, but to reality everywhere around the world, to this time and to all times. I will limit myself to such.

Chapter 10 of *A Theology of Liberation*, which qualifies as "the foundation stone" of liberation theology, contains a beautiful series of reflections on the gospel and particularly on the parable of the Good Samaritan and the vision of the Last Judgment (Matthew 25:31–46). This is Gutiérrez at his best. As I also tried to show in chapter 3 above, Gutiérrez concludes from the commandment to feed, clothe, and shelter Christ in the poor that a political obligation is involved:

Charity is today a "political charity," according to the phrase of Pius XII. [Actually, my point was that the obligation was one not merely of charity but of justice, at least for those who had superfluous goods, and that it was an obligation that was personal, political, *and* economic.— J.C.C.] Indeed, to offer food or drink in our day is a political action; it means the transformation of a society structured to benefit a few who appropriate to themselves the value of the work of others. This transformation ought to be directed toward a radical change in the foundation of society, that is, the private ownership of the means of production.[95]

What is this radical change? It is the *elimination* of private ownership. Lest we think that Gutiérrez may have changed his mind about this since he wrote the book in 1971 or saw it published in English in 1973, consider a statement from *The Power of the Poor* (1983):

[The] revolutionary struggle . . . questions the existing social order in its very roots and insists on the involvement of popular power in the construction of a society of genuinely equal and free persons. It insists on a society in which private ownership of the means of production is eliminated, because private ownership of the means of production allows a few to appropriate the fruits of the labor of many, and generates the division of society into classes, whereupon one class exploits another. It insists on a society in which, by appropriating the means of production, the masses appropriate their own political management as well, and definitive freedom, thereby occasioning the creation of a new social consciousness.[96]

The first sentence and the declarative part of the second sentence seem to refer to the revolutionary struggle in Latin America, but the rest of the second sentence, the rationale for all the rest, is clearly for Gutiérrez, as it was for Marx, a universal principle. The question has been raised as to whether Gutiérrez includes land under the term "means of production." One naturally assumes that he does. If he does not, he should make that clear without delay. Latin America's economy is primarily agricultural and most of the peasants are laborers on the plantations of the rich, or at best, tenant farmers. What they want is a piece of land of their own. There is no question about that. In none of Gutiérrez's books that have been translated into English, including the most recent ones, *We Drink from Our Own Wells* (Orbis, 1984) and *On Job* (Orbis, 1987), does he depart from the classical Marxist position stated in *The Power of the Poor* that private ownership of the means of production, presumably including land, should be "eliminated."

In a book he co-authored with Richard Shaull in 1977 Gutiérrez, in almost the same language, justifies the same goal: "private ownership of the means of production will be eliminated."[97] So it is evident that this is a basic, strongly held tenet of his political economy. Luis Segundo agrees on this point, or did in 1974, when he could see only two options, either capitalism, which he emphatically did not want, or a socialism that he defined as taking away from "individuals and private groups. . . the right to possess the means of production."[98] Since private groups would cover worker cooperatives, this means that Segundo was preferring the most rigid kind of Marxist communism to pre-Marxian and post-Marxian socialism, and could not even concede that the latter is an available option. Or, second possibility, perhaps he was just too ignorant of socialist history to know the difference.

Other liberation theologians disagree with these statements of Gutiérrez and Segundo, or so I am informed by Harvey Cox. He notes that the Boff brothers, Leonardo and Clodovis, have strongly supported the Brazilian bishops in their fight for a land reform program that would break up the great haciendas and give land to the peasants to have and to hold. He further reports that on May 10, 1986, Father Josima Morais Tavares was assassinated by a hired gunman for his activity on behalf of the Pastoral Land Commission, the Church's agency that is pressing the Brazilian government for action.

Cardinal Paolo Arns of Brazil, perhaps the most prestigious defender of liberation theologians, has also expressed disagreement in this interesting remark, which Michael Novak records from memory:

> One thing is clear. . . we must reject capitalism, which is based on selfishness. We believe in the right of workers to own their own land and to keep their profits for themselves, and therefore we incline toward socialism.[99]

So some confusion and division exists on a very important point. Let me pursue this point by referring to the founding convention of Christians for Socialism at Santiago (Chile) in 1972. This convention was composed largely of Latin American priests; its "final document" was written by a committee that included Gutiérrez and two other prominent liberation theologians—Hugo Assmann and an Italian priest, Giulio Girardi.[100] The document nowhere mentions the peasants, even as "farm laborers," but there are many references to "the proletariat" and "the working class." The large Chilean delegation came in with a report that does mention the peasantry, but mainly to rebuke them because they are "attached to the ownership of land," a value that is "part and parcel of the dominant bourgeois ideology." The document also rebukes "many segments of the proletariat" because "they have been led astray by a tradition of labor unionism that is *economics*-oriented" [emphasis added].[101] Heaven forbid.

Liberation theologians, including Gutiérrez, contrast their method, which, they say, proceeds inductively from "the praxis of the poor" toward theoretical conclusions, with the deductive methods of European theologians, who allegedly impose their theoretical conclusions from above onto the praxis of the poor.

I suggest that Gutiérrez is doing something similar himself. He is imposing the European abstractions, or conclusions, of Karl Marx onto the Latin American peasants, whose actual "praxis" cries out for land of their own and by no means wants to be submerged in some vast collective owned and operated by the state. Let us review some of those Marxist, European abstractions and conclusions.

You may recall that in chapter 9 in the section on Tillich I quoted at length from Marx to the effect that "wages and private property are identical" and that the only way the workers could ever enjoy "real human life" and rid themselves of alienation, estrangement, and "all the muck of ages" was to make a revolution that would do away with private property and the wage relationship on which it depended so that we could all "hunt in the morning, fish in the afternoon, rear cattle in the evening, criticize after dinner, just as [we] have a mind, without ever becoming hunter, fisherman, shepherd or critic."[102]

In the process, you see, division of labor, another alienating phenomenon, would also be done away with because, as Marx confidently assured us, "private property and division of labor are identical expressions."[103] Of course, Marx did not live to enjoy life in the Soviet Union or any other Marxist country where wages and division of labor exist very happily, or unhappily, without private property.

If all this sounds rather foolish, that is because it is, and we can't begin to understand why it is so foolish until we rip away the veil of illusion that has been draped over the figure of Karl Marx and has persuaded so many people that because he was a genius, because he could write so profoundly about Hegel and Feuerbach, because he could turn out good, readable histories of the Revolution of 1848 and the Paris Commune, because he could fill three unreadable volumes (*Capital*) with statistics about the horrors of English capitalism in the nineteenth century and murky theories about surplus value, sliding back and forth between a formula based on subsistence wages and another based on actual wages, theories that all together were not as enlightening as the medieval notion of just wage/just profit/just price, because finally— give him credit—he was consumed with a great, burning hatred of injustice and knew how to communicate it to others in a flaming phrase, that therefore— *therefore*—he *really knew* the life of men and women working in the world.

He did not. As I noted above, he suffered from Godwin's Disease, the intellectual equivalent of AIDS—a fatal deficiency of common sense. Intellectuals themselves have a word for it, "reductionism," but this only covers one part of the full, deadly pathology.

Take, for example, those absurdities about private property and wage labor. Marx, as far as we know, never worked for a wage in his life, but five minutes of careful thinking should have told him that the wage relationship is simply one more power relationship among thousands, not as common or as potentially abusive as the husband-wife relationship or the parent-child relationship, but very common and potentially very abusive, or subject to abuse.

(Personal note: I once argued briefly with Gutiérrez about the wage relationship. My Spanish is nonexistent and his English is good but not perfect, but my impression was that he was maintaining that the wage relationship is bad "of necessity," which would be a good, classical Marxist position. Afterwards, it occurred to me that I should have pointed out that his own professor-student relationship is a power relationship that is subject to abuse, but that it doesn't therefore follow that it must be abused of necessity any more than that the wage relationship must be abused of necessity.)

Actually, the wage relationship can be, and often has been, abused by *wage earners*, as in the case of powerful, shortsighted unions that force employers to pay wages that are unjustly high, thereby forcing consumers to pay unjust prices and sometimes forcing employers out of business and union members into unemployment.

Let us concede that in the case of Marx in England in the nineteenth century, or Gutiérrez in Peru in the twentieth, the abuse of wage relationships by employers was and is probably so common that the natural temptation is to believe that if one could do away with it, injustice and alienation might perish from the earth. But how? By making the state the universal employer? No chance.

Jean Jaures, the great French non-Marxist socialist who was assassinated in 1914, was sensible enough to see that. He wrote:

Delivering men to the state, conferring upon the government the effective direction of the nation's work, giving it the right to direct all the functions of labor, would be to give a few men a power compared to which that of the Asiatic despots is nothing, since their power stops at the surface of the society and does not regulate economic life.[104]

Michael Harrington put it more succinctly when he reminded us that "any fool can nationalize."[105]

Of course, the individual employer or corporation could be replaced with a workers' cooperative, and the workers, on the basis of one-person-one-vote instead of the capitalists' one-share-one-vote, could elect the board of directors. This is a better idea than state ownership because it is real economic democracy. The best short definition of socialism is the extension of democratic process from the political to the economic sphere. Then we must quickly remind ourselves that if the cooperative is to survive, the board of directors must appoint a competent manager who has *power* to insist on performance by the workers. And the cooperative must pay a regular *wage* to the members, in addition to their sharing any profits (or losses). Finally we should consider that a cooperative, if it is a true cooperative and not a creature of the state, is a form of *private property* and considerably more private than a corporation owned by stockholders who usually don't care at all about the company beyond the size and frequency of its dividends. True, it is not *individual* private property. It cannot be bequeathed to one's children. It is *socialized* private property.

CLASS STRUGGLE—PRO AND CON

We come now to the question of class struggle, an aspect of liberation theology that particularly disturbs Cardinal Ratzinger. Gutiérrez points out that class struggle has been and remains a historical reality. This is true. From the beginning of time there has been struggle between the rich and the poor in economic, political, and social aspects of life, between workers and unjust employers, rich or poor, even between workers and just employers when disputing over conditions of employment. One of the weaknesses of Ratzinger's first Instruction is its dismissal of the reality too quickly and lightly in its eagerness to get at the Marxist doctrine behind the words "class struggle." Ratzinger writes, "it cannot be taken as the equivalent of 'severe social conflict,' in an empirical sense."[106] Ah, but it is so taken and more careful consideration should have been given to this confusion.

Marx and Gutiérrez go further than the notion of class struggle as a historical reality—much further. Ratzinger missed the boat when he summarized the Marxist notion of class struggle as the claim that if a person "belongs to the objective class of the rich he is primarily a class enemy to be fought."[107] The Marxist doctrine, shared by some liberation theologians and, apparently, by Gutiérrez as well, is not that such persons are class enemies if they belong to the rich, but that they are class enemies if they are *employers*, since the employer-employee relationship is of necessity a bad, alienating, enslaving, exploitive relationship. By limiting the class struggle to the rich-vs.-the-non-rich, Ratzinger conceded far too much to Marx and liberation theology. After all, Jesus had a very poor opinion of the rich. Remember the camel and the needle's eye.

No, Marx did not merely exclude the rich from his secular heaven. He excluded all employers, rich or poor. And this exclusion is a far, far more difficult position to reconcile with Christianity than exclusion of the rich—not simply because it flies in the face of the whole Judeo-Christian tradition, but even more because it flies in the face of common sense and everyday experience. For common sense and everyday experience have taught us that employers and employees do, yes, have important things in conflict, but they also have important things in common and they do, yes, frequently work out a just relationship that is abused by neither side, no more nor less than any other power relationship is abused in this permanently imperfect world where live and work permanently imperfect human beings.

Why do I say that Gutiérrez *apparently* shares Marx's view of class struggle? I am thinking particularly, not just of the quotations cited above about the elimination of all private employers, but of pages 272–279 of *A Theology of Liberation*, a section entitled "Christian Brotherhood and Class Struggle" and of several reference notes on pages 284 and 285, notably nos. 51, 56, and 57.

Perhaps the most significant passage is the following (p. 277), which quotes Louis Althusser, the hard-line French Communist:

> Understood in this way, the unity of the Church is *rightly* [emphasis added] considered by Althusser as a myth which must disappear if the Church is to be "reconverted" to the service of the workers in the class struggle: "For this to happen," he asserts, "it would be necessary that the myth of the 'Christian community' disappear, for it prevents the recognition of the division of society into classes and the recognition of class struggle. One can foresee serious divisions occurring in the Church precisely around the theme of the *recognition* and the *understanding* of social classes and the class struggle, the recognition and the understanding of a reality which is incompatible with the *peculiarly religious myth* of the 'community of the faithful' and the (catholic) universality of the Church" [emphasis in the original].

Insofar as Cardinal Ratzinger, however imperfectly, is saying that the *Marxist myth* of class struggle reflected in that passage is indeed incompatible with the *reality* of "the community of the faithful," I cannot denounce him but can only agree. For what Althusser and Gutiérrez are saying is that the private employer-employee relationship, as contrasted with the public employer-employee relationship, is so intrinsically evil and sinful that the employer cannot qualify for admission to the community of the faithful. This is, quite simply, an irrational statement.

In 1984 Gutiérrez responded to Ratzinger's first Instruction in an article entitled *Teología y ciencias sociales* (Theology and Social Sciences). He writes this:

> The present painful situation, which forces us to see some as our adversaries, does not absolve us from loving them, quite to the contrary. For this reason, when we speak of social opposition, we are referrring to social groups, classes, races, and cultures, but not to persons.[108]

You cannot, however, separate classes or groups from the persons who make them up. Or better, you cannot engage in a justified struggle unless you are struggling against persons who are unjust or, despite good will, caught in an unjust "painful situation." And what is that situation, in Gutiérrez' view? From all his arguments and premises one can only conclude that it is the wage relationship, the employer-employee relationship. If the conclusion is wrong, then Gutiérrez should make it clear without delay. If right, he is standing on very soggy ground indeed.

That the conclusion is correct would follow from the more explicit view of one of the more impressive exponents of liberation theology, Enrique Dussel:

> When you work for another person and come to depend not on work offered up to God but on work demanded by an employer for your daily bread, a kind of idolatry takes place. The institutionalization of this employee-employer relationship has resulted in the domination of one over another. Such domination is sin.[109]

Contrast this with St. Paul in Romans 13:2: "Let every person be subject to the governing authorities. For there is no authority except from God." Isn't this also "domination of one over another"? Life is full of legitimate dominations, parent over child, teacher over student. Are these all of necessity sinful? Domination is not sin. The abuse of domination is sin. Since human nature is weak and domination, like Lord Acton's power, tends to corrupt, it is better that in the work situation there should be as little domination as possible. That is why the worker cooperative is a better situation than the employer-employee situation, but even in a cooperative there must be some form of domination. Otherwise anarchy, inefficiency, failure. It is significant that Gutiérrez dreams of, and apparently believes in the possiblility of, here in this world, not in heaven, "a society that exercises no kind of coercion, from whatever source."[110]

This is indeed dream stuff, the same dream stuff that addled the brains of Marx and Engels and persuaded them that, once the private ownership of the means of production had been eliminated, human nature would be changed as if by magic and the state would "die out"[111] and we would see "a society that exercises no kind of coercion, from whatever source." Do we need another Reinhold Niebuhr to disabuse us of that dangerous dream?

GUTIÉRREZ AND DEMOCRACY

One can understand why Gutiérrez and most liberation theologians are cynical about "bourgeois democracy" as practiced in the United States, or, more to the point, practiced *on* our neighbors to the south. Gutiérrez, now and then, expresses his approval of "real" or "genuine" democracy, but he nowhere, to my knowledge, explains precisely what he means. The frequent putdowns for "reform" and "compromise" are not reassuring. Reform and compromise are of the essence of genuine democracy. In truth, they are of the essence of life. It is all very thrilling and *macho* to call for "revolution, revolution," but after the revolution, what?

The Final Document of the founding convention of Christians for Socialism, which Gutiérrez helped write, contains this remarkable paragraph:

The revolutionary process is in full swing in Latin America. Many Christians have made a personal commitment to it. But many more Christians, imprisoned in mental inertia and categories that are suffused with bourgeois ideology, regard this process fearfully and insist on taking the impossible pathway of reformism and modernization. The Latin American process is all-embracing and one in character. We Christians do not have a peculiar political approach of our own to offer, and we do not wish to have such an approach. The realization that the process is all-embracing and one in character makes us comrades, uniting all those who are committed to the revolutionary struggle.[112]

I would respond: "But, comrades, you do have a peculiar political approach of your own to offer. You have just expressed it: Down with reform and up with revolution. You have an approach. What you do not have is some clear idea of where you are going, other than toward the same beautiful vision of freedom and justice that even the most pro-capitalist Christians profess. (Michael Novak has just recently published a book entitled *Freedom with Justice*.) Once into politics, which is where you are obviously determined to be, the only responsible, the only intellectually competent course is to tell the voters exactly what you have in mind. Otherwise, you should stay out of politics."

The conclusion sounds harsh. The conclusion is harsh, something like the harshness of a jealous lover. I am jealous, envious, of Karl Marx because he has won the affections of a lot of learned, eloquent, dedicated Christians whom I would like to see dedicated to a brand of socialism that is more rational, realistic, and unambiguously democratic.

Gustavo Gutiérrez is certainly one of the most learned, eloquent, and dedicated of them all—in spite of all. And in spite of all, all the arguments, debates, and distinctions raised by critics like myself, there remain certain incontestable facts and certain incontestable principles of our Christian faith that cry out for action. These are expressed more sharply than I could express them by Otto Maduro, a sociologist of religion from Venezuela, in the April 1987, issue of *Maryknoll*, the magazine of that society of missionaries that has devoted so much time, thought, energy, and sacrifice to consideration of those facts and principles:

> In the years after Medellín nearly 100 clergy and religious . . . have been killed for their commitment to the Latin American poor. . . . In the same period nearly 1,000 clergy and religious were imprisoned, tortured or exiled. But that's only the tip of the iceberg because they are people covered by the media. No fewer than 100,000 lay people have been murdered: peasant lay leaders and parishioners who were beginning to understand their faith in a new, active way . . .
>
> Today, as every day, 35,000 children under five in the world will die of malnutrition. Matthew, in chapter 25, says we must give food to the hungry, water to the thirsty, clothing to the naked. If we read Matthew and know that today 35,000 children will starve, can we honestly think that Christ's call has nothing to do with our responsibility to stop this suffering? There is no other commitment more important than saving those lives when the earth is filled with wealth. Reading the Bible among the oppressed makes us ask if we can honestly say that Christians have no responsibility in the face of military spending, death by malnutrition and the call of Jesus to commit ourselves to the hungry, thirsty and homeless of the earth. There is an absolutely urgent connection. The call doesn't come from liberation theologies, but from Christ. Liberation theology attempts to articulate that call.[113]

That is why, despite the legitimate concerns raised by his *peritus*, Cardinal Ratzinger, Pope John Paul II in April, 1986, weighed the positive against the negative and wrote the Brazilian bishops that "we are convinced that the theology of liberation is not only timely but useful and necessary." That is why both Ratzinger and the Pope have given their blessing to the Christian base communities which, inspired largely by liberation theology, have proliferated throughout Latin America and proved once again that Canon Cardijn's technique of small groups and See-Judge-Act can be a powerful engine for realization of the Gospel.

In recent years, as more Latin American countries have freed themselves from military dictatorships and revealed to their people, and to liberation theologians, the advantages *even* of "bourgeois democracy," some of those theologians seem to have changed their minds somewhat on the subject of democracy Western-style. Students as opposite in their sympathies as Paul Sigmund and Michael Novak agree on this. More explicit expression of this change would help in turn to change the negative perception of liberation theology that is currently held by such secular socialists as Irving Howe, who once said,

> The notion that democracy, even in its most corrupted forms, is anything but a precious human conquest, that it's just a facade for the rule of the oppressors: this serious people can no longer believe.[114]

Unfortunately, Howe was wrong. Serious people in Latin America and many countries of the Third World do still believe it. The fact that more are coming to disbelieve it is reason for hope.

THE FRANKFURT DECLARATION

I have emphasized the importance of the Frankfurt Declaration of the newly reconstituted Socialist International in 1951. Just as the popes and bishops of the sixties, seventies, and eighties have come to recognize and acknowledge the change in the thought and action of socialists over the years, so the democratic socialists, even earlier, came to recognize and acknowledge the change in the thought and actions of Catholics. The united front of Catholics and socialists in the European Resistance to the Nazis, and after the war to the Stalinists, doubtless was important in preparing the ground for this development.

For the first time a Socialist International clearly distinguished socialism from Marxism, as follows:

> Socialism is an international movement which does not demand a rigid uniformity of approach. Whether Socialists build their faith on Marxist or other methods of analyzing society, whether they are inspired by religious or humanitarian principles, they all strive for the same goal—a system of social justice, better living, freedom and world peace.[115]

The acceptance of this distinction obviously came hard, for only three paragraphs before, in a repudiation of communism which *should* be most welcome to Catholics, the framers of the Declaration apparently forgot themselves and wrote this:

> Communism falsely claims a share in the Socialist tradition. In fact, it has distorted that tradition beyond recognition. It has built up a rigid theology which is incompatible with the critical spirit of Marxism.[116]

The repudiation is fine, but the implication that Marxism is the major ground on which socialists repudiate communism is certainly not consistent with the distinction made a few paragraphs later.

I would submit that, except for the momentary lapse noted above and possibly a slightly heavier emphasis on public ownership, there is no *essential* difference between the Frankfurt Declaration and the economic and political preferences expressed by Catholic popes and bishops, first by Leo XIII and then more clearly and surely by those of the twentieth century. Consider the following statements from the Frankfurt Declaration:

- Without freedom there can be no Socialism. Socialism can be achieved only through democracy.
- Every dictatorship, wherever it may be, is a danger to the freedom of all nations and thereby to the peace of the world.
- Socialist planning can be achieved by various means. The structure of the country concerned must decide the extent of public ownership and the forms of planning to apply.
- Public ownership can take the form of the nationalization of existing private concerns or the creation of new public concerns, municipal or regional enterprise, consumers' or producers' cooperatives. [The inclusion of cooperatives under "public ownership" is another slip. A cooperative is a form of private ownership.]
- Socialist planning does not presuppose public ownership of all the means of production. It is compatible with the existence of private ownership in important fields, for instance in agriculture, handicraft, retail trade and small and middle-sized industries. [Most U.S. enterprises would fall in these categories.]
- Socialist planning does not mean that all economic decisions are placed in the hands of the government or central authorities. Economic power should be decentralized wherever this is compatible with the aims of planning.
- All citizens should prevent the development of bureaucracy in public and private industry by taking part in the process of production through their organizations or by individual initiative. The workers must be associated democratically with the direction of their industry.[117]

Note in these last two paragraphs the emphasis on several values central to the notion of "subsidiarity," which popes and bishops have promoted over the years and which Richard Goodwin expressed perhaps most succinctly in the *New Yorker* some years ago: "The general rule should be to transfer power to [or retain it in] the smallest unit consistent with the scale of the problem."[118]

THE RESPONSIBILITY OF THE UNITED STATES

"The United States represents the most powerful single factor in the international economic equation."[119] This sentence is from the U.S. bishops' pastoral message, *Economic Justice for All: Catholic Social Teaching and the U.S. Economy*. These statements precede and succeed the above quotation:

In short, the international economic order (like many aspects of our own economy) is in crisis; the gap between rich and poor countries and between rich and poor people within countries is widening. . . . But even as we speak of crisis, we see an opportunity for the United States to launch a worldwide campaign for justice and economic rights to match the still incomplete, but encouraging, political democracy we have achieved in the United States with so much pain and sacrifice.

How much the United States is responsible for poverty in the Third World is a subject of endless debate. The U.S. bishops, after long, painstaking consultation with many experts on all sides of the question, have concluded that U.S. responsibility is major, if not as totally damning as some maintain.

American Catholics—Christians of every denomination—are no more immune to considerations of self-interest than Americans of other or no religious faiths. The difficulty of persuading Americans to pay higher taxes and cut "defense" expenditures in order to do more for the poor of this and other countries—this needs no demonstration. The bishops do far better than I could to make the argument. Let me cite instead a clearer, cleaner example from the past—a real-life parable—of how greedy, shortsighted policies on both the national and international front can ultimately be devastating to a nation's self-interest.

By 1924 the punitive Treaty of Versailles had reduced Germany to a state of political chaos and financial bankruptcy. Hitler's Beer Hall *Putsch* of the year before had been stopped and Hitler imprisoned, but his movement was growing rapidly amid the chaos. Brought to their senses, the Allies forsook revenge and came to Germany's rescue in 1924 with the Dawes Plan, named for the American banker Charles Dawes, who was subsequently elected vice-president under Calvin Coolidge. The Dawes Plan loosened the vise of reparations that the Allies had tightened at Versailles, made available a large loan (mostly U.S. money), and led to the evacuation of the Ruhr Valley by the French. With such a fresh start, the German economy rebounded and U.S. investments poured in. By 1928 the country had recovered its equilibrium and the Nazis, who had won thirty-two seats in the Reichstag in 1924, had only twelve in 1928. However, in the same year, U.S. investors, dazzled by the "boom" profits that followed on the laissez-faire policies of Coolidge and Hoover, began to withdraw their money from Germany to invest it in the United States. The following year, of course, came "the bust," the Great Crash of 1929, and the beginnings of a worldwide depression, which sent Germany into a second economic tailspin.

Result: The Nazis increased their representation in the Reichstag from twelve in 1928 to two hundred thirty in 1932, and the following year, in coalition with fifty-two deputies from the conservative Nationalists, gained a clear majority and forced Von Hindenburg to name Hitler chancellor. So began the introduction and observance of the Nazi Program, of which Point 4 read,

"No Jew can be regarded as a fellow countryman." Point 24 provided for freedom of religion, but only if the religion did not "offend against the moral or ethical sense of the Germanic race," which Point 4 had already made certain that any truly Christian religion must.

Consider further: Every honest economist *should* agree that those laissez-faire, supply-side policies of the U.S. government during the 1920s led not only to the withdrawal of American capital from Germany in 1928 but also to the collapse of the U.S. economy and that of Germany, not to mention other countries all over the world. The U.S. government, elected by the American people, a people then even more "Christian" than it is now, did everything it could to encourage investors and producers: little or no taxation, no protection for union organization, no charge on profits for social security, unemployment compensation, welfare, health insurance. All supply-side, no demand-side, no need-side. It is therefore reasonable to ask ourselves: Did we, the American people, not contribute significantly to the rise of Adolf Hitler, World War II, and the Holocaust? I think of St. Paul's reminder: "We are all members one of another" (Rom. 12:5). The world is one body; if gangrene is allowed to develop in one limb, all the limbs and the whole body may sicken and die.

One is also reminded that Charles Frankel's comment about Rousseau's *Social Contract*, transposed, fits the Bible, the question of Christian socialism, *and* the relationship of the United States to its own poor and to other nations of the world: The Bible "is an incitement to revolution because it does what a revolutionary book has to do: it joins justice and utility, and shows people that their interest and their duty are on the same side."[120] Or, "Seek ye first the Kingdom of God and his justice, and all these things shall be added unto you" (Matt. 6:33). Conversely, neglect it and all these things shall be taken away.

"THE RIGHT REVEREND NEW DEALER"

Of course, what is meant by "revolution" remains a question to discuss and thus while away the hours in academia. The U.S. Catholic bishops do not use such words, but their splendid pastoral on the U.S. economy says much the same thing in more careful language. The bishops did not, of course, create Catholic teaching from scratch. Not only did the bishops have the authoritative documents emanating from Vatican City, they also had a rich tradition tailored to American conditions. John A. Ryan, as noted, was a major architect of that tradition. Richard Ely hailed Ryan's first book, *The Living Wage* (1906), as "the first attempt in the English language to elaborate what may be called a Roman Catholic system of political economy."[121] By 1909 Father Ryan was criticizing Father Cathrein's *Socialism and Christianity* on the ground that Catholics were

> so preoccupied refuting socialism and defending the present order, that they go to the opposite extreme, understating the amount of truth in the

claims of the Socialists and overstating the rights of property and the advantages of the present system.[122]

In 1910, the *Catholic Encyclopedia* printed Ryan's article on labor unions, which justified, under certain circumstances, the use of force by pickets in preventing "scabs" from taking their jobs. (In the 1930s Ryan, as well as Bishop Gallagher of Detroit, came to the defense of the sitdown strikes in situations where workers were entirely dependent on their jobs and employers could afford to pay decent wages but would not.) His article went beyond labor legislation to such advanced proposals as public ownership of public utilities, mines, and forests, control of monopolies—either by breaking them up or fixing their prices—progressive income and inheritance taxes. This was twenty-one years before *Quadragesimo Anno*. The *Program of Social Reconstruction* that Ryan wrote for the bishops in 1919 anticipated Roosevelt's New Deal by fifteen or more years, as well as the bills enacting protection for the workers' right to organize, minimum wages, social security, abolition of child labor, public housing, unemployment, and health insurance. The program also urged that "more consideration than it has yet received [be given] to government competition with monopolies that cannot be restrained by the ordinary anti-trust laws."[123] In short, public ownership. This is from Ryan's autobiography, *Social Doctrine in Action*:

> Early in the 1920's I entered two organizations which have done valiant service in the movement for public ownership of public utilities, namely, the National Popular Government League and the Public Ownership League of America. For many years I have been a member of the executive committee of the former and a vice-president of the latter. My prominence in these organizations exposed me occasionally to the epithet "socialist."[124]

In response to the epithet, Ryan later quoted *Quadragesimo Anno*'s statement that "certain forms of property must be reserved to the state." An interesting angle to this controversy is that Carl Thompson, president of the Public Ownership League, was a Protestant minister who had been a contributing editor of *The Christian Socialist* and, during World War I, secretary of the Information Department of the Socialist Party. Father Ryan did not seem to care.

Several of the Program's proposals were not part of the New Deal:

> Labor ought gradually to receive greater representation in . . . the control of processes and machinery, nature of product, engagement and dismissal of employees, hours of work, rates of pay, bonuses, welfare work, shop discipline, relations with trade unions.[125]

The majority [of the workers] must somehow become owners, at least in part, of the instruments of production . . . through cooperative productive societies and co-partnership arrangements. . . . These ends will have to be reached before we can have a thoroughly efficient system of production.[126]

The last two sentences of the 1919 Bishops' Program are these:

The employer has a right to get a reasonable living out of his business, but he has no right to interest on his investment until his employees have obtained at least living wages. This is the human and Christian, in contrast to the purely commercial and pagan, ethics of industry.[127]

THE U.S. BISHOPS' PASTORAL MESSAGE

Rarely, if ever, has any group—Catholic, Protesant, Jewish, or atheist—made such a thorough, exhaustive study of the U.S. economy as did the five Catholic bishops, headed by Archbishop Rembert Weakland of Milwaukee, who wrote the pastoral message *Economic Justice for All: Catholic Social Teaching and the U.S. Economy*. The long process of consultation began on November 15, 1981, and the fourth draft was approved five years later on November 13, 1986, by a vote of 225 to 9 at a meeting of all U.S. bishops.

The five bishops had a staff of five, seven regular consultants, and listened to 148 experts over the five years, during which they made public three preliminary drafts and read thousands of pages of good and bad advice on all three. The experts included theologians, economists, corporate executives (18), top representatives of the Jewish community (6) and the Protestant community (8), representatives of the Third World (15), including eight bishops from Latin American countries.

The footnotes alone comprise one of the most complete, up-to-date bibliographies ever assembled on both Catholic social teaching and the U.S. economy.

The painstaking and open process, so rare in the history of any religious denomination but particularly rare in Catholic history, is one of the reasons the pastoral merits the rating of "magnificent." Before I mention a few disappointing features, let me list some of the positive features.

From the start the bishops place themselves firmly in favor of "the preferential option for the poor." Using that perspective, they are extremely critical of U.S. capitalism. They cite its successes, but also its "failures—some of them massive and ugly" (3). (The numbers after quotations here represent paragraphs in the Nov. 27, 1986, issue of *Origins*, the national Catholic documentary service.) Among these they highlight the fact that 8 million Americans cannot find jobs and another 6 million have either given up looking or can only find temporary or part-time work. They conclude, "The acceptance of present unemployment rates would have been unthinkable twenty years ago. It should be regarded as intolerable today" (152).

Another massive and ugly failure, in the bishops' opinion: in this richest of all nations more than 33 million Americans are poor by the Reagan government's official definition and "poverty has increased dramatically during the last decade" (171). They conclude: "That so many people are poor in a nation as rich as ours is a social and moral scandal that we cannot ignore" (16).

The bishops note that "today one in every four American children under the age of six, and one in every two black children under six, are poor" and that "the number of children in poverty rose by 4,000,000 over the decade between 1973-1983, with the result that there are now more poor children in the United States than at any time since 1965" (176).

By contrast with these shocking figures the bishops emphasize that in 1983 the 2 percent of U.S. families whose annual income was over $125,000 also possessed 54 percent of all financial assets, exclusive of homes and other real estate. And further: "In 1984 the bottom 20 percent of American families received only 4.7 percent of the total income of the nation . . . [whereas the top 20 percent] received 42.9 percent . . . the highest share since 1948" (184).

A fascinating conclusion follows from these figures. We often hear it said that if we were to take the riches of the rich and spread them among the poor, the problem of poverty would not be solved. Totally false. These figures show that if we were to take only one quarter of the income of the richest 20 percent, not to mention their wealth, and spread it among the poorest 20 percent, the income of the poor would be increased by 114 percent, more than doubled. And that money would be spent mostly for food, clothing, and housing, which in turn would employ many more people than if a few rich people spent the money for oil paintings, rare coins, precious jewels, and mink coats.

The bishops do not draw this conclusion, but they do conclude that these massive, ugly failures of the U.S. economy (capitalism) do not meet "the converging demands of [the] three forms of basic justice" (73). These forms, traditional in Catholic social theory, are commutative justice, as between private individuals or groups; distributive justice, involving "the allocation of income, wealth and power in society [evaluated] in light of its effects on persons whose basic material needs are unmet" (70); and social justice, which "implies that persons have an obligation to be active and productive participants in the life of society and that society has a duty to enable them to participate in this way" (71).

There are too many good things in the pastoral to detail in the space available here. Most of them are applications to the U.S. of principles enshrined in Old and New Testaments, patristic writings, the writings of Thomas Aquinas, of Vatican Council II, and recent encyclicals. The skewed priorities of the American people and the American government are highlighted by the bishops as they note that while children go hungry and die "the hundreds of billions of dollars spent by our nation each year on the arms race create a massive drain on the U.S. economy as well as a very serious 'brain drain' " (148).

"And beyond our own shores, the reality of 800 million people living in absolute poverty and 450 million malnourished or facing starvation casts an ominous shadow" (4) while "the United States, once the pioneer in foreign aid, is almost last among the seventeen industrialized nations . . . in percentage of gross national product devoted to aid" (266), budgeting "more than twenty times as much for defense as for foreign assistance. . . . Nearly two-thirds of the latter took the form of military assistance" (289).

TWO DISAPPOINTMENTS

The first draft of the letter included this great passage:

In order to create a new kind of political democracy [the founders of our nation] were compelled to develop ways of thinking and political institutions which had never existed before. . . . We believe the time has come for a similar experiment in economic democracy: the creation of an order that guarantees the minimum conditions of human dignity in the economic sphere for every person."

Not that there was anything very radical about this, or novel. After all, way back in 1797, Albert Gallatin, secretary of the treasury under Thomas Jefferson, said this: "The democratic process on which this nation was founded should not be restricted to the political process, but should be applied to the industrial operation as well." Nor would this appeal be surprising to anyone who followed Catholic social teaching from Leo XIII's defense of trade unions, the first step in economic democracy, through Pius XI's vocational groups or industry councils, which the U.S. bishops hailed in 1948 as "a Christian and American type of economic democracy," all the way up to 1981 and John Paul II's call for a new system in which "on the basis of his work each person is entitled to consider himself a part-owner of the great workbench at which he is working with every one else."

After the first draft was made public in November 1984, the McNeil-Lehrer TV program invited Archbishop Weakland and Michael Novak to discuss it. Michael Novak is a Catholic layman and prolific author who was once a progressive Democrat, but eventually became a sort of house theologian for the Reagan administration, a bastion of the American Enterprise Institute (a conservative think-tank), and organizer of a "lay commission of Catholics" (consisting mainly of corporate executives), which issued a counter-pastoral in defense of capitalism even before the bishops had published their first draft. In spite of all this, Novak was the first "expert" invited by the bishops in 1981 and he appeared before them twice more, more times than any other invitee.

During the TV interview McNeil pressed Novak for specific criticisms of the draft. Finally Novak singled out the above appeal for "economic democracy" and added, "That's an Olof Palme phrase." By this he meant a *socialist* phrase, because the late Olof Palme was then the Socialist prime minister of Sweden and a leader of the Socialist International.

The phrase "economic democracy" has been used affirmatively by so many Catholic theorists and authorities, including, as noted, the U.S bishops in 1948, that Novak could just as well have said, "That's a Catholic phrase." Nevertheless, as this book and this chapter have taken pains to emphasize, the phrase is in fact, since the Frankfurt Manifesto of 1951, a good working, short definition of democratic socialism.

"Socialism" is still a dirty word in the United States. Perhaps the fear that this dirty word might be used to besmirch the pastoral moved the bishops' committee to strike the phrase. The second and final draft read: "We believe the time has come for a similar experiment in securing economic rights, . . ." (95). Of course, if the experiment is similar, then it must, by definition, be a system of economic democracy. In fact, the final draft also says this: "A new experiment in bringing democratic ideals to economic life calls for serious exploration of ways to develop new patterns of partnership among those working in individual firms and industries" (298). The bishops also express a favorable view of the most perfect form of economic democracy, "cooperative ownership of the firm by all who work within it" (300).

Nevertheless, I can't help thinking that the deletion of a perfectly honorable, praiseworthy phrase in paragraph 95 represented a failure of nerve on the bishops' part. Just because Michael Novak can publish another book every year, that's no reason why he should be allowed to dictate to the U.S. bishops. It's not good for his self-image, or for theirs.

The irony of all this is that the incident does furnish supporting evidence for the title of this chapter. Socialism and Catholicism, or at least Catholic social teaching, *are* converging, embarrassing as this fact may be for both parties.

Second disappointment: The bishops failed to carry through to the logical conclusion of their argument for full employment, which they define, so accurately, as "the foundation of a just economy" (136). And in another place: "Work with adequate pay for all who seek it is the primary means for achieving basic justice in our society" (73).

True to the long history of Catholic social theory, the bishops insist on the responsibility of government to protect the individual's right to a job wherever and whenever private industry is unable to do so. Their pastoral is full of factual evidence that private industry is unable and/or unwilling to provide decent jobs at decent pay for all those who want and need them. They insist further that

> government should assume a positive role in generating employment and establishing fair labor practices, in guaranteeing the provision and maintenance of the economy's infrastructure, such as roads, bridges, harbors, public means of communication and transport.

They might have added health and educational facilities, parks, recreation and a dozen other services necessary to a decent society. And further:

Government may levy the taxes necessary to meet these responsibilities, and citizens have a moral obligation to pay those taxes. The way society responds to the needs of the poor through its public policies is the litmus test of its justice or injustice (123).

The bishops quote John Paul II's great statement made during his visit to Canada in 1984:

The needs of the poor take priority over the desires of the rich; the rights of workers over the maximization of profits; the preservation of the environment over uncontrolled industrial expansion; production to meet social needs over production for military purposes" (94).

They appeal to a sensible regard for self-interest when they note that every percentage point of unemployment means a $40 billion increase in the federal deficit. All this being so, and so well said, it is cause for bafflement that the bishops cannot bring themselves to write the words, "Government must be the employer of last resort" and the further words, "If all of us who can afford it have to pay higher taxes in order to guarantee this most basic of human rights, the right to work, then we must pay higher taxes. It is the only Christian, the only human, the only just and honorable thing to do."

Ockham's Razor is relevant here. William of Ockham, the fourteenth-century Franciscan, and Duns Scotus first began to twist Catholic theories of property away from the sound doctrine of Aquinas. William of Ockham did, however, leave us a valuable piece of intellectual property: his razor. This was the principle of logic that there is no point in looking for a complex explanation of any phenomenon if a simple explanation is adequate.

The simple, adequate explanation of unemployment in the United States is that the more affluent citizens of this country are unwilling to do away with it, even though they can easily afford to do so, and plenty of good, meaningful, necessary work needs to be done.

Once we abandon the simple explanation and start looking for more complex explanations we are on a slippery slope that ends in a morass, a swamp of argument and excuses, where slither and sport all manner of experts talking of fiscal policy, monetary policy, defense policy, OPEC prices, capital flight, free trade, protectionism, inflation, deflation, stagflation, drought, and sun spots. It is not that we do not need experts. We need more and better ones. They have vital roles to play in making it possible for private industry to create and maintain as many jobs as possible. But first things first. Putting the unemployed to work should come first.

THE CASE OF CANADA

I have already referred to the excellent study by Gregory Baum on the relations between Catholicism and socialism in Canada (*Catholics and Cana-*

dian Socialism, Paulist Press, 1980). Since socialism in Canada is a stronger reality in the country's political life than it is in the United States and since about half Canada's population is Catholic (overwhelmingly so in French-speaking Quebec), this study is well worth reading for anyone who wants a real-life history of the action and reaction of these two major movements in an industrialized democracy of the modern world.

For most of its history Canadian politics has been dominated by the Liberal and Conservative parties, roughly analogous to the U.S. Democrats and Republicans. In 1944 a socialist party, the Cooperative Commonwealth Federation (CCF) won major elections in Canada's Western province of Saskatchewan and became the official opposition in three other provinces: British Columbia, Manitoba, and Ontario. It appeared to be on the way to replacing one of the older parties as the second or even first most powerful party of Canada. Its national progress was halted largely because of Catholic opposition. As of 1987, its successor, the New Democratic Party (NDP), held 30 seats in the Canadian parliament, compared to 40 for the Liberals and 212 for the Conservatives.

Socialism in Canada was mainly British and Protestant in its origins, and only tertially Marxist. When socialism first began to grow in the country at the turn of the century, its most successful organizer was George Wrigley, a Christian socialist.

The CCF was founded in 1932 at Calgary in Alberta, a merger of independent labor parties from the western provinces and some radical farmers' organizations. The farmers were responsible for a non-Marxist insistence that the program include "security of tenure for the farmer on his use-land,"[128] that is, the land that the farmer actually farmed. They weren't so concerned about absentee landlords.

The leading personality in those years was J. S. Woodsworth, a former Methodist minister. He was an intelligent, charismatic figure, who had founded one of the labor parties in Winnipeg, Manitoba, and had represented a Winnipeg district in the House of Commons at Ottawa since the early 1920s.

Woodsworth fashioned a species of socialism that was even less Marxist than the British Labour Party. He had the help of the League for Social Reconstruction, a group of Protestant ministers and academics from the eastern provinces, which in 1932 modeled itself on the British Fabian Society. Many of the same people had, in 1931, created the Movement for a Christian Social Order, which then became the Christian Socialist Movement, insisting that "the teaching of Jesus Christ, applied in an age of machine production and financial control, means Christian socialism."[129]

In 1934, the CSM, spreading from Toronto to Montreal and Ottawa but picking up a bit of caution en route, became the Fellowship for a Christian Social Order, which lasted to the end of World War II. Despite the change in name it remained a socialist organization.

All this activity was of course directly related to the onslaught of the Great Depression, which had hit Canada as painfully as it had the United States, its country of origin. In February 1933, Woodsworth initiated a debate in Parliament with his resolution that

> the government should immediately take measures looking to the setting up of a cooperative commonwealth in which all natural resources and the socially necessary machinery of production will be used in the interest of the people and not for the benefit of the few.[130]

Henri Bourassa, an outstanding member of parliament (MP) from Quebec, defended Woodsworth from the cries of "Communism!" that immediately greeted his speech in the Commons. To his fellow Catholics he said,

> Do not raise your hands in horror and say, "Oh no, we have nothing in common with these men from the West, these semi-Bolsheviks, these quarter-Communists." When you make use of the papal encyclicals to denounce the CCF, why do you not read that part . . . which denounces the system that has been built, maintained and protected by the two great historic parties since Confederation?. . . . Let us admit that there is much good in the program of the CCF.

Despite this he did not join.

The CCF was clearly a party like the British Labour Party, which Cardinal Bourne, the primate of England, had defended as not coming under the interdict of Pius XI in *Quadragesimo Anno*. The Catholic bishops of Australia and New Zealand had also cleared the Labour Parties of those countries which, as in England, were recognized as bona fide socialist parties.

What was the reaction of the Catholic Church in Canada? Unfortunately, the Canadian situation was complicated by the fact that the French-speaking minority, largely Catholic, was suspicious of a party that came out of the Protestant, English-speaking world and that favored a strong national government, which the people of Quebec feared as a threat to their autonomy.

On March 9, 1933, the *journée des treize* (Day of the Thirteen), thirteen ecclesiastics met in Montreal under the auspices of the *École sociale populaire*, under the dominant influence of the Dominican Father Georges-Henri Lévesque. Lévesque's analysis of the CCF in relation to Pius XI's condemnation of socialism—in particular, in relation to the three "vices of socialism": class warfare and violence, the abolition of private property, and the materialist conception of society—was the basis for the Thirteen's conclusions and for subsequent positions taken by the Canadian bishops.

The Day of the Thirteen occurred a few months before the Regina convention of the CCF, at which the Marxist radicals of British Columbia were outvoted on four important positions adopted by the majority: (1) exclusion of social change by violent means, (2) limitation of public ownership to the "principal means of production," (3) exclusion of land from socialization, and (4) compensation for owners when private property is confiscated.

By reason of his ignorance of CCF history and by using a selective choice of quotes from CCF left-wingers, Lévesque was able to make a plausible case for the position that the CCF represented the brand of socialism condemned by Pius XI.

In the fall of 1933, a conference of Canadian bishops, without mentioning the CCF explicitly (apparently the French-speaking bishops wanted to and the English-speaking bishops did not), approved a pastoral letter that implied that the CCF was socialist in the bad sense.

Murray Ballantyne, editor of *The Beacon*, the English-language Catholic newspaper of Montreal, and Henry Somerville, editor of *The Catholic Register*, diocesan newspaper of Toronto, took the opposite view. Ballantyne had to face the wrath of his archbishop, the conservative Georges Gauthier, who in company with the even more reactionary Cardinal Villeneuve of Quebec City, had issued explicit condemnations of the CCF.

Father Lévesque, however, was too intelligent to cling to his irrational conclusions of 1933. In 1939 he changed his mind and was actually successful, finally, in persuading Cardinal Villeneuve to support a new statement of the Canadian bishops that gave explicit permission to Catholics to vote for the CCF. But that was not until 1943. The damage had been done and the CCF would have to struggle to sell its moderate brand of socialism to the Catholics of Canada, and especially to the French-speaking Catholics of Quebec.

By 1983, however, modes of thought in the Canadian hierarchy had so drastically changed that the Espicopal Commission for Social Affairs could issue a statement implying that the New Democratic Party (formed by the merger of the CCF and the Canadian Congress of Labor in 1961) was the *only* party that an intelligent Catholic could join.

Consider these excerpts:

From the standpoint of the Church's social teachings, we firmly believe that present economic realities reveal a "moral disorder" in our society. . . . The present recession appears to be symptomatic of a much larger structural crisis in the international system of capitalism. . . . Capital is reasserted as the dominant organizing principle of economic life. This orientation directly contradicts the ethical principle that labor, not capital, must be given priority in the development of an economy based on justice. . . .

What would it mean to develop *an alternative economic model* that would place emphasis on socially useful forms of production: labor-intensive industries, the use of appropriate forms of technology, self-reliant models of economic development, community ownership and control of industries, new forms of worker management and ownership, and greater use of the renewable energy sources in industrial production? [emphasis added].[131]

I cannot read this as anything less than an anticapitalist statement calling for a non-Marxist brand of democratic socialism consistent with the Frankfurt

Declaration of the Socialist International. Not a clarion call perhaps, phrased as it is in the form of a question, but a call nonetheless.

THE PERCEPTIVE FATHER CULLINANE

Canada, which has about one-tenth the population of the United States and which receives little attention on the world stage, tends to be ignored by the residents of its neighbor country to the south. That should not be. There are important lessons to be learned from Canada.

What some of those lessons might be are summed up in a quotation from Father Eugene Cullinane, an American by origin who became a Basilian priest and dedicated member of the CCF in Canada. After detailing all the non-Marxist characteristics of the CCF, which he had confirmed by personal investigation, he summarizes his study. His words clearly could apply to Catholics in the United States and, in fact, to almost all Americans in their reaction to the *word*, as opposed to the *reality* of socialism.

The mentality of most Catholics I have met across Canada, including the clergy, is infected with a terribly distorted view of the CCF *reality*. The result is that Catholics generally are afflicted with a deep rooted, though unconscious, prejudice against the CCF. It is virtually identical with the kind of prejudice against Catholics found in the typical Ontario Protest-ant of twenty years ago. Catholics by and large condemn the CCF for something it is not; they are enslaved by the tyranny of a single word— "socialism." If I may generalize on the fairly large sample I have inter-viewed across the continent, then the overwhelming majority of Catholics are unconsciously banded together in a compact political unity based on an illusion (I suspect that this is not true of Nova Scotia due mainly to the enlightened leadership given the people by the priests of St. F.X.) [St. Francis Xavier University in Antigonish]. The result is that Catholics tend to fall into a mould of political and economic thought quite out of line with that of the encyclicals. Enslaved mentally by the tyranny of that awful word, they are virtually forced to devour with great avidity all the "anti-socialist" propaganda dispensed so generously and freely by the forces of reaction. And we come to the sad and tragic paradox where we find that Canadian Catholics, by and large, have divorced themselves from those constructive and creative forces about which Maritain has written so well, and which are the only hope we have of winning the peace.[132]

THE ANTIGONISH MOVEMENT

The reference to the priests of St. Francis Xavier University in Antigonish, Nova Scotia, is mainly to two enlightened men, Fathers J. J. Tompkins and M. M. Coady, who, starting around 1930, created a vital movement and gave voice to a radical critique of capitalism. They were able to join academics with farmers and fisherfolk in the development of successful credit unions, consumer and producer cooperatives. Though constantly accused of being socialist (which, according to the concepts of this book, they were), the two priests just as constantly denied this and avoided any indication of sympathy with the CCF.

Father Coady, despite the success of Antigonish with producer cooperatives, makes a case for the proposition that the workers will never be able to regain control of production, stripped from them by the Industrial Revolution, "unless they attack the problem from the consumer end." He uses an argument that I haven't seen elsewhere, namely, "what the common man has to sell, his labor or his primary products, is not his with that absolute ownership which he has over the money in his pocket." He points out that the farmer's wheat and the fisherman's lobster may be halved in value by "conditions over which they have no control."[133] Unfortunately, the same is true of the money in their pockets, though perhaps not with the same rapidity as wheat or lobster.

The argument has merit, but there are more compelling reasons why it is not convincing. Admittedly the ideal would be a society in which both producer and consumer cooperatives share dominance in the economy. Producer co-ops can exploit the consumer like any capitalist, just as consumer co-ops can exploit their workers. Except, however, in a really impoverished society one simply cannot arouse the interest in consumer services that one can create in production, by reason alone of the amount of time a worker spends in production as compared with the purchase of goods.

Marx was wrong about a lot of things, but his emphasis on the control of production as against consumption was not one of them. Ultimately, we cannot escape the fact that those who control production also control consumption. Control of production must remain the worker's primary goal.

CHAPTER 12

Protestants and Prospects

Meanwhile, what have the Protestants been up to? Actually, until the 1960s the history of Christian socialism in the modern era has been mainly a Protestant history. Only during the last thirty years has it become a Catholic history to any significant extent. I have dealt at length with Protestant socialism in England (granted the Anglicans don't regard themselves as Protestants), in German-speaking Europe, and in North America. Let me fill in the French situation very briefly.

The first one to use the word "socialism" was, you may recall, the French Protestant theologian, Alexandre Vinet, in 1831. Over the next eighty years few Christian socialists would have described themselves as Protestants; not many of the pioneers who built their socialism on Christian foundations would have described themselves as Catholics either—men like Saint-Simon, Considérant, Cabet, or even Buchez, though he did return to the Catholic Church on his deathbed.

Professor Paul Passy reports from France in the American *Christian Socialist* of June 22, 1911, that there are "a dozen well-organized Christian socialist centers" in France, but no paid help. In a letter to the editor, the Rev. Edward Carr, he notes that on religious questions "my point of view is much more orthodox than yours." In the issue of December 1, 1913, Passy writes again that "our little French Union of Christian Socialists is growing steadily," numbering six hundred, including some Catholics and Christian Scientists, but mainly "Baptists and Presbyterians, with a good sprinkling of Methodists." Passy is editing a monthly, *L'Espoir* (Hope), which has 1800 readers. That is the good news. The bad news is that Passy has been fired from the faculty of the University of Paris for his oppositon to a bill requiring three years of military service.

In more recent times the stand-out Protestant among French Christian socialists was André Philip, (1902–70), professor and politican, who served as minister of economy and minister of finance in the French cabinets of 1946 and 1947. Writing in his book *Les Socialistes* (Paris: Seuil, 1967) of the heady days of the Popular Front government of Léon Blum in 1936, which put through twelve pieces of social legislation in ten days, including the first paid vacations for many, Philip states: "Those who lived through that period will never forget the emotion of old workers going on vacation, discovering the sea and the mountains which they had never known."[1] Another important book by Philip is *La Gauche, mythes et réalités* (Paris: Aubier, 1964).

THE WORLD COUNCIL OF CHURCHES

"I do not pray for these only, but also for those who believe in me through their word, that they may all be one; even as thou, Father, art in me and I in thee . . . even as we are one" (John 17:20–22).

The dream of Christian unity, which has been lying, shattered and scattered in a thousand pieces for over four hundred years, has in the past forty years been taking shape and substance once again in the impressive reality of the World Council of Churches.

Founded only in 1948 at its assembly in Amsterdam, the Council has more than doubled its membership. By the time of its sixth assembly in Vancouver in 1983 it represented over 400 million Christians in over three hundred churches in over one hundred countries. From being a mainly European and North American body, the Council has now achieved strong representation from First, Second and Third Worlds.

The principal non-members have been the fundamentalist churches, such as the Southern Baptists of the United States, and the 840 million members of the Roman Catholic Church. Over a score of official Catholic observers attended the Vancouver assembly and Pope John Paul II sent warm greetings, assuring the Council of his "deep pastoral interest and closeness in prayer" and acknowledging that the Council had "affirmed our common belief that Jesus is the crucified Saviour, the Redeemer of all, the Lord of life who was designated Son of God in power according to the Spirit of holiness by his Resurrection from the dead (Rom. 1:4)."[2]

One of the preparatory documents for the Vancouver assembly was written by a group of Catholic theologians called to Rome by the Vatican's Secretariat for Promoting Christian Unity. This document makes several significant points:

God shows that, in his love for all humanity and everything that is human, he is on the side of the humble and weak, the victims of the powerful. . . . A church which breaches its solidarity with the poor can no longer claim to mirror the gospel.[3]

And perhaps even more significant:

The first task of the churches is, then, that of unity, that full *koinonia* [community or fellowship] of all those who are dignified by the name of Christians, just because of the gospel of God. The life of the world requires it.[4]

The World Council, most wisely, has refrained from pontificating on such controversial matters as abortion, divorce, homosexuality, and the Real Presence in the Eucharist. Its constitution provides that it "shall not legislate for the churches" and "may take action on behalf of constituent churches only in such matters as one or more of them may commit to it and only in behalf of such churches."[5]

All this being so, one may logically ask, "Why, in the name of all that is good, holy and Christian, doesn't the Catholic Church affiliate with the Council?" One of the Vancouver assembly documents reveals that "the 1972 answer to the [R.C.] membership question—'not in the immediate future'— still stands and the question is not yet ready to be taken up again."[6]

Of course some difficult problems would have to be worked out. Notably, how do you give fair representation to a church whose 840 million members would constitute a substantial majority of the entire Council and how do you, simultaneously, prevent that church from swallowing up the Council? But such matters are manageable where there is the spirit of sweet reason and sweeter Christian love. As the Vatican's own theologians put it, "The life of the world requires it."

WHY THIS DIGRESSION?

The reader may wonder how the question of Catholic affiliation with the World Council of Churches fits into a history of Christian socialism. The answer is that both the Catholic Church and the World Council have been moving in the direction of a socialist option, if not preference, and the sooner they pool their strength and influence, the sooner that option becomes viable in such pivotal nations as the United States.

Just as the recent history of Catholic social teaching shows a growing similarity to the language of the Frankfurt Declaration of the Socialist International, so does the language approved by assemblies of the World Council of Churches (Amsterdam, 1948; Evanston, 1954; New Delhi, 1961; Uppsala, 1968; Nairobi, 1975; Vancouver, 1983). With some differences.

Let us take a few samples from the first and last assemblies, at Amsterdam and Vancouver. Amsterdam:

There are conflicts between Christianity and capitalism. The developments of capitalism vary from country to country and often the exploitation of the workers that was characteristic of early capitalism has been corrected in considerable measure by the influence of trade unions, social legislation and responsible management. But (1) capitalism tends to subordinate what should be the primary task of any economy—the meeting of human needs—to the economic advantages of those who have most power over its institutions. (2) It tends to produce serious inequalities. (3) It has developed a practical form of materialism in Western nations in spite of their Christian background, for it has placed the greatest emphasis upon success in making money. (4) It has also kept the people of capitalist countries subject to a kind of fate which has taken the form of such social catastrophes as mass unemployment.

The Christian churches should reject the ideologies of both communism and *laissez-faire* capitalism, and should seek to draw men away from the false assumption that these extremes are the only alternatives. Each has made promises which it could not redeem. Communist ideology puts the emphasis upon economic justice, and promises that freedom will come automatically after the completion of the revolution. Capitalism puts the emphasis upon freedom, and promises that justice will follow as a by-product of free enterprise; that too is an ideology which has been proved false. It is the responsibilty of Christians to seek new, creative solutions which never allow either justice or freedom to destroy the other.[7]

As we read this statement, entitled *The Church and the Disorder of Society*, and as we come across such sentences as "Our modern society . . . underestimates both the depth of evil in human nature and the full height of freedom and dignity in the children of God,"[8] we think, "Doesn't this have a familiar ring?" Sure enough, the chairperson of the committee that wrote the first draft was Reinhold Niebuhr. Other members of what may have been one of the more distinguished committees of thinkers and theologians ever assembled were Nicholas Berdyaev, Emil Brunner, Jacques Ellul and John C. Bennett. Of the fifteen members, all male, however, only one was from the Third World, a layman from India, M. M. Thomas.

Very different was the composition of the committee that headed the "issue group" that prepared the equivalent statement of the Vancouver assembly: an American woman was moderator, a Brazilian woman and a Soviet Baptist were vice-moderators, two *rapporteurs* came from Sierra Leone and Korea, and a staff assistant was from Pakistan.

Their first draft was, however, rejected by the assembly and sent back to the committee, which was asked to submit a revised statement (title: "Struggling for Justice and Human Dignity") to the WCC Central Committee of 150 members. This body later approved a statement from which these excerpts are taken:

Since Nairobi [1957] we have struggled towards the vision of a just, participatory and sustainable society.

The machine of the prevailing economic order starves millions of people to death and increases the number of unemployed every year. Science and technology are misused to oppress the people and to destroy the earth in an insane arms race. More and more people are detained and "disappear," tortured, deprived of religious liberty, forcibly displaced or exiled.

We interpret this development as idolatry, stemming from human sin, seduced by satanic forces. We are not in a usual situation, where only prophetic and intercessory actions of the churches are sufficient. . . .

Some fundamentalist sects and church people, political parties and governments, would legitimize this development as "Christian." These groups militate against the identification of the churches with the poor in their witness to God's kingdom. . . .

The so-called Christian arguments defend exploitative transnational systems, the uncritical applications of science and technology and the production of mass nuclear weapons. . . .

A special manifestation of this injustice is the prevailing international economic order. It has institutionalized domination by Northern economies of trade, finance, manufacturing, food processing and knowledge. Handled mainly through transnational corporations, this economic order subordinates and renders dependent the Southern economies.

In sum, we live today to witness the emergence of a new type of abuse of power. As never before, economic interests, military might, technological knowledge and international alliances form a constellation of forces arrayed against the dignity of life in the world: Jesus Christ Himself! The consequences are formidable: immense human suffering, degradation and death. . . .

[Note in these last two paragraphs the identification, perhaps unintended, of the Southern Hemisphere with "Jesus Christ Himself" and the Northern Hemisphere with "a constellation of forces arrayed against" Jesus Christ Himself. And yet, even if unintended, the analogy has validity. Jesus did identify himself with the poor (Matt. 25:40, 45) and there is reason to identify the Northern Hemisphere with Dives and the Southern with Lazarus.]

Churches are called to enable people who resist oppression, combat the roots of injustice and take risks in the search for a new society. . . .

Economic domination and unjust social structures suppress the socioeconomic rights of the people, such as the basic needs of families, communities and the rights of workers.

The assembly recommended, among other things:

That member churches demonstrate their international ecumenical solidarity in combatting unjust economic structures, through:

1. Theological reflection on the principles of work and human dignity, and on a new economic paradigm aiming at a just, participatory and sustainable society;

2. Engaging in an intensive process of education of their members regarding the nature of oppressive economic structures and their own complicity in bolstering them;

3. Exposing the role of transnational corporations in buttressing unjust economic structures, in undergirding racist regimes, in exploiting
women as cheap labor resources and in using technologies which result
in the expulsion of laborers from their jobs, thus creating unemployment.[9]

Several things are noteworthy about this statement, in addition to the
apocalyptic style in which it is written, a style with a sense of life-or-death
urgency that is less evident in Catholic statements that are composed by popes
and bishops of the Northern Hemisphere.

One, the statement is violently anti-capitalist, even though the word "capitalism" is never mentioned. Two, unlike the Niebuhr statement at the Amsterdam assembly in 1948, there is no mention of communism, either explicitly or
implicitly, or if implicitly, the implication is so faint as to be virtually invisible.
Three, there is a woeful lack of economic analysis and specificity in the
indictment of transnational corporations and the Northern economies in
general, "the constellation of forces arrayed against" Christ Himself. This is
not so true of current Catholic statements.

Northern moneybags have been guilty of extortion in forcing desperate
Southern nations to borrow money at usurious interest rates. In justice the
North should forgive a significant part of Southern debt. In its own self-
interest, not to mention concern for Judeo-Christian values and/or human
decency, the North should forgive more than that. But the South still has a job
to do in providing the specific argumentation to persuade the North that it is a
question as much of justice as of charity and, if possible, self-interest. Apocalyptic indictments without specifics are not going to do it.

A fourth characteristic of the Vancouver statement is the omission of
references to "democracy" or "socialism." In place of "democratic" we find
an even more ambiguous term, "participatory," but at least the thrust is in the
right direction. In place of "socialism" we see references to "a new society"
and "a new economic paradigm aiming at a just, participatory and sustainable
society," which, by repeated insistence, will be very different from current
models of capitalism. It seems reasonable to conclude that the paradigm will
resemble some model of socialism. Once again, specificity is noteworthy by its
absence.

THE SUBMERGED DEBATE

As we study the documents of the Vancouver assembly we sense a submerged, inexplicit debate going on over the more Marxist-Leninist aspects of
liberation theology. On the one side, the side that still retains the Niebuhrian
emphases and distinctions of 1948, would be, for example, the Moderator
(chairman) of the assembly, the Most Rev. Edward W. Scott, Anglican archbishop of Canada. His address strongly criticized "the two major competing
ideologies—capitalism and communism." Both are

materialistic . . . tend to place emphasis upon persons as units of production and consumption . . . are no longer satisfying the deepest human aspirations, and neither is displaying the power to galvanize adherents and so provide unity, direction, standards and courage to their respective communities.[10]

On the other side we might place José Míguez Bonino, formerly one of the six presidents of the Council, a Methodist lay theologian from Argentina, and author of *Christians and Marxists*. His viewpoint is understandably very different from that of Archbishop Scott, coming as he does, as he put it, from

a continent where torture and assassination have become the "normal" means of political control, where millions are condemned to marginalization, starvation and death in the name of "the law of economy," where the genocide of Indians and peasants is considered a "reasonable" price to pay for "order."[11]

We might say that the debate between Leninism and some form of democratic socialism as alternatives to capitalism is not only going on inside the World Council of Churches, but is going on inside the mind of José Míguez Bonino. His book *Christians and Marxists* condemns Stalin's version of Leninism as "the very negation of humanism."[12] He criticizes Marxist political thinking because it

has not yet developed adequate forms of control of the exercise of power in order to prevent arbitrariness, the "cult of personality," the appropriation by a clique or a bureaucracy of a total control of society, the exclusion of the very proletariat from the shaping of the process and the determination of its direction.[13]

Yet the very same book declares that

the communist [Juan] Rosales is right when he says that . . . "it should be inconceivable for progressive Christians" to envisage a revolution "without the orientating contribution of Marxism-Leninism."[14]

Fortunately, the progressive Christians of the Philippines, in a situation very similar to that in Míguez Bonino's continent, were able to envisage a revolution "without the orientating contribution of Marxism-Leninism." In fact, their orientation was about as contrary to Marxism-Leninism as one could possibly imagine. One can't help wondering if their example has moved Professor Míguez Bonino, who is obviously a high-minded, intelligent Christian, to reconsider his evaluation of Marxism-Leninism as a necessary ingredient of successful revolutions.

Meanwhile, of course, the horrors of Latin America and South Africa, and other sections of this sad old world, continue. As I write this, the morning news reveals that the U.S. House of Representatives has voted $100,000,000 in support of the horror represented by the Contra war against the legal government of Nicaragua. This from the most powerful and prestigious *democracy* in the world. No wonder that the progressive Christians of Latin America and Africa are tempted to turn their backs on democracy Western-style and look to the Soviet Union, to Cuba, to any kind of Marxist-Leninist leadership to save and deliver them from such horrors.

No wonder that reasonable men and women everywhere are tempted to ignore what remains, in spite of all the horror and betrayal, the sound and essential wisdom of Karl Popper's aphorism: "The use of violence is justified only under a tyranny which makes reforms without violence impossible, and it should have only one aim—to bring about a state of affairs which makes reforms without violence possible."[15] The Filipinos have added their own aphorism, which might be expressed this way: "Revolutions without violence are also possible, and Christian faith, prayer and love can be powerful revolutionary weapons." For as Christians we should all agree with Dom Helder Camara, "I would a thousand times rather be killed than to kill."

It will be interesting to see how the debate within the World Council of Churches, and within the mind of José Míguez Bonino, turns out. It is regrettable that the Catholic Church, which could contribute eloquent voices to both sides of the debate, cannot do so as part of the Council.

The World Council of Churches, representing the vast majority of non-Catholic Christians, remains today the primary locus and hope for some realization *soon* of Jesus' prayer that we "all may be one." In addition, its leaders, the studies it has sponsored, and the positions it has taken, have been making significant contributions to the development and practice of Christian socialism.

One of the most significant contributions is the analysis by Konrad Raiser, deputy general secretary of the WCC, in his essay included in the collection called *Perspectives on Political Ethics*, a volume compiled in preparation for the Vancouver assembly. In recounting the history of the Council's pursuit of "a just, participatory and sustainable society" and its development from the concept of "a responsible society" first enunciated at Amsterdam in 1948, Raiser contributes this summary of past agreements and current disagreements:

The concept of the responsible society reflects the changes which have taken place in social and economic life and which have rendered the choice between *laissez-faire* capitalism and communism unacceptable. Both these are seen as challenging the basis for the affirmation of responsible freedom and the concern for a just distribution of wealth. Thirdly, the responsible society represents an attempt to come to terms with the new form of power and the concentration of power by insisting on an order which guarantees the distribution of power and the control of state power by the people, including the possibility of legitimately and peacefully introducing basic changes. The responsible society was an attempt to keep in balance the demands of freedom and justice within the framework of democratic order, based on the recognition of essential human rights.

This concept, which was developed further at following Assemblies, in particular at Evanston in 1954, has proved to be an important point of synthesis and crystallization of ecumenical social and political thinking. But increasingly its roots in the tradition of Western liberal democracy were being challenged. The first challenge came from Asia. In particular in India the experience of economic and social development after independence led to a new appreciation of the role of the state and to the search for *a "third way" in terms of democratic socialism*. In other newly independent countries also the task of nation-building and rapid social and economic change led to questions about the basic assumptions of the concept of the responsible society with its bias for constitutional, democratic change. The main challenge came in the 1960s from Latin America, calling in question the theological, economic and political assumptions underlying the concept of the responsible society [emphasis added].[16]

If the World Council of Churches could put together the *democratic* assumptions of the "responsible society," the challenge of post-liberation India, Karl Popper, and the Filipino Revolution of 1986, it might find a way to resolve disagreements and respond to most of its challenges.

PROSPECTS FOR THE FUTURE

Prospects for the future of Christian socialism, and perhaps for the future of socialism itself, depend more on what happens inside the Catholic Church and other Christian churches than on any existing organizations or movements that bear the name of Christian socialism.

This is not to disparage them, for some have shown remarkable signs of vitality and growth over the last few decades. Of these the most noteworthy has been the movement that has circled the world and that goes under the broad name of liberation theology. It is not an organized movement, really, although there are organizations of liberation theologians such as Theology in the Americas, the Association of Latin American Theologians, and the Ecumenical Dialogue of Third World Theologians, all of which are headquartered in New York City and have the same executive secretary, an exiled Chilean priest, Sergio Torres.

Liberation theology has also given birth to several organizations designed for non-theologians. One of these is Christians for Socialism, founded in Santiago, Chile, in 1972, just before the fall of Allende. CFS spread to Europe and Asia, notably the Philippines, and for nine years (until 1983) had a U.S.

affiliate, which at one point had eight local chapters. The European affiliates, after initial success, have shown a similar lack of staying power. They tended to lean toward far left parties of Leninist complexion, and as these have dwindled in Western Europe, CFS has followed suit.

In Holland during the 1970s CFS's first preference was the Communist Party because, as one leader put it, the CP "is the only socialist revolutionary party of some weight."[17] The CP lost weight thereafter.

Another organization that has worked closely with CFS and liberation theology is the Centre Oecuménique de Liaisons Internationales, known by its acronym COELI, with headquarters in Brussels. A capable staff publishes an intellectual quarterly in both French and English. In January 1984, COELI organized an impressive World Assembly of Christians in Liberation Struggles, which met in Barcelona.

This brought together, by invitation only, about one hundred Christian socialists from thirty different countries and all major continents. Although invitations went out to a few Eastern Europeans, none showed up. But Eastern Europe was well represented nonetheless. An effort to criticize the Soviet Union and specific Eastern transgressions, notably in Afghanistan and Poland, ran into heavy opposition and was voted down. Pablo Richard, an eloquent liberation theologian from Chile, led the opposition, which protested that it was not opportune to criticize countries that have been the major support of people who have been the victims of U.S. imperialism and aggression. Another argument, in Richard's words, "To place the fight of the Central American people in an East-West perspective is absurd; it just helps conceal the South-North confrontation that is happening there."[18] No one could dispute this truism.

Of course, by refusing to protest even worse acts of aggression and oppression in the East the assembly did, in fact, place the South-North confrontation precisely in the middle of an East-West perspective, taking its stand firmly on the side of the East. But since no one was there to speak for the Afghans, the Poles, the Hungarians, or the Czechs, since the hall was full of people only too anxious to indict the current sins of the United States, and, finally, since it is an incontrovertible fact that the East bloc has been the main supplier of guns and money to liberation struggles in the Third World and the U.S. a major opponent, what other outcome could be expected?

A similar scenario played itself out in several other world congresses of Christian socialists in 1983 and 1986. These were organized by the International League of Religious Socialists, mainly with funds and facilities contributed by the Swedish Social Democrats. The ILRS has existed since 1929, most of that time composed of affiliates in Scandinavia, Germany (now West Germany only), German-speaking Switzerland, Austria, and the Netherlands. Since 1983 it has added affiliates in the United States (the Religion and Socialism Commission of the Democratic Socialists of America) and England (the Chrisitian Socialist Movement).

In Bommersvik, Sweden, in August 1983, the ILRS congress was truly international for the first time, bringing together delegates from twenty-seven countries. Pablo Richard was prominent in debate here as well and, despite the efforts of U.S. delegates, his "East-West-perspective-is-absurd" arguments carried the day.

In Managua, Nicaragua, in October 1986, Pablo Richard was not present, but his viewpoint was strongly represented by other delegates from sixteen countries. However, by dint of persistence and the threat by one U.S. delegate to walk out, the final statement did include one inexplicit reference to the Soviet Union: "We are concerned about the increasing arrogance of the superpowers towards small nations and towards the principles of the international legal system." In addition Evert Svensson, the ILRS chairman, and another featured speaker, Christian Ahlund, were bold enough to mention Afghanistan explicitly.

Fairness demands that we note that in 1983, after the Bommersvik congress, the ILRS board, in condemning the U.S. invasion of Grenada, also denounced the Soviet invasions of Czechoslovakia and Afghanistan. On balance, however, one would have to conclude that the Soviet Union, by reason of its assistance to liberation struggles (where these do not involve liberation from its own oppression) is rapidly out-distancing its rival superpower in the World Popularity Contest, even among those—Christian democratic socialists—who should be most sympathetic to oppression wherever it occurs, East or West, North or South. Whether this trend can be reversed by a new U.S. administration in 1988 is one of the more fascinating and serious questions that confront us.

ILRS AFFILIATES

In comparing the ILRS and such organizations as Christians for Socialism that owe their origins more directly to liberation theology, the ILRS appears to be stronger. Founded in 1929, it has demonstrated staying power, and since 1983 it has further demonstrated the ability to take advantage of the impetus given to Christian socialism by liberation theology.

Previous chapters have mentioned ILRS affiliates in Germany, Austria, England, and the United States. The major source of its organizational and financial strength has been its Swedish affiliate, which enjoys the strong support of the Social Democratic Party of Sweden. Christian socialism in Sweden goes back to 1924 and the activity of the Rev. Bertil Mogard, who since 1920 had maintained contact with the English movement. In 1929 Mogard organized the *Broderskaprörelsen* (Brotherhood Movement), also known as the Swedish Association of Christian Social Democrats, of which he was president until 1954. Since 1968, Evert Svensson, who with about ten other members sits in the Swedish parliament, has served as president and more recently as ILRS chairperson. Bertil Zachrisson, national postmaster and cabinet member, is its most prestigious member. Bo Nylund, a professor at the University of Uppsala and author of *Kristendom och Socialism*, is the principal theoretician of the movement. He served as moderator of the Managua Congress/Seminar. Ingvar Paulsson is the Brotherhood's efficient general secretary.

The *Broderskapröelsen* has about a thousand members in two hundred groups and is an affiliate of the Social Democratic Party. Its lively newspaper, *Broderskap*, appears twenty times a year.

OTHER AFFILIATES

A regular attendant at ILRS conferences is the cheerful Elma Jaatinen of the Christian Social Democratic League of Finland. With help from its Swedish counterpart the league was organized in 1946 and is an affiliate of its own SDP, which publishes the six thousand copies of its quarterly *Veljeys* (Brotherhood), free copies of which go to the more than five hundred pastors in Finland. Since 1966 its chairman has been the Finnish MP, Sakari Knuuttila, and since 1968 its secretary and *Veljeys* editor has been Pekka Lampinen.

Of the fifty-seven socialist MP's, twelve are affiliated with the Christian movement, which is organized in fifteen chapters spread around the country, with a total membership of about a thousand, mostly Lutheran. The movement has a part-time secretary whose salary is paid by the Social Democratic Party.

The Christian Socialist Association of Norway dates from 1939. During the 1950s its membership rose to five thousand, of whom twelve sat in the Norwegian parliament. Both figures have fallen off since then. Gerd Grenwold, author of sixteen books, is its full-time official and editor of its bimonthly magazine, which has a circulation of 2,500. She was a delegate at the Managua Congress.

Harry Rasmussen is chairman of the League of Danish Christian Social Democrats, which was organized in 1947. It has a semi-official relationship with the Social Democratic Party and is regularly invited to attend congresses of the SDP. It holds an annual conference and in 1985 reported 5 percent increase in membership over 1984. A major stimulant of interest in Christian socialism in the early 1960s was Torben Christensen's excellent book on the Christian socialism of Ludlow, Maurice, and Kingsley, *Origin and History of Christian Socialism, 1848-54* (Copenhagen: Universitetsforlaget, 1962).

The Woodbrookers is the curious name of the Christian socialist movement in the Netherlands. It is the oldest such organization in the world, dating back to 1902, when a group of Dutch ministers attended a retreat at a place called Woodbrook in England and came back fired with enthusiasm for Christian socialism.

The Woodbrookers' excellent periodical *Tijd en Taak* (Time and Task) is also the oldest such publication in the world, even older than Switzerland's *Neue Wege*. It was begun in 1902.

Before World War II socialism in Holland was represented by a Marxist party, the Social Democratic Workers, hostile to religion. The Resistance and the concentration camps, as in other countries, brought together persons of secular and religious background; after the war these combined to form a more tolerant Labor Party, the PVDA (*Partei van der Arbeit*). A Protestant minister/theologian and author of many books on social science, Dr. W. Banning, was one of the more influential founders of this party in 1946.

The Woodbrookers enjoy close relations with the PVDA, which has actually given them responsibility for recommending party platforms. They have a full-time staff of three members, led by Bert Barends, who also serves as secretary of the International League of Religious Socialists. One of their members, a journalist named Harry Peer, has visited the United States and published an impressive study of socialism and religious socialism in this country (in Dutch).

Another expression of religious socialism in the Netherlands has been the Center for *Weltanschauung* (World View) and Politics, which during the 1970s was headed by a Dominican priest, David van Ooijen. The Center organizes meetings in which ideas are exchanged by Christian, Jewish, Islamic, and humanist members of the PVDA on questions of concern to the party and the various faiths.

Although not affiliated with the ILRS, an organization that deserves mention is the ASCE (*Azione Socialisti Cristiani Europei*, European Christian Socialist Action). Organized in 1976 by a group of Milanese Catholics within the Socialist Party, it publishes an ambitious periodical, *ASCE News*, and organizes international conferences, both of which feature prominent European Christian socialists. *ASCE News* publishes articles in Italian and English and occasionally in French, German, and Spanish.

The dominant personality in ASCE is Alfredo Luciani, an earnest intellectual who has published a five-volume work, *Cristianesimo e Movimento Socialista in Europa* (from 1789 to the present).

During the early 1980s intensive efforts were made to promote a merger between ASCE and the International League of Religious Socialists, but these ended in failure.

Under the influence of the Marxist Antonio Gramsci (1891–1937), socialism in Italy, and even communism, has been far less intolerant of religion than has been the case in other countries. Italian communism has also, since the 1950s, been more independent of the Soviet party line, and these factors have made it possible for Christians and Catholics to be more active in both parties.

CHAPTER 13

Conclusions

What can we conclude from this long, long story, from Moses to the present moment, the story of those who have reflected on the imperatives of the Judeo-Christian tradition and sought to apply them to the temporal order?

Let me deal with that question by responding to some questions raised by a Christian who read most of this manuscript and still disagreed with the idea that a Christian could, not to mention should, be a socialist.

1. "Can you extract a political program from the gospel? Is feeding the hungry and clothing the naked identical to the systematic redistribution of wealth? Can the spirit of Christian love ever be reduced to a political imperative?"

Answer: Concentrate the mind on the old saw: "Give a man a fish and you feed him for a day; teach him how to fish and you feed him for a lifetime." Then ask yourself, "Which is more in keeping with the spirit of the gospel?" The answer is obvious. From there it is a short step in logic to a further conclusion: even more in keeping with the letter and spirit of the gospel, especially in the modern era, is the construction of a political economy that makes it possible for every man or women who needs a job to work at a decent job so that he or she may feed, clothe and shelter him or her self and his or her children. The physical, psychological, spiritual, economic, and political advantages of this reading of the gospel—as opposed to one that is exclusively personal and individual—seem too obvious to need further repetition. The simpler reading *may* have been appropriate for Jesus' time. There is evidence that it was not appropriate even then. It is certainly not appropriate for our time.

Several quotes from the Catholic bishops' pastoral letter on the U.S. economy are relevant:

The responsibility for alleviating the plight of the poor falls upon all members of society. As individuals, all citizens have a duty to assist the poor through acts of charity and personal commitment. But private charity and voluntary action are not sufficient. *We also carry out our moral responsibility to assist and empower the poor by working collec-*

tively through government to establish just and effective public policies [189, emphasis added].

And from the very last paragraph:

Jesus taught us to love God and one another and that the concept of neighbor is without limit. . . . Love implies concern for all—especially the poor—and *a continued search for those social and economic structures that permit everyone to share in a community that is part of a redeemed creation* (Rom. 8:21-23) [365, emphasis added].

The "spirit of Christian love" cannot be reduced to a political imperative, granted, but it most certainly has a political dimension. Feeding the hungry and clothing the naked are not precisely identical with a systematic redistribution of wealth, but in the present situation, of gross inequality, obscene wealth and wretched poverty, they most certainly cry to heaven for both systematic and unsystematic redistribution.

2. "What is it that you are for? How is the 'socialization' of property to be effected without the Marxist solution of a strong central government ('the vanguard of the proletariat')? What is the engine of your implementation of the social gospel?"

Answer: There is no need to socialize all forms of property. There should be more rather than fewer people who enjoy the benefits of private property, both productive and consumer property, than we presently have, even in the United States, where property is so concentrated in the hands of a small minority.

There is no one "engine" for the implementation of the social gospel, unless it be called Democratic Process. An old saw is relevant here: "Never underestimate the intelligence of the average, ordinary person and never overestimate his or her knowledge." Democratic process, democracy, is based on the assumption that *given the facts*, the ordinary person will make the right decisions most of the time. Another part of the democratic assumption is that the ordinary person not only has enough intelligence, but he or she also has enough basic human decency. A few more relevant quotes, some of which have appeared before, but can bear repetition:

Reinhold Niebuhr: "Man's capacity for justice makes democracy possible, but man's inclination to injustice makes democracy necessary."[1]

Winston Churchill: "Democracy is the worst form of government except for all those other forms that have been tried from time to time."[2]

E. B. White: "Democracy is the recurrent suspicion that more than half the people are right more than half the time. It is the feeling of privacy in the voting booths, the feeling of communion in the libraries, the feeling of vitality everywhere . . . It is an idea that hasn't been disproved yet, a song the words of which have not gone bad."[3]

Lord Acton: "Power tends to corrupt and absolute power corrupts absolutely."[4] This saying holds both in political and economic life. Therefore power—whether political or economic—must be well distributed. The best, most effective form of distribution in economic life is the producer cooperative—one-person-one-vote. Just as it is the most democratic form of productive enterprise, it is also, like democracy, one of the most difficult. However, we now have enough examples of successful cooperative enterprise to use this particular "engine" with some confidence. Of these the most sensationally successful is the Mondragón Group in the Basque country of Spain.[5]

Full implementation of economic democracy calls for democratic structures at the level of the individual enterprise, such as the producer cooperative, but at many other levels as well, the industry level, the state, regional and national economic level. Guild socialism had some good insights. So did the vocational group plan of Heinrich Pesch and Pius XI. So did the CIO Industry Council Plan. So does the West German practice of *Mitbestimmung* (co-determination: worker representation on boards of directors) and the French practice of *autogestion* (self-management). So do a number of American experiments with worker participation in management—joint production committees, quality-of-life circles—which have proven so attractive to both labor and management that even corporations like General Motors and unions like the United Auto Workers have accepted them. Every trade union, incidentally, every union contract, is an "engine" for the implementation of the social gospel.

One of the major curiosities of economic and political discourse in the 1980s is the selection of John Stuart Mill as an ideological hero by Michael Novak, the Catholic champion of "democratic capitalism," the oxymoron to end all oxymorons. (Oxymoron: "A rhetorical figure in which an epigrammatic effect is created by the conjunction of incongruous or contradictory terms; for example, 'a mournful optimist' " [*American Heritage Dictionary*].) Mill not only identified himself finally as a socialist, but in the very work that Novak memorializes as some sort of justificiation for capitalism Mill gave one of the most eloquent arguments for pre-Marxian socialism, now well on the way to becoming post-Marxian socialism as well. Interestingly enough, this was published in 1848, the same year as Marx and Engels's *Communist Manifesto*. Mill speaks first of the advantages of "an association of the laborers themselves on terms of equality, collectively owning the capital with which they carry on their operations." He continues:

The mode in which cooperation tends . . . to increase the productiveness of labor, consists in the vast stimulus given to productive energies by placing the laborers, as a mass, in a relation to their work that would make it their principle and their interest (at present it is neither) to do the utmost, instead of the least possible, in exchange for their remuneration. It is scarcely possible to rate too highly this material benefit, which yet is as nothing compared with the moral revolution in society that would accompany it: the healing of the standing feud between capital and labor; the transformation of human life, from a conflict of classes struggling for opposite interests, to a friendly rivalry in the pursuit of a good common to all; the elevation of the dignity of labor; a new sense of dignity and independence in the laboring class; and the conversion of each human being's daily occupation into a school of the social sympathies and the practical intelligence."[6]

What am I for? I am for all the things that the popes (and the World Council of Churches) have been for. I call it "democratic socialism" and call to the witness stand the Socialist International to support that designation.

In the last manifestation of his annual book production my old friend Michael Novak does me the honor of associating my name with this kind of democratic socialism. Then he quotes Ludwig von Mises:

If anyone likes to call a social idea which retains private ownership of the means of production socialistic, why, let him! A man may call a cat a dog and the sun the moon if it is pleases him.[7]

To which I respond, "Same to you, Ludwig, and the same to you, Michael! If anyone likes to call capitalism democratic, socialism communism and communism socialism, if anyone chooses to ignore all pre-Marxian socialism and all post-Marxian socialism, if anyone chooses to deny that the Socialist International has some faint claim to define what socialism really is, why, let him! A man may call a cat a dog and the sun the moon if it pleases him."

The fear of God is the beginning of wisdom, but the fear of communism has too often been the beginning of foolishness. If the Novaks and the Miseses really feared communism in a sensible way, they would be more appreciative of the Socialist International and those who are concerned about freedom for the affluent, within reason, but also and primarily, as Christ taught us, about justice for the poor.

Cardinal Arns said it very well and with magnificent brevity:

One thing is clear . . . we must reject capitalism, which is based on selfishness. We believe in the right of workers to own their own land and to keep their profits for themselves, and therefore we incline toward socialism.[8]

Socialism has been defined in many ways, many of them inaccurate, but many accurate and not necessarily contradictory. "Socialism is the opposite of individualism." This was the definition of Alexandre Vinet, the French Protestant who used the word for the first time in 1831. "Production for use and not for profit" is all right, but a rewording, "Production primarily for use and only secondarily for profit" would be more in keeping with the definition of the Socialist International. "Socialism is the extension of democratic process from the political to the economic sphere." Excellent. "Socialism is the vision of a pluralist society in which the advantages of competition, a free market and political democracy are reconciled with the maximum socialization of production and the demands of justice, full employment and the realization of that minimum of worldly goods for all which Thomas Aquinas told us is necessary for a life of virtue." If I have to pick one definition among them, let it be that, but I like the idea of retaining all of them.

3. "If Christian socialism is grounded ultimately on faith, . . . how is that socialism viable in a pluralist, secular democracy?"

Answer: Despite the trace of skeptical condescension in what I wrote about the natural-law reasoning of Cathrein, Pesch and Nell-Breuning, I do agree fundamentally with them that there is in human nature, on average, a kind of unwritten law of decency—Niebuhr's "capacity for justice." All the basic tenets of Christian, democratic socialism can find some motivation and support in that unwritten law.

In the United States, Christian socialism starts—or restarts—with an additional advantage. The *New York Times* for December 11, 1984, ran the following news item:

> In recent years researchers have consistently found that about 40 percent of Americans attend religious services weekly, three-quarters of them pray at least once a day, and more than 90 percent profess belief in God.

Most of these people get whatever religion they have from the Bible. The reactionary preachers who dominate the television screen tell them that the Bible teaches us that "government should get off the back of business," that the nuclear bomb is the Christian's best friend, that our present economy is the best possible economy in the world. They are wrong. The Bible teaches nothing of the sort. All we have to do is to tell them what the Bible really teaches, persuade them to believe it, and—who knows?—the kingdom of God may yet come on earth as it is in heaven, at least insofar as poor, weak human nature is capable, with the help of God. This is precisely what Jesus taught us to pray for, and work to make real. He also told us that God, our God, would indeed help us. As Eberhard Arnold said to the religious socialists at Tambach in 1919, responding to the discouragements of Barth, "Karl Barth is right. Human action goes nowhere. But if God tells us to do something, is that just human action?"[9]

And God has told us to do something.

Notes

INTRODUCTION

1. Cited by William Ebenstein and Edwin Fogelman, *Today's Isms* (Englewood Cliffs, N.J.: Prentice Hall, 1980), p. 248
2. *The Philippine Times,* May 18–24, 1978, p. 3.
3. *Reinhold Niebuhr: His Religious, Social and Political Thought,* ed. Charles Kegley and Robert Bretall (New York: Macmillan, 1917), p. 226.

Richardson, incidentally, an early English disciple of Niebuhr, is the author of a limerick which alone should qualify him as an exegete not to be taken lightly:

At Swanwick, when Niebuhr had quit it
A young man exclaimed, "I have hit it!
Since I cannot do right
I must find out tonight
The right sin to commit—and commit it."

(Cited by Richard W. Fox, *Reinhold Niebuhr: A Biography* [New York: Pantheon, 1985], p. 181.)

CHAPTER 1: THE QUESTIONS AND THE ISSUE

1. Quoted in Introduction to Adam Smith, *The Wealth of Nations* (New York: E. P. Dutton, 1937), vol. I, p. vii.
2. Ibid., quoted on jacket of Modern Library Edition.
3. Ibid., Introduction, p. vi.
4. Ibid., p. 79.
5. Ibid., p. 128.
6. Ibid.
7. Ibid., p. 423.
8. Ibid., p. 508.
9. Ibid., Introduction, p. ix.
10. Ibid., p. 745.
11. Ibid., p. 726.
12. Ibid., p. 754.
13. Ibid., p. 724.
14. Max Weber, *The Protestant Ethic and the Spirit of Capitalism* (New York: Charles Scribner's Sons, 1958), pp. 17, 21.
15. Quoted in ibid., pp. 48–50. The two paragraphs are from Benjamin Franklin, *Works* (Sparks Edition), vol. II, pp. 87ff. and p. 80.

16. Quoted in Weber, p. 193, n. 7.

17. Ibid., pp. 51–52.

18. Ralph Ketcham, ed., *The Political Thought of Benjamin Franklin* (New York: Bobbs-Merrill, 1965), p. 358.

19. Quoted in Weber, p. 73.

20. Ibid., pp. 79, 204–212, notes.

21. Quoted in R. H. Tawney, *Religion and the Rise of Capitalism* (New York: Harcourt Brace, 1926), p. 105.

22. John Calvin, *Institutes of the Christian Religion,* trans. J. Allen (1838), vol. II, pp. 128–129 (Bk. III, Ch. XXI, par. 7) and p. 147 (Bk. III, Ch. XXIII, par. 7).

23. Quoted in Weber, *The Protestant Ethic,* p. 101.

24. Willian Tyndale, *The Parable of the Wicked Mammon* (Parker Society, 1848), p. 97.

25. Richard Baxter, *Christian Directory* (1678), vol. I, p. 111a and pp. 378b. 108b; vol. IV, p. 253a.

26. Quoted in Tawney, p. 246, from Richard Steele, *The Tradesman's Calling* (1684).

27. Weber, p. 235, n. 79.

28. Ibid., p. 121.

29. Tawney, p. 112.

30. John Wesley, *Thoughts Upon Methodism, Works,* vol. I, p. 441.

31. John Wesley, Sermon 50 in *The Use of Money, Works,* vol. I, pp. 445–446.

32. Weber, pp. 39–40.

CHAPTER 2: THE OLD TESTAMENT

1. See José Miranda, *Marx and the Bible* (Maryknoll, N.Y.: Orbis, 1974), pp. 46–47.

2. See Miranda, p. 14ff. Also Julio de Santa Ana, *Good News to the Poor* (Maryknoll, N.Y.: Orbis, 1979), p. 5.

3. See Gustavo Gutiérrez, *A Theology of Liberation* (Maryknoll, N.Y.: Orbis, 1973), p. 360.

CHAPTER 3: THE NEW TESTAMENT

1. St. Gregory the Great, Homily 40 in Migne, *Patrologiae Cursus—Series Latina* 76, cols. 1304–05.

2. J. Dupont, "Les Pauvres et la Pauvreté dans les Évangiles et les Actes," in *La Pauvreté Evangélique* (Paris: Ed. du Cerf, 1971), p. 52.

3. Pie-Raymond Régamey, *Poverty* (New York: Sheed and Ward, 1950), p. 11.

4. P. Seidensticker, "St. Paul et la Pauvreté," in *La Pauvreté Evangélique,* p. 102.

5. Ibid., pp. 131–133.

CHAPTER 4: THE FATHERS OF THE CHURCH

1. *Funk & Wagnalls New Encyclopedia* (Funk and Wagnalls, 1973), vol. 9, p. 384.

2. St. Gregory of Nazianzus, *Sobre el Amor a los Pobres,* MPG, T. XXXV, col. 909, in Julio de Santa Ana, *Good News to the Poor* (Maryknoll, N.Y.: Orbis, 1979), pp. 75–76.

3. In Walter Shewring, *Rich and Poor in Christian Tradition* (London: Burns and Oates, 1948), p. 6.

4. St. Basil, *Homilia VII,* 1, 3, and 4, MPG, T. XXXI, Cols. 280–281, 288, 289–292.

5. St. Basil, *The Rich Fool,* Migne, *Patrologiae Cursus—Series Graeca,* 31, cols. 261–277, in Shewring, p. 58.

6. St. Basil, *Homilia II,* MPG, T. XXIX, cols. 325–328, in Julio de Santa Ana, p. 75.

7. St. John Chrysostom. *On Lazarus,* Homily 11, in P. Evodokimov, *Theology Digest* 18:1 (1970), p. 49.

8. St. John Chrysostom, *1 Corinthians,* Homily 10.3, in P. Evodokimov, p. 49.

9. Ibid.

10. José Miranda, *Marx and the Bible* (Maryknoll, N.Y.: Orbis, 1974), pp. 10–14.

11. R. M. Grant, *Augustus to Constantine* (1970), p. 268.

12. St. John Chrysostom, *Fall of Eutropius,* 2.3, in Shewring, p. 35.

13. St. John Chrysostom, Homily X, *1 Thessalonians,* MPG, T. LXII, col. 462.

14. St. Ambrose, quoted by St. Thomas Aquinas, *Summa Theologiae,* II-II, 66, 7 (*Decretum Gratiani,* Dist. XLVII).

15. St. Ambrose, *De Nabuthe, Patrologiae Cursus—Series Latina,* PL 14, col. 747.

16. St. Ambrose, *Duties of the Clergy,* 1. 132, translation based on NPNF 10.22.

17. St. Ambrose, *De Nabuthe,* in Shewring, p. 70.

18. St. Ambrose, in R. Gryson, *Le Prêtre selon St. Ambrose* (Louvain: Ed., Orientaliste, 1968), p. 301.

19. St. Clement of Alexandria, *The Rich Man's Salvation,* in Shewring, p. 15.

20. St. Jerome, Carta 120, PL, 22, col. 984.

21. Reinhold Niebuhr, *Christian Realism and Political Problems* (New York: Scribners, 1953), p. 123.

22. St. Augustine, *De Trinitate,* PL 42, col. 1046.

23. St. Augustine, *Commentary on the Psalms,* MPL, T. XXXVI, col. 293, in Julio de Santa Ana, p. 72.

24. St. Augustine, Sermon 50, No. 3, in Régamey, *Poverty* (New York: Sheed & Ward, 1950), p. 12.

25. St. Augustine, in Shewring, pp. 35–36 (En. in Ps. 72, para. 26).

26. Régamey, p. 76.

27. St. Augustine, *Sermon* 87.1–2, "Patristic Social Consciousness—The Church and the Poor" by William J. Walsh and John P. Langan, in John C. Haughey, ed., *The Faith That Does Justice* (New York, Paulist Press, 1977), p. 133.

28. St. Augustine, *Sermon* 128.4, in Haughey, p. 133.

29. St. Gregory the Great, Reg. Past. III, 21, Shewring, p. 29.

30. St. Leo, *Sermon X,* Migne, PL 54, cols. 164–166, in Shewring, pp. 98–99.

31. St. Isidore, Migne, PL 83, cols. 728–30, in Shewring, pp. 112–114.

CHAPTER 5: THE MIDDLE AGES AND THOMAS AQUINAS

1. St. Ambrose Autpert, in Shewring, *Rich and Poor in Christian Tradition,* p. 117–118.

2. St. Bernard of Clairvaux, in Shewring, p. 132.

3. St. Catherine of Siena, in Shewring, p. 159.

4. A. P. D'Entrèves, ed., *Aquinas: Selected Political Writings* (New York: Macmillan, 1959), pp. 27ff.

5. *Summa Theologica,* Prima Secundae, Qu. 95, The Division of Human law, Art. 4, in D'Entrèves, pp. 131–133.

6. Aristotle, *Politics,* in *Basic Works of Aristotle* (New York: Random House, 1941), p. 1156 (Book II, 5, 1263a22–27).

7. *Summa Theologica* (also entitled *Summa Theologiae*), translated by Marcus Lefebure, O.P. (London: Blackfriars, 1975), II-II, 66, 66, 2, ad 1, p. 69.

8. In D'Entrèves,l p. 115.

9. *Summa Theologica,* II-II, 66, 66, 2, ad 1, p. 69.

10. D'Entrèves, p. 169.

11. Ibid., p. 81, from chap. XV, *De Regimine Principum.*

12. *Summa Theologica,* II-II, 66, 7, p. 83.

13. D'Entrèves, p. 71.

14. St. Thomas Aquinas, in *II Politics* (Commentary on the Politics of Aristotle), 8, 87.

15. Tommaso de Vio Cajetan, *S. Thomae . . . Summa Theologica cum commentariis Thomae de Vio Cajetani,* t. 6 (Rome, 1778), II-II, 118, 3, p. 188.

16. St. Thomas Aquinas, *Summa Theologiae,* Blackfriars Edition, *op. cit.,* II-II, 77.4, vol. 38, p. 229.

17. Ibid., vol. 34, pp. 257–258.

18. St. Thomas Aquinas, *Summa Theologica,* II-II, 57, 2 (trans. Thomas Gilby, O.P. [Blackfriars, 1975], vol. 37, p. 5).

19. William of Ockham, *Opus Nonaginta Dierum,* in *Guillelmi de Ockham,* ed. R. F. Bennett, and J. C. Sikes, trans. Mary Emil Penet (Manchester: University, 1940) vol. 1, p. 311.

20. Leo XIII, *Rerum Novarum,* par. 15 (Daughters of St. Paul, pp. 6, 9).

21. Raymond Miller, C.Ss.R., *Forty Years After* (Radio Replies Press).

22. See Henri Pirenne, *Economic and Social History of Medieval Europe* (New York: Harcourt Brace, 1937), pp. 189–206.

CHAPTER 6: THOMAS MORE AND THE RADICAL REFORMERS

1. William Roper, *The Life of Sir Thomas More Knighte,* edited by E. V. Hitchcock (New York: Oxford University Press, 1935), pp. 58–59. Also in *The Life of Sir Thomas More* by an author known only as "Ro. Ba.," written about 1599 (New York: Oxford University Press, 1950), pp. 89–90.

2. Roper, p. 48.

3. Frank E. Manuel and Fritzie P. Manuel, *Utopian Thought in the Western World* (Cambridge, Mass: Harvard University Press, 1979), p. 149.

4. Roper, p. 100.

5. Quoted in R. W. Chambers, *Thomas More* (Ann Arbor, Mich.: University of Michigan Press, 1958, originally published in England, 1935), p. 349.

6. Acts 5:29.

7. *The Marx-Engels Reader,* ed. Robert C. Tucker (New York: W. W. Norton, 1972), p. 109.

8. Ibid., p. 607, n. 2.

9. Karl Kautsky, *Thomas More* (1890), p. 340.

10. Thomas More, *Utopia,* translated and edited by H. V. S. Ogden (Appleton-Century-Crofts, 1949), pp. 25–26.

11. Ibid. p. 26.

12. Ibid. p. 32.

13. See the magnificent Holbein portrait of More in the Frick Museum, New York City.

14. Desiderius Erasmus, *Opus Epistolarum* IV, ed. P. S. and H. M. Allen (Oxford: Clarendon Press, 1922), p. 16, Erasmus to Ulrich von Hutten, July 23, 1519.

15. *Utopia,* p. 71.

16. Acts 2:44–46; 4:32.

17. *Utopia,* p. 83.

18. Ibid., p. 9.

19. Erasmus, p. 16.

20. *Utopia,* pp. 80–81.

21. Ibid., p. 81.

22. Ibid., p. 33.

23. Ibid., p. 35.

24. Ibid., p. 37.

25. Ibid., p. 29.

26. Ibid., p. 31.

27. Ibid., p. 39.

28. Ibid., pp. 32–33.

29. Ibid.

30. Ibid., p. 42.

31. Ibid., p. 33.

32. Ibid., p. 42

33. Ibid., pp. 32, 34.

34. Ibid., p. 33.

35. Ibid., p. 75.

36. Ibid., pp. 71, 72.

37. Manuel and Manuel, p. 63.

38. *Utopia,* pp. 81–82.

39. I. A. Richter, ed. *Selections from the Notebooks of Leonardo da Vinci* (New York: Oxford University Press, 1952), pp. 213–214.

40. Ludovico Agostini, "L'Infinito," book I, part II, sec. 130, quoted in Firpo, *Lo Stato ideale della Controriforma,* p. 275.

41. Ludovico Agostini, *La Repubblica Immaginaria,* ed. Luigi Firpo (Turin, 1957), p. 63.

42. Friedrich Engels, "Socialism: Utopian and Scientific," in *Marx-Engels Reader,* p. 607, and in *The German Revolutions,* ed. Leonard Krieger (Chicago: Univ. of Chicago Press, 1967), pp. 29, 30, 46ff. for Engels's appraisal of Müntzer.

43. Thomas Müntzer, *Schriften und Briefe,* ed. Günther Franz (Gütersloh: G. Mohn, 1968), p. 251.

44. Ibid., p. 471.

45. Ibid., p. 394.

46. Manuel and Manuel, p. 187.

47. Müntzer, *Schriften und Briefe,* p. 329.

48. Ibid., pp. 454–455.

49. Ibid, p. 548.

50. Manuel and Manuel, p. 198.

51. Ulrich Zwingli, *Huldreich Zwinglis Sämtliche Werke* (Leipzig, 1808), vol. II, p. 511.

52. John Hostetler, *Hutterite Society* (Baltimore, Md: John Hopkins University Press, 1974), p. 34.

53. Ibid., p. 143.

54. Quoted in John Horsch, *The Hutterian Brethren* (Goshen, Ind.: Mennonite Historical Society, 1931), pp. 131–132.

55. Quoted in Horsch, p. 232.

56. Hostetler, p. 142.

57. Ibid., p. 166.

58. Ibid., p. 147.

59. Quoted in Manuel and Manuel, p. 255.

60. In ibid., p. 260.

61. In ibid., p. 239.

62. Ibid., p. 309.

63. Ibid., p. 410.

INTRODUCTION TO PART II

1. Tommaso de Vio Cajetan, p. 188 (see chap. 5, n. 15 above).

2. John Locke, *Two Treatises of Government* (New York: Cambridge University Press/Mentor, 1963), p. 395 (*Second Treatise,* chap. IX, sec. 124).

3. Ibid., p. 327 (*Second Treatise,* chap. V, sec. 25).

4. Ibid., p. 328 (sec. 27).

5. Ibid., p. 329.

6. Ibid., p. 406 (chap. XI, sec. 138).

CHAPTER 7: FRANCE

1. *A History of Civilization,* ed. Crane Brinton et al. (Englewood Cliffs, N. J.: Prentice-Hall, 1960), vol. II, p. 52.

2. G. D. H. Cole, *A History of Socialist Thought* (London: Macmillan, 1953), vol. I, p. 219.

3. Cited in Joseph N. Moody, ed., *Church and Society* (New York: Arts, 1953), p. 84, n. 31.

4. Henri Daniel-Rops, *The Church in an Age of Revolution* (Garden City, N.Y.: Doubleday, 1967), vol. II, p. 31.

5. Ibid.

6. François Fénelon, *Télémaque,* trans. Littlebury and Boyer (London; 1726), p. 169.

7. Ibid., p. 184.

8. Quoted in Jacques Droz, *Histoire générale du socialisme* (Paris: Presses Universitaires, 1972), vol. I, p. 109, trans. J.C.C.

9. André Biéler, *Chrétiens et socialistes avant Marx* (Geneva: Labor et Fides, 1982), p. 275, trans. J.C.C.

10. Manuel and Manuel, p. 561.

11. P.-J.-B. Buchez and P.-C. Roux-Lavergne, *Histoire parlementaire de la Révolution Francaise* (Paris: 1834), vol. II, p. ii, trans. J.C.C.

12. Romain Rolland, *The Living Thoughts of Rousseau* (Longman Green, 1939), p. 5.

13. Ibid., p. 40.

14. Ibid., p. 47.

15. Jean Jacques Rousseau, *The Social Contract* (New York: Hafner Publishing, 1947), p. 5.

16. Ibid., Introduction, p. xvii.

17. Rousseau, p. 5.

18. Ibid., Introduction, p. xxvii.

19. Rousseau, p. 91.

20. Ibid., pp. 9–10.

21. Ibid., p. 20.

22. Ibid., p. 22.

23. Ibid., p. 123.

24. Ibid., 120.

25. Quoted in Manuel and Manuel, p. 574.

26. *Marx-Engels Reader,* p. 359.

27. Mercier de la Rivière, *Ordre naturel* (Paris: New Edition, 1910), p. 338, quoted in Parker Moon, *The Labor Problem and the Social Catholic Movement in France* (New York: Macmillan, 1921), p. 10.

28. Pierre Du Pont in Preface to Quesnay's *Physiocratie* (Paris, 1767–68), p. lxxxi, quoted in Moon, p. 10.

29. Du Pont, *De l'origine et des progrès d'une science nouvelle,* reprinted in Daire's edition of *Les Physiocrates* (Paris, 1846), vol II, p. 347, quoted in Moon, p. 10.

30. Moon, pp. 7–9

31. Villerme, *Tableau de l'état physique et morale des ouvriers employés dans les manufactures de coton, de laine et de soie* (Paris, 1840), vol. II, p. 91, quoted in Moon, p. 9.

32. Emile Durkheim, *Socialism* (New York: Collier, 1962), pp. 127–46.

33. *The New Encyclopedia of Social Reform,* ed. W. D. P. Bliss (New York: Funk and Wagnalls, 1908), p. 1088.

34. Henri Saint-Simon, *Selected Writings,* ed. Keith Taylor (New York: Holmes and Meier, 1975), p. 103.

35. 2 Thessalonians 3:10.

36. Henri Saint-Simon, *Nouveau Christianisme* (Paris: Bureau de Globe, 1832), pp. 10–11, trans. J.C.C.

37. Ibid., p. 12.

38. Ibid., p. 18.

39. Ibid., pp. 19–20.

40. Ibid., p. 23.

41. Ibid., pp. 25–31.

42. Ibid., p. 40.

43. Ibid., pp. 48–62.

44. Ibid., p. 76.

45. Ibid., p. 71.

46. Saint-Simon in *La Politique* (newspaper), 1919, quoted in Droz, vol. I, p. 341, trans. J.C.C.

47. Cole, vol. I, p. 56.

48. *Retraite de Ménilmontant* (Paris, 1832), p. 15, quoted in Manuel and Manuel, p. 619.

49. *Souvenirs littéraires* (Paris, 1883), vol. II, p. 124, quoted in Manuel and Manuel, p. 635.

50. Alexander Gray, *The Socialist Tradition* (New York: Harper, 1946 and 1968), p. 168.

51. *Marx-Engels Reader,* p. 388.

52. Durkheim, pp. 39–63. I have simplified Durkheim's definitions.

53. Cole, vol. I, pp. 189–201.

54. Jean Bruhat in Droz, vol. I, p. 379.

55. Quoted in Alexander Vidler, *Prophecy and Papacy* (London: SCM Press, 1954), pp. 71–72. An excellent book on Lamennais and his differences with Gregory XVI, from which most of the following facts about Lamennais are derived.

56. M. Kaufman, *Christian Socialism* (London: Kegan Paul, 1888), p. 38.

57. Quoted in Daniel-Rops, vol. I, p. 223.

58. Vidler, p. 161.

59. Ibid., 194.

60. Ibid., pp. 200–201.

61. *The Papal Encyclicals,* ed. Claudia Carlen (Wilmington, N.C.: McGrath, 1981, "Original Translation"), vol. I (1740–1878), p. 236.

62. Ibid., p. 237.

63. Ibid., p. 238.

64. *Dignitatis Humanae* (Declaration on Religious Freedom), in *The Gospel of Peace and Justice,* ed. Joseph Gremillion (Maryknoll, N.Y.: Orbis, 1976), p. 339.

65. *The Papal Encyclicals,* pp. 238–239.

66. Ibid., p. 234.

67. *Populorum Progressio,* in Gremillion, p. 396.

68. *The Papal Encyclicals,* p. 240.

69. Vidler, p. 244.

70. *The Papal Encyclicals,* pp. 249–250.

71. Ibid., p. 234. For the worthlessness of these assurances, see Daniel-Rops, vol. I, pp. 277–281.

72. Félicité Lamennais, *The Words of a Believer* (London: Cousins, 1832), pp. 44–45.

73. Ibid., p. 61–63.

74. Vidler, pp. 285–286, trans. J.C.C.

75. Ibid., pp. 277ff.

76. Daniel-Rops, vol. I, pp. 259-277.

77. Ibid., p. 277.

78. Kaufman, p. 54.

79. Daniel–Rops, p. 277.

80. From *Le Livre du peuple* (The Book of the People), 1837, quoted in Albert Samuel, *Le Socialisme* (Lyon: Chronique Sociale, 1981), p. 81, trans. J.C.C.

81. Quoted by Jean Bruhat in Droz, p. 380, trans. J.C.C.

82. Ibid., 401.

83. Samuel, p. 84.

84. Ibid.

85. Ibid.

86. Quoted in Samuel, p. 85.

87. Victor Considérant, *Le Socialisme devant le vieux monde* (Paris, 1848), pp. 69–70, trans. J.C. C.

88. P.-J.-B. Buchez and P.-C. Lavergne, *Histoire parlementaire de la Révolution Française* (Paris, 1834), vol. I, p. 1, trans. J.C. C.

89. Armand Cuvillier, *P.-J.-B. Buchez et les origines du socialisme chrétien* (Paris: Presses Universitaires, 1948), p. 19, trans. J.C. C.

90. George Lichtheim, *The Origins of Socialism* (New York: Praeger, 1969), p. 66.

91. Cuvillier, p. 81.

92. Buchez, *Introduction à la science de l'histoire* (Paris: Paulin, 1833), p. 254.

93. Buchez, *L'Européen* (Oct. 6, 1832), in Barbara Petri, trans., *The Historical Thought of P.-J.-B. Buchez* (Washington, D.C.: Catholic University, 1958), p. 12. This is probably the only study in English of Buchez's life and thought.

94. Ibid.

95. Andre Biéler, *Chrétiens et socialistes avant Marx* (Geneva: Labor et Fides, 1982), p. 68. This is a gold mine of facts and quotations from the Buchezians, trans. J.C. C.

96. Buchez article in *L'Européen* (December 17, 1831), in Cuvillier, p. 42.

97. Cuvillier, p. 64.

98. Considérant, p. 101.

99. Quoted in Petri, p. 120.

100. Considérant, p. 69.

101. Buchez, *Traité de politique et de science sociale* (Paris: Amyot, 1866), vol. I, p. 330.

102. Ibid., p. 332.

103. Ibid., pp. 338–339.

104. Buchez, *Introduction à la science de l'histoire,* vol. I, p. 8, quoted by Petri, pp. 23–24.

105. Quoted in Cuvillier, p. 38.

106. Buchez, from preface of *Histoire parlementaire,* vol. 32, quoted in Cuvillier, p. 39.

107. Cuvillier, p. 41.

108. Ibid., p. 44.

109. Ibid.

110. Petri, p. 110.

111. Ibid, pp. 73–74.

112. Cuvillier, p. 33.

113. Frédéric Arnaud de l'Ariege, *La Révolution et l'Église* (Paris, 1869), p. 14.

114. Auguste Boulland, *Doctrine politique du christianisme* (Paris, 1845), pp. 298–299.

115. Ibid., pp. 244–245.

116. *L'Atelier* (January 1848), p. 76.

117. C. -F. Chevé, *Catholicisme et démocratie, ou le règne du Christ* (Paris, 1842), pp. 12–14.

118. Anthime Corbon, *Pourquoi nous vous délaissons* (1877), p. 5.

119. Corbon, *Le secret du peuple de Paris* (Paris, 1863), pp. 320–321.

120. Henri Feugueray, *L'Association ouvrière, industrielle et agricole* (Paris, 1851), unpaged preface.

121. Feugueray, *Revue Nationale* (1848), p. 393.

122. Feugueray, *L'Association,* p. 24.

123. Désiré Laverdant, *Socialisme catholique: La Déroute des Cesars* (Paris, 1851), p. xi.

124. Ibid., p. xiv.

125. Auguste Ott, *Revue Nationale* (1847), p. 57.

126. In Biéler, p. 67.

127. Alexander Gray, *The Socialist Tradition* (New York: Harper, 1946 and 1968), p. 193.

128. Charles Fourier, *Archives Nationales,* 10 AS8 (4), in Frank E. Manuel, *The Prophets of Paris* (Cambridge: Harvard University, 1962), p. 235.

129. Lichtheim, p. 74.

130. Ibid.

131. Considérant, *Le Socialisme,* p. 142.

132. Ibid., p. 60.

133. Ibid., p. 1.

134. Ibid., p. 9.

135. Ibid., p. 28.

136. Ibid., p. 124.

137. Ibid., p. 90.

138. Ibid., p. 106.

139. Ibid., p. 102.

140. Ibid., p. 78.

141. In Biéler, p. 273.

142. Considérant, pp. 165–166.

143. Ibid., p. 210.

144. Ibid., pp. 204–205.

145. Ibid., p. 220.

146. Biéler, p. 27.

147. Étienne Cabet, *Le Vrai Christianisme suivant Jésus Christ* (Paris, 1847), p. 363, trans. J.C. C.

148. Ibid., p. 5.

149. *The New Encyclopedia of Social Reform,* p. 593.

150. Ibid., p. 594.

151. *Marx-Engels Reader,* p. 8.

152. Quoted in Droz, vol. I, p. 14.

153. Cabet, p. 131.

154. Ibid., p. 114.

155. Ibid., p. 624.

156. Ibid., p. 114.

157. Ibid., p. 633.

158. *Marx-Engels Reader,* p. 381.

159. Cole, vol. II, p. 92.

160. Karl Marx, preface to *A Contribution to the Critique of Political Economy,* in *Marx-Engels Reader,* p. 4.

161. Two examples from *Capital,* in *Marx-Engels Reader,* pp. 250–251, 255.

162. Cole, vol. II, p. 94.

163. *Marx–Engels Reader,* p. 380.

164. *Critique of the Gotha Program,* in *Marx-Engels Reader,* p. 393.

165. Ibid., p. 393–394.

166. A. R. Vidler, *A Century of Social Catholicism* (London: S.P.C.K., 1964), p. 34.

167. Biéler, p. 225.

168. Ibid.

169. Vidler, pp. 50–51.

170. Biéler, p. 50.

171. Vidler, p. 48.

172. A.R. Vidler, *The Church in an Age of Revolution* (Grand Rapids: Eerdmans, 1961), p. 41.

173. *The Papal Encyclicals,* p. 296.

174. Ibid., p. 300.

175. Ibid., p. 301.

176. Ibid., p. 296.

177. Ibid., p. 299.

178. Ibid.

179. Ibid., p.371.

180. Ibid., p. 283.

181. Ibid., p. 250.

182. Ibid., p. 279.

183. Ibid., p. 384.

184. Jean-Baptiste Duroselle, *Les Débuts du catholicisme sociale en France* (Paris: Presses Universitaires, 1951), pp. 705–706. François–Auguste Ledreuille (1797–1860) was a priest-protegé of Archbishop Affre, a popular preacher and the outstanding personality of the society of St. Francis Xavier, an organization of Catholic workers which in 1845 had fifteen thousand members in Paris and three thousand in Lyons alone. Christian socialists gave lectures at many of the Society's meetings. *L'Univers* was the newspaper of the Catholic right, edited by the able but disastrously reactionary Louis Veuillot.

CHAPTER 8: ENGLAND

1. N. C. Masterman, *John Malcolm Ludlow: The Builder of Christian Socialism* (Cambridge University Press, 1963), p. 8.

2. Ibid., p. 21.

3. Ludlow's unpublished *Autobiography* (chapter XVII), in Torben Christensen, *Origin and History of Christian Socialism: 1848–54* (Copenhagen: Universitetsforlaget, 1962), p. 58.

4. Ibid., p. 59.

5. Masterman, p. 60.

6. William Shakespeare, *King Henry VI,* Part II, Act IV, Scene 2.

7. In Michael Harrington, *Socialism* (New York: Bantam, 1973), p. 26.

8. Christensen, p. 69.

9. Brenda Colloms, *Victorian Visionaries* (London: Constable, 1982), p. 121.

10. *Charles Kingsley: His Letters and Memories of His Life,* edited by his wife (London: 1877, 4th ed., pp. 156–7.

11. Ibid., p. 156.

12. Christensen, p. 75.

13. Ibid., p. 306.

14. Ibid., pp. 76–77.

15. *The Marx-Engels Reader,* edited by Robert C. Tucker (New York: W. W. Norton, 1972), p. 12, from "The Critique of Hegel's *Philosophy of Right.*"

16. Christensen, p. 81.

17. Ibid., p. 89.

18. Ibid., pp. 86–87.

19. Ibid., p. 87.

20. Ibid., p. 100.

21. Ibid., p. 127.

22. Masterman, p. 89.

23. Ibid., p. 92.

24. Christensen, p. 145.

25. Ibid.

26. Masterman, p. 95.

27. Christensen, pp. 133–34.

28. Ibid., p. 253.

29. Ibid., p. 254. These words appeared in January 1852, in the *Journal of Association,* the Christian socialist newspaper that had succeeded *The Christian Socialist,* the weekly that Ludlow edited from November 1850 to December 1851, at which point disagreements with Maurice, his unhappiness over the trend of Neale and others toward consumer cooperation, led to his resignation and the change of name. Ludlow used to say, "If you appeal to consumption, you appeal to the belly. God is the eternal producer." (Masterman, p. 118). Maurice by 1852 had become increasingly embarrassed by the name *Christian Socialist,* as it became evident that his vague notion of socialism was not shared by Ludlow, Goderich, and others. The *Journal of Association* lasted until June 1852, mostly under the editorship of Tom Hughes.

30. Christensen, pp. 257–58.

31. Ibid., p. 258.

32. Ibid., p. 263.

33. Ibid., p. 264.

34. Ibid., p. 365.

35. Ibid., p. 364.

36. Masterman, p. 207.

37. Ibid., p. 250.

38. Christensen, p. 366.

39. Gilbert C. Binyon, *The Christian Socialist Movement in England* (New York: Macmillan, 1931), p. 84.

40. From Preface to Shaw's *Plays Pleasant* (London: Penguin, 1946), quoted in Peter d'A. Jones, *The Christian Socialist Revival: 1877–1914* (Princeton, N.J.: Princeton University Press, 1968), p. 99.

41. Ibid., pp. 175–76.

42. Ibid., p. 75, n. 30.

43. Ibid., p. 419.

44. Ibid., p. 182.

45. G. B. Shaw, Preface to *Androcles and the Lion* in *Complete Plays with Prefaces* (New York: Dodd, Mead, 1963), vol. V, p. 381.

46. Jones, p. 120.

47. Ibid., p. 146.

48. Ibid., p. 146, n. 105.

49. Ibid., p. 134.

50. Ibid., pp. 160–61.

51. Ibid., p. 116.

52. Ibid., p. 164.

53. Quoted in Maisie Ward, *Gilbert Keith Chesterton* (New York: Sheed and Ward, 1943), pp. 163–64.

54. G. K. Chesterton, *Autobiography* (New York: Sheed and Ward, 1936), p. 169.

55. Jones, p. 166.

56. Ibid., p. 222.

57. Ibid., p. 246.

58. Ibid., p. 243.

59. Ibid., p. 248.

60. Ibid., p. 248.

61. Conrad Noel, article in *The Country Times,* June 1912.

62. Conrad Noel, *Socialism in Church History* (Milwaukee: The Young Church-man, 1911), pp. 15–16.

63. Jones, p. 188.

64. Donaldson, quoted in Jones, p. 187.

65. Maurice B. Reckitt and C. E. Bechhofer, *The Meaning of National Guilds* (London: Cecil Palmer, 1918), pp. xiii–xiv.

66. Maurice B. Reckitt, *As It Happened* (London: J. M. Dent, 1941), p. 114.

67. S. G. Hobson, *National Guilds and the State* (London and New York: Macmillan, 1920) and G. D. H. Cole, *Guild Socialism Restated* (London: Parsons, 1920). The same is true of A. J. Penty's *The Restoration of the Guild System* (London: Swan Sonnenschein, 1906). Penty identified himself as "a Christian socialist."

68. Reckitt and Bechhofer, p. xii.

69. Alexander Gray, *The Socialist Tradition: Moses to Lenin* (New York: Harper/Torch, 1946), p. 115.

70. G. B. Shaw, Preface to *Androcles and the Lion* from *Nine Plays* (New York: Dodd, Mead, 1935), p. 904.

71. Ibid., p. 880.

72. Anne Fremantle, *This Little Band of Prophets* (New York: Mentor Books, 1960), p. 231.

73. Reckitt, *As It Happened,* p. 107.

74. Shaw, *The New Age,* February 15, 1908, p. 310.

75. Jones, p. 353.

76. Ibid.

77. Ibid., p. 458.

78. Ibid., p. 459.

79. Cited by Ronald Preston in Introduction to William Temple, *Christianity and Social Order* (New York: Seabury, 1977), p. 23.

80. Ibid., p. 100.

81. Joseph Fletcher, *William Temple* (New York: Seabury, 1953), p. 263.

82. Ibid., p. 247.

83. Ibid., p. 184.

84. See Fletcher, pp. 277–78.

85. Ross Terrill, *R. H. Tawney and His Times: Socialism as Fellowship* (Cambridge: Harvard University Press, 1973), pp. 60–61.

86. Ibid., p. 51.

87. Gary J. Dorrien, *The Democratic Socialist Vision* (Totowa, N.J.: Rowman & Littlefield, 1987), p. 28.

88. Ibid., p. 32.

89. Temple, p. 53.

90. Ibid., p. 80.

91. Terrill, p. 126.

92. *London Times,* November 28, 1960.

93. Terrill, p. 3.

94. Ibid., p. 276.

95. Ibid., p. 253.

96. Ibid., p. 53.

97. Ibid., p. 53.

98. R. H. Tawney, *Religion and the Rise of Capitalism* (New York: Harcourt Brace, 1926), p. 280.

99. Terrill, p. 59.

100. Tawney, pp. 12–13.

101. Ibid., p. 267.

102. Ibid., p. 317, n. 32.

103. Terrill, p. 185.

104. Ibid., p. 51.

105. Ibid., p. 3.

106. Ibid., p. 82.

107. Ibid., p. 41.

108. Ibid., p. 63.

109. Ibid., p. 30.

110. Ibid., p. 340, n. 57.

111. Ibid., p. 151.

112. Ibid., p. 160.

113. Ibid., p. 55.

114. Ibid., p. 277.

CHAPTER 9: GERMAN-SPEAKING EUROPE

1. G. D. H. Cole, *A History of Socialist Thought,* vol. 1, p. 222.

2. Edmund Wilson, *To the Finland Station* (Garden City, N.Y.: Doubleday, 1940), p. 165.

3. Ibid., pp. 166–68.

4. Weitling, *The Poor Sinner's Gospel* (London: Sheed and Ward, 1969), p. 17.

5. Ibid., p. 119.

6. Ibid., p. 120.

7. Ibid., p. 130.

8. Ibid., p. 153.

9. Ibid., p. 182.

10. Carl Wittke, *The Utopian Communist: A Biography of Wilhelm Weitling* (Baton Rouge: Louisiana State University Press, 1950), p. 136.

11. The entire text of the *Circular Against Kriege* is included in Henri Desroche, *Socialisme et sociologie religieuse* (Paris: Cujas, 1965), pp. 319–33. This quote is from p. 321, trans. J.C. C.

12. Ibid., p. 328.

13. Ibid., p. 326.

14. Ibid., p. 318.

15. *The Communist Manifesto* in *The Marx-Engels Reader,* ed. Robert C. Tucker (New York: Norton, 1972), p. 354.

16. Edgar Alexander, "Church and Society in Germany," in *Church and Society: Catholic Social and Political Thought and Movements, 1789–1950,* ed.

Joseph N. Moody (New York: Arts, 1953), part IV, p. 395.

17. Ibid.

18. Ibid., p. 403.

19. Ibid., p. 399.

20. Ibid., p. 400.

21. Ibid., p. 403.

22. Ibid., p. 398.

23. Wilhelm von Ketteler, *The Social Teachings of Wilhelm Emmanuel von Ketteler,* trans. Rupert J. Ederer (Washington, D.C.: University Press, 1981), p. vi.

24. Ibid., pp. 109–11.

25. Alexander, p. 409.

26. William Hogan, *The Development of Bishop Wilhelm Emmanuel von Ketteler's Interpretation of the Social Problem* (Washington, D.C.: Catholic University, 1946), p. 40.

27. Ketteler, p. 10.

28. Ibid., pp. 11, 12, 15.

29. Ibid., p. 16.

30. Ibid., p. 15.

31. Ibid., p. 13.

32. Ibid., p. 18.

33. Ibid., p. 32.

34. Ibid., p. 34.

35. Hogan, p. 116.

36. Ibid., p. 101.

37. Ibid., p. 107.

38. Ketteler, p. 410.

39. Ibid., pp. 441, 442, 444.

40. Ibid., p. 444.

41. Ibid., p. 406.

42. Hogan, p. 171.

43. Ibid., p. 147.

44. Ibid., p. 266.

45. Ibid., p. 137.

46. Ibid., p. 119.

47. Ibid.

48. *Marx-Engels Reader,* p. 397.

49. Cited in David Goldstein and Martha Avery, *Socialism* (Boston: Flynn, 1911), p. 95.

50. *Berlin Volksblatt* (1890), n. 281.

51. Goldstein and Avery, p. 148.

52. Cited in Victor Cathrein, *Socialism* (New York: Benziger, 1904), p. 216.

53. W. B. Yeats, "The Second Coming," in *Poetry of W. B. Yeats* (New York: Macmillan, 1983), p. 187.

54. Ketteler, p. xi.

55. Hogan, p. 18.

56. Cited in James Bentley, *Between Marx and Christ: The Dialogue in German-Speaking Europe, 1870–1970* (London: NLB, 1982), p. 18.

57. Ibid., p. 22.

58. Ibid., p. 5.

59. Ibid., p. 62.

60. J. L. Adams in *Metanoia,* (September 1971), pp. 2–3.

61. Bentley, p. 23.

62. Ibid., pp. 23–24.

63. Ibid., p. 23.

64. Ibid., p. 24.

65. Christoph Blumhardt in *Metanoia,* p. 6.

66. Bentley, p. 28.

67. *Metanoia,* p. 14.

68. *Signs of the Kingdom: A Ragaz Reader,* ed. and trans. Paul Bock (Grand Rapids: Eerdmans, 1984), Introduction, p. xiv.

69. Bentley, pp. 64–65.

70. Bock, pp. 47–48.

71. Ibid., pp. 43, 49, 50, 54, 55.

72. Ibid., p. 84.

73. Ibid., pp. 28–31.

74. Maurice Friedman, *Martin Buber's Life and Work: The Middle Years, 1923–45* (New York: Dutton, 1983), p. 99.

75. Buber, *Pointing the Way* (New York: Harper, 1957), p. 112.

76. Friedman, p. 99.

77. Bock, p. 100.

78. Eduard Buess and Markus Mattmüller, *Prophetischer Socialismus* (Prophetic Socialism): Blumhardt, Ragaz, Barth (Freiburg: Edition Exodus, 1986), p. 73, trans. Gabriel Grasberg.

79. *Karl Barth and Radical Politics,* ed. George Hunsinger (Philadelphia: Westminster, 1976), pp. 19, 30, 36.

80. Cited in Bentley, p. 62.

81. Cited in ibid., p. 25.

82. Cited by Joseph Bettis in Hunsinger, p. 165.

83. K. Barth, *The Word of God and the Word of Man* (Boston: Pilgrim Press, 1928), p. 276.

84. K. Barth, *The Epistle to the Romans,* trans. E. C. Hoskyns (London: Oxford, 1933), p. 480.

85. Cited in Hunsinger, p. 208, from 1st ed. of *Römerbrief* (Epistle to the Romans), p. 390.

86. M. Mattmüller in *Als Christ Sozialist,* ed. Jurgen Finnern (*Bund der Religiösen Sozialisten Deutschland e.V.* [Association of Religious Socialists of West Germany], 1983), p. 17.

87. Ibid., p. 18.

88. Cited in Hunsinger, from preface to Karl Barth, *Community, State and Church* (New York: Doubleday, 1960), p. 11.

89. *The Epistle to the Romans,* p. 353.

90. Cited by Richard W. Fox, *Reinhold Niebuhr* (New York: Pantheon, 1985), p. 123.

91. Bock, p. xix.

92. Karl Barth, "No Christian Marshall Plan," in *Christian Century*, December 8, 1948, pp. 1330–32.

93. Pierre Benoit, *Jesus and the Gospel* (New York: Herder & Herder, 1973), p. 42.

94. Niebuhr's address is a chapter (pp. 105–17) in his *Christian Realism*

and Political Problems (New York: Scribner's 1953), p. 109.

95. Ibid., p. 116.

96. Cited by Eberhard Busch in *Karl Barth* (Philadelphia: Fortress, 1976), p. 383.

97. Ibid.

98. K. Barth, *The Christian Century* (March 25, 1959), p. 355.

99. Reinhold Niebuhr, *The Christian Century* (February 11, 1959), p. 168. (This date precedes the above because Niebuhr was commenting on a partial report printed elsewhere. A fuller translation appeared in the March 25 issue.)

100. *The Christian Century* (December 31, 1969), pp. 1662–63.

101. *The Epistle to the Romans,* p. 509.

102. Wilhelm and Marion Pauck, *Paul Tillich: His Life and Thought,* vol. I, (New York: Harper and Row, 1976), p. 23.

103. *Time,* March 16, 1959, p. 47.

104. Pauck and Pauck, pp. 40–41.

105. *Time* (March 16, 1959), p. 47.

106. Pauck and Pauck, p. 41.

107. Ibid., p. 229.

108. P. Tillich, *Systematic Theology,* vol. II (University of Chicago Press, 1957), p. 160.

109. Pauck and Pauck, p. 126.

110. Ibid., p. 70.

111. P. Tillich, *Political Expectation,* ed. James Luther Adams (New York: Harper and Row, 1971), p. 81.

112. *Metanoia,* p. 5.

113. Ibid., p. 9, trans. J. L. Adams.

114. *Political Expectation,* p. 79.

115. P. Tillich, *The Socialist Decision* (New York: Harper and Row, 1977), p. 67.

116. *The Marx-Engels Reader,* ed. Robert C. Tucker (New York: Norton, 1972), pp. 65, 66, 98.

117. "The German Ideology," in ibid., p. 157.

118. Ibid., p. 124.

119. *The Socialist Decision,* p. 159.

120. *Time,* May 17, 1963, p. 69.

121. *Political Expectation,* p. 41.

122. John R. Stumme, *Socialism in Theological Perspective: A Study of Paul Tillich, 1918–1933* (Missoula, Montana: Scholars Press, 1978), p. 33.

123. Günter Ewald, "Christians in the Labour Movement," in March/April issue of *ASCE News,* periodical of European Christian Socialist Action, an organization of southern European, mainly Italian, Christian socialists.

CHAPTER 10: THE UNITED STATES

1. Charles H. Hopkins, *The Rise of the Social Gospel in American Protestantism, 1865–1915* (New Haven: Yale University, 1940), p. 9.

2. James Dombrowski, *The Early Days of Christian Socialism in America* (New York: Columbia University, 1936), p. 5.

3. John K. Galbraith, *The Age of Uncertainty* (Boston: Houghton Mifflin, 1977), p. 49.

4. Quoted in Louis Adamic, *Dynamite* (New York: Viking, 1931), p. 23.

5. Robert T. Handy, *The Social Gospel in America, 1870–1920: Gladden, Ely, Rauschenbusch* (New York: Oxford, 1966), p. 60.

6. *The Dawn,* January 1, 1891.

7. Charles and Mary Beard, *The Rise of American Civilization* (New York: Macmillan, 1939), vol. II, p. 174.

8. Ibid.

9. See chapter 1 above, pp. 15–17.

10. Dombrowski, p. 80.

11. Hopkins, p. 43.

12. Ibid.

13. Ibid., p. 44.

14. Dombrowski, p. 81.

15. Ibid., p. 83.

16. Ibid., p. 80.

17. Hopkins, p. 255.

18. Washington Gladden, *The Working People and Their Employers* (Boston: Lockwood, Brooks, 1876), p. 44.

19. Ibid., pp. 18, 19.

20. Gladden, *Reflections* (Boston: Houghton Mifflin, 1909), p. 309.

21. Ibid., p. 308.

22. Handy, p. 166.

23. *Working People,* p. 233.

24. Handy, p. 139.

25. Ibid., p. 140.

26. Ibid., p. 61.

27. Ibid., p. 55.

28. Ibid., p. 69.

29. Edward Bellamy, *Looking Backward* (New York: New American Library, 1888 and 1960), pp. 53–58.

30. Ibid., p. 53.

31. John E. E. Dalberg-Acton, letter to Bishop Mandell Creighton, 1887.

32. Dombrowski, p. 94.

33. Bellamy, *Equality* (New York: Appleton, 1897), p. 341.

34. Ibid., p. 259.

35. Dombrowski, p. 87.

36. Ibid., pp. 94–95.

37. Ibid., p. 50.

38. Handy, p. 173.

39. Ibid., p. 186.

40. Ibid., p. 203.

41. Dombrowski, p. 50.

42. Ibid., p. 51.

43. Handy, p. 215.

44. Hopkins, p. 170.

45. *The Dawn,* February 1894.

46. Ibid., May 15, 1889.

47. Ibid.

48. Ibid., December 4, 1890.

49. Ibid., November 1890.

50. Ibid., February 12, 1891.

51. *The Dawn,* June 15, 1889.

52. Ibid., December 1894.

53. Ibid., June 15, 1889, "SCS Declaration of Principles."

54. Dombrowski, p. 172.

55. George Davis Herron, *The Christian Society* (New York: Johnson Reprint, 1894 and 1969), p. xv, Introduction by Milton Cantor.

56. Dombrowski, p. 186.

57. Ibid.

58. Herron, pp. 24–25.

59. Hopkins, p. 187.

60. Dombrowski, p. 177.

61. Ibid., p. 177.

62. Ibid., p. 178.

63. Ibid., p. 180.

64. Goldstein and Avery, *Socialism,* p. 4.

65. Ibid., p. 275.

66. Ibid., p. 274.

67. Ibid., p. 280.

68. Ibid., pp. 282–83.

69. Ibid., p. 310.

70. Ibid., p. 107.

71. *The Christian Socialist,* February 15, 1910.

72. Ibid., July 20, 1911.

73. Ibid., October 15, 1905.

74. Ibid., June 15, 1905.

75. Ibid., January 26, 1911.

76. *Chicago Tribune,* August 15, 1911, quoted in *Christian Socialist,* August 17, 1911.

77. *The Christian Socialist,* August 31, 1911.

78. Eugene V. Debs, "Jesus, the Supreme Leader," in *The Coming Nation,* March 1914.

79. *The Christian Socialist,* September 28, 1911.

80. Ibid., May 1, 1907.

81. Ibid., February 1918.

82. Ibid., March 15, 1910.

83. Ibid., April 1, 1905.

84. Ibid., December 1918.

85. Ibid., August 1921.

86. Reinhold Niebuhr, *An Interpretation of Christian Ethics* (New York: Harper, 1935), p. 1.

87. Reinhold Niebuhr, "Walter Rauschenbusch in Historical Perspective," in *Religion in Life* (Fall 1958), a paper read at a colloquium celebrating the fiftieth anniversary of Rauschenbusch's most important book, *Christianity and the Social Crisis,* November 22, 1957.

88. Paul Merkley, *Reinhold Niebuhr* (Montreal: McGill-Queen's, 1975), p. 74.

89. Niebuhr, "Intellectual Autobiography" in *Reinhold Niebuhr: His Religious, Social and Political Thought,* ed. Charles Kegley and Robert Bretall (New York: Macmillan, 1956), p. 13.

90. Dores R. Sharpe, *Walter Rauschenbusch* (New York: Macmillan, 1942), p. 154.

91. Ibid.

92. Walter Rauschenbusch, *A Theology for the Social Gospel* (New York: Macmillan, 1917), p. 277.

93. Letter from A. W. Beaven to Mrs. Rauschenbusch in 1937, quoted by Max Stackhouse in his introduction to Walter Rauschenbusch, *The Righteousness of the Kingdom* (Nashville: Abingdon, 1968), p. 15.

94. Walter Rauschenbusch, *Christianity and the Social Crisis* (New York: Macmillan, 1907), p. 408.

95. Ibid., pp. 409–10.

96. Rauschenbusch, *Christianizing the Social Order* (New York: Macmillan, 1912), p. 454.

97. Sharpe, p. 415.

98. Ibid., p. 448.

99. Ibid., p. 54.

100. Rauschenbusch, *Christianity and the Social Crisis,* p. 238.

101. Sharpe, pp. 61 and 80.

102. Rauschenbusch, *Christianizing the Social Order,* p. 91–92.

103. Ibid.

104. Ibid., pp. 98–99.

105. *Christianity and the Social Crisis,* p. 107.

106. *Christianizing the Social Order,* p. 358.

107. *Christianity and the Social Crisis,* p.164.

108. *Christianizing the Social Order,* p. 241.

109. *A Theology for the Social Gospel,* p. 86.

110. Ibid., p. 90.

111. *Christianizing the Social Order,* p. 127.

112. Ibid., p. 353.

113. Ibid., pp. 321–22.

114. Sharpe, p. 86.

115. Handy, p. 282.

116. Ibid.

117. *Christianity and the Social Crisis,* p. 396.

118. Handy, p. 309. The speech appeared in the *Rochester Democrat and Chronicle,* February 25, 1901.

119. Ibid., p. 311.

120. Ibid., p. 318.

121. Ibid., p. 320.

122. *Christianizing the Social Order,* p. 152.

123. Ibid., p. 357, from J. S. Mill, *Principles of Political Economy* (1868), vol. II, p. 357.

124. *Christianity and the Social Crisis,* p. 271.

125. Conference, New York City, March 16–17, 1985, sponsored by *Dissent* magazine and the Institute for Democratic Socialism.

126. *The Christian Socialist,* July 1, 1905.

127. *Christianizing the Social Order,* p. 175.

128. Ibid., p. 178.

129. Handy, p. 282.

130. *Christianizing the Social Order,* p. 178.

131. *Christianity and the Social Crisis,* p. 281.

132. *Christianizing the Social Order,* p. 347.

133. George Washington Woodbey et al., *Black Socialist Preacher,* ed. Philip S. Foner (San Francisco: Synthesis, 1983), p. 243.

134. Ibid., p. 261.

135. Ibid., p. 260.

136. Ibid., p. 297.

137. Ibid., pp. 353–54.

138. Ibid., p. 269.

139. Ibid., pp. 275, 279.

140. Ibid., p. 284.

141. Ibid., p. 289.

142. Ibid., p. iii.

143. James H. Cone, *The Black Church and Marxism* (New York: Institute for Democratic Socialism, 1980), p. 10.

144. Cornel West, *Prophesy Deliverance! An Afro-American Revolutionary Christianity* (Philadelphia: Westminster, 1982), p. 115.

145. Mari Jo Buhle, *Women and American Socialism, 1870–1920* (Chicago: Univ. of Illinois, 1983), p. xiv.

146. Ibid.

147. Ibid., p. 51.

148. Ibid., p. 49.

149. Ibid., p. 64.

150. Ibid., p. 80.

151. Ibid., p. 81.

152. *The Christian Socialist,* February 1, 1905, p. 1 in ibid., p. 80.

153. Vida Dutton Scudder, essay in *The Privilege of Age* (New York: E. P. Dutton, 1939), p. 129, published originally in *The New Leader,* 1929, under the title "Problems of Socialism: From a College Window."

154. Scudder, *On Journey* (New York: Dutton, 1937), pp. 162–63.

155. Ibid., p. 155.

156. Ibid., p. 165.

157. *Christianizing the Social Order,* p. 298.

158. Vida Dutton Scudder, *Socialism and Character* (Boston: Houghton Mifflin, 1912), pp. 132–34.

159. Ibid., pp. 364–65.

160. Rosemary Ruether, "An American Socialism: A Just Economic Order" in *Religious Socialism*, Summer/Fall 1983, p. 22.

161. Ibid., *Religious Socialism*, Spring/Summer 1983, p. 10.

162. Democratic Socialists of America pamphlet, *For a More Livable World*, available from DSA Religion and Socialism Commission, 45 Thornton Street, Roxbury, MA 02119.

163. Reinhold Niebuhr, *Reflections on the End of an Era* (New York: Scribner's, 1934), p. ix.

164. Arthur Schlesinger, Jr., "Reinhold Niebuhr's Role in Political Thought," in Kegley and Bretall, p. 149.

165. Quoted in June Bingham, *Courage to Change* (New York: Scribner's, 1972), p. 12.

166. *Reflections on the End of an Era,* p. 269.

167. Merkley, p. viii.

168. Bingham, p. 277.

169. Emil Brunner, "Niebuhr's Work as a Christian Thinker," in Kegley and Bretall, p. 29.

170. Kegley and Bretall, pp. 22–23.

171. Ibid., p. 439.

172. Ibid., p. 226.

173. Ibid., p. 438.

174. Reinhold Niebuhr, *The Children of Light and the Children of Darkness* (New York: Scribner's, 1944), p. xiii.

175. Niebuhr, in John A. Hutchison, ed., *Christian Faith and Social Action* (New York: Scribner's, 1953), p. 226.

176. Kegley and Bretall, p. 11.

177. Bingham, pp. 22–23.

178. Merkley, p. 21.

179. Ibid., p. 18.

180. Ibid., p. 63.

181. Hutchison, p. 227.

182. *The World Tomorrow,* February 1932.

183. Merkley, p. 76.

184. Reinhold Niebuhr, *Moral Man and Immoral Society* (New York: Scribner's, 1932), p. 144.

185. Ibid., p. 177.

186. Ibid., pp. xxii–xxiii.

187. Niebuhr, *The Nature and Destiny of Man* (New York: Scribner's, 1941), vol. I, p. 208.

188. Niebuhr, *Reflections,* p. 156.

189. Cited in Irving Howe, *Socialism and America* (New York: Harcourt Brace, 1985), p. 69.

190. Niebuhr, *Reflections,* p. 172.

191. Ibid., p. 175.

192. Norman Thomas, *A Socialist's Faith* (New York: Norton, 1951), pp. 5, 7.

193. In W. A. Swanberg, *Norman Thomas* (New York: Scribner's, 1936), p. 407.

194. Merkley, p. 149.

195. Ibid., p. 148.

196. *Christianity and Society,* Summer 1940.

197. *Radical Religion,* Summer 1938.

198. Niebuhr, *The Children of Light,* pp. 103–118.

199. Ibid., p. 103.

200. Ibid., p. 116.

201. *Christianity and Society,* Fall 1948.

202. Merkley, p. 191.

203. Ibid., p. 199.

204. *Christian Century,* December 31, 1969.

205. Reinhold Niebuhr, *Man's Nature and His Communities* (New York: Scribner's, 1965), pp. 81, 89.

206. Reinhold Niebuhr, *The Irony of American History* (New York: Scribner's 1952), p. 101.

207. Reinhold Niebuhr, *Christian Realism and Political Problems* (New York: Scribner's, 1953), p. 14.

208. Niebuhr, *The Irony,* p. 115.

209. Ibid., p. 126.

210. Quoted in Bingham, *Courage to Change,* frontispiece.

211. Anthony P. Dunbar, *Against the Grain: Southern Radicals and Prophets, 1929–1959* (Charlottesville: University of Virginia, 1981), p. 60.

212. Ibid., p. 250.

213. Ibid., p. 110.

214. Ibid., p. 154.

CHAPTER 11: THE CONVERGENCE OF SOCIALISM AND CATHOLICISM

1. Pius XI, *Quadragesimo Anno* (New York: Paulist Press, 1939), p. 32, n. 131.

2. Cited in Joseph N. Moody, ed., *Church and Society* (New York: Arts, 1953), p. 84, n. 31.

3. Leo XIII, *Quod Apostolici,* in *The Papal Encyclicals,* ed. Claudia Carlen (Washington, D.C.: McGrath, 1981), vol. 2, p. 11.

4. Ibid., pp. 14–15.

5. In Francesco Nitti, *Catholic Socialism* (London: Swann and Sonnenschein; New York: Macmillan, 1895), p. 154.

6. Cited in Hervé Chaigne, O.F.M., "The Catholic Church and Socialism," *Cross Currents* (Spring 1965), p. 151.

7. Leo XIII, *Rerum Novarum* (Washington, D.C.: National Catholic Welfare Conference, 1942, original date 1891), p. 6, no. 6.

8. Ibid., p. 18, no. 38. See John Coleman, S.J., "Development of Catholic Social Teaching," *Origins* (Jan. 4, 1981), for more on Leo's shaky Thomism plus an excellent summary of papal teaching.

9. Leo XIII, *Rerum Novarum,* p. 8, no. 14.

10. Ibid., p. 7, no. 10.

11. Ibid., p. 9, no. 15.

12. Ibid., pp. 23–25, nos. 53, 56.

13. Chaigne, p. 151.

14. Leo XIII, *Rerum Novarum,* pp. 33–34, no. 77.

15. Ibid., p. 24, no. 54.

16. Ibid., pp. 24, 26–28, nos. 53, 54, 56, 59–64.

17. Ibid., p. 23, no. 52.

18. Ibid., p. 22, no. 51.

19. Ibid., p. 13, no. 28.

20. Coleman, p. 37.

21. Cited in Giancarlo Zizola, *The Utopia of Pope John XXIII* (Maryknoll, N.Y.: Orbis, 1978), p. 301.

22. Leo XIII, *Rerum Novarum,* p. 28, no. 63.

23. Victor Cathrein, in Moody, p. 492.

24. Cited in Victor Cathrein, *Socialism* (New York: Benziger, 1904), p. 5.

25. Oswald von Nell-Breuning, S.J., *Reorganization of Social Economy* (New York: Bruce, 1936), p. 35.

26. Cited in Richard E. Mulcahy, S.J., *The Economics of Heinrich Pesch* (New York: Holt, 1952), p. 6.

27. Ibid., p. 15.

28. Ibid., p. 16.

29. Ibid., p. 23.

30. Ibid., p. 25.

31. Ibid., p. 40.

32. Ibid., p. 175.

33. Ibid., p. 169.

34. Ibid., p. 170.

35. Ibid.

36. Franz Mueller, in *Social Order* (April 1951), p. 149.

37. Mulcahy, p. 168.

38. Nell-Breuning, p. 16.

39. Piux XI, *Quadragesimo Anno,* p. 27, no. 107.

40. Ibid., pp. 27–28, nos. 111, 113,116,117.

41. Ibid., p. 18, nos. 70, 71.

42. Ibid., p. 30, no. 125.

43. Coleman, p. 38.

44. In *The Labor Leader* (ACTU newspaper), March 16, 1942, p. 3.

45. Pius XI, *Quadragesimo Anno,* p. 9, no. 31.

46. "The Christian in Action," Nov. 21, 1948, in *Pastoral Letters of the American Hierarchy, 1792–1970,* ed. Hugh J. Nolan (Huntington, Ind.: Our Sunday Visitor, 1971), p. 411.

47. George Morris, in the *Daily Worker,* Jan. 8, 1948, p. 6.

48. William Z. Foster, *Labor and the War,* 1942.

49. Oswald von Nell-Breuning, in *Sacramentum Mundi* (New York: Herder & Herder, 1970), vol. IV, p. 102.

50. Pius XI, *Quadragesimo Anno*, pp. 31–32, no. 130.

51. Ibid.,. p. 30, no. 121.

52. Ibid., p. 27, no. 107.

53. Gregory Baum, *Catholics and Canadian Socialism* (New York: Paulist Press, 1980).

54. Pius XI, *Divini Redemptoris* (New York: Paulist Press), p. 25. no. 61.

55. Ibid., p. 13, no. 32.

56. Cited in John Hellman, *Emmanuel Mounier and the New Catholic Left, 1930– 50* (Toronto University, 1981), p. 5.

57. Hellman, p. 252.

58. Ibid., p. 9.

59. Ibid., p. 31.

60. Ibid.

61. Eric Gill, recalled by members of the Catholic Worker.

62. Cited in Hellman, p. 112.

63. Ibid., p. 11.

64. Ibid., p. 246.

65. Ibid., p. 239.

66. Pius XII, *Christmas Message of 1944* (New York: Paulist Press), pp. 7–8.

67. Cited in Boniface Hanley, O.F.M., *Ten Christians* (Notre Dame, Indiana: Ave Maria Press, 1979), p. 235.

68. Marie Fernier, "La Crise Chronique (et Mortelle) de la JEC," in *Esprit,* April/ May 1977, p. 82. The "Mortelle" seems to be exaggerated.

69. Jean Lesturel, "La Vie Nouvelle," in *Esprit,* April/May 1977, pp. 163–64.

70. Michael Harrington, *The Politics at God's Funeral* (New York: Holt, Rinehart and Winston, 1983), pp. 205–6.

71. John XXIII, *Mater et Magistra,* in *The Gospel of Peace and Justice,* ed. Joseph Gremillion (Maryknoll, N.Y.: Orbis, 1983), pp. 159–60, no. 75.

72. Ibid., p. 163, no. 93.

73. John XXIII, *Pacem in Terris,* in Gremillion, pp. 235–36, no. 159.

74. Paul VI, in Gremillion, p. 499, no. 31. This was not an encyclical, but an "apostolic letter" or allocution entitled *Octogesima Adveniens.*

75. Gremillion, p. 304, no. 68.

76. Ibid., p. 305, no. 68.

77. Ibid., p. 307, no. 71.

78. John Paul II, *Laborem Exercens* (Boston: St. Paul Edition), p. 18, II, 7.

79. Ibid., p. 28, III, 12.

80. Ibid., pp. 35–37, III, 14.

81. Ibid., pp. 42–43, III, 18.

82. Cited in *Religious Socialism* (Winter 1982), p. 3.

83. Ibid.

84. Cited in Zizola, p. 90.

85. First published in *Témoignage Chrétien* (Paris, August 31, 1967).

86. Interview in *The Sign* (July/August 1976), p. 12.

87. Frei Betto, *Fidel and Religion* (New York: Simon & Schuster, 1987), p. 212.

88. *Populorum Progressio,* in Gremillion, p. 396, nos. 30–31.

89. Karl Popper, *The Open Society and Its Enemies* (Princeton, N.J.: Princeton University Press, 1962), vol. 2, p. 151.

90. Paul VI, *The Pope Speaks*, vol. 13, no. 1 (1968), p. 256.

91. Cited in Michael Novak, "Liberation Theology and the Pope," *Commentary,* June 1979, p. 60.

92. In Gustavo Gutiérrez, *The Power of the Poor in History* (Maryknoll, N.Y.: Orbis, 1983), p. 164, no. 44.

93. *The New York Times,* Feb. 18, 1979.

94. Dow Kirkpatrick, "Liberation Theologies and Third World Demands," *Christian Century* (May 12, 1976).

95. Gustavo Gutiérrez, *A Theology of Liberation* (Maryknoll, N.Y.: Orbis, 1973), p. 202.

96. Gutiérrez, *The Power of the Poor,* pp. 37–38.

97. Gustavo Gutiérrez, *Liberation and Change* (Atlanta: John Knox, 1977), p. 76.

98. Luis Segundo, cited by Michael Novak, ed., *Liberation South, Liberation North* (Washington, D.C.: American Enterprise Institute, 1981), p. 22; appeared originally in *Concilium 96,* 1974.

99. Cited by Michael Novak, *Will It Liberate?* (New York: Paulist Press, 1986), p. 29.

100. John Eagleson, ed., *Christians and Socialism* (Maryknoll, N.Y.: Orbis, 1975), pp. 141–42.

101. Ibid., p. 78.

102. Robert Tucker, ed., *The Marx-Engels Reader,* (New York: W.W. Norton, 1972), pp. 65, 66, 98, 124, 157.

103. Ibid., p. 124.

104. Michael Harrington, *Socialism* (New York: Bantam/Saturday Review Press, 1970), p. 242.

105. A quote from Harrington's public speeches.

106. Joseph Ratzinger, *Instruction on Certain Aspects of the 'Theology of Liberation,'* Origins (Sept. 13, 1984), VI, 8, p. 199.

107. Ibid., IX, 7, p. 201.

108. Gustavo Gutiérrez, *Paginas*, September, 1984, p. 4ff.

109. Cited by Novak, *Will It Liberate?*, p. 52.

110. Gustavo Gutiérrez, *We Drink from Our Own Wells* (Maryknoll, N.Y.: Orbis, 1984), p. 27.

111. Friedrich Engels, "Socialism: Utopian and Scientific," in *The Marx-Engels Reader*, p. 635.

112. Eagleson, p. 162.

113. "Call for Liberation Comes from Christ," *Maryknoll*, April 1987, pp. 11–12.

114. Cited by John C. Cort, *Commonweal*, July 21, 1978. Howe made the statement at the 1977 convention of the Democratic Socialist Organizing Committee (DSOC) in Chicago.

115. *The New International Review*, (Winter 1977), pp. 6, 7.

116. Ibid., p. 6.

117. Ibid., pp. 7–9.

118. Richard Goodwin, *The New Yorker*, Jan. 4, 1969.

119. *Economic Justice for All: Catholic Social Teaching and the U.S. Economy* in *Origins*, Nov. 27, 1986, p. 440, no. 290.

120. Charles Frankel, Introduction to Rousseau's *The Social Contract* (New York: Hafner, 1947), p. xvii.

121. Cited in Francis L. Broderick, *Right Reverend New Dealer* (New York: Macmillan, 1963), p. 46.

122. Ibid., p. 53.

123. John A. Ryan, *Social Reconstruction* (New York: Macmillan, 1920), p. 229.

124. Ryan, *Social Doctrine in Action* (New York: Harper, 1941), pp. 228–29.

125. Ryan, *Social Reconstruction*, p. 232.

126. Ibid., p. 235.

127. Ibid., p. 239.

128. Gregory Baum, *Catholics and Canadian Socialism* (New York: Paulist Press, 1980), p. 15.

129. Ibid., p. 50.

130. Ibid., p. 15.

131. Ibid., pp. 123–24.

132. Ibid., pp. 164–65.

133. Moses M. Coady, *Masters of Their Own Destiny* (New York: Harper, 1929), p. 70.

CHAPTER 12: PROTESTANTS AND PROSPECTS

1. Quoted by Michael Harrington, *Socialism* (New York: Bantam, 1972), p. 239.

2. *Gathered for Life:* Official Report, Sixth Assembly, World Council of Churches, Vancouver, 1983, ed. David Gill (Grand Rapids: Eerdmans, 1983), p. 210.

3. "Roman Catholic Consultation Memorandum," in *The Lord of Life*, ed. William H. Lazareth (Geneva: WCC, 1983), p. 22.

4. Ibid.

5. *Gathered for Life*, p. 325.

6. Ibid., p. 119.

7. *The First Assembly of the WCC* (New York: Harper, 1949), p. 80.

8. Ibid., p. 74.

9. *Struggling for Justice and Human Dignity,* Document GR6, World Council of Churches, Vancouver Assembly, 1983, pp. 1–3, 6–8.

10. *Gathered for Life,* p. 190.

11. *The Lord of Life,* p. 70.

12. José Míguez Bonino, *Christians and Marxism* (Grand Rapids: Eerdmans, 1976), p. 81.

13. Ibid., p. 132.

14. Ibid., p. 16.

15. Karl Popper, *The Open Society and Its Enemies* (Princeton University, 1962), vol. 2, P. 151.

16. *Perspectives on Political Ethics,* ed. Koson Srisang (Washington, D.C.: Georgetown University Press, 1983, for WCC), pp. 2–3.

17. *International Communications,* March/June 1984, COELI, p. 29.

18. Ibid., p. 11.

CHAPTER 13: CONCLUSIONS

1. Reinhold Niebuhr, *The Children of Light and the Children of Darkness* (New York: Scribner's, 1944), p. xiii.

2. Winston Churchill, *Barnes & Noble Book of Quotations,* ed. Robert I. Fitzhenry (New York: Harper & Row, 1983), p. 85.

3. E. B. White, *The Wild Flag* (Boston: Houghton Mifflin, 1954), p. 31.

4. John Dalberg-Acton (Lord Acton), Letter to Bishop Mandell Creighton, April 5, 1987.

5. There is a sizable literature on Mondragon. One short treatment: "The Marvels of Mondragon," John C. Cort, in *Commonweal,* June 18, 1982, pp. 368–71.

6. John Stuart Mill, *Principles of Political Economy,* Revised Edition, Book IV, Chapter VII, Sec. 6, pp. 280–81, 295 (New York: Colonial Press, 1900). This tribute does not appear in earlier editions.

7. Novak, *Will It Liberate?,* p. 175.

8. Ibid., p. 29.

9. Told to me by Hans Meier, a Hutterian elder at the Norfolk, Conn., *bruderhof,* who knew Arnold.

Bibliographical Essay

A more complete bibliography may be found in the reference notes. A really complete one would run to thousands of books. The following are the ones I found most useful:

INTRODUCTION

For my understanding of what the Bible and Jesus Christ teach I used *The New Oxford Annotated Bible with the Apocrypha* (New York: Oxford University Press, 1977). For definitions of socialism I relied on the dictionaries mentioned in the text and also on a number of the works discussed in the following paragraphs.

Above all others, I relied on the Frankfurt Declaration of the Socialist International, first voted in 1951 but still recognized and enshrined in the International's statutes. At the last congress of the International in Lima, Peru, in June 1986 a new declaration was discussed, but there was no final authorization. Michael Harrington, its principal author, has assured me that it will in no way alter the basic principles of the Frankfurt Declaration and will, as he put it, "clearly differentiate socialism from communism and insist upon the critical importance of freedom, as means and end."

I used the text of the Frankfurt Declaration that is given in *The New International Review* (vol. 1, no. 1 [Winter 1977]: 5–10). If this is not available, check library catalogues under "Socialist International" or "Frankfurt Declaration."

Other sources on socialism: G. D. H. Cole, *A History of Socialist Thought,* 5 vols. (London: Macmillan, 1953–60). I found this objective and refreshingly free of Marxist bias. For a good anthology of Marx's basic writings, see *The Marx-Engels Reader,* ed. Robert C. Tucker, 2nd. ed. (New York: W. W. Norton, 1978); my references are to the first edition (1972). Despite its over-emphasis on philosophy as opposed to politics and economics, Leszek Kolakowski's *Main Currents of Marxism,* 3 vols. (New York: Oxford University Press, 1981) is must reading for the serious student of Marxism. Kolakowski is an exiled, Polish, ex-Marxist philosopher. Also useful: Arthur F. McGovern, *Marxism: An American Christian Perspective* (Maryknoll, N.Y.: Orbis, 1980).

Probably the most useful, and certainly the best written, book on these subjects is *Utopian Thought in the Western World,* by Frank and Fritzie Manuel (Cambridge: Harvard University Press, 1979). A witty, monumental masterpiece, even though highly secular in viewpoint.

The Democratic Socialist Vision, by Gary J. Dorrien (Totowa, N.J.: Rowman & Littlefield, 1986), is a good Christian, non-Marxist treatment of its subject, with special attention given to William Temple, Norman Thomas, Michael Novak, and Michael Harrington.

In 1982 the American Enterprise Institute, a conservative think tank in Washington, D.C., published a seventy-five-page antisocialist monograph by Bernard Murchland, *The Dream of Christian Socialism: An Essay on Its European Origins.* If you can ignore its bias, it is not a bad summary of developments in England, France, and Germany during the nineteenth century, and, as far as I know, it was the first work to deal with the subject in English on more than a one-country basis since Conrad Noel's *Socialism in Church History* (Milwaukee: The Young Churchman, 1911).

CHAPTER 1: THE QUESTIONS AND THE ISSUE

For Adam Smith's *Wealth of Nations* I used the E. P. Dutton edition, 2 vols. (New York, 1934), and also the Modern Library edition (New York, 1937).

The ground-breaking pioneer in analysis of the relationship between religion and capitalism is certainly Max Weber in *The Protestant Ethic and the Spirit of Capitalism* (New York: Scribner's, 1958). Unfortunately, Weber was totally incapable of resisting the temptation to add interminable comments in the notes. I counted a dozen wordy references from one page alone. For that and more substantial reasons, a better, more readable book on the same subject is R. H. Tawney's *Religion and the Rise of Capitalism* (New York: Harcourt Brace, 1926). Other comments on these works appear in the text.

CHAPTERS 2 AND 3: THE OLD TESTAMENT AND THE NEW TESTAMENT

Here I used *The New Oxford Annotated Bible* (see above). I also used: *Cry Justice: The Bible on Hunger and Poverty,* ed. Ronald J. Sider (New York: Paulist, 1980); *The Faith That Does Justice: Examining the Christian Sources for Social Change,* ed. John C. Haughey (New York: Paulist, 1977); Julio de Santa Ana, *Good News to the Poor: The Challenge of the Poor in the History of the Church* (Maryknoll, N.Y.: Orbis, 1979); and José Miranda, *Marx and the Bible* (Maryknoll: Orbis, 1974). The last-named includes impressive scholarship and an absurd conclusion, namely, "God will be only in a world of justice, and if Marx does not find him in the Western world it is because he is indeed not there, nor can he be" (p. 296). So read with caution.

CHAPTER 4: THE FATHERS OF THE CHURCH

Good quotes and commentary are in Walter Shewring, *Rich and Poor in Christian Tradition* (London: Burns and Oates, 1948), and in the Haughey and Santa Ana books mentioned under chapters 2 and 3, above.

CHAPTER 5: THE MIDDLE AGES AND THOMAS AQUINAS

I used Shewring (see above) for the early period, and then *Aquinas: Selected Political Writings,* ed. A. P. D'Entrèves (New York: Macmillan, 1959) and, as acknowledged in my text, the research of my mentor, Sister Mary Emil Penet, IHM, which features Aquinas's *Summa Theologica* (London: Blackfriars, 1975), trans. Marcus Lefebure.

CHAPTER 6: THOMAS MORE AND THE RADICAL REFORMERS

The Manuels (see above) have an excellent chapter on Thomas More, and there are many biographies. I still like R. W. Chambers's *Thomas More* (Ann Arbor: University of Michigan Press, 1958), but you may prefer one of the more recent, and critical, ones. You should certainly read *Utopia,* which is only eighty-three pages in the Appleton-Century-Crofts paperback.

For Müntzer I leaned heavily on the Manuels, and for the Hutterites on John Hostetler, *Hutterite Society* (Baltimore: Johns Hopkins University Press, 1974), and on *God's Revolution: The Witness of Eberhard Arnold* (New York: Paulist, 1984).

CHAPTER 7: FRANCE

English Books

G. D. H. Cole (see above) and the Manuels (see above) contain valuable material. Also Henri Daniel-Rops, *The Church in an Age of Revolution, 1789–1870,* 2 vols. (Garden City, N.Y.: Doubleday, 1967). Alexander Vidler, *Prophecy and Papacy* (London: SCM, 1954), is very good on Lamennais. Both Daniel-Rops, a French Catholic, and Vidler, a British Anglican, are kinder to Gregory XVI than the facts in their books would warrant. Lamennais's short bombshell, *The Words of a Believer,* is available in an old English edition (London: Cousins, 1832). Barbara Petri's *The Historical Thought of P.-J.-B. Buchez* (Washington, D.C.: Catholic University of America Press, 1958) is the only book I could find in English about the man I regard as the founder of authentic Christian socialism in the modern era. Alexander Gray, an antisocialist historian, has some fascinating material in *The Socialist Tradition: Moses to Lenin* (New York: Harper, 1968). There is a woeful lack of English translations of French socialists, Christian and otherwise, but Saint-Simon, *Selected Writings,* ed. Keith Tayler (New York: Holmes and Meier, 1975), is one exception. Some useful things are in Parker Moon, *The Labor Problem and the Social Catholic Movement in France* (New York: Macmillan, 1921). For relevant papal encyclicals in English, the best work is vol. 1 (covering 1740–1878) of *The Papal Encyclicals,* ed. Claudia Carlen (Wilmington, Del.: McGrath, 1981).

A good overview of "The Papacy" and "Catholicism and Society in France, 1789–1950" (pp. 21–277) can be found in *Church and Society: Catholic Social and Political Thought and Movements, 1789–1950,* ed. Joseph Moody (New York: Arts, 1953). Moody not only edited the volume but also wrote the above-named articles. Could be stronger on Christian socialism.

French Books

Far and away my best source was André Biéler, a Swiss Protestant, and his *Chrétiens et socialistes avant Marx* (Geneva: Labor et Fides, 1982). I don't like the organization of his material, but the material itself is great and for the most part is, as far as I know, unavailable elsewhere. For primary sources of Buchez's thought I relied mainly on his *Traité de politique et de science sociale* (Paris: Amyot, 1866) and on Armand Cuvillier's *P.-J.-B. Buchez et les origines du socialisme chrétien* (Paris: Presses Universitaires, 1948). Saint-Simon's *Nouveau christianisme* (Paris: Bureau de Globe, 1832) is only one hundred pages long and worth reading. Étienne Cabet's *Le Vrai christianisme suivant Jésus Christ* (Paris, 1847) is 636 smaller pages and requires more commitment. But my favorite is Victor Considérant's *Le Socialisme devant le vieux monde* (Paris, 1848). Some great writing. Albert Samuel's *Le Socialisme* (Lyon: Chronique Sociale, 1981) devotes a chapter of forty-five pages to *le socialisme chrétien*; the chapter covers some of the founders plus more modern movements such as Emmanuel Mounier's Personalism, liberation theology, and Christians for Socialism. Jacques Droz's *Histoire générale du socialisme* (Paris: Presses Universitaires, 1972) is a multi-volume, multi-author, comprehensive history with an excellent chapter (in volume 1) by Jean Bruhat on French socialism from 1815 to 1848; that chapter gives good coverage to the Christians.

CHAPTER 8: ENGLAND

For the founders I liked best a Danish work in English by Torben Christensen, *Origin and History of Christian Socialism—1848-54* (Copenhagen: Universitetsforlaget, 1962). It gives overdue credit to John Ludlow, whose unpublished autobiography some smart publisher should make available. I also liked and used extensively Peter d'A. Jones's *The Christian Socialist Revival—1877-1914* (Princeton, N.J.: Princeton University Press, 1968). If you have access to a library with back copies or microfilm of *The New Age* for 1907 and 1908, you will enjoy the debate between the Chesterbelloc and the Shawells. For Archbishop Temple, I used mainly Joseph Fletcher's *William Temple* (New York: Seabury, 1953), and the Temple chapter in Gary Dorrien's book (cf. *Introduction*) and for Tawney I used Ross Terrill's *R. H. Tawney and His Times* (Cambridge: Harvard University Press, 1973). Gilbert C. Binyon's *The Christian Socialist Movement in England* (New York: Macmillan, 1931) has material that Jones's history omits, but otherwise is of lesser quality.

CHAPTER 9: GERMAN-SPEAKING EUROPE

English Books

G. D. H. Cole (see above under Introduction) is very useful, also *Church and Society* (see above under the listings for chapter 7), particularly "Church and Society in Germany," by Edgar Alexander. For Wilhelm Weitling, I relied on his *The Poor Sinner's Gospel* (London: Sheed & Ward, 1969) and Carl Wittke's biography, *The Utopian Communist* (Baton Rouge: Louisiana State University Press, 1950). And for Weitling's disciple, Hermann Kriege, I relied on Henri Desroche's *Socialisme et sociologie religieuse* (Paris: Cujas, 1965), which is one of the few places to find the entire text of *Circular Against Kriege,* one of the more significant items in Marxist literature.

Archbishop Ketteler's life and work are adequately dealt with in *The Social Teachings of Wilhelm Emmanuel von Ketteler,* trans. Rupert J. Ederer (Washington, D.C.: University Press, 1981) and in William Hogan, *The Development of Bishop Wilhelm Emmanuel von Ketteler's Interpretation of the Social Problem* (Washington, D.C.: Catholic University of America Press, 1946). *Signs of the Kingdom: A Ragaz Reader,* ed. and trans. Paul Bock (Grand Rapids: Eerdmans, 1984) is a welcome recognition at last of the importance of the man who was once the leading Christian socialist on the European continent.

There is copious literature on and by Karl Barth in English. I used mainly his *Epistle to the Romans* (London: Oxford, 1933); his *The Word of God and the Word of Man* (Boston: Pilgrim, 1928), which includes the famous Tambach speech; *Karl Barth and Radical Politics,* ed. George Hunsinger (Philadelphia: Westminster, 1976); James Bentley's *Between Marx and Christ: The Dialogue in German-Speaking Europe, 1870-1970* (London: NLB, 1982) and Eberhard Busch's *Karl Barth* (Philadelphia: Fortress, 1976), an English version of a longer German work.

For Tillich I relied on the biography by his friends, Wilhelm and Marion Pauck, *Paul Tillich: His Life and Thought* (New York: Harper & Row, 1976), and on his own *The Socialist Decision* (New York: Harper & Row, 1971); *Political Expectation,* ed. James Luther Adams (New York: Harper & Row, 1971); and *Systematic Theology,* vol. 2 (University of Chicago Press, 1957). I also found some interesting material in John R. Stumme, *Socialism in Theological Perspective: A Study of Paul Tillich, 1918-1933* (Missoula, Mont.: Scholars Press, 1978).

German Books

Als Christ Sozialist, ed. Jürgen Finnern (Bielefeld: Bund der Religiösen Sozialisten Deutschland, 1983) is an excellent, short summary of the history of religious socialism in Germany and Switzerland (those topics are covered mainly by Markus Mattmüller, Ragaz's biographer) and of the present situation of the Association of Religious Socialists in West Germany.

Walter Bredendiek, *Christliche Sozialreformer des 19 Jahrhunderts* (Leipzig: Koehler und Amelang, 1953), is a useful anthology of the lives and thought of early Christian socialists: Baader, Huber, Wichern, Ketteler, Todt, and Naumann. Another valuable source ("an encyclopedic dictionary of theology and religious sociology") for material on the above and others—a source that also contains a useful article on "Christian Social" movements and personalities—is *Die Religion in Geschichte und Gegenwart: Handworterbuch für Theologie und Religionswissenschaft,* 7 vols. (Tübingen: J. C. B. Mohr [Paul Siebeck], 1957-1965), ed. Kurt Galling, Hans Freiherr von Campenhousen, et al. A valuable new book is *Prophetischer Socialismus: Blumhardt, Ragaz, Barth* by Eduard Buess and Markus Mattmüller, the biographer of Ragaz (Freiburg, Edition Exodus, 1986).

CHAPTER 10: THE UNITED STATES

Of general histories that feature one or more Christian socialists, I would recommend: Charles H. Hopkins, *The Rise of the Social Gospel in American Protestantism, 1865-1915* (New Haven: Yale University Press, 1940); James Dombrowski, *The Early Days of Christian Socialism in America* (New York: Columbia University Press, 1936); Robert T. Handy, *The Social Gospel in America: Gladden, Ely, Rauschenbusch* (New York: Oxford, 1966); and David Goldstein and Martha Avery, *Socialism* (New York: Benziger, 1911). The last-named is wildly biased writing by Catholic converts from socialism, but it contains material you won't find elsewhere and is a useful example of the intensity of anti-socialist propaganda by the Catholic church. It carries the imprimatur of William Cardinal O'Connell of Boston.

If you can get your hands on copies of old Christian socialist periodicals, these make fascinating reading and introduce you to most of the major figures. The major ones are: W. D. P. Bliss's *The Dawn* (1889-1896); Edward Ellis Carr's *The Christian Socialist* (1905-1922); and Reinhold Niebuhr's *Radical Religion* (1935-1940) and *Christianity and Society* (1940-1948). Since 1977 there has been *Religious Socialism,* a quarterly published by the Religion and Socialism Commission of the Democratic Socialists of America at 45 Thornton St., Roxbury, MA 02119.

For Rauschenbusch, *Christianity and the Social Crisis* (New York: Macmillan, 1907) is clearly the best of his books. Mari Jo Buhle has good material on Mary Livermore and Frances Willard in her *Women and American Socialism, 1870-1920* (Chicago: University of Illinois Press, 1983). Vida Scudder's autobiography, *On Journey* (New York: Dutton, 1937), is also well worth reading. For early black Christian socialists, the best book available is *Black Socialist Preacher,* ed. Philip S. Foner (San Francisco: Synthesis, 1983), and, for more recent developments, Cornel West's *Prophesy Deliverance!* (Philadelphia: Westminster, 1982).

Highly recommended: *Against the Grain: Southern Radicals and Prophets, 1929–1959,* by Anthony P. Dunbar (Charlottesville: University of Virginia Press, 1981). Also: Morris Hillguit and John A. Ryan, *Socialism: Promise or Menace* (New York: Macmillan, 1914).

There is a voluminous literature by and about Reinhold Niebuhr. Among those books by him, I found the most enjoyable to be *Leaves from the Notebook of a Tamed Cynic* (Hamden, Conn.: Shoe String Press, 1956; first printing 1929). The most valuable in terms of ideas is clearly *The Children of Light and the Children of Darkness* (New York: Scribner's, 1944). Both are short, and easy reading. My favorite among those books about him is Paul Merkley's *Reinhold Niebuhr* (Montreal: McGill-Queen's University, 1975), but Richard Fox's *Reinhold Niebuhr* (New York: Pantheon, 1985) has a good deal more information. None of the Niebuhr biographies appreciate the importance of the Barth–Niebuhr debate, mainly in *The Christian Century* (10/27/48, 12/8/48, 2/16/49 and 2/23/49).

CHAPTER 11: THE CONVERGENCE OF SOCIALISM AND CATHOLICISM

For socialism, see the books recommended above under Introduction. For Catholicism, perhaps the best comprehensive treatment is Donal Dorr's *Option for the Poor: A Hundred Years of Vatican Social Teaching* (Maryknoll, N.Y.: Orbis, 1983). For exhaustive lists of (1) Catholic social documents and (2) major studies of same, see respectively note 1 of chapter 1 and note 17 of chapter 2 of the U.S. bishops' pastoral letter, *Economic Justice for All: Catholic Social Teaching and the U.S. Economy* (in *Origins,* Nov. 27, 1986 [Washington, D.C.: National Catholic News Service]). For North Americans the pastoral itself is an excellent summary of Catholic socialistic teaching. The best short treatment I have seen is John Coleman, "Development of Catholic Social Teaching" (in *Origins,* Jan. 4, 1981).

Except for the fact that it doesn't address the two radical pamphlets highlighted in my text, Richard E. Mulcahy's *The Economics of Heinrich Pesch* (New York: Holt, 1952) gives the best available account in English of Pesch's work. Oswald von Nell-Breuning's *Reorganization of Social Economy* (New York: Bruce, 1936) provides insights into the mind of the man who wrote most of Pius XI's *Quadragesimo Anno* (1931), which in some respects I still think was the most significant of all the social encyclicals to date. The book is also an extended commentary on the encyclical.

For liberation theology I depended mainly on Gutiérrez' five books published in English and cited in the text. Michael Novak's *Will It Liberate?* (New York: Paulist Press, 1986) has some useful quotes from other theologians. Curt Cadorette kindly loaned me a chapter from his forthcoming *In the Heart of the People: The Theology of Gustavo Gutiérrez* (Oak Park, IL: Meyer-Stone, 1987), which includes his own translation of the Spanish article by Gutiérrez, *Teologia y ciencias sociales* (*Paginas* 9/84).

Recommended biographies: of John A. Ryan, *Right Reverend New Dealer,* by Francis L. Broderick (New York: Macmillan, 1963); and *Emmanuel Mounier and the New Catholic Left 1930–1950,* by John Hellman (Toronto University Press, 1981).

CHAPTER 12: PROTESTANTS AND PROSPECTS

For the World Council of Churches (WCC), I used: *The First Assembly of the WCC* (New York: Harper, 1949); *Gathered for Life: Official Report, VIth Assembly, WCC, Vancouver, 1983,* ed. David Gill (Grand Rapids: Eerdmans, 1983); *The Lord of Life,* ed. William H. Lazareth (Geneva: WCC, 1983); and *Perspectives on Political Ethics,* ed. Koson Srisang (Washington, D.C.: Georgetown University Press, 1983, for WCC).

José Míguez-Bonino's *Christians and Marxism* (Grand Rapids: Eerdmans, 1976) is a persuasive statement of liberation theology from an intelligent, moderate, Protestant point of view.

Index

Compiled by William E. Jerman